D0916709

VICTIMS, VICTORS

FROM NAZI OCCUPATION
TO THE CONQUEST OF GERMANY
AS SEEN BY A RED ARMY SOLDIER

by Roman Kravchenko-Berezhnoy

translated by Marina Guba

with a foreword by David M. Glantz

WITHDRAWN

No longer the property of the
Boston Public Library.
Sale of this material benefits the Library

THE ABERJONA PRESS
Bedford, Pennsylvania

Editor-in-Chief: *Patricia K. Bonn*
Editor: *Lars Gyllenhaal*
Translator: *Marina Guba*
Technical Editors: *Lars Gyllenhaal, Keith E. Bonn, and Scott McMichael*
Cartographer: *Tom Houlihan*
Printer: *Mercersburg Printing, Mercersburg, Pennsylvania*

Except where noted, all photos are from the author's collection.
(LG) is for the Lars Gyllenhaal Collection.

© 2007 by Roman Kravchenko-Berezhnoy
All rights reserved.
Printed in the United States of America
14 13 12 11 10 09 08 07   5 4 3 2 1

ISBN 10: 0-9717650-6-5
ISBN 13: 978-0-9717650-6-1

On the front cover: The portrait of the author was taken in Bernau, Germany, in 1947 (author's collection). Soviet citizens stand in line before German occupiers. (National Archives, College Park, MD). The flag was hoisted from the *Reichstag* in Berlin as a sign of the fall of Berlin. (National Archives, College Park, MD)

On the back cover: This photo of the author was taken in 1942, while he and his family lived in Kremenets under German occupation (author's collection).

For the victims

Contents

FOREWORD

Military historians attempting to reconstruct a complete and accurate record of the Soviet-German War (1941–45) have encountered a formidable array of obstacles to their work. The most imposing have been the pervasive German bias that has permeated most Western histories of the war; an acute shortage of Soviet archival materials; political and ideological biases present in virtually all Soviet military histories; the language barrier barring access to Soviet (Russian) sources; and the near total absence of memoirs by rank-and-file Red Army soldiers. The demise of the Soviet Union and the emergence of a new Russia in 1991 have eliminated some, if not all, of these obstacles. Beginning shortly after 1991 and accelerating sharply thereafter, the Russian government has released from its military archives vast quantities of formerly classified materials related to the war and has authorized publication of unexpurgated versions of previously published, but highly censored memoirs written by famous wartime Red Army military leaders. Only now, however, are the memoirs of rank-and-file Red Army soldiers beginning to appear in print.

Precious few Red Army soldiers had either the opportunity or the courage to record their memoirs on paper during the war because the penalty for keeping diaries or taking notes during wartime could be most severe. Even after the war ended, soldiers who spoke too frankly about their combat experiences faced harsh official condemnation, outright prosecution, or even imprisonment for "tarnishing the Red Army's reputation" by their candor. Sadly, even today, a time when political conditions have become conducive to greater frankness, too many veterans have died—and most of those who remain are simply too old or feeble to write coherent memoirs or have forgotten their experiences. As a result, Russian memoir literature about the war today consists largely of the recollections of famous wartime generals such as Zhukov, Konev, Rokossovsky, and Batov; the wartime experiences of several official war correspondents; and precious few memoirs written by lower-ranking officers who achieved general officer rank in the postwar years.

There are, however, some exceptions to this rule, most notably, the memoir of famed Red Army war correspondent, Vasily Grossman, entitled *A Writer at War* (published in English in 2006), and the recollections of a handful of junior officers who served in the Red Army during the war. The most prolific of these is Dmitri Loza, the commander of a tank brigade who rose to general officer rank after the war's end and wrote two books about his own experiences—*Fighting for the Soviet Motherland* (University of Nebraska Press, 1998) and *Commanding the Red Army's Sherman Tanks* (University of

Nebraska Press, 1996)—and edited a third, *Attack of the Airacobras* (University Press of Kansas, 2002), which recounted the experiences of several veteran air force officers. Supplementing Loza's works are memoirs by Evgeni Bessonov, who wrote about his experiences in the 4th Guards Tank Army in his book, *Tank Rider: Into the Reich with the Red Army* (London: Greenhill, 2003), and Evgenii Moniushko, who began the war as a teenager besieged in Leningrad but later was evacuated from the city, graduated from an artillery school, served in an antitank regiment in 1944–45, and wrote of his experiences in *From Leningrad to Hungary* (Frank Cass, 2005).

As attractive as they are, all six of these books fall well short of providing candid soldierly perspectives on the privations of wartime service in the Red Army. Despite laudatory reviews, Grossman's popular memoir lacks the insights and feelings of a common soldier. An accomplished novelist before the war began, Grossman served as a war correspondent for the Red Army's official organ, *Krasnaia Zvesda* [Red Star] and propagandist whose primary mission was to observe the war and, through his writing, inspire the Red Army's soldiers and the Soviet population to endure until victory was achieved. Although his private notes in the memoir are certainly more candid than his public pronouncements, the memoir fails to give us the candid perspective of the common combat soldier. Similarly, as interesting and accurate as they are, the memoirs by Loza, Bessonov, and Moniushko contain little about the lives and trials of the average Red Army infantryman, the army's "cannon-fodder," the men who made up well over 80 percent of its overall strength and suffered up to 90 percent of its appalling wartime casualty toll.

Roman Kravchenko-Berezhnoy's *Victims, Victors* surpasses the value of previous memoirs in several important respects. First, unlike earlier works in this genre, the breadth of its view is unprecedented and exceptional because it is written by a man whose experiences spanned life in German-occupied territories, service as a private in the wartime Red Army, and finally, military service as an NCO during the immediate postwar years in Soviet-occupied Germany. Second, unlike the majority of Red Army veterans who committed little or nothing to paper, while spending the first three years of the war living as a youth in German-occupied Ukraine, Kravchenko began the practice of taking daily notes about his experiences in enduring the German occupation and, thereafter, continued doing so in the form of reminiscences written some years after the war. Third, because he lived in German-occupied territories where he was subject to German propaganda, rumors born of life in relative isolation behind the front, and the competing influences of the Communist underground in the Ukrainian cities and towns and the ubiquitous bands of Soviet and Nationalist Partisans roaming the Ukrainian countryside, Kravchenko provides us a unique birds-eye perspective of the course of the war, replete with the rumors and innuendo born of isolation.

Finally, Kravchenko's service as a rifleman in the Sixty-First Army's 356th Rifle Division, interrogator of German POWs during wartime, and his experiences with German concentration camps and the Soviet military administration in Germany during the immediate postwar period far exceeds the limited perspectives of an infantryman about the rigors of war. In terms of its breadth, perspective, and candor, Kravchenko's memoir is truly unique.

David M. Glantz
January 2007

Colonel David M. Glantz, USA (Retired), received degrees in history from the Virginia Military Institute and the University of North Carolina at Chapel Hill then entered active service with the US Army in 1963. His military career included membership in the history faculty of the United States Military Academy from 1969 through 1973. In 1987, he founded The Journal of Soviet Military Studies. *In 1993, Glantz retired from the US Army with the rank of Colonel and converted his journal into* The Journal of Slavic Military Studies, *including the states of Central and Eastern Europe as well as the former Soviet Union.*

Perhaps the most significant American scholar of the Eastern Front over the past twenty years, Glantz was one of the first westerners to gain access to the Soviet military archives, and has been prolific on topics about the Eastern Front focused on the Red Army's operations.

Editor's Introduction

History without faces is just some names, dates, and maps. Reading someone's diary and personal recollections, as you are about to do, not only makes history more tangible, but is necessary to get an idea of how history was perceived at the time, while the historic events were unfolding.

The personal angle ensures that particular places, battles, and units—because of an eloquent and credible witness—will be remembered even in a distant future. Life in prewar Austria and the tasks of an enlisted soldier in the German Army become clearer through *The Good Soldier* by Alfred Novotny, an Austrian veteran of the *"Grossdeutschland"* Division.[1] The life of a schoolboy in Nazi Germany who becomes a frontline soldier of the *Waffen-SS* becomes very "real" by reading *Black Edelweiss* by Johann Voss.[2]

You have probably already learned about the life of the enlisted World War II infantryman in the American and German armies from hundreds of films, books, and websites. You may even be aware of minute details about their training, uniforms, and weapons.

Very few, shockingly few, people in the West, however, have ever heard or read the words of a Red Army private. Memoirs of Soviet WWII *officers and non-commissioned officers* have been published in English, notably the memoirs mentioned by David Glantz in his foreword. What about the overwhelming majority, though, the Red Army privates who bore the brunt of all the fighting on the Eastern Front, the front where two-thirds of the permanent losses of the German Armed Forces occurred?

Only in 1998 a memoir by a rank-and-file Red Army soldier (who became an NCO during the war) was made widely available in English, *My Just War* by Gabriel Temkin, followed in 2004 by *Red Road from Stalingrad* by Mansur Abdulin.[3] However fascinating and valuable, the authors of these books are not Russians, but a Polish Jew and a Tatar (part of a Turkic people living in the Soviet Union). The author of the book you are now holding was and is undoubtedly Russian. In fact he was more Russian than the average Red Army soldier as he was raised in a home much more Russian than Soviet.

This book, however, contains not only a Russian soldier's view of the final stage of history's greatest clash of military forces. More than half of the book lets us see the German occupation of Eastern Europe as it was perceived at the time, through the eyes of a very history-conscious teenager—the author on his road to the Red Army through the different stages of German rule.

---

1. Alfred Novotny, *The Good Soldier* (Bedford, PA: Aberjona, 2002).

2. Johann Voss, *Black Edelweiss* (Bedford, PA: Aberjona, 2002).

3. Gabriel Temkin, *My Just War: The Memoir of a Jewish Red Army Soldier in World War II* (Novato, CA: Presidio, 1998); Mansur Abdulin, *Red Road from Stalingrad* (Barnsley: Pen & Sword Military, 2004).

Having distinguished himself as a brave combat commander under the last Russian czar, the author's father's actions ensured that his family would be treated with suspicion and sometimes be persecuted by the Soviet regime. This aspect of Roman's diary was also why only some of its excerpts were published in the Soviet press. Incidentally, in these articles the author was said to be deceased.

In some ways, Roman's teen diary may even be compared to Anne Frank's. She gave the world an image of what life was like in occupied Western Europe. Roman paints a vivid canvas of a German-ruled Eastern European community through the eyes of a teenager. As Roman was not a Jew, however, he was able to snoop around and report to his diary to an extent to which Anne could only dream. Roman was able to write a unique record of how the Jewish population of Kremenets was systematically abused and ultimately exterminated.

When the young author wrote his diary under Nazi occupation, he could not always grasp the whole picture of what was happening and at times misunderstood events due to faulty rumors or propaganda (surprisingly often, though, the author's reports and forecasts were correct). In this book you will, therefore, also find passages explaining misconceptions. To clearly show where the front lines and borders actually were at certain points of the war, the publishers have added maps to help understanding.

Having lost around 27 million citizens to German bombs, bullets, racial policy, and, initially, very poor Soviet leadership, the Soviet Union was marked by WWII like no other nation. This is the reason why, 60 years later, the gigantic events of 1941 to 1945 are still highlighted, and now also debated, in Russian society more than anywhere else.

Not only is WWII very present in Russian society even today, but WWII veterans like Roman Kravchenko-Berezhnoy are still in 2007 taking an active part in the economic and social life of their country. Roman has chosen not to retire, but to keep on serving the Russian Academy of Sciences in the Arctic until his body capitulates.

As a civilian, but due to his experience as a military interpreter, Roman even became involved, most unexpectedly, in an act of airline terrorism in the Soviet Union. He thus involuntarily came to visit the editor's homeland, Sweden. As Roman says, however, "all this will be related in due time."

As you read this book, you'll get to know a very much alive Russian gentleman who, as a consequence of his wise and loving parents, at the time of my writing these words is still able everyday, through his behavior, to pass on the best aspects of pre-revolutionary Russia.

I would like to acknowledge the assistance of Marina Guba for her excellent translation of the manuscript; Peder Axensten, Tom Houlihan, Yan Mann,

Scott McMichael, Terry Poulos, and Marc Rikmenspoel for their invaluable input during the translation and editing stages; and David Glantz for his insightful comments in the foreword of the book.

During all stages of editing this book I have also benefited from the huge support of my wife, Ann-Sofie, and editor-in-chief, Patricia K. Bonn. Thanks to Patti's husband, the late Keith E. Bonn, the translation and editing of *Victims, Victors* was initiated. Kit Bonn's attitude towards history will always inspire me.

Lars Gyllenhaal
January 2007

Preface

Some time ago, I was riding a bus from our train station to downtown. The bus was almost empty. A fare collector, walking freely up the aisle, approached me. My wife has told me that in such situations I don't have to demonstrate my identification—anybody could tell I was a senior so I could ride the bus for free. My vanity, however, drove me to pull out my ID and open it up. I just felt like doing it! The lady stared at the little gray booklet and with some confusion she asked, "What's that?"

"My ID certifying that I participated in the Patriotic War," my vanity kept pushing on and I continued without catching a breath, "of 1812," referring not to the Great Patriotic War (as we call World War II), but to the Patriotic War (the repulse of Napoleon's invasion in 1812).

The expression on her face showed she was even more confused now. She smiled slightly, still unsure. Another woman, sitting in a front seat, said loudly and clearly without even turning her head, "You're certainly well preserved." The situation was relieved to everybody's pleasure.

The inclination to make jokes using any opportunity and to make sarcastic self-comments has gotten me into trouble many times, yet I still keep acting like that and there is no way to stop me from doing so. As my life experience has taught me, this fortunate gift is not a common one, and it feels good to belong to such a particular minority.

When I think about it, the joke that I cracked in that bus was not at all nonsensical. For today's younger generation just entering their adult life, the events of half a century ago—or for that matter almost two centuries ago—are melted into one distant past. My granddaughter asked me one day what the "USSR" was, yet this was the reality of only fifteen years ago.

How is it that I have come to live such a long life? To begin with, I believe that a man's life is much easier with joy in his heart. I think that this joy extends longevity. Recently a foreign visitor was surprised when he learned how old I was. I used this occasion to explain my "preservation theory": in northernmost Russia (where I live) the average temperatures are quite low, and in this environment a body is preserved longer (like a piece of refrigerated meat). The bottom line is that it doesn't go bad, especially if the body in question doesn't indulge in alcohol or tobacco. Additionally, I do my morning exercises, treadmill, water treatment, and so on. The academic circles where I have spent some five decades now have no argument against this theory.

I was destined to have a long life, and for me, just like for other witnesses to the German occupation whose numbers sadly keep decreasing, the WWII period has not yet become a part of the past. It is a part of our own lives, seemingly brief, but nonetheless significant and meaningful! Many of those who live today do so because of the millions who covered the fire-spewing guns of that war with their bodies.

⸻◦◦◦⸻

I didn't start out to write a memoir. This, in fact, began as a diary of my experiences under German occupation. To it I have added a collection of "snapshots" from my memory. Whole years may leave no trace, but occasional moments leave their images and remain with us until the end of our lives. I have tried to reproduce these "snapshots" as they were, without any retouching, maintaining the Russian principle of "the truth, only the truth, and nothing but. . . ."

My diary presents a composite picture of how I viewed the prelude to the end of the world—as it seemed then. That was the kind of time in which we lived. I keep writing now about the time rather than about myself. More precisely, I am writing about the time as perceived in my mind.

Our glorious Marshal Zhukov, one of the most important Soviet military commanders of World War II, titled his war memoirs *Memories and Reflections.* I had the honor to fight under his standards for almost a year, from the summer of 1944. He was a marshal and I was a private. He told his story many years ago. Now I wish to tell mine.

In a sense I started to write the book you are now holding in your hands way back in 1941. In 1944 I stopped writing in my diary when I joined the Red Army. I almost forgot about it until something unexpected happened in the year of 1958. . . .

Prologue:
A Nationwide Search Ends

Life occasionally provides a great surprise: an unexpected "sign" seems to herald potential trouble, and you face this omen armed with negative emotions. Only with hindsight do you realize that you should have rejoiced rather than given in to dread. I experienced a clear example of this in 1958.

I came home from work. A subpoena was waiting for me in our mailbox. I was ordered "to appear on the date so-and-so [the very next day] at 3:00 PM at the Department of Internal Affairs [also called the militia and meaning the Soviet police], Room number so-and-so. By order of [name], Major of Militia."

One Guards Captain once told me, "In uniform, you report to your superiors, you do not just 'appear.' 'Appearing' is for Christ, as when he 'appeared' before the people!" (He was referring to the painting "The Appearance of Christ before the People," a famous masterpiece by Alexander Ivanov, now in the Tretyakov Gallery, in Moscow, Russia.) I'd been out of the military for a while by 1958, though, and my encounters with the militia (that is, the Soviet police) were limited to visits to the office for domestic ID cards. So what was going on? I was in my own country in my hometown above the Arctic Circle. I was a full-fledged and law-abiding citizen. Why was I upset and anxious having received that subpoena? Perhaps because it reminded me of how things had once been? There *had* been police encounters in my life, and injustice, but that was in the past.

The major was young, athletic, and polite. There was a little diamond-shaped university alumni badge on the breast of his uniform. He invited me to sit down. He didn't offer me the chance to smoke, but on second thought, I wouldn't have anyway.

"Your name?" he began.

"Roman Alexandrovich Kravchenko-Berezhnoy," I replied.

"You have a double last name. Is it a pen name?"

"Usually pen names are results of some literary, or as they say, some creative activity of actors, poets. I can't boast of any achievements in that domain yet. I got the last name from my parents. Generally speaking, from my ancestors."

"Do you write at all?"

"I would say no."

"You would say, . . ." he continued. "So, your place of birth is Kremenets. That is in Western Ukraine. Bandera gangs were raging there, in 1944, until, perhaps, 1950. [Stepan Bandera (1909–1959), head of the Organization of Ukrainian Nationalists (OUN). At the beginning of the German-Soviet war in 1941, the OUN announced the establishment of a new independent Government of Ukraine. Later the Germans disbanded this government and arrested its members. Bandera was sent to Sachsenhausen in Germany where he spent the remainder of the war. The OUN continued struggling against the Soviet authorities well into the 1950s. *Ed.*] Where were you then?"

The Major has obviously done his homework.

"In the spring of 1944 I joined the Red Army and was deployed to the front. I was in active military service until 1950, stationed in Germany. When I got back it was pretty calm. Sometime in the late 1940s, though, my aunt, Nadezhda Vassilievna, and Volodya, her son, were caught by the bandits, tied up with barbed wire, and buried alive."

"I see. . . . Do you have any other family in Kremenets?" he asked.

"My mother, Yuliya Yakovlevna, and brother, Yuri, live there. My father Alexander Vassilievich is buried there."

"Did you all live there during the occupation?"

"From July 1941 through March 1944, we lived all together in Kremenets, not moving anywhere."

"You weren't hurt, were you? Everybody survived. . . ."

Sounds like we had done something wrong.

"Yes, and I'm still amazed by this," I said.

"Were your brother and father in the military?"

"After the liberation, my brother was designated to be a communications technician. He had been a student before the war, that is, I mean, prior to 1939. He was a student at Warsaw University and he was very much into amateur radio. Now he is the chief of the communications center in Kremenets. My father was in the military in the First World War; he served in the old Russian Army. In 1944 he no longer qualified for induction, although he attempted to. . . ."

Well, that should be enough. He hardly wants a lecture anyway.

He went on, "Before 1939 the area was Polish territory. Your parents were Russian. So, then they were . . . like immigrants?"

"Exactly so. One of the results of the Polish-Soviet war of 1920 was that borders "moved" east. My parents simply remained in their own home, in Kremenets. My father was a disabled war veteran and a former Czarist officer, which was not an advantageous thing to be in Soviet Russia, nor in the Poland of that time. Comrade Major, may I ask you . . . ?"

He cut my question off, "Everything will be explained in due time, Roman Alexandrovich. [The second name used here is the patronymic one, denoting the first name of Roman's father, Alexander. *Ed.*] Tell me more about your town of Kremenets. How many residents are there? You do visit the place, don't you?"

"There were over 30,000 people before the war, almost 40,000 when refugees from the West started flooding in. Now there are some 20,000 people."

"How's that?"

"The Germans," I answered. "During their occupation, the Nazis slaughtered almost 15,000 people."

"Jews? This was a part of the former Pale of Settlement," he said, referring to the zone singled out for Jewish residence in the areas annexed from Poland and Turkey.

Did the Major get his degree in history or what?

"Not only Jews." I responded. "Ukrainians, Poles, Russians, even Czechs used to live there. It was that kind of a place. Everybody got their share of suffering during the German occupation."

"Your parents were originally from there. The town was small; you must have known everybody there."

"Yes, and everybody knew us. My parents knew a lot of people in the area."

"Were there by any chance other families named Kravchenko?"

"Never heard of any."

"What did they call you as a child?"

"Usually—Romka."

"Did you go by your double last name when in the military, too?"

"No, I didn't. I went by Kravchenko only. There was no time for such peculiarities and double names mean a lot of hassle, even today. Moreover, in the military, . . ."

"So you could just as well be called Romka Kravchenko? I mean back then, in Kremenets."

"That was the only name I went by then."

"I see. Roman Alexandrovich, you're not in a hurry, are you? Could you sit here and wait for half an hour or so? I could summon you again, but let's get it all straight right away. I will have to talk now to some people, and will get back to you."

The Major seemed to have relaxed somewhat.

"Well, of course, if it is necessary."

"So, you don't write anything nowadays, do you? What about earlier? Any notes, diaries?" he asked.

Ah, here we go!

"Yes. I kept a diary during the years of the occupation. I maintained it from 1941 through 1944."

"What happened to that diary?" the Major asked.

"I hid it away when leaving for the front. I wanted to keep it secret. Later, from the front, I wrote home to my father. The diary was submitted to the State Commission on Investigation of Nazi War Crimes. The diary included numerous records of such. My father wrote me later that the diary was included in the materials of the Soviet prosecution at the Nuremberg Trials. My parents received a letter from the Prosecutor-General's Office stating that fact and expressing appreciation for it. The diary was then returned. Now it's kept in Kremenets, in a local museum, together with the letter."

"Yes. It's very interesting. Could you please sit here, in the reception lounge? I will invite you in."

"I will invite you" rather than "I'll call for you." That's some progress.

About half an hour later the Major finished his conversation with Moscow.

"So, Roman Alexandrovich, the Ministry of Internal Affairs announced a nation-wide search. To be more exact, the search originated from the Ministry's Central Archive. They are looking for a Romka Kravchenko from Kremenets, who kept the diary during the war. I believe we can report the writer as found?"

"I wasn't lost anywhere, you know."

The Major smiled tightly, for the first time during our meeting. "I reported on our conversation. They send you their best regards and ask you to wait for an official query. They would like to publish your diary; a writer found its copy in the Archive. Yes, I have to admit that when it comes to a nationwide search, it is very rare that the individuals in question are wanted for positive reasons. So, this case ends with a most pleasant twist."

Thus, the Major provided an unexpected twist as well. I had come feeling no enthusiasm whatsoever. It truly does happen to everyone. You expect the worst, but the actual outcome can be the opposite—or not. It depends.

The Major shook my hand. When I first walked in, he wouldn't. He didn't know me then. Can one person really know another? Can anyone know even oneself well?

As a result of this conversation I was invited to Moscow, to the Central State Archive of the October Revolution, where I met very friendly people. They requested a copy of the original diary from Kremenets, and then I was busy comparing the original text with the typewritten copy. At the end of this work, a copy of my diary was presented to me.

Excerpts from the diary were published in the Soviet press. Large parts of the diary could not be published as they were not "politically correct" at the time.

Before I let you open my wartime diary, however, it is appropriate to go further back in time, to see why I became so interested in following world events. . . .

Early Years

1935: War Enters My Thoughts

My story begins in what was then Poland, in a largely Ukrainian district in the time between the world wars. My Russian parents-to-be had found themselves there as the result of the upheavals of the Russian Civil War, when people and borders migrated. My parents were born at the end of the nineteenth century in the same area as I was—but it was then not part of Poland, but the Russian Empire. I came into the world in 1926.

As I grew, the first thoughts that really troubled my soul had to do with the word "Abyssinia." Then, in 1935, the dictator of Italy, Benito Mussolini, was waging a war against Abyssinia, which is today's Ethiopia. Mussolini wanted to turn Italy into a vast and powerful colonial empire.

My family's interest in Abyssinia was because of Russia's ties there. Russian Orthodox priests had served as missionaries in Abyssinia. There had been Russian doctors there, too, in a Russian hospital, helping Abyssinia. Czar Peter's own servant Hannibal, Pushkin's ancestor, was originally from those lands. [Alexander Sergeyevich Pushkin (1799–1837), a poet and writer viewed as Russia's greatest poet. According to tradition, among the ancestors of the poet there was an Abram Hannibal, a princeling from Abyssinia bought as a slave by Czar Peter the Great. *Ed.*] I learned all of this then, when I was only nine years old, and mostly from my father. My father knew everything, I thought.

I can't say today for sure which side the Polish media generally was taking at the time, but the *Wieczor Warszawski*—the evening paper in Warsaw, which my classmate Tadek Vrona brought us daily [his mother, *Pani* (Madame) Vrona, owned a newsstand at the corner of Targova and Vilenska Streets]— obviously took the side of the victim of the aggression. In my family, the attitude toward the political situation was the same (as they would put it today, affected by the fourth estate!). The events in faraway Africa were discussed enthusiastically, and I got hooked on reading the paper. Even though I was just nine years old at the time, I read every news report that I could about the war in Abyssinia. I got excited when the Italians initially were defeated. I was outraged when they used gas in their attacks—my father had inhaled poison gas in the trenches of the World War and I knew about this deadly weapon from his stories. I was anxious when the heroically fighting, barefoot, and poorly armed troops of Emperor Hailie Selassie began losing the war.

Many years later I saw the Emperor in Sevastopol during his state visit to the USSR after his victorious return to Addis Ababa. There in Sevastopol, the city of everlasting Russian military glory, I happened to be present when Hailie Selassie arrived, and we actually looked each other in the eye, if only for a moment. It was a glance that he may have instantly forgotten, but one that I still carry around within me. In addition to his glance I will never forget how I saw him descend to the warship that would take him back and the impressive salute that was then fired in his honor. With the thunder of the naval guns still ringing in my ears I went back into the wonderful city and experienced one of those spectacularly beautiful evenings that can be had only in Sevastopol.

Even then, in my childhood years, my father's stories about the World War and the Russian Civil War seemed like accounts of something long gone in history. I thus understand how distant the Second World War seems to today's generation. In those years, however, it was approaching, and we couldn't avoid talking about it.

Alexandra Vassilievna, my granddaughter, was named after her great-grandfather. If it had been a boy, he would have been named Alexander. Well when I was Alexandra's age, my head was swimming with various then-current events—Abyssinia, gas attacks, and so on. I wonder whether hers does, too. Or do they, the children of today, have it all different now? We felt we were *on the eve* then.

On the Eve

Our kitchen smelled heavily of something unusual—it smelled of tar, leather, horse sweat, and something else that reminded one of traveling and brought on anxiety. Uncle Petro was sitting on a stool, in the center of the kitchen. [Uncle, a common form of address from children to an adult man (not necessarily related). An adult woman would be called Aunt. *Trans.*] He sat slouching, with his legs wide apart, and tapped his whip handle on his boot. The smells came from Uncle Petro.

Petro explained, "You see, your honor, *Pan* (Mister) Kravchenko, it's seventeen *verstas* (18.2 kilometers) one way, and then you stay overnight there. Two *zlotys'* (cents) worth of oats alone will be needed. In the meanwhile, I could make two runs to the station, to meet the Warsaw train, or some other, and make some money, and the horses do not get wasted. Let's agree on three *zlotys*—and let's set out on Saturday; with God's help, why not?"

My father responded, "You say, 'runs', but what if you don't get any passengers? There is a fight for every passenger at the station. In Kushlin, though, your horses will graze, you will save your oats, and you will get meals yourself, so what are three *zlotys* for?"

When Uncle Petro spoke, I felt that one couldn't but agree with him, as it all seemed so logical and right. When my father spoke, though, it also seemed right and reasonable, and Uncle Petro should even have to pay for taking us on such a trip. I had wished they wouldn't bargain. Uncle Petro might have gotten upset and left, and then we wouldn't go to Kushlin. In Kushlin there were cherries and there were beehives, and Granny would bring honey still in the combs, lying on a plate, warm and smelling scrumptiously, with a fuzzy bee stuck on them. The bee would buzz angrily. I couldn't see its wings, only a trace of them, as if from a propeller. If it would get free, then beware! Granny would pick the bee cautiously with her hardened fingers and set it free outside the door. Additionally she would bring in a big round loaf of bread with a cabbage leaf design on the top of it, a special touch to her homemade bread—so warm and tasty, too! You could never have bread like this in the city, even in Warsaw. Granny would send me into the cellar, which was in the garden, to bring a jar of sour cream. It was dark inside the cellar, and the earthen floor was cold. The year before something inside there leaped with a splashing noise toward a distant corner, and everybody laughed when I bolted out of the cellar, calming me with, "Those are just frogs, hiding from the heat." If you ask me, frogs don't splash that loudly.

"Uncle Petro, are you going to let me hold the reins?" I asked.

"What if the horses bolt, shall we call for your Mama?" he answered. "Well, when we get out of town, we'll see. Go ahead, kid. Go and check how the horses are doing. Someone may even have stolen them already."

"Go, go. Maybe we are not going anywhere!" Mama then said. I thought it was so typical of Mama to have to stop our trip. We had promised Granny we'd come; we hadn't seen her for a year, how could we "not go"? Well, I thought I could go and take a look at the horses. It would keep me busy, but who would care to steal them, anyway? Their faces were set deep in bags, up to the very eyes, and they were crunching oats. Their eyes were big, brown, friendly looking, and winking at me. In Warsaw, the cabbies would put on special leather horse-blinders so that their horses didn't look around and get scared by cars and trams. In Kremenets, there was no need for blinders. A bus owned by a local pharmacist, *Pan* Leshchinsky, rode around making so much noise and racket that one always had enough time to run outside and take a look at it. Any cabby had plenty of time to maneuver, since he, too, heard the bus approach from a mile away. There was a taxi in town, too—a long cabriolet—but it spent most of the time in the garage getting repaired. It was an old car left from the Great War. My father had a picture in which he is shown sitting in one like that, during the war. In our family museum, we even kept the klaxon from that car—three shiny horns with a red rubber bulb. The signal it made was loud and wonderful! Father once joked, "Thus, one part after another, we'll collect the complete car. In some forty years."

Petro must have painted his carriage recently. It smelled of varnish and fingers would still leave prints. Using such prints, police could have easily tracked down a thief. If the carriage had been found, however, the prints would not have been needed any longer. No, wait, the carriage could be found, but the thief could have run away with the horses. So they'd still have use for fingerprints when searching for him.

"So, young man, are the horses there?" Uncle Petro asked, as he came up behind me.

"Uncle Petro, are we going to Kushlin? Did you reach an agreement?"

"We agreed, why wouldn't we?" he replied. "Two and a half zlotys, and off we go, with God's help. Go get ready."

My father and Uncle Petro had known each other for a long time, for some 20 years. They both fought on the Austrian front in the Carpathian Mountains, in the same regiment. Then there was the German front, which was much more lethal still. When we would leave Warsaw to spend the summer in Kremenets, Uncle Petro always would take us home from the station. Then every year we went to Granny's, to Kushlin, and he would take us there. They would bargain every time, most likely, to seem formal. Uncle Petro said about Dad, "He was a good and a fair commander. The soldiers liked him."

On Saturday, we rode solemnly along Shirokaya Street in Kremenets. Mama and Father rode on the back seat, while my brother, Yuri, and I sat on a bench across from them, behind Uncle Petro's back. Yuri was seven years older than I and attended an academic middle school. He remained haughty, pretending that he was here for no reason. When Mom didn't look, he would give me a bonk on the head. Then he would call me a sneak. He was never home, but always out somewhere. One should find out more about where he spends his time. . . .

As we would ride through town, Father would tip his Panama hat from time to time, and Mama would nod at people. Everybody knew that we were off to Kushlin. It was late July and the heat rose from the cobblestone street and pavements. All different shapes and sizes of houses crowded the street, with their little wooden attics, fancy balconies, and outside stairways. Many of the homes contained modest businesses. There were shoemakers, tailors, and metal workers. It was a true human beehive of the poor, small-town Jewry, with many children and much noise. Usually you could hear banging hammers in almost every home: shoemakers at work from dawn to dusk. There were two shoe factories in town and hundreds of home-based shoemakers worked for the factory owners. As we drove through, there were almost no hammers to be heard because it was Saturday, the Jewish Sabbath, when it was a sin for Jews to work.

I liked that small town. We were all born there, although when my father took a job in Warsaw, we stopped living in Kremenets. We returned there to spend only the summer months, until we finally moved back there just before the war started in 1939. Nevertheless, when we walked along Shirokaya, the men tipped their hats, stopped, and said, "Hello, Alexander Vassilievich. You are back again; you haven't forgotten our town. And this young man, is he your son? He's so big, time flies fast indeed."

Dad began building a house here the year I was born. I would be ten years old soon, but the construction was still in progress. Dad said there was no money as we two "brats" were growing, and we required money for clothes and for education.

Shirokaya (Wide) Street was anything but wide, but it was a very long street, spreading out for a few kilometers. There were houses along it, with gardens behind them, and mountains and forests behind the gardens. While we were rolling on and on along the street, Dad would tell us how during the Russian Civil War, control of Kremenets changed hands 18 times between competing factions. A pogrom was the first thing they organized after taking over the place. ["Pogrom," from the Russian word meaning "devastation." These were mob attacks against the persons and property of a religious, racial, or national minority. The term is most commonly refers to the persecution of Jews in Russia and Eastern Europe. *Trans.*] They persecuted officers who had returned from the front, yet were not in a hurry to take sides in the Russian Civil War and join either the Whites (Czarists) or the Reds (Bolsheviks). Together with Dad, every summer we would go to the monastery wall. There, behind a metal fence, was a small cross and an inscription on a tombstone, a prayer from the fallen officers: "We lived because it was Thy will. We died because Thou told us so. Now save us, because Thou can." Here the Bolsheviks executed officers, my father's comrades-in-arms, who, being disciplined men, had come to get "registered" as ordered. They were buried here as well. My father hadn't appeared, however.

A window in the little apartment where he and Mama lived after they got married had reached down to slightly above the ground, facing the woods. Getting down from the window ledge, my father would run, limping slightly, and hide in the woods every time new "officer hunters" started to bring down our door. They wouldn't touch Mama, who was pregnant by then; a semblance of a "code of conduct" was nevertheless maintained in those days.

Human life was so cheap at the time that it was as easy to shoot a man as to give a catcall to a streetwalker, as my dad once colorfully put it, confounding me. Every summer, therefore, we would bring flowers to the grave near the monastery wall, and stand for a few minutes in silence there. Those events took place so long ago, I thought at the time (1935), when the rule of the *Rzeczpospolita Polska* (Republic of Poland) was only just becoming permanent in Kremenets and the Russian border was then some forty kilometers away to the east, along the Zbruch River. Actually, it wasn't even "Russia" any more; it was "the Soviet Union."

When in Warsaw, my dad seldom shared his memories of the events of that time; I could never persuade him to tell me anything. When we would come over here, though, he would get more cheery and kind. That was another reason why I liked Kremenets so much more.

That autumn I would begin my schooling. Until this point, I had been schooled at home. My parents supposed I was now big enough to be able to deal with some troubles I might have at school connected with my Russian ethnicity. "We can't delay it any more," Dad said. I couldn't get into the *gymnasium* (academic secondary school) without a certificate of completion of six years of school. I didn't want to go to school, and would even get sick when I thought about it. I had two days at my Granny's ahead of me, though. Also, it was still more than a month until September, when school would start. It was so quiet and wonderful here.

As we left town on our way to Kushlin, having passed by the last houses in the street, the carriage would take a long, slow climb up the hill, and finally stop. Petro would whistle something to his horses and foamy puddles would spread out from under the wheels. We would look away civilly. We would look down at our town of Kremenets. It was an ancient place. The invading Tatars of Khan Baty had come down this road in the thirteenth century, laying siege to a nearby castle standing on a mountain. They could not capture it, so they spent a night in villages surrounding it and rolled on into the Carpathian Mountains, toward the Hungarian plains. There are residents in those villages who even today are slightly slant-eyed. Later, amorous couples would stroll by the old castle walls and from above, the town looks like a model; you can sit there observing its slow-paced life for hours. Kremenets had its own smell. It smelled of leather and hides soaking in barrels, and of peat-coal smoke. This smell was the first thing that would greet those arriving into town at the train station. Then, there would come a horde of cabbies, attacking the passengers, just like Baty's nomadic Tatars who once swept through this region.

There was another event in 1935 that has left a trace in my memory: I saw a dead man for the first time in my life. Only a few years later, there would be so many of them, way too many, everywhere and anywhere. People lined up to see this one, however. It was dark when we joined the endless line, several rows wide. The line meandered to the royal castle, where a coffin had been set up on a slightly raised platform. The May night was cold. We warmed ourselves by coal-filled barrels arranged along the streets. Then slowly we passed by the elevation, and I looked at a familiar face with a white moustache, recognizable from countless portraits. These were the remains of our chief, Marshal Jozef Pilsudski, "Grandfather of Poland." [The word for "chief" in the original Russian, *vozhd,* is also generally used to describe leaders like Stalin, thus it can be said to be synonymous with "dictator." *Ed.*]

After that, two portraits hung above the blackboard in our classroom, flanking the crucifix: one of the old leader and one of the new one, the latter without any moustache and with a shaven head. We learned to sing a song, "Our Marshal Smigly-Rydz, our beloved and brave chief . . ." in honor of our new leader. The idea of a national chief was popular in the Europe of that day. The cute little songs we sang in our class were all militaristic and cheery. We sang about a cavalry officer who was falling off his horse so handsomely. We sang loud and clear, *"Pulk ulanuv stoi w lese, rym-cym-cym!"* "The cavalry regiment stopped in the woods, rym-cym-cym!"

"Rym-cym-cym" was sounded by the cymbals of a brass band that had been polished until they were shining like gold. Those were festive, invigorating sounds. Each Sunday an infantry regiment marched along Zigmuntovska Street toward Saint Florian's Church, going to mass. The soldiers wore helmets and marched handsomely, stomping their boots on the cobblestones. On horseback, a little behind the commander, there was Lieutenant Colonel Puchalski, the father of my fourth-grade classmate, Jozek. The horses trotted slowly, in time with the martial music: *rym-cym-cym.*

It was Jozek who was the first to demonstrate to me that "might is right."

In a classroom he was sitting right behind me. During a lesson, he whispered barely audibly, without moving his lips, "Quiet. Don't jerk." At the same time he pricked my lower back with the point of his pen. I was sitting, my teeth clenched, and tried my best not to cry or show that it hurt. That torture happened almost daily, ever since I came to the class and they learned that I was an ethnic Russian. The class observed this act in silence. They were afraid of Jozek. His dad was a "legionnaire." [A member of the Polish legions in WWI, Polish military formations that from 1914 to 1917 acted on the side of the "Central Powers"—Germany, Austria and Hungary, on the territory of the "Polish Kingdom." The legions were mainly infantry units under the command of Jozef Pilsudski (until his retirement in 1916). *Ed.*] Jozek was named after Poland's "grandfather," Pilsudski, and Jozek was extremely proud of it. He voiced his opinion of the Abyssinian situation very simply, "Italy is strong. It can do as it likes." Most likely, their family was reading different newspapers than my family read.

Panna (Miss) Javorska, our class mistress, treated me well, but also acted as if she never noticed Jozek's actions. Complaining about it meant to be disgraced in front of the whole class. I tried playing hooky—once I put a thermometer into a boiling kettle because I wanted it to appear that I had a fever.

The thermometer exploded and I had to tell my parents everything. Dad's face whitened, he patted me silently on my back and left. In a minute he was back, and told me not to go to school that day.

I was back in class a week later. Nothing had changed. That day, in all lessons, *Panna* Javorska was calling Tadek Vrona, a chronic flunkie, to the board all day long. Usually he was dozing in the back row, and was seldom bothered. That day, when during the last lesson of the day he got another F, the teacher suddenly announced, "If things go on like this, Vrona will never finish school. Vrona will immediately move from the back desk. Vrona will sit together with . . . say with Kravchenko (being Polish, she distorted it and pronounced it "Krav-CHEN-ko") Romek is a good student. Maybe together, as a joint effort, we'll be able to help Vrona?"

The class observed all this with tense silence. With noise and wheezing, Vrona got out of his desk, then pushed in next to me. He smelled of printing ink. He was one of a few classmates who visited our home. He brought the newspapers, and Mama always tried to treat him with something tasty. Those private contacts never affected our relationship in the classroom, though; he simply ignored me there. Somehow he was never called "Tadek," but always *Vrona* (raven); perhaps because his last name could serve just as well as a nickname since he was big and kind of dark. The following day after Vrona's installation by my desk, however, no sooner had I jerked from another prick, as the sound of a smack followed. *Panna* Javorska turned back slowly from the board and asked the class, "Children, what happened?" The class was quiet and solemn. Jozek was covering up his nose with his hand, and pink snot was running down his sleeve.

From then on, they left me alone. The traces of that pricking have survived until today, though, on the relevant area of my body, as the proof of torture carried out in the 1930s by a little *pilsudchik* (Polish nationalist).

━━━◈◈◈◈◈━━━

My dad knew everything—languages, history, botany, the Holy Scripture, and so on. We always had people in our home. Our small apartment had only two rooms, but a lot of people, of all sorts, came to see us: students (Yuri's friends); priests who we knew (an Orthodox church was nearby); an old Jewish lady that kept bringing old books in hope of selling them; and Lyda, a lifelong student, who would tell us how she survived by eating sauerkraut and fish oil, both being very cheap. Yech!

The conversations in our apartment were in Russian. It was a little corner of Russia. It was not advisable to speak Russian in the street; people could swear at you. It was forbidden to speak Russian in school.

In the evenings, Father Ignatius, a former captain in the czar's personal guard, would settle into an old wingback sofa. He had taken monastic vows after the Civil War. He sat there, smoking incessantly. He was extremely skinny, and when seen through tobacco smoke in his black robe, he reminded me of Don Quixote and Satan at the same time. Perhaps he could have told a lot about his war experiences in Russia, against the Bolsheviks, but he didn't like to share that. Mostly he kept silent, thinking about something that seemed to weigh heavily on his mind. Mama said he had consumption [tuberculosis. *Ed.*]. He would call me up, rumple my hair, and pull a candy from his deep pocket. He wore pinstriped pants under his robe, like everyone else.

"Do you study?" he would ask me.

"Yes, I study," I'd respond.

"Study, lad. Learning makes people wise. Do they bully you at school?"

"They call me a Bolshevik. A 'damned Bolshevik'."

Father Ignatius would smile strangely at some thought of his. "Be patient, lad. They once suffered from us. Take, for example, Alexander Vassilievich Suvorov, your father's idol and namesake. [Alexander Vassilievich Suvorov (1729–1800), Russian military commander, still much admired in Russia for his achievements in the Russian-Turkish War of 1787–91 and the French Revolution. *Ed.*] Here he fought Poles as a brigadier general. He certainly was involved with the division of Poland.

"So, what now, eye for an eye, tooth for a tooth?" Dad would butt in, and get all wound up. "We oppressed them, and now they oppress us? And Ukrainians, Byelorussians, and Jews? And on and on, until the end of time?"

"Why until the end of time?" Father Ignatius would retort, covering himself up in the clouds of smoke. "Attempts are made to overcome national intolerance. Look at the very same Bolsheviks. Can't judge how successful they are, though. Here, more than a third of the population of the *Rzeczpospolita* is comprised of ethnic minorities. There are six million Jews alone. The oppression of minorities does not help strengthen this country! 'Love one another', the Savior commands us, in no way suggesting separation into pure and not so pure." Then suddenly changing the subject, Father Ignatius would say, "By the way, what was the name of the division headed by Suvorov in 1768 during the Polish campaign?"

"He led his Suzdal Regiment," Dad would answer. "Later on, however, he was in charge of a brigade."

"And later, by what name was that glorious regiment known?" asked Father Ignatius.

No answer.

"The 77th Tenginsky Infantry Regiment, your Honor! The very same regiment that later accepted Mikhail Lermontov, our great Romantic poet, into its ranks." Father Ignatius would laugh with satisfaction, inhaling smoke and choking on his cough. Sitting in the corner of the sofa, behind that smoky curtain, you could not tell for certain whether it was a monk speaking or the brave officer who had served under General Denikin against the Bolsheviks in the Russian Civil War.

A few years later, General Denikin addressed the Russian émigrés with an appeal not to support Nazi Germany in its war against the USSR

1938: Determining My Homeland

"Tell me, is a homeland a place where one was born?" I would ask my father.

"Well, it is not that simple, . . ." he'd reply. "What's the Polish word for 'homeland'?"

"Ojczyzna," I'd say.

"Right, *ojczyzna,* fatherland, the land of our fathers. It is not necessarily the land where one was born. It is the land with which a person is connected through generations, with one's family roots, the land that is considered the most dear. Take Poles, for example. For centuries they were deprived of their statehood, and even the name 'Poland' was discontinued, but they remained Poles. They considered Poland their homeland, and not the region near the Vistula, or the Russian, German, or Austrian-Hungarian Empires. History showed that such oppression does nothing but enhance the feelings of patriotism and love toward one's homeland."

"And our homeland. . . ." I'd say.

"Yes, and how you are doing at school?" he'd say, trying to change the subject. "Show me your report book, let's take a look."

I would bring him my report book. "I was born in Poland. And they still call me a *Moskal,* a Bolshevik, and beat me up. . . ." [*Moskal,* a derogatory name for a Russian person; used in Ukraine (especially, Western), and Poland. *Trans.*]

Dad would sigh and push my report book aside. In it everything was in order; it couldn't be otherwise. "You see, these are all very complicated issues, and you're too young to try to understand them. There was the time when the Poles were going with fire and sword across Russia, putting a Czar of their choosing on the throne in Moscow. You learned about *Hetman* Chodkiewicz and *Hetman* Zolkiewski in history class, didn't you?"*

Hetman is a military title that was used in the Polish-Lithuanian state (during the sixteenth to eighteenth centuries). Later, in the Ukrainian National Army, which borrowed titles from Poland, the *Hetman* was commonly the chief of the armed forces and the chief commander in the absence of the king in the battle. Jan Karol Chodkiewicz (1560–1621) was a Polish general, noted for his remarkable victories against Swedes and Turks. Stanislaus Zolkiewski (1647–1720), was Chancellor of Poland and a talented military commander.

"We did," I'd reply.

"See, they teach you to be proud of them for those deeds," he'd continue. "Almost 200 years later, Suvorov assaulted Warsaw and took it over, and ever since, the Russian emperors have considered these lands as their own. So the Poles passed hatred of the Russian emperors on, from one generation to another. Additionally, those who were not so smart passed hatred toward anything Russian. There are always many fools in this world. Now we have to suffer for their foolishness."

"But the Bolsheviks," I'd say, "they killed the Czar, and. . . ."

"Yes, lad. You've done your homework? Then, go to bed, it's getting late."

This would happen every time. Dad still thought I was too young and he could not discuss any serious things with me. I was eleven and a half years old, though, and Dad didn't have to worry that I would say something I shouldn't at the wrong occasion. I had certainly done so a few years before, when Father Victor was visiting us. He had sneakily made up little horns from remains of his gray hair, scaring me. I started crying; he got scared and gave me ten *grosh* (cents) to buy an ice cream. Through my tears I asked him, "The coins are not fake, are they?"

His laughter roared throughout our apartment. I began crying even more, from hurt feelings, and he kept laughing, "Right! You have a child with quite materialistic inclinations!"

Mama began fussing around me, "Aren't you ashamed of yourself? Father Victor is a priest, how can you say such things?"

I went on, "So, then if he is a priest, why did he scare me with horns, looking like a devil?" What followed then is better left unsaid!

Even later, when Father Victor would come back, he'd wink at me and put his fingers to his head like a devil, making sure Mama didn't see him.

One day Tanya, a girl in my class, had a new lace collar on her dress. She even glanced at me in class. She seldom smiled, but whenever she did, it made me feel good. Unlike me, they didn't bully her in class. Perhaps because she was a girl, and a pretty girl at that. Also, her last name—Makedonska—sounded quite Polish. They had to twist mine into Krav-CHEN-ko, though. They always stressed the second to last syllable. The French stress the final syllable. In Russian, and *theoretically* in all other languages, it's pronounced KRAV-chen-ko.

Father's cool hand touched my forehead. Every night he would check to see if I had a fever. Or perhaps he did so instead of saying "good-night." Father knew everything. Mama wanted me "to speak fluent French," because she said that it was "a language of high society, understood and spoken every-where." In Kremenets they made me go to Old Lady Wengrinowska all sum-mer long. Mama said that the madam speaks with a real Parisian accent. I wished they had taught me music instead. Music lessons were expensive, though, while French lessons were cheap, as there were many who wished to give French lessons. They were immigrants, all of whom were elderly and needy. Colonel Wengrinowsky was very old. He was my godfather.

The next day I would again go to school. Tanya would be there. If it hadn't been for her, I would have called in sick and stayed home.

I wasn't afraid of the Polish language exam. In one of the final lessons in the academic year, having returned our composition books, *Panna* Javorska said, "Romek (another way of saying my first name) wrote the best composition. It is unpleasant for me to admit the fact that the best composition in the class was not written by a Polish student. I'm sure Romek will have no difficulty in passing the admission tests to the *gymnasium.*" These words earned me a few punches in the restroom, from Puchalski and his pals; they held me while he beat me.

The entrance exams for the public *gymnasium* passed by in a flash indeed.

"The next is Krav- . . . Krav-CHEN-ko, Roman. What an odd last name."

"*Pan* Professor, my last name is pronounced KRAV-chen-ko."

"What? You are telling me how to pronounce? Well, tell me, Krav-CHEN-ko, . . ." he retorted.

Five minutes later, a handwritten conclusion was put across my test paper: *Nie zdolny do pojmowania nauk* (Not capable of understanding sciences.) With this summary I went back home.

These adventures brought me to a private Russian, rather than a public Polish, *gymnasium.* There, in the Russian *gymnasium,* for the first time ever I felt as if I was an equal of the other students. I was equal among the disad-vantaged. This *gymnasium* didn't issue Certificates of Maturity (diplomas); the graduation exams still had to be taken in the public Polish *gymnasium.* My brother, Yuri, had passed it and he was in his second year of studies at the Physics and Mathematics Department of the University of Warsaw, feeling very significant indeed.

Walking into the classroom, in the doorway I bumped into Tanya. For the first time ever she said, "Hello, Roma!" and smiled as if all had been planned and organized the way she had wanted. I was so taken aback that I couldn't find words to answer her. I stayed there, blinking, moving my lips and blush-ing. I had a feeling that she enjoyed my behavior.

On Sundays, the entire student body of the *gymnasium* marched to the morning service in an Orthodox Church in the Praga district of Warsaw. Keeping our ranks, our band played "Farewell of a Slavianka," a sad Russian march from the Great War era. We marched proudly, under the standard of our *gymnasium,* the Russian tri-color (horizontal bars of white, blue, and red) with the double-headed Russian eagle. Passers-by stopped and some faces seemed to register surprise. On Sundays all schools of the city marched off to pray to God. Our column was not like any other, however, and in those minutes we didn't feel ourselves in any way disadvantaged. In church, we stood in careful disciplined ranks—boys to the left and girls to the right. When required, we crossed ourselves, and in due time, we knelt down. We exchanged glances. We whispered. We passed messages to each other. Those who didn't come to the church would have to be able to present a note from their parents the next day, explaining to the homeroom teacher the reasons why their child had been absent. The same practice existed in that Polish school that I had just finished, and there we had to fight for the right to attend the Orthodox services, and not march together with everybody else to the Catholic Church. I was granted that, under the responsibility and supervision of my parents.

Later in life, during *Komsomol* (Young Communists' League) events, I would observe certain parallels and similarities.

At that particular moment, however, we were thirteen years old. The beginning of World War II in September 1939 was approaching. For some people on this planet, it was the eve; for others it was the beginning. There were other people for whom it was the end. Tanya died in Warsaw, during German bombings, in the first days of September.

1939: War Hits Poland

There was no one in the office, and I rushed to Dad without knocking on the door. "You know, Dad, we didn't even have two lessons today and. . . ."

My father was standing by his desk, looking at me without a blink, and his face grew pale. He had returned from the war with six wounds and contusions, and this was one of their consequences. Shell fragments still worked their way out of his body. I felt somebody's stare at the back of my head, and a bone-chilling guess rushed through my head, while a queasy, sinking feeling descended in my stomach. I turned slowly around. *Pan* Zagorowski is sitting in a chair in the corner of the room. His face was turning red, his white beard trembled, and his lips unexpectedly began to widen in a smile.

"Dzien dobry, panie dyrektorze. Przepraszam" ("Good day, Mr. Director. I beg your pardon"), I said.

Dad's hand was on my shoulder, and he gently pushed me toward the door, "Go home, son. I will be home soon."

Dad spoke in Russian, quietly and very calmly. He spoke *Russian,* in his office, in the presence of Director Zagorowski.

"Go home, kid, go. Your father will soon be home. He will have plenty of free time. You will tell him everything then," Director Zagorowski said.

It turns out that *Pan* Director speaks Russian.

I dragged my feet home. Mama opened the door, looked at me in silence for a moment, and then asked in a whisper, "What happened?"

"I was at Dad's office, and I spoke Russian there. *Pan* Zagorowski was there, but I didn't see him. He said that Dad will have plenty of time now."

Mama stepped back and sat down. There was nothing else to say. The year before, *Pan* Director had called my father in to his Department and expressed his dissatisfaction with my entry to the Russian *gymnasium,* following in my brother's steps. "To speak Russian at home, he probably knows it well enough. He will need Russian nowhere else. Nowhere and never!" Dad's story of how I was flunked when entering the public *gymnasium* had caused him only to smile, "You should have told me, and everything would have been taken care of." *Pan* Zagorowski was a department head in the Ministry of Religious Confessions and Education.

Indeed, Dad came home almost right after me. He was unexpectedly cheerful.

"You helped out *Pan* Director a lot there! He had spent the whole hour beating around the bush. In August we have to leave the apartment. Come on, cheer up! What will be, will be. It's good that our house in Kremenets is almost complete, and we'll find jobs there. Yuri will transfer to the university in Lvov. They won't have you at the lyceum, that's for sure, but there is a private *gymnasium.*" We're so fortunate with private *gymnasiums.*

The Kremenets lyceum was known in interwar Poland as an elite institution, a center of culture in *Kresach wschodnich,* in the Eastern lands, as that part of Poland was known.

There were but a few days left until the end of that world.

———✦———

Thus we returned to Kremenets, in August 1939. Soon, the broadcasts of Warsaw radio were interrupted, and an announcer repeated, in a steady and formidable tone, "Attention, attention! Approaching! Attention, attention! 46–38 (code numbers sending a message to the Polish Armed Forces in the area that were meaningless to civilian listeners). Passed!" German bombers were locked onto their course toward Warsaw.

On one of those September days, closer to mid-month, I witnessed the appearance of some of those German aircraft in a very dramatic way.

I watched as a plane dove on a procession of black limousines that had lost their shine. Long-nosed Buicks, Packards, Plymouths, and Chevrolets drove in a line toward the southeast along Shirokaya, our cobblestone street that had witnessed so much in its long existence. Somebody managed to see inside one of the cars the familiar, gray-haired head of Ignacy Moscicki, the President of the *Rzeczpospolita*. Perhaps it only seemed so, though. . . .

Of course the radio didn't broadcast that the government had fled Warsaw and tried to reach the Romanian frontier via roads filled with fleeing refugees. It was just then, however, that the "information service" that always began its broadcasts with the phrase "they say that" informed the inhabitants of Kremenets about the escape of the government. Since August the same ancient service had advised everyone of the urgent need to stock up on kerosene, matches, and soap supplies, there was no reason to doubt the validity of this source.

The German command, obviously, had the information not only about the attempted exodus, but also about the route and schedule of the government procession. As a result of a confluence of these two currents of information, we all met—the President, a "Stuka" dive-bomber pilot, and me. I was outside in the street watching the absolutely atypical car traffic of our small town, and demonstrating my profound knowledge of car brands to my provincial friends. The motorcade was moving along its route. The plane reached the point at which its bombs would be released.

Suddenly, the street noises overlapped with a roaring crescendo from above. The plane was diving directly at me. I saw its shadow contours along the axis of a bank: a circle of a propeller, wings at an odd angle, and under them, what appeared to be the claws of a predatory bird. The plane was falling and growing in size, its multiple voices roaring, turning into an unbearable shriek that seemed to pierce my body. During those seemingly endless seconds I experienced, for the first time, a feeling of freezing, paralyzing fear, terror, helplessness, and an utter pity for myself. Why me?

At that moment, the plane let go of its heavy burden, its shriek changed into a deep bellow, and two explosions instantly resonated in my head, ears, and body. I bolted off toward our hillock, toward home, toward my mother, who was already running toward me, running to save me.

That year we didn't hear any more sounds of combat. For me and for my little town, the war of 1939 began and ended with that single Junkers and its two bombs that exploded in some vegetable patches nearby. Other sounds of war soon flooded our town, however, as thousands of refugees and a sea of rumors arrived. Then there were my mother's reddened eyes. There was also a sickening feeling of anxiety that planted itself somewhere within, deep within my stomach, from the very first day when Dad left. He left on the first day of war, on 1 September, when huge, almost yard-long posters appeared on all walls, with a profile of a white eagle and a black word, *"Mobilizacja"* (mobilization).

The town fell ill with those posters. The squadrons of a cavalry regiment clomped on their way along Shirokaya; the horses danced to the sounds of a cheery song, *"Jak to na wojence ladnie, kiedy ulan z konia spadnie!"* (What a pretty sight it is, at war, when a cavalry officer falls off his horse.) Everything was well thought over in case of war, everybody knew their place, and since spring the walls had been full of gaily-colored posters, *"Silni, zwarci, gotowi!"* (Strong, united, ready!) During the spring term in Warsaw, we enthusiastically dug out a shelter in the schoolyard to be used in case of enemy air raids. In the night, at home, I listened, terrified, to the roar of planes on training missions in the black sky above the darkened city. They were imitating night bombing raids and wooden blocks hit the ground noisily. It wasn't very clear where the enemy was—to the east? Or to the west? What if they came from both sides, at the same time? But then, Stalin and Hitler were enemies, weren't they?

In our backwoods village we hadn't yet grasped that they had become friends. Then it all started: from the west and north, from East Prussia, and from the south, from prostrate and downtrodden Czechoslovakia. The previous year Poland, too, had grabbed a piece of that country, Zaolzie, which suddenly turned out to be a historically Polish region. Now the Germans poured in from everywhere. Only in the east was it still quiet. The Polish horse cavalry managed to cross almost the whole country and on the day when the government limousines drove across our town, they charged the enemy in mounted formations somewhere there, in the west. We watched as a *KOP* battalion from the Border Protection Corps marched west. Boys cried out *"niech zyje!"* (Live long!). Adult men kept a gloomy silence, while women cried.

Who was holding the border with the Soviets? March music was broadcast from Warsaw, where a Polish Army colonel ended his daily addresses with a clear appeal, "Soldiers! Aim and shoot well! Don't waste the bullets!" For some reason neither these addresses, nor any military updates provided any actual information about the current situation at the front. The marches were interrupted, and a familiar announcer's voice would go on, slowly and clearly, *"Uwaga, uwaga! Nadchdzi!"* (Attention, attention! Approaching . . .) and recite some code numbers. The feeling of anxiety grew only worse. Müller, a German *gymnasium* teacher, was arrested. The police found a transmitter; it was said that he was helping to direct German bombers. Rumors spread: the Government had fled; the High Command had fled; Warsaw was encircled;

the Germans were rolling eastward unhindered and they wouldn't stop at the Zbruch; they would go on, against the Soviets.

Then, like a bolt out of the blue, the Red Army crossed the Polish border. The Germans were not coming to our town!

Tense silence filled the town. Shirokaya seemed dead. At noon, from the east, a few armored vehicles arrived, followed by a slow moving convoy of open trucks of then-unknown types. Soldiers in gray overcoats and deep helmets rode in those trucks, holding rifles with thin bayonets tipped by blue steel. A car stopped by the curb; I didn't know its make. The men made gestures, telling me to come up. There were four men in the car. They wore Sam Browne belts, but had no shoulder boards. They had red little squares on the corners of their collars. They were obviously officers. One addressed me in an unfamiliar language. A confused pause followed. He persistently repeated one Russian word, *"voenkomat"* (abbreviation for *Voenny Commissariat,* Military Commissariat, a Soviet military draft board). Ah! I guess that this man is their interpreter, and he is trying to speak Polish to me. An Army recruiting center? That would be a *PKW—Powiatowa komenda wojskowa—* not far from here, I answered them in Russian. The one who sat in front held a map in his lap, and I recognized the contour of Kremenets on it. My dad had taught me how to read maps. I learned about them as a scout, too. I tried to point and show on the map, but his hand covered it. Their faces were unsmiling. I heard somebody say, "He is from the Whites," and the car left.

"From the Whites. . . ." I recalled the mass grave by the monastery wall.

⸺∘◦∘⸺

My father was gone for about three weeks in that awful, brief war in 1939. He came back home, riding a bicycle, unshaven, his face ashen. He was dressed in civilian clothes. Though it was planned that upon arrival to Modlin (a fortress near Warsaw, where he was assigned as a reserve officer) he would be issued a uniform, ammunition, and weapon, he couldn't even reach his assigned destination. He didn't get to fight again. Everything was over by the time he arrived. Had he managed to get a uniform and receive an officer ID instead of his civilian passport, he would have spent his time until the spring of 1945 in a German *OfLag* (POW camp for officers). Or he would have remained forever in the Katyn trenches, together with thousands of other Polish officers, mostly reservists, who were captured during the Red Army's "Polish campaign." [The Katyn massacre was a mass execution that took place outside Katyn in eastern Poland (now Belarus). The victims were 4,000 Polish officers that had been taken prisoner by the Red Army in 1939. *Ed.*]

Father had had his fair share of fighting in World War I. By the age of 22 he had risen from enlisted volunteer to the rank of junior captain and battalion commander. He was highly decorated and had received a gold-plated dagger engraved "For bravery." He also preserved with much pride a plate with the imperial monogram: a crown, the letter N, and a Roman numeral two (II). He brought that plate as a keepsake from the Winter Palace where the Royal family gave a reception in honor of those front veterans who were Companions of the Order of St. George and who were treated in Petrograd hospitals. The Poles, when ascribing my father into the Polish reserve officer corps, had reduced his rank and that hurt him a lot. Although that setback was only one among the many he had in his lifetime, he viewed it as the most painful one, because he was very proud of his Army youth. Throughout all of my life I frequently have felt a pang of pity when thinking about my father. I wish he were here today; he would have been only a little older than one hundred. He could have seen Sputniks, men landing on the moon, and computers. He also would have witnessed much of what I didn't want to see, however—how vulnerable this world would become at the end of the twentieth century.

1939–1941: Intermission

Intermissions usually aren't very long, but this one lasted almost two years, from the fall of 1939 to June 1941. It was during this time that I finally got a feeling for my homeland. Schools were opened in Kremenets—Ukrainian, Jewish, one Polish, and one Russian. I was sent to the sixth grade, although they could have assigned me to the seventh, but that's not vital anymore. In our class there was even a boy from Georgia, Gogi, the son of a commander from a new Soviet military garrison. Now instead of the cavalry, a tank regiment was stationed by our town. It was *strictly* forbidden to talk about it—it was a military secret, but why? Everybody knew about it.

In the classroom nobody would reproach others for being of this or that ethnicity, and that felt so good! The "eastern" children were brought to school from the garrison on a GAZ truck, manufactured in the Soviet Union at the Gorky Automobile Plant (Russian abbreviation, GAZ). The emblem on the radiator looked very much like that of Ford's, that is, a similar oval with the letters GAZ inside, instead of FORD. This was most probably due to the fact that the machines that made the trucks in the Gorky Automobile Plant were purchased from the Ford factories. Nonetheless the truck was Soviet. Lusya, a daughter of the regimental commander, was also in my class, as well as three other kids, including Gogi. He was assigned to the same desk as I. He immediately began picking on me because of a bicycle, "How come you have two bicycles at home? You're capitalists, you should be dispossessed!" We settled that my bicycle would be as if a common, joint property: Gogi would ride it as much as he wished, on school breaks, after school, and on the weekends. I would ride it to school and at home because I lived far away. That was how we resolved the matter.

I got my bicycle from my brother, Yuri. He now worked in a village, teaching arithmetic to kids. He was denied admission to the University in Lvov, to continue his studies. Some *commission,* having looked into his personal background information, made a decision: he was a "class-alien" element (meaning that he represented a non-Soviet class). They advised him to seek employment in a rural area, their requirements being lower. Back in the *gymnasium,* Yuri had become interested in amateur radio; he spent hours over circuits, soldering and brazing them. This continued and perhaps kept his mind free of sad thoughts. He was already an adult and he understood it all well. His hobby would play a significant role in the life of our family.

Dad found a job as an accountant in a school for glider pilots. There the cadets wore uniforms and Dad got to bring home rations. Unfortunately, this only lasted for two months. He was called in somewhere, had a talk with someone, and he was told to start looking for another job. We had never made a secret of our family's background. Perhaps we should have?

Around this time, our friend, Rostislav visited us. He was the "fifth member of the family" who lived in a house behind the hillock.

An ancient friend of my parents and a student of Warsaw University, Rostislav was an ever-present participant in our evenings in the little apartment. Later, he earned a Master of Economic Sciences and Theology degree, and became an exceptional government official. When I was ill, he would bring me an orange. Since those childhood years, I have associated the festive smell of oranges with something infinitely pleasant and in particular, a chance to avoid going to school, where they beat me and called me names. I had always perceived Rostislav, an elegant gentleman and a stubborn bachelor, as a member of our family. I suppose that once, in his student years, he had fallen in love with our mother, and it turned out to be a one-sided-love-for-a-lifetime, or at least for a few decades, but this was a supposition. They have all been united forever in the cemetery behind the monastery wall.

In August of that very long 1939, we left Warsaw while Rostislav remained behind, promising us to come on his holiday in the coming fall. In September a new border appeared separating us, along the Bug River. Nonetheless, in early winter, Rostislav knocked on our door, skinny, unshaven, in a worn coat, with an empty knapsack on his back. We were waiting for him, and having crossed the Bug walking on its ice, he came, as he had promised. He had returned home, just like us. Here, at home in Kremenets, the Soviets were already in power. In Warsaw, he told us not without amusement how during the Russian Civil War as a 16-year-old student, he had been put against a wall by the Reds to be executed: his father was a "his Excellency," the principal of a *gymnasium*. The Reds had subjected him to a mock execution, aiming slightly away, since he was just a kid. Nevertheless, the bits of stone that chipped off the wall hurt him quite badly. Even so, he came to us in the Soviet zone, fleeing from Hitler and the Nazis. Rostislav was not the only one fleeing from the occupied, Nazi-ruled General Government in occupied Poland, and the Soviet bureaucratic "system" was already in place with various restrictions for "class aliens": he was issued a residency permit instead of a passport. This included mandatory monthly "invitations" to certain offices. He got a job as an accountant in the Mining Directorate. That's the kind of family we were then according to our personal background information—not part of Soviet society, but a family of class aliens.

This is despite the fact that I attended a normal Soviet school, where everybody spoke Russian.

Lusya and Toma shared the front desk. When a teacher called me up to the blackboard, they intentionally stared at me. I became confused and blushed, and they enjoyed it. Lusya had a clean white face, and a braid, very fair-colored and very thick. Lusya kept braiding its end continuously with her thin, white fingers. Tomka (as we called Toma) had a short haircut and her hair was messy and sticking out in all directions. Tomka had a mischievous look, while Lusya looked calm and gentle. Both of them wore red scarves, as did Gogi and Slavka. They were all the Pioneers (Communist scout organization for boys and girls) we had. We, the rest of the class, were locals. There were also the refugees from the west among us, from Poland, or from the former Poland. They were fleeing from the Germans. The papers didn't write bad things about the Germans. They were writing bad things about those against whom the Germans fought—the Western capitalists and "plutocrats." We heard about joint parades by units of the Red Army and *Wehrmacht* in Brest and Lvov held right after the end of the campaign to conquer Poland. In art class, I drew a big red star against the backdrop of a black German eagle. I got an "A" for that piece of work.

Fast fighter planes were flying in the sky above the town, diving, shining in the sunlight. They were blunt-nosed and short-winged. We watched movies about Maxim, tractor drivers, Chapayev (one of the early commanders of the Red Army, a Soviet hero of the Civil War immortalized by classic Soviet movies). We heard new songs, sad and cheerful, serious and funny ones. Tank commanders wearing handsome, mustard-colored overcoats walked along Shirokaya (now officially renamed "Stalin Street"), their leather shoulder belts squeaking. We quickly learned to discern their ranks, as well as how to recognize all the new brands of cars and trucks in the streets.

A military classroom was established in our school under the supervision of a retired Red Army sergeant with a "saw" in his collar patch (four triangles arranged so that it looked like a saw; this denoted his military rank later called *starshina*) and badges over his entire chest. We studied a Mosin-Nagant rifle manufactured in the 1930s according to a pattern from 1891. On revolutionary holidays, we carried highly realistic wooden replicas of precisely that rifle, bravely passing in review for the leaders of our region and shouting choruses of hurrahs in response to slogans sounding from the reviewing platform.

We all loved our military teacher, and we studied the Mosin-Nagant rifle in infinite detail. Once, in response to his order to disassemble and assemble the bolt, I blurted out cheerfully, "Yes, sir, your honor!" He rebuked me, "You, Kravchenko, should forget this pre-Revolutionary attitude! Now we don't have any officers or "sirs" here!" Later, at a school assembly, the principal vetoed my request to join *Osoaviakhim* (the first Soviet association for the support of the armed forces), asking me the fatal question, "What was your father doing prior to 1917?"

The mass grave by the monastery wall was suddenly unmarked, replaced by anonymous, featureless flat ground. The only trace of its existence was that the grass hadn't grown in yet, like everywhere else. Later, when the grass did grow, it was a green bed of oblivion. During my visit to Kremenets much, much later, the staff of the local historical museum (who treated me a bit like a relic) were surprised when they learned about the mass grave near their building. Then again, there are too many places where our compatriots have been buried in near and faraway lands throughout the twentieth century. They could be almost anywhere one digs.

Nonetheless, those nearly two years, from September 1939 through June 1941, remain a bright, colorful picture in my album of memories. The belief in a bright future settled in my kid's heart, open to anything good. I was sure that there was a bright future for me and for everyone else, in a world of equality and justice. I didn't want to notice manifestations of injustice, above all those that were directed against my father or my family.

June 1941: War Again

In the final days of June 1941, when the menacing roar was coming from three sides, and the east side was the only one that was relatively quiet, I met our military instructor on silent, emptied Shirokaya. Answering my unspoken question, he swept his palm through my hair and said, "We'll be back nonetheless." After a second's pause, he added, "Well, you take care, Romka. Think kindly of me!" For some reason he was walking not on the sidewalk, but along the middle of the street, away toward the east, with his duffel bag and a small-bore training rifle on his shoulder, not the rifle that we had assembled and disassembled, which was educational; it had no firing pin and had a hole in the rifle breech, so that it definitely couldn't fire.

They were leaving. We were left behind. We, the locals, were not yet considered their fellow countrymen. Again the border controls were set up on the former posts on the Zbruch to prevent the flow of refugees that had reached us from the west by then, in September, from going further.

Some time in mid-June there was an order to turn over the house registers to the municipal councils. These books listed the owners and residents of each house.

At the crack of dawn on 23 June, the second day of the German invasion, Soviet authoritics arrested my father and Rostislav. Somebody had knocked loudly on our door, too loudly. When the door was opened, two men entered the room: a soldier in a long overcoat carrying a rifle with a fixed bayonet and a lieutenant with a gun in his hand and three pips in his NKVD collar patches. [The NKVD, the People's Commissariat for Internal Affairs, was the predecessor of both the KGB (the State Security Service) and the MVD (the Ministry of Internal Affairs).] Having asked a few questions—in fact, having read them off a list—the lieutenant ordered them to get ready. My father and Rostislav got dressed. Mama tried to push a quickly packed bundle into their hands. My father said, "We don't need it." After making the sign of the cross at Mama, Yuri, and me, they all moved out. A GAZ-AA truck was parked in the street, behind the hillock. Men dressed in civilian clothes were sitting in the back of the truck, and a soldier with a rifle stood by the driver's cab. My father and Rostislav were told to climb to the back and take seats, and again my father made the sign of the cross at me, now from a distance. Perhaps he was making the sign at everything by the hillock that he was leaving behind. When the truck was lost out of sight, I walked back to the house. My soul felt empty.

A week later, when a distant artillery roar could be heard clearly, they came back. My father returned first, followed by *Rostyu* (as we all called Rostislav at home). Father told us that the NKVD guards had disappeared, Soviet tankers were everywhere in the prison courtyard, and a boyish second lieutenant entered his cell and listened to my father's simple story. After hearing it, the lieutenant told him he could leave and go XXXX his XXXX, adding "your honor" to it. [Expletives deleted.] It was the first time that I ever heard unsavory expletives out of my father's mouth. Rostislav—to prove his innocence—had to mention his portrait hanging on the Board of Honor in the Mining Directorate, not far from the prison. One soldier ran there and had a look; the portrait was still on the Board; everybody had been too preoccupied to remove it. Rostislav regained his freedom from this oversight.

Having taken control of the town, the new Ukrainian and German rulers soon returned the house register. In our book, checkmarks had been pencilled in next to the names of my father and Rostislav. According to these marks, at dawn on 23 June, a wave of arrests swept throughout the town. Why didn't executions follow the arrests? I could only guess that the relevant order was delayed somewhere, as the *Wehrmacht* drove eastward with unexpected speed. As I later found out, in those areas where the parties in charge of the execution of orders stayed behind, the operations of arresting those whose names bore checkmarks in the registers were carried out in full, that is, they were taken into custody and shot.

The arrest of my father by the Soviet authorities would change the life of our family during the coming years of German occupation. The men in our family were now labeled as "victims of the Bolsheviks" and that fact some-what neutralized their barely concealed antipathy toward the German invaders and their helpers. Following the arrest, Father should have turned "White," that is, anti-Soviet, which automatically would have made him a supporter of the "New Order," but my father had always been a non-con-formist. He was simply too sincere, and didn't have the moral flexibility to take on values simply because they were advantageous at this or that particu-lar time.

The German invasion began differently for different people, but this was how it began for us. At night, wagons rattled along the paved street behind the hillock, followed by slowly crawling tanks. Our boys were leaving. *Our* boys.

Generally it was believed that "we won't surrender an inch of our lands" and that we would defeat the enemy on his own territory. Well, the latter part did come true, at the cost of almost four years of the worst of wars, and of approximately 27 million lives on the Soviet side alone.

———◦◦◦———

The first German soldiers started to arrive in the morning.

I know a woman who, as a girl, saw her first German ever as he approached her family's wagon on the Stavropol steppe. He was a tall, sweaty fellow, and he offered her candy he had in his hand. He actually was the only German soldier she ever saw; the refugee caravan she was in pulled into the mountain foothills, and the refugees spread out across the villages. Ultimately her family settled in that German-occupied territory, but there were too few Germans to occupy every town, so they never saw another one, and life went on almost as before. They even had a Soviet New Year tree with a red star on its top. Her memories of "German occupation," so very different from mine, are basically the heat of the steppe, the squeaking of rolling train carriages, endless star-studded skies, the smell of sheepskin, air bombardment (as it later turned out, by our own air force), and the darkened face of her mother. This girl—who later became my wife—for many years was posed a common post-war official question, "Did you stay in the territories temporarily occupied by the Nazi German invaders?" She answered with a "yes," a reply that didn't ease her life afterward. In particular, it closed the doors of Moscow State University to her, which had an honor school program to which she wished to be admitted. Well, if it were otherwise, our paths wouldn't have crossed. Later, this question about the occupied territories disappeared from official forms and questionnaires, along with many other unnecessary things. It was no longer shameful to tell a story like that of the German soldier and his candy. For her, that was a childhood recollection and all she saw of the German war machine.

The first German soldier that *I* encountered carried a peculiar digging implement that resembled giant pliers This happened on 2 July. The German slowly climbed over our fence, and walked carefully along the path between our rows of vegetables. He walked past Mama, saying something that sounded throaty, out of which we only recognized a few words like *"fleissig"* (industrious) and *"tüchtig"* (efficient), so obviously he was saying something like, *well, you did a good job weeding,* implying that he was impressed with our gardening. His facial expression corresponded to our understanding of what he was saying. We nodded in agreement. He walked with a measured step toward the opposite fence wall, cut the wire fence with his metal shears, and stepped over to the neighbor's lot. There, using his excavating device, he dug out a deep narrow pit with an amazing speed. He pushed the pliers straight into the ground, pressed the handles, and pulled a clump of dirt out, held in between two shiny blades. Having left a molehill of dirt, he went on further, and I followed to check out the resultant hole in the ground. It was ideally round, smooth, and at least a meter deep. Closer to noon, other German soldiers came and drove poles into the excavations, then stringing shiny copper wires above our vegetable patch. They spiraled endlessly, from west to east, in coils; on the first pole, dielectric cups were installed on both sides, while on the next pole they were on one side only, and so on.

The thick, tarred poles were meant to stand forever, in one straight communication line—toward the east.

Meanwhile, German columns, menacing in their discipline and purposefulness, were rolling along Shirokaya for the whole week. Could our boys withstand them?

That was how the long night of two years and eight months began for us.

SECRET DIARY

My Secret Diary
1st Notebook, 1941–1942

The words of my wartime diary, pretty much the same as I wrote them so many years ago, shows events and feelings just as I experienced them at the time.

First, however, I wish to clarify something about a recurring theme: the wave of Ukrainian nationalism that broke out after the German invasion. I got to know various types of nationalism in my life—Polish, Ukrainian, and Russian—and I became acquainted with fascism and anti-Semitism not through secondary sources. I got to know them through my life, through practice, through my own, as they say, skin, if one recalls the exercises of my classmate, Jozek Puchalski. If I am asked a question in the course of an interview, on what I like most of all, I will most likely have to think hard. If I was to be asked what I hate the most, however, I would say instantly: nationalism. Or if putting it wider, any demonstration of intolerance. Many things come to people over the years—one gradually forms preferences, sympathies, and antipathies. My dislike of nationalism was formed back in my childhood, under the impression of things witnessed and experienced.

Things I experienced then, in the years of occupation, led to a strong distaste for Ukrainian nationalism, which in those years was associated with collaboration with the invaders. Here lies the source of all my sarcasm and gloating because of the failed hopes of the nationalists to get independence and statehood out of the enemy's hands, seen here and there throughout the diary entries. And while nationalists and Ukrainians occasionally seem to be synonymous to the young author, this should be explained by the microclimate in which we had to live in our small Western Ukrainian town (which, as you may recall, had just been Soviet-Ukrainian and before that Polish and further back part of the Russian Empire).

May the reader of any nationality forgive the youthful use of superlatives by the diary's author. It is an ailment of childhood.

The diary text will appear in sans serif type and sometimes there will be contemporary elaboration about something you have just read in the diary.

11 July 1941
Many thoughts trouble me. I often lie in my bed, unable to fall asleep, and keep thinking. Yes. It is my fortune or misfortune that I happen to live in times when events don't follow one another gradually, but instead they come in a fleeting, flashing instant. We now re-live the era of Napoleon, though on a much larger scale.

Adolf Hitler, the leader of the German National Socialist Party and the dictator of Germany, is this "new Napoleon." The Germans have demonstrated their amazing ability to get organized. Germany, crushed by the Treaty of Versailles, managed not only to get back on its feet, but felt strong enough to resume the fight against its old enemies, England and France. The short-term goal of Germany in this war is to establish a "new Europe," the nations of which will develop irrespective of the "Island" [the United Kingdom, *Ed.*].

The long-term goals of Germany or its leader will become clear with time, when the war is over. This war, which has already outgrown the war of 1914–1918, began on 1 September 1939, with Germany attacking Poland, an ally of France. The war lasted for two weeks and ended with the Red Army also entering Polish territory (it could no longer be referred to as Poland, since its government was gone, having fled into Romania and beyond) as well as the parts of Ukraine and Belarus that were part of Poland, too.

12 JULY 1941

Now I'm getting down to the most important parts of it all. Germany began actively transferring its troops to the Soviet border following its campaign in the Balkans. The USSR followed suit. Finally, on 22 June, bombarding Kiev, Odessa, and Sevastopol, Germany began the war against the USSR. During that time, the German radio announcements in Russian were quite interesting. Germany accused the Soviet Union of breaching commitments of the treaty, of negotiating secretly with England, and essentially of getting ready to attack Germany. I heard through the grapevine of a military council in which Stalin opposed war, yet the military council insisted on it. If that is true, then it was useless; now, after three weeks' time, we are living in "Liberated Ukraine."

For two days, the Red Army tried to contain the German attacks. There was heavy fighting everywhere. The Soviet units managed to withstand them for quite a long time, maintaining the southern sector of the front, including Kremenets. Some talented commander must have been in charge there. Several times they managed to throw back the Germans. Those were quite the days for us! Then, getting surrounded from the north, the Soviet units had to retreat. The second-to-last division left in the small hours of 2 July, blasting the highway behind them. The very last division had to temporarily fill in the ditch to be able to leave. The blown highway didn't stop the Germans, however. On 1 July, we bade farewell to Soviet rule.

I will write more tomorrow. For now, I'll include a few more impressions from today. I went downtown in the morning. I saw how people were erecting an arch proclaiming *"Es lebe die unbesiegbare deutsche Armee!"* or "Long

Live the Invincible German Army!" A similar arch was erected to welcome the Bolsheviks, perhaps by the very same enthusiastic "welcomers." The addresses posted everywhere call for us to help the *"Führer"* in his fight against the "Muscovite horde." The grapevine reports the occupation of Kiev; I don't believe it, however. The future will tell. All radio receivers in town have been confiscated, thus no news except marketplace rumors is available.

In the evening they drove Soviet prisoners of war along the street. The men were treated worse than a herd of animals. They were beaten with sticks right in front of local residents. That's true German *"Kultur!"*

That's about it.

P.S. I have to hide my diary. Now one could be executed for such "free-thinking." I keep it under a crate, which I lift with difficulty every time I put it there. Now, if the diary is found and read, they will know where I'm hiding it. Enough philosophy!

[Kiev fell on 19 September, two days after the last Soviet troops in the city had been ordered to leave the Ukrainian capital. The evacuation order never reached the last defenders. *Ed.*]

13 JULY 1941

In the morning I went downtown. I stopped by at F.'s, and together we went to the Lemberg's. They were still in turmoil after the recent pogroms. F. went back to our place with me. She picked a few roses, but didn't stay long, because her home is in turmoil, too, and her parents don't want her out of the house now. She came to me "illegally." Some "friends" laugh at me for hanging around with a Jewish girl. Now, indeed, I can tell who is my true friend, and who is, well, a "friend." Let them laugh. This demonstrates their type better. There is a good proverb—"He laughs best who laughs last." Recently I had the following conversation:

"Your girlfriend. . . . It seems she was killed," I was told.

"She wasn't," I said.

"She wasn't?" said with disappointment. "You won't go out with her any-more, though, will you?"

"Yes, I will." I replied. "Why shouldn't I go out with her?"

"Oh!" The "friend" left without saying goodbye.

I found out from "well-informed sources" that the USA has entered the war. The future will tell.

New appeals are being posted. I read the address by Archbishop Alexis who announced our "most merciful blessing" and "his ascension to the throne." [Archbishop Alexis retained the title of the archbishop in the years of the German occupation of Western Ukraine; and on the Episcopal Assembly in November 1941, he was elected the *Exarch* (the high priest) of (Western) Ukraine. *Ed.*] People seem so thrilled! In these addresses the USSR is referred to only as the "Moscow Empire". Based on this, the Russian monarchists should be satisfied that they have lived to see the resurrection of the empire.

I saw a Soviet plane. It flew very high. The Germans shot at it, but missed. This should be enough to prove that the situation at the front may not be so bad, if they take their time to fly over Kremenets. I don't think I will write any more today—people come here too often and disturb my concentration.

[The rumors from which the author surmised the United States had entered the war were probably construed from the fact that on 7 July 1941 the US Armed Forces took over the occupation of Iceland from British troops, who had been sent there after the German invasion of Denmark on 9 April 1940. Iceland at the time was still united with Denmark. The USA, however, did not enter the war against Germany until Germany declared war on the USA on 11 December 1941. *Ed.*]

14 JULY 1941

In the morning I had visitors—F., her friend, and an unfortunate admirer. The rest of the day I spent upstairs reading.

There is no news about world events. Now I know for certain that the USA is in the war. [See explanation above. *Ed.*] Today, a Soviet plane was above us again, and again the Germans shot at it. A distant booming has been heard throughout the day: somebody is bombing someone. This is a good sign: if the Germans are bombing the Bolsheviks, it means that the Bolsheviks are not distant. Otherwise, it means that the Bolsheviks are not doing so badly, either, and have time to devote efforts on our Shumskoye Highway (the booming sounds were coming from there). We are doing fine, but what about the people over there?

15 JULY 1941

There is really nothing to write about today. I spent the day at home, but it was fun. Dad brought F. to visit us. She spent the whole day with us. We played volleyball and ate currants. I walked F. home, and on the way back I got into the rain and was soaked through.

No news. The absence of a radio is terrible. I would like to know what is going on in the world and to listen to some music. The marketplace news becomes more and more fantastic; knowing nothing for certain, the saleswomen apply all their imagination. News picked up there is as follows:

1. "Reports from England" (Reuters, no less): Polish General Sikorski, who lives in England, has been sent to the USSR to organize military units out of prisoners of war captured during the occupation of the Western Ukraine.

2. All former Czarist army officers have been inducted in the USSR. Over 3,600 immigrant officers have been sent from England to the Soviet Union. This piece of news doesn't seem as unrealistic as the following one

3. "Reports from Moscow"—The Atheistic Society has been dissolved and public praying has been instituted. That's some twist! It must be the "news" from some very "godly" granny.

In fact, news reports 1 and 3 were the closest to reality, while unfortunately the second piece wasn't. General Wladyslaw Anders, Commander-in-Chief of the Polish forces in the Soviet Union, led his men, salvaged with great difficulty from Soviet POW and labor camps and missing thousands of officers, into the Middle East in early 1942, to serve alongside British forces in North Africa and Italy. The Russian Orthodox Church was given previously undreamed of freedoms during the war.

F. (Frida)

She was a petite platinum blonde with a small straight nose and serious dark eyes.

Somehow it happened that Gogi moved to another desk and Frida took his place in the classroom, sitting next to me. This was the last school year before the war began. It became the very last year for many in our class.

I think that our—Frida's and my—friendship, from both ends, was a demonstration of eager aspirations for equality and justice. Such friendship had simply been impossible prior to September 1939, for either party involved, under the conditions of *that* Poland. Now it became possible, and we used this opportunity! In spite of everyone who thought differently. It was more than a regular friendship. It was a demonstration!

For us, it was a sunny, blissful time with no explanations needed. We were fifteen years old. We wanted to share one desk in class. On weekends we wanted to go together into the mountains. We wanted to be together, that was all.

Earlier that day I had experienced a very unpleasant episode with my school principal. He had called me in to his office. Tapping his fingers on the desk, he had said, "Do you know that a group of the best students is going to Kiev?"

"Yes, I heard them speak about it" I replied.

"You're not included in the group," he declared. I was silent.

"Do you understand?" he asked.

"Yes, I understand. May I leave now?" I asked.

"Yes, go." I understood perfectly why I was not allowed to go; the reason was my father's officer past in the Tsarist army.

On our mountain on this clean and sun-washed day, being with Frida cleared away the aftertaste left by that upsetting conversation.

Early in the morning, Frida and I went into the mountains. The Kremenets Mountains is the actual geographic term. Their height from the foot to the flat top does not exceed 100 meters, but to us, they are mountains all right. The town of Kremenets winds among them, like a long serpent, and from the top it looks like a toy town. Human figures moving along the sidewalks on Shirokaya Street are barely recognizable; carts and wagons move somewhat faster, but just as quietly, along with the occasional cars. All sounds from the town are melted into one, and from the mountains this sound is but a lulling, non-irritating noise. It is the kind of noise that bees make inside their hive on a sultry summer day, busy with their endless work.

We sat together, side by side, on a ridge, among the young birch trees, and looked down at our town. Her hand rested on my knee, and I touched her fingers gently. We never spoke about it, either before that day, or after. We simply felt good about being together and we tried to be together as much as possible. Under favorable circumstances, with time, such friendship perhaps could have grown into something significant and serious. The circumstances as they were would not be favorable, however. That is why my memory preserved this feeling of warmth coming from her shoulder, along with the freshness of the forest.

A cloud tumbled by, followed by the rustling of fleeting rain among the leaves. Then came a sound that caused some inexplicable anxiety, the sound of a plane, low, vibrating, and with an unusual tone. Among the patches of clouds we saw an unclear image that disappeared, and the sound of the plane was gone. Only birch trees were rustling in their greenery. The side of the mountain got lighter, sparkling with myriad droplets on grass and leaves, enhancing the freshness, but the vague anxiety lingered, and it made us hurry back home.

What follows is the exact record I made in the summer of 1942 trying to recall the first impression of the news about the German-Soviet war on 22 June 1941.

The main street, which after the rain looked much tidier than usual, was filled with people, dressed in their best; the crowd slowly floated along the sidewalks, exchanging comments, talking. The faces were excited, with traces of surprise and shock, mixed with fear. In front of the post office the crowd filled the street. It was quiet here. Then the public speaker on the roof began broadcasting: "Attention! Attention! Moscow speaking! Moscow speaking! We shall broadcast a pre-recorded address of the Deputy Chairman of the Council of People's Commissars and the Commissar of Foreign Affairs, Comrade Vyacheslav Mikhailovich Molotov." The voice in the speaker went silent, and the crowd rumbled composedly; then this noise was overcome by some hissing sound from the speaker and all quieted down, tense with expectations: "Men and women, citizens of the Soviet Union. . . ."

That's how I remembered the beginning of the war. We stood in that crowd and I held Frida's hand in mine.

Then they played some marches. I ran home and Frida ran home, too, in the opposite direction. Our families needed us and waited for us there, now, at our homes.

Our little town was some 160 kilometers from the state border on the Bug River. We didn't realize that Kremenets was in the path of the major attack of the Germans' Army Group South. So, by the time I had my next meeting with Frida only three weeks later, it was in the world where the "new order" had already been established.

In those days my father would occasionally bring Frida into our house behind the hillock.

In the circumstances of Nazi occupation a father encouraging his son's friendship with a Jewish girl was an extraordinary thing in itself. Then, of course, it could be our plain childhood simplicity—we didn't know what fascism really meant. In those days, we simply didn't know very much at all. If asked today about my father, I would say that throughout his life he was never trying to be slick. Perhaps that was even his life-saving feature during the twenty changes of rule that happened in his lifetime, none of the successive powers really considered him one of their own. He always maintained a somewhat doubtful attitude toward the happy propaganda that was proclaimed by supporters of each new regime. It was obvious that remaining true to himself in conditions of frequent changes of authority was, for my father, the only acceptable way to adapt.

17 JULY 1941

I went to F. in the morning. The order is posted throughout the town, proclaiming that all Jews now have to wear a white armband with the Star of David on it. They are being turned into slaves of Germany. Poor F. What will happen to her?

I feel awful, going around with a heavy heart. This feeling doesn't leave me for a second. What will happen next? The nationalists are being nasty and loutish. I was in line to get some bread. The "militia" applies force with no reservation. (I'm even embarrassed to call them "militia"—they are actually local bandits with knives sticking out from under their coats.) When I see it all, I feel anger rising inside me, along with the desire to hang them myself. These are very difficult times. Shall we survive it? And how should Jews, F., feel now? She tells me she wants to be killed.

My records now are brief. There is practically nothing to write about, no news from the front, and this makes the situation worse altogether. The German radio broadcasts say that serious tank battles are taking place around Smolensk and Bobruisk, but these cities have not been taken yet. People say that the British Navy is in the Black Sea. This is a typical peculiarity of all today's news; they start with the words, "people say." This is the result of radio news being unavailable. Sometimes the news is good, but it is difficult to trust it since the sources of the information are not known.

18 JULY 1941

I was downtown and met F. She was standing in the line to get bread. She is not looking good lately. It results from sleepless nights when every minute you're expecting either nationalists or Germans to break in and vandalize everything. There have been instances when they broke into houses in the middle of the night demanding that young girls be turned over to them. Could these bandits and marauders even be compared with the men of the Red Army? The Germans practice the following system. You come to a German officer and tell him that a German soldier robbed you. In response the officer punches you in the face and says that the soldiers of the German Empire do not rob; the Bolsheviks are the only ones who can rob people. *"Heil"* to the liberators!

19 JULY 1941

The rumors are absolutely rampant. Some say that the Bolsheviks have taken Zdolbunov back; others say that the Germans are in Smolensk. It's all very confusing.

F. came by today. She came only to make me mad. She is very petty and vindictive.

Today is the anniversary of Dzerzhinsky's death. He is hated for having ordered the executions of many people. I think he was fighting for an idea. When executing people he believed them to be enemies of the revolution, and remembering the experience of the French revolution that pampered its enemies, he executed them all. The French revolution failed because of this trifling. Studying the experience of the French revolution, Lenin decided to destroy all of his enemies; it was ruthless but inevitable. Another issue is in having gone too far. The GPU [State Political Directorate], then the NKVD [the People's Commissariat of Internal Affairs], and finally the NKGB [the People's Commissariat of State Security] shot people or sent them into exile without any discrimination. In fact, they persecuted more sympathizers of the revolution (my dad, Rostislav, and so on) than enemies! *They*, the GPU, and so on, were thus the worst enemies of the revolution since they produced 10 enemies for every "enemy" they shot. This put things in direct proportion. A tragic proportion!

In the summer of 1941, a Soviet calendar for the year was still hanging on the wall of our kitchen. I took various historical dates and references from it, which I then commented on from my own understanding of things. When reading my diary many years later, Natasha, my daughter, observed, "You were rather pinkish then!" It is quite an understatement! I believed virtually everything that we had been told by the Soviet authorities during the previous year and nine months, and I wanted to believe it all! I tried to ignore new and more numerous "flies" that were ruining the Soviet propaganda ointment. Eventually, I was no longer able to accept it, but the road to that hard realization would be long and difficult.

Reading again the words of the fifteen-year-old author of the diary about *fighting for an idea*, I am amazed at how readily I accepted the legitimacy and even the necessity of physically annihilating opponents of an idea. At first, there would be liquidation of the idea's real enemies, followed by the extermination of imaginary or pretended ones, with the selection based primarily on demographic data—class and race; ethnic background; choice of religious confession; and so on. The chosen method was common for Lenin, Stalin, Hitler, and other dictators.

Today, when my twentieth century is over, I am absolutely confident about one thing: *no idea* can justify the need for physical destruction of those who disagree with it. The road to happiness can never be paved with corpses. *Never and nowhere.*

The way Communism was instituted in the twentieth century included, above all, an "image of an enemy" and continuous terror. Without either of these two, it would have been impossible to bring the idea to life. The death of Stalin on 5 March 1953, followed by the breakaway from the tradition of bloody oppression signaled the beginning of the end of this global experiment. Thus this process is not a wholly modern one, as its roots stem from 1953. How about "Democratic Communism" then? This is something new, tempting, but not verified in practice, or rather, there is no proof of its viability, as the search for it (under the slogan of *perestroika,* that is, restructuring) collapsed in the former USSR in the early 1990s. And that is a pity.

20 JULY 1941

No news from the front. I become desperate. I spend my days walking as if in a fog. Visited F. She is sick, but will stay home because of those armbands mentioned earlier. She wants to wait until people get used to the sight of them.

I stood in line to get bread. Getting bread has almost become impossible. The administrating "militia" men allow their friends to go in first, followed by the impudent who violate the line, and then those standing in the line. There is a Jewish man in the line; he gets close to the precious door with broken glass. A "militia" man walks up to him, and moves him back to the very end of the line. Half an hour later the story is repeated. Eventually, the man gives up and walks away, back home to his crying and starving children.

22 JULY 1941

It's been a month now since the war began. The rumors have it that last night Kiev was taken. Well, rumors are in the air . . . no other news, and if things progress that way, I'll soon have to make one record for several days.

Yet there is one interesting thing to write today. I visited F. She told me they had a fast yesterday, and the reason for it was as follows. Three days ago someone—I think it was the ritual [that is, kosher] poultry slaughterer—was tortured and killed. They buried him somewhere on Stream Street [which was the street the author lived on, *Ed.*]. Then the day before yesterday three men saw the victim in their dreams—the Rabbi and some other important Jewish leaders in the community. The murdered man seemed to have asked them to bury his body in the Jewish cemetery, and asked all the faithful to keep a fast the following day. If they did as told, in two weeks' time they would be rid of the Germans.

Who could have imagined that Kremenets plays such an important part in the second imperialistic war!

23-25 JULY 1941

I haven't written anything for two days, and have accumulated some "material" now. This system has but one deficiency—my forgetfulness. I will definitely forget something.

The *Gestapo* called up all members of the Jewish intelligentsia on 23 July. They were all detained at the *Gestapo* office. Now some of them have been released, and some of them have been executed. Over 600 people have already been arrested in Kremenets. A few days ago one local Jewish leader was arrested and was released the very same day in good health, except for four knocked-out teeth. He was ordered to return the following day, at the very same time. Most likely, he was to get another dose of the same treatment. Today things progressed even further. I came out of the house and saw that a flyer with big red letters had been posted. It read something like this: "From the moment of arrival of the German Security Police, all law enforcement authority in the town is transferred to its supervision. No longer do any local police or militia formations have any law enforcement authority." They won't even be allowed to guard lines, poor souls! That's a good one!

Another thing: the notorious Bandera, a murderer and the self-proclaimed head of the "Ukrainian Government" has been arrested for the "declaration" he issued in which the name of Hitler was put after his own. So much for a "Free Ukraine." Fools!

Now, on to the international developments. "All is quiet on the Eastern Front." This formula reflects precisely the bottom line of all news from the past two weeks. Now, no matter how you look, the Germans are marking time. If so, it means that the situation is no good for them, and that means that all is tip-top (for me, personally). The Germans bomb Moscow heavily, the Kremlin is in ruins. Barbarians!

[Moscow was indeed bombed and the Kremlin damaged, but not to the extent that the author surmised. *Ed.*]

26 JULY 1941

Early in the morning I learned about the latest local news: "somebody" set the synagogue on fire. The *Gestapo* will perhaps search for arsonists, but I'm certain they won't find anyone. Had they come to me, I could have pointed out the arsonists without leaving my bed . . . and would then surely have ended up in the *chevaux-de-frise* [meaning, in this case, prison] of Dubenskaya.

I'm writing the following later in the day. Looks like I was wrong. It doesn't mean that I can't name the arsonists, but there is no longer a need for that. All details of last night's fire are known now.

I heard shots at night. At that time the synagogue was already on fire, and the Germans were shooting, overjoyed. They obviously performed a savage dance around it. In the morning when a crowd gathered around the synagogue, an officer came by and told everybody to step aside. He pulled out a hand grenade, showed off by spitting on it, and tossed it through a window. The roof collapsed after that. By the way, the local firemen (obviously following the orders of their German masters) worked really "well" on site; they dragged all combustible materials inside (most likely, to help it burn down faster—a new way of tackling fires).

27-28 JULY 1941

Nothing of significance. Hitler made a speech in which he announced that the capture of Moscow has been postponed for another month, due to bad road conditions. I feel very sorry for him! Poor devil, he didn't know that the roads were bad in Russia! I wonder what excuse he will find when 22 August finally comes? Perhaps the rains will be in his way. I wish it would pour down. And if, God forbid, it won't, what will we do then? We will have to wrack our brains hard!

Well, the above words should suffice to guarantee my execution!

29 JULY 1941

There are two events to write about—one of them significant, the other commonplace.

All day long we heard the booming of artillery. This was somewhere far— 100 to 150 kilometers—away from here, and that was good; very good! Now, Messrs. Germans, there have been no changes near Kiev, have there?

The second bit of news is something now seen daily. Rostislav saw how Germans beat up a local "militiaman" until he was bleeding and barely alive. He had been ordering people around in the line, not to the Germans' liking. They called him a Ukrainian swine at that. Now they have yet another enemy, unless they get rid of him. . . .

30-31 JULY 1941

The most recent, shocking news: the Germans are in Ryazan, and they have cut off Moscow from Leningrad!

Shots are heard, but infrequently. Today, I was out of town and heard explosions. They most likely bombed Dubno. On the road I counted ten Red Army tankettes and tanks. One was totally burned out. There are huge amounts of Red Army artillery pieces throughout the fields. It is a rather unpleasant and depressing landscape. Yesterday I went to the river and took a swim. There were many tanks around there, too. They are all in a pitiful state; the locals saw to that.

I wish there were at least some news from the front! The silence is encouraging, but in the long run it gets frustrating. It is difficult to live in this world, notwithstanding the fact that the Germans are taking such good care of us, easing our lives—by easing us off the surface of the earth. Ah, that was an adage worthy of my greatness! I'm bored. Perhaps I should try writing some poetry? I have a liking for it, but no talent, and a liking for rude poems only, sort of "Malbrouck goes off to war. . . ." Period.

No, no finite punctuation mark yet. I had a sad encounter today: a new meter reading clerk came by. It was Baupret, our chemistry teacher. What a career move!

1 August 1941

Today is the international anti-war day. A nice joke, indeed. Bravo!

They say that the German retreat is general, along the whole front line, and that the Germans have given up Minsk. Furthermore, the Germans are screaming their heads off at the Japanese, cursing them because they are ruining the situation at a critical moment: they are letting American transports into the USSR.

Now here are my personal observations regarding the situation at the front: 1) the *Gestapo* has departed, leaving a few men behind to be seen, but not even our old ladies can be fooled that easily; 2) the latter refuse to take German marks any more; and 3) cars loaded with suitcases go west. Because of these events I believe that the Germans are about to retreat. In the morning the artillery booming was heard with increasing strength.

I will have to change my estimate about schooling this year; seems like we will meet Baupret again in our chemistry class.

In two days is the deadline for the prophecy in the Rabbi's dream. If by then the Bolsheviks will have Kremenets back in their hands; that would really be something noteworthy.

2 August 1941

Yesterday the first issue of a new German-controlled newspaper was published. It is called the *Kremyanezky Visnik* (The Kremenets Courier), but the Kremenets news in it is rare and spread out. Actually, everything printed there could be guessed without even touching it; the whole paper is dedicated to descriptions of "the Bolshevik murderers" and praises of Hitler and Company. Not a single word about what is taking place at the front. This is not surprising; you can't write about retreats or failures. Now, as I'm writing, I can hear the distant roar of the artillery.

"The Bolshevik murderers" refers to the mass executions (by the NKVD), such as Katyn, that were, as I now know, actually performed during the first days of the German-Soviet war. No such shootings took place in Kremenets, however. In other places graves were later opened and shown to newspapermen, who saw them and took pictures that were published.

2 August 1941 (continued)

A new directive has hit town: from now on food will be rationed. We shall get 400 grams of bread per person a day, and Jews 300 grams. Other food products will be distributed, too. I haven't read the directive in detail yet. Perhaps it is good, since it will stop the chaos.

I have spent the whole day at home, reading Twain's book. He has written some excellent satirical stories. I read a lot until my eyes get sore. (My father's library contained, among others, a several volumes edition of Mark Twain works in Russian, beginning from *Tom Sawyer, A Connecticut Yankee in King Arthur's Court, Innocents at Home, Innocents Abroad,* and so on. At that time I read them all.)

3 AUGUST 1941

The battles continue, somewhere in the area of Shumsk, and shots are heard. In addition, a few farmers wounded by shells were brought from there. In contrast, there is a total calmness in town. The Germans obviously have settled here for a long stay. They get furniture from warehouses or take the things they need from the local population.

There are certain contradictions in my notes: one day I write they are leaving and the next day I suppose they are getting "winter accommodations." Oh gosh, I really don't understand a damn thing about it. I write down everything as is, and do not attempt to comment now. I will get confused and won't get out of it. I'll leave it to the future to sort things out.

I finally read the directive about the rationed food distribution in detail. First, the products will be distributed among Christians, then among Jews. According to the directive, they will get enough. There is this passage, however, and especially these words: in case of food deficit, the distributors retain the right to change the rations. Surely there won't be enough food to distribute to the Jews, because they will be the last ones to receive their rations. They have no reason to expect 300 grams of bread a day.

There has been an autumnal drizzle all day long. The nights have gotten cold. Fall in the beginning of August! The same thing is happening to nature that is happening with people—it's going insane.

My mood corresponds exactly to the weather—apathy. I don't feel like doing anything. The only thing I want to do is to sit and think of nothing. Today's notes show a definite contrast compared to yesterday's. The future seems to be colored in gloomy hues. My dreams, university, all of this, are so far away now.

4-6 AUGUST 1941

A great event has happened: today, the second issue of the *Kremyanezky Visnik* published a communiqué from the German command. It was dated 28 and 29 July. According to it, "the Bolsheviks are about to meet their death." Right. I wonder just who will "meet their death." I will cut out the summaries on the front situation, and paste them into this book. One day I'll sort them through, but right now I mainly have to collect material.

My mind is kind of slow today. I cannot think of anything more. Aha! I have it! I just held a Soviet pamphlet in my hands, dropped from an airplane. In this pamphlet they appeal to us to hang in here, while the Red Army is approaching. We'll see how accurate this announcement is. The booming was heard the other day and yesterday. I didn't pay attention to it today.

7-10 AUGUST 1941

Another issue of the paper, but I'll cut things out tomorrow. I was reproached by the family members the last time that I chopped the "public" paper.

I learned now that the booming was the echo of the Soviet advance. As far as I know, it was thrown back, but not all the way to their original positions. Smolensk was won back, and the Germans have been thrown out of Estonia. They were thrown as far as 150 kilometers away from Smolensk.

Neither any battle for Smolensk nor for Estonia took place then. It was just the author's wishful thinking.

7-10 AUGUST 1941 (CONTINUED)

This advance, as the Germans themselves are saying, was of a previously unseen strength. The two sides have suffered huge casualties. Of course, the Bolsheviks had ten times worse casualties. Perhaps a million, or even two. The Germans didn't, though. They don't die at all.

Well, the international update is over. There was nothing significant among the local events. It is an interesting observation: when there is a lot of news, I'm brief; but when there is nothing really to speak of, I can come up with two pages of various rubbish that may seem to be noteworthy. What a talent! I even amaze myself. I wish I lived in New York and not in Kremenets. Oh well, my presence is God's gift to this place, and when I die, the town will become a popular tourist attraction. Tourists will flock in, to gaze at the Kremenets prison.

14 AUGUST 1941

I haven't written for a while, but I have an excuse: I was sick for two days, stayed in bed and looked truly miserable. That was also the reason why I didn't buy the newspaper when it came out, and if I get it, I'll paste a piece from it in its proper place.

Well, Gentlemen Nationalists, it is your turn now! I commence my speech. "Dear *Pans* [Ukrainian Gentlemen]! I have the honor of congratulating you with having established the Ukrainian statehood in our lands, as well as with the triumph of our sacred cause, and so on, and so forth. (Endless shouts of "Glory!") We have been incorporated into *Grossdeutschland* (Greater Germany)."

I imagine how their jaws drop—and enjoy the sight [the "I told you so" effect. *Ed.*].

The thing that I just jotted down has not been officially announced yet, but it is expected any day now, and it is very good. At least, this "militia" with knives in their belts and bandit faces won't be seen everywhere. A new issue of the paper should probably come out tomorrow. Well, I'll get it for sure.

17 AUGUST 1941

No news. It is very frustrating. I got the paper—the issue dated 9 August. Two articles are worth special attention.

One has it that the Soviet government is signing deals with the Polish puppet government located in London. Sikorski heads this government. Noteworthy is the fact that the market news could be trusted after all to a certain degree; it has been circulating for a long while now that Sikorski heads the Polish Legion, and so on.

The second article is funny, though. It is titled, "Stalin's son was captured." The essence and the subject of the article are obvious from its title, and there is no need to relate it.

So, congratulations to you, Comrade Stalin, on your male newborn. Not just any newborn, but one ranked as a lieutenant. And this newborn was captured instantly as well. The moment he was born, he became a lieutenant, and was taken prisoner. As if he was born only to be taken prisoner, and to announce that he believes resistance is impossible and useless. I used to be impressed by the abilities of the German high command, but now I have trembled respectfully ever since I learned of its ability to make others give birth to children.

During the war, we knew only about Stalin's daughter by his second wife, Svetlana. The existence of his son by his first wife, Yakov (Yasha) Dzhugashvili (Stalin's birth name, used before he changed his name to "Stalin," meaning "Man of Steel.") was somehow kept quiet and was unknown to us. Yasha fought in the war and was, indeed, captured by the Germans. He seems to have comported himself with dignity while in German captivity. Details of his POW life are in the memoirs of the Polish officer Aleksander Salacki, *Jeniec wojenny Nr 335,* published in Polish by the Wydawnictwo Ministerstva Obrony Narodowej (1973). The author claims that the Americans liberated Stalin's son in the spring of 1945, but then he just vanished. The version of his death by the hands of Nazi torturers was more simple and understandable. The brand "former POW" would cast a shadow on the sacred image of the "greatest genius of all times and people." Today they claim that Yakov Dzhugashvili committed suicide by throwing himself against high-voltage barbed wire.

Is there yet another version?

18 AUGUST 1941

Lots of news. It hasn't been verified officially, but I heard it today from three people, so I guess I can believe it, more or less. The essence is as follows: there has been a coup in France. Daladier has become the head of the state. The Italian garrisons in the French Mediterranean ports are being destroyed. At the same time, English assault troops took over Le Havre. This was accompanied by bombing of the northern shoreline of France. Five thousand planes took part in the action. There are serious losses, of course. General Weygand was appointed the army commander in France. In Africa, the command is assigned to General de Gaulle. The news is of a very sensational nature; everybody speaks about it, with every imaginable detail, so we shall see.

They also say that Khrushchev was executed (shot), but I don't believe this part, since they have previously reported about executions of Voroshilov, Timoshenko, and Budenny. If everybody had been shot, who is left? Most likely, everybody.

Voroshilov, Timoshenko, and Budenny were among the most prominent Soviet political and military figures in the pre-WWII period. They had not been shot, nor had Khruschchev, who became a postwar leader of the USSR.

21 AUGUST 1941

I got two issues of the paper. They are filled with venom. They are filled with praises of the German successes. They have gotten to the point of stating that all Ukraine, all the way to the Dnieper, has been taken over by them. What about Odessa and Kiev? They forgot all about them among the triumphant chimes. They also report that the Soviet 6th, 18th, and some other armies were defeated. Considering that the USSR has a total of eighteen armies, fifteen are left. In my opinion that should be sufficient.

Later I will happen to serve in the 61st Army.

21 AUGUST 1941 (CONTINUED)

The very same paper reports that the Bolsheviks bomb Eastern Germany and even Berlin. Bravo! Some plane was flying about us here the other day and was shot at.

Now to the most important news: action No. 2 against the Jews. An announcement is posted, in Yiddish and German, with the following contents: beginning 20 August, Jews are forbidden to walk on sidewalks, due to high traffic. They should walk along the curb. Furthermore, if a Jew meets a German on his/her way, the Jew should make a detour of no less than 4 yards away. The first-time violation of the new order will result in the Jewish community paying 10,000 rubles. If the violation is repeated, all Jews will be deported out of the town. I won't comment on this punishment; it is as clear as it sounds.

We are not a part of Germany. Galicia is. It is almost the same.

As far as the events in France are concerned, however, I think it's all a bunch of lies; there are not the slightest hints to prove it true.

Well, that's it; I have written quite enough.

By the way, my mood is lousy.

23 August 1941

I completely forgot that yesterday was two months since the war started, and this prominent anniversary was not marked in any way. On the other hand, how to mark it? Perhaps by killing a German in honor of the "belated anniversary"?

Today a new issue was out (issue 7). It had two sensational pieces of news in it. "The Destruction of the Soviet Navy"! Seems like they charged Odessa and sunk three merchant ships, a destroyer, and two submarines. How is one to believe the Bolsheviks after this one! They announced to the whole wide world that they had a powerful navy, and it turns out that it was comprised of three transport ships, a destroyer, and two submarines. The world was fooled as never before! The second piece of news reads: "The Destruction of the Stalin Canal." This one is even better! One attack, and the canal is gone, totally wiped off the face of the earth. They are great at lying! The bottom line: there is a new victory for every day, I wonder how come the war is not over yet? Period.

25 August 1941

Now the troublesome days have begun—240 of our paratroopers landed the other night in Shumsk. A high alert has been announced. Fourteen were captured, and will be executed by hanging. The others will create problems for the Germans. This is not all, however. Yesterday, a group of paratroopers landed nearby, in Smyga, and today two paratroopers were arrested in Kremenets.

Yesterday, a new "edict" against Jews was issued. They are ordered to give away all their valuables—gold and anything else. They can leave wedding rings only (I'm not sure whether Jews wear wedding rings?) Totally, the Jews of Kremenets have to yield 8 kg of gold to add to the gold reserves of Germany.

Another piece of news: we got a radio back. It is not our radio, and it is so bad that it can't receive broadcasts even from Moscow and Kiev. Well, that's all so far. What will tomorrow bring us?

26 AUGUST 1941

Again there are two events worthy of writing down. Last night, around 7 o'clock, one of our parachutists landed in Pyatenka, some half a mile away from our house. He was noticed, but they only managed to find his parachute. The parachutist himself hid in the woods. There are already results of their activities everywhere: many wires have been cut, communications disrupted; the Germans in their cars fly around like madmen.

The second piece of news is a new "decree." It turns out that in certain aspects the Jews are not too much oppressed. For example, in the "golden" respect, they are almost equal to the Aryans in their rights. Not because the gold will not be taken away from them, but because it will be taken from the Aryans as well. That is, currently they only register it, in order to make it easier to collect it all later. Without the chaos and confusion, so to speak.

If readers are familiar with the artistic style of Mikhail Mikhailovich Zoshchenko, they cannot avoid noticing its effect on the style of the diary's young author. [Zoshchenko (1895–1958), a popular Soviet humorist, was expelled from the Union of Soviet Writers in 1946. His works were then banned and not published again until 1956. *Trans.*] The stories and satirical sketches by Zoshchenko were hugely popular among Russians living abroad. I was fond of them as well and such quotes from him as "Your complexion is way too indifferent, perhaps you should go take a bath" settled down in my mind similarly to the later quotes by Iliya Ilf and Evgeny Petrov. [*The Golden Calf* is the sequel to *The Twelve Chairs* relating a story of antics and adventures of O. Bender in Soviet Russia. *Trans.*] By the way, *The Golden Calf* was in my duffel bag when I left to the front. I picked it up in the first days of the occupation out of a heap of books piling high in the yard of our former library, to be burned. They hadn't set it on fire yet and the book found its place on a shelf of my father's library. Many an enjoyable evening was spent in the house by the hill reading aloud from this book by the light of a kerosene gas lamp.

27 AUGUST 1941

I'm totally bored. There is no news. It drizzles unpleasantly. This drizzle also brings certain joy, however; now the Germans are having it tough! Wait until winter is here—they will then fear to share the fate of Napoleon, after whom Hitler likens himself so much.

The power is out for the second day in a row. Most likely we got the radios back to serve as furniture ornaments only. This one is rather pretty, of a modern style.

There is news! And not just any news, but a stunning piece of news! It seems that according to the German radio broadcast the Bolsheviks are occupying Persia (Iran). Hip-hip-hurray—in case it's true!

The electric power station is no longer in operation. As it seems because they are afraid of sabotage. They say that our paratroopers land daily in the area of Kremenets.

30 AUGUST 1941

Today one of the remaining Soviet persons came over to our place. It seems like she didn't have the time to leave, or perhaps she didn't want to leave; though I suspect it's more like the former. According to what she says she shouldn't have stayed behind. She was a Komsomol member, and now she can't get a job. Everybody points out she is Russian. She is surprised, saying, "They invent some kind of differences among nations." Her heavily criticized Soviet upbringing showed. She cannot imagine that there could be differences among nations and that not all are equal. She went on, "In the Soviet Union, everybody can work, even has to. . . ." There was some sadness heard in her tone, but pride was above it all. As if she was saying, "You could curse it as much as you want, but I prefer the Soviet Union." It was a good thing she said these things to Rostislav and not somewhere in the street, but in our home. Otherwise, she would have been dead. Looks like she cannot be "cured." Good girl!

The rumors about the occupation of Iran proved true. I heard this yesterday, first-hand, on the radio.

Tomorrow will be the holiday of the "Ukrainian statehood." There will be speeches, prayers, parades, and so on. A Jewish pogrom will probably be scheduled for dessert. At least they say so.

31 AUGUST 1941

Today we managed to tune in to Moscow. We listened to "Eugene Onegin." ["Eugene Onegin" is the famous opera by P. I. Tchaikovsky, based on Pushkin's novel in verse. *Ed.*] Then we turned off the radio, and now we can't tune back to anything at all. Darn!

There is a new issue of the paper. It says that the USSR and England "attacked Iran treacherously" without declaring a war. And who has so far been attacking exclusively that way? Bastards! (Pardon my French, but this comes from the bottom of my heart.) There is nothing else in the paper, besides abuse.

Today's a celebration. A lot of "patriots" wearing Cossack costumes, riding wretched nags. All kinds of prayers and services are held followed by the "parade." I can imagine what it looked like, their "cavalry." Nothing about the pogrom yet, but the drunk are already seen all over the place. To be continued. . . .

I wonder why the Bolsheviks needed Iran and what the next issue will be? The Germans say, "the attack on Iran was not justified by anything." I'm sure they are just glib talking. If the German Navy fails to leave the Black Sea, that will be a riot!

1 September 1941

I congratulate you, citizens, on the occasion of the arrival of fall and also the start of the new academic year of 1941–42, which in our lands, so fortunate to be under the German jackboot, will be somewhat delayed.

I tuned in to Moscow and listened to a program for schoolchildren. Notwithstanding the progressing enemy, the academic year in Moscow began on schedule; life goes on. I listened to the latest news. The army is retreating, but it costs the Germans a lot! On 29 August, 125 German planes were brought down while the Bolsheviks lost 24. The nation resists heroically. Hitler will lose many hundreds of thousands of his troops there and the results of the war are far from known. No, not at all! I'm certain we'll have our life back again—because the situation that we are in now could hardly be qualified as a life.

The weather today is totally fall-like. The Germans most likely want to be back home, in their fatherland, especially in such weather. This little but persistent rain will wash away the notorious Russian roads completely, and their tanks and armored vehicles will get stuck anywhere and everywhere, and then we'll see what the outcome of the war will be. They don't seem to like Russian bayonets much.

Well, there is nothing much to write about although this kind of weather brings my writing mood on.

3 September 1941

It's been raining for three day in a row, so I stay indoors. Another development in town—the Jews were allowed back on the sidewalks, most likely for the 8 kilos of gold and one and a half tons of silver that they had gathered following the order of the German authorities! Or perhaps it was issued by a new commandant; rumor has it he is smarter than the previous one. In any case, the pedestrians were in the way of the traffic on the streets.

The radio that we got back was of such poor quality that Yuri had to fix it twice (which, by the way, didn't improve its quality a bit). In any case, I listened today to the news from Kiev (RF-9). For some reason RF-97 doesn't work; I can't ever tune in to it.

Judging by the German news, it is either quiet at the front or they have run out of luck. Although yesterday they captured some huge trophies: two anti-aircraft guns! You expected two battleships, right?

4 September 1941

Again, about the radio: it will be taken away. Today the orders were posted: to turn in all radio receivers. The death penalty awaits those who fail to do so. The deadline is set at 10 September. At least that's good, a couple more days we can listen to it, before turning it in.

The second order is to turn in all weapons and ammunition no later than 10 September, with penalty of death for those who disobey. This is most likely an effect of the partisans. There are loads of them throughout the forests. They are armed with machine guns and grenades, and they don't let the Germans sleep peacefully at night. No wonder the Germans are getting mad at them. There might just as well be a machine gun and two anti-tank guns in my cellar; I'll have to turn them in! And on my pencil there is a tip made out of a rifle cartridge. I'll have to bury it, otherwise they will execute a poor innocent soul who wishes them only the best, that is, back in Germany.

Well, that's enough of bitterness. That's the effect of the weather on me.

The radio. It is hard to say whether the new commandant was any smarter than the previous one, but the fact remained that for two weeks the population was freely listening to the radios. Perhaps it was the commandant's abundant confidence in victory? Well, it didn't last for long anyway. Following the menacing decree regarding radio receivers and radio parts, and with the tacit consent of our elders, we set off on a night mission. We dug a pit in our garden and buried a carefully packed bundle with radio parts that had accumulated over the years through my brother's interest in amateur radio. Just in case. Until things became clear.

8 September 1941

Public life is in bloom. Parties have appeared. They fight and squabble among themselves. There are "Bandera-men" and there are "Melnykites" [opposing factions of the Organization of Ukrainian Nationalists. *Ed.*] One of the groups posts a proclamation; the other group chases them and tears down the proclamation. It is obvious now that there is a state, or at least some semblance of one. Little by little one side shoots down the other one.

The Bandera-men were chased out of the eastern regions, and they now do all they can to get what they desire in the western regions. That's all the Germans seem to need. Let them squabble; we have used it before and we'll keep on using it.

They say that on 15 September the secondary school will begin its classes. I miss school, but I don't look forward to going to this one. The good times are gone! Here, there will be raw nationalism, the law of God, and so on, and I will have to bear it all! Oh damn it.

The easy-going attitude with which the young author accepted anti-religious principles, formulated in O. Bender's unforgettably succinct quote, "there is no God, and this is a scientifically proven fact," can be explained not so much by the mandatory and formal religiousness of my earlier years, but also by my personal experience. Here is another snapshot.

When I was a *gymnasium* student back in Warsaw, I not only diligently marched on Sundays to the mass, but I also performed some work in the church. I wore my acolyte's vestment, went into the altar section, and there in the corner I lit up the incense in the incensory, handing it all over with a bow to the priest. I also lit the candles in tall candlesticks and brought them out at the necessary moment. Once during the mass I was sitting in my corner while the priest in his shiny golden robes was standing in front of the see, and the altar gates behind his back were closed. The choir was singing. Suddenly the priest coughed up, spit out, and smeared the spit with his boot—right there in the church, at the altar, in front of the see. I shrunk in expectation of the collapsing walls and the dome, but nothing happened. Having cleared his throat, the priest went on with the holy Eucharist. The choir went on singing. This happened some sixty years ago, but I still remember the name of the priest: Vedybida-Rudenko. He was the first one to plant seeds of anti-religiousness into the susceptible boy's soul. Fortunately, those were not the seeds of atheism. With the years my perception of God, who is above all formalities invented by humans, grew only stronger.

11 SEPTEMBER 1941

Amazing things happen. For a few days now we haven't seen any of the ever present "freighters"—cargo planes. If they appear, they fly at very high altitudes. The postal planes are gone, too, I think, flying with the speed of 180 to 200 kilometers per hour. The bombers have become more frequent and 5 minutes ago a reconnaissance aircraft appeared, of the kind that flew above us during the fighting and that disappeared when they rolled further to the east. All these things considered together makes one deeply suspicious. We'll see.

They've been saying for a few days now that Turkey has declared war against Germany. If this is seen as a consequence of the occupation of Iran, this could have been expected, though I feel skeptical about it now. It could be from the same category as "the coup in France"; as it turned out, though it is not quite calm there, there was no coup.

I also noticed that once radios disappear and nothing can be proved or denied, some stunning news begins to circulate. Perhaps people find some consolation in it. Somebody starts spreading something like the above, the following day he hears the news in which he cannot see his own hand, he believes it, and it comforts him.

[Turkey actually declared war on the Axis on 23 February 1945, as a precondition to joining the United Nations. The author's comments show he understood that ever-more-fantastic rumors were spreading, and was frustrated with the inability to verify or deny them. *Ed.*]

13 SEPTEMBER 1941

There was a first-class surprise last night! A new decree was issued in the German and Ukrainian languages. It begins with the words, "Kremenets and its twelve districts are a *German* Commissariat." Further on, it goes, "*All* political parties are banned; any political propaganda, *regardless of purpose,* is viewed as a crime against Germany. All power in the town is transferred to the German authorities."

Now Kremenets is a German Commissariat, which means, farewell to the "grand, united Left Bank and Right Bank Ukraine! [the OUN vision to unite the western and eastern halves of Ukraine into one nation. *Ed.*]

All political parties are banned, which means, farewell to the OUN. Any propaganda and agitation is considered a crime, which means it is not advisable even to talk out loud about an independent Ukraine any more. This is the decisive decree and true to German nature. If they ban the "Official Organ of the Kremenets Committee of the OUN" [the *Kremyanezky Visnik, Ed.*] because of the decree, I'll be satisfied—almost. How are you doing, gentlemen of the ex-OUN? God forbid, your stomachs do not ache, do they? Ah, they do. What a pity! Take some cyanide, it'll help.

Just now a thing flew by. Never seen that one before! I saw a huge plane with three very small planes flying ahead. I thought it must be some six-engine bomber and some fighter planes. As they approached, though, I didn't believe my own eyes! What is this contraption? This huge plane was an airframe, and it was towed by regular Junkers-88—"small" planes! What a sight! These three huge bombers were barely pulling it ahead, and they were some five times smaller than it was. Perhaps that monster could fit a whole armored division inside. (That's what I first thought; now I would adjust the number to two dozen tanks only.)

17 September 1941

I haven't held a pencil for a while; there was nothing to write about. Today is a sort of anniversary. Ah! The Soviet authorities didn't last even two years here, the poor devils!"

On 17 September 1939, the Red Army divisions set off to the west, toward the *Wehrmacht,* as it became known, due to the good accord between the two leaders.

17 September 1941 (continued)

Today a new announcement appeared—about school admission. They are opening a *gymnasium* and three elementary schools. We'll apply and see what the outcomes will be.

The latest news! I'm writing and it's already evening. The posters about school admission have already been torn down; something must have failed to meet approval.

The latest about our local paper: it has already changed its look; the notice of it being "the OUN organ" is gone. Moreover, part of the text is now in German: notices, decrees. Soon, I think, it all will be in German.

19 September 1941

About the posters: they were torn down following the order of the military government. They were in Ukrainian while they should have been put out in German first, followed by the text in Ukrainian.

I handed in my application, and on 22 September I will sit in for an exam. Oh, what will happen to us? It is obvious that the administration will attempt to admit as few "foreigners" as possible. Well, nothing is new for me here; I already sat for exams to get into the Polish Public *Gymnasium,* and failed; they didn't like my not-so-Polish last name. Well, it's going to be this way or the other; but for the time being I have to cram Ukrainian.

20 September 1941

The announcements on the town walls say that the Germans took Kiev and Poltava. There will, therefore, be a special thanksgiving service today in the cathedral. Damn them all! I could wring their throats, the priests, and all of those with them, with great pleasure. Bastards!

22 SEPTEMBER 1941

I wrote a dictation today. They had to try hard to find an appropriate text and this one was very difficult. Besides, the person dictating it did everything possible to confuse us. That is why I have some five errors. It will be graded as "mediocre."

We got together at the school by 8 AM. We had to wait through to 9 AM (it is a common practice in all schools, and at all times to round students together an hour, and sometimes two hours prior to the appointed time), and then we were marched like a herd of sheep into the church. Principal Vesselovsky (a complete bugger, though he is part of the "Ukrainian intelligentsia") announced that, "The students who do not belong to the Orthodox faith do not have to go to church if they do not wish to do so. It is, however, imperative for the Orthodox students to go to church." So the Orthodox students went, imperatively.

A little priest read an appropriate homily, mentioning "Jesus Christ, our Lord" after every other word. Naturally, the service was in Ukrainian; moreover a Gospel quote translated into Ukrainian was read out from a plain notebook, placed on top of a big, copper (or perhaps, golden) framed Bible in Church Slavonic, due to the unavailability of the Ukrainian-language Bible.

After all this, we went back to school where we were told to sit and wait till 11 AM when the tests began. Naturally, we waited through half past one. Tomorrow we have to come at 10 AM (read: 1 PM), to continue.

[Slavonic, tracing its origins to the Russian that was spoken in the Middle Ages, is the equivalent of Latin to the (Russian) Orthodox Church. *Trans.*]

25 SEPTEMBER 1941

I was right; it continued at 1 PM sharp. It went ok. Tomorrow I will learn of the results and find out whether I am admitted or not.

It's been three months since the war started. The Germans are amazingly fortunate. Any way you look at it, they are winning. It is obvious that their advance throughout Ukraine, after crossing the Dnieper, has been progressing well. Donbass and Kharkov are in danger. Losing Donbass will mean losing the entire coal reserve. It is bad enough that Krivorozhye has already been lost. I don't know what they are thinking; they should have transferred military command into the hands of one of the brighter generals that surely still must be around. It is also clear, however, that the current command cannot control the situation.

[Donbass in the Donetsk Region in Eastern Ukraine, an area rich in coal, and one of the major traditional mining resources in Europe. Krivorozhye, the area around Krivoy Rog, Dniepropetrovsk Region in Eastern Ukraine, a mining area rich in metals and other natural elements. *Ed.*]

25 SEPTEMBER 1941 (CONTINUED)

I wish I didn't have to go to this *gymnasium,* but I will have to go. There are no changes to be expected in the foreseeable future.

Then there are those two articles, printed in the recent issue of the Kremenets rag.

One report speaks about American paratroopers landing in Spitsbergen and taking over the islands, notwithstanding the fact that the islands had been under the supervision of German military forces. There were some hurt feelings in those words—how could this happen? The Americans didn't have the right! Amusing!

The second piece related that Roosevelt has ordered the US Navy to fire at Axis ships. As a result of this action, a part of the US Navy maneuvered to the battle zone in the eastern Atlantic. What's going to be next?

There was another piece: Roosevelt has addressed the "Papa" (not mine, but the one in Rome) with the suggestion to declare the war on National Socialism. Naturally, the Pope refused. It's a no-brainer. Where does the Pope live? In Rome. Does the Pope want to live? By all means. The Pope wants to remain being the Pope, too. This explains everything.

A few more words about Vesselovsky, the principal of our *gymnasium.*

This episode happened back under Polish rule, in the Kremenets Lyceum. The aforementioned Vesselovsky was teaching Ukrainian there. There was a Russian student, a girl named Filimonova, in one of his classes. At one of the lessons Vesselovsky started arguing with Filimonova, "You all keep saying, 'Russian literature, Russian literature!' Gogol? Gogol was a Ukrainian writer. Pushkin? Pushkin cannot be named a Russian writer. Pushkin was a Moor!" (Pushkin had some measure of Muslim/Middle Eastern ancestry.)

These are the words of the brightest representative of the Ukrainian emigration intelligentsia. "Great and United Left Bank and Right Bank Ukraine" will go far with people like him.

29 SEPTEMBER 1941

On 27 September new "signs of distinction" were introduced for local Jews: yellow circles some 10 centimeters in diameter worn on the chest and back. It's an awful sight. What will come next and how will it all end? [There were at first no consistent requirements as to the color and shape of the symbol that Jews were forced to wear; it varied from a white armband to a yellow star. *Ed.*]

I study German. My tutor is a Jewish refugee from Silesia.

I have to go to school and find out whether I was admitted or not. Classes are supposed to start tomorrow, but I don't believe too much in that; they have already postponed it twice, could do it for a third time in a row. God favors the trinity.

30 SEPTEMBER 1941

Classes started today. Of course, the principal addressed us all with an appropriate speech. He is a fool, a total fool. As it is customary always and everywhere, he expressed hope that our school would be the best in the Volhyn, and so on. In addition, as expected, he prohibited students to talk anywhere in any other language but Ukrainian. Two teachers from our old school, Kleonovsky and Baupret got in here, too. Poor Baupret! Not knowing Ukrainian, he desperately tries to compensate knowledge with gestures. No Polish students were admitted. Perhaps my Ukrainian last name helped me get in. Although today they got disappointed; on the first lesson we had to state our nationalities our nationalities and faiths. I signed in as a Russian, the only one in the whole class.

I witnessed a scene today that has become commonplace these days. Bandits from the "militia" attacked the marketplace when people were shopping and selling. Christians were ordered to leave, while Jews were grabbed and searched for butter, eggs, and other banned products. Those who attempted to escape were caught and beaten violently. There was one wild chaotic chase along Shirokaya, accompanied with screaming and hooting. This is called an "inspection."

2 OCTOBER 1941

I go to school. It's insanely boring. I don't know if I will be able to last for a month. It is very difficult. The principal—and I haven't met another rascal like him before—tries to do all he can to make my life miserable every step of the way. When I signed in as a Russian, he got mad, and told me that perhaps I come from near Moscow or Tula since I consider myself Russian. He knows my Dad perfectly well, and knows all too well where I come from. Our anatomy teacher entered the classroom, took a seat and announced, "Man is God's creation." That's what I call Anatomy! I rest during math class, taught by our old teacher Kleonovsky.

4 OCTOBER 1941

No news except for the Commissioner's decree banning the sale of milk, oil, butter, and eggs at the marketplace. Until now this ban concerned Jews only, which made the non-Jews gleeful. Yes and how do you feel now? We'll gradually come down to bare bones covered with skin. God willing, I won't get too skinny, I suppose. Again my notes have grown short; but there is no material to write about.

7 OCTOBER 1941

I am gradually getting used to the school. I met a couple of formerly Russian students in our class who are Ukrainian now. They were Russians during the Soviet rule when all nationalities were treated the same. I have to be careful around these Russians who are now Ukrainians; since they were so fast and carefree to trade their nationalities, they may be just as fast and carefree to go to the *Gestapo* if need be.

"Ukraine" is disappearing at an hourly, rather than daily, rate. Most likely the Germans, who no longer see the need in nationalists' help, decided to end their illusions.

Now Jews get 150 grams of bread instead of 200. What is next?

Today a gypsy camp passed through town. They were in rags, hungry. I spoke to one, or rather he talked to me. He asked me for a smoke. I don't smoke. I gave him 5 rubles, but they are worth little these days. Perhaps their value is closer to the value of the old 50 kopecks. With one difference, though: one could buy something for 50 kopecks then, while now you can buy nothing for 5 rubles.

9 OCTOBER 1941

The latest issues of the papers had no news from the front, only a speech by Hitler. Promises, promises, promises. It turns out that he had offered twice to conclude peace with England. England denied his two proposals. Her people are holding out well.

Since yesterday the bread ration is down to 300 grams per person, and this is not the last word. In school I heard from one farm boy that the Germans ordered his family to bring in the entire grain reserves into town, leaving only the amount needed for the coming year's crops.

12 OCTOBER 1941

The weather is rather appropriate: rain mixed with snow. The temperature does not rise above 4 degrees Centigrade. That's also today's political analysis.

The other day I called in "sick" and went to the movies, sitting in the front row, at 5 rubles' admission. Later I bitterly regretted my decision. The movie was about the invincible German army, and so on. I don't plan on going to the movies again in the foreseeable future, but I do plan on being "sick" more frequently.

I got the paper. New "progressive" decrees of the Commissioner are of interest. Selling potatoes is banned. Who could have imagined such poverty? The second decree demands that all posters and announcements issued by all others than the Commissioner, to be removed off the walls of houses, fences, and so on, no later than 14 October. All new announcements and proclamations are banned unless preapproved by the Commissioner—a new slap in the face for local Nationalists.

16 October 1941

The dates of my notes correspond to the dates of the new issue of the paper. It is not surprising as all days are so murderously alike; it is unbearable to be living in this world. The paper isn't exactly improving my mood either. Even if I believed half of what it says, or even a quarter, it is still clear that the situation is tragic. One blow follows another. After the great German victory near Kiev, military actions are focused on the Azov Sea, and from there, to the center of the country. Another breakthrough, Orel is taken! My father is certain that in the end the Germans will be defeated, but I don't have the slightest hope for that. It is obvious that the Red Army's best divisions have been defeated. How could weaker ones tackle the Germans?

If one adds Russian winter and the infinite Russian space, however, the situation could be viewed in a slightly different perspective. But—this "but" is everywhere—if we suppose that the war doesn't end by the Germans reaching the Urals or taking Moscow, they are unlikely to take a risk and tread into Siberia during winter. The German plans of a Germany extending to the Urals, and Russia behind the Urals, could become true. Japan, however, has its own plans, of a Japan stretching all the way to the Urals, and where does that leave Russia? All this is based on supposing that the war ends with a German victory. Winter is not here yet, the weather is dry, and I want to kill myself. I wish I had something like a gun.

I write this just so that . . . I don't really know why, . . . but if I had to die, and I knew that National Socialism would rule Europe at least for a couple of decades, I wouldn't feel sorry for my life at all.

I saw German postcards with a map of Europe where Germany spreads out all the way to the Urals; I know the German song, *"Deutschland, Deutschland, über alles!"* and I know that Hitler has never changed his intentions and plans before.

I don't know what local nationalists expect from Hitler. There seems to be not a single man among them with a bit of brains. They trust in Hitler as in God. Fools! They don't know that he is a ranting and promising babbler and they believe everything he says in his speeches is true.

The same could be said about Russian nationalists as well, though. That's how they imagine their future: the war ends, the Germans re-institute a Romanov (from the Germans) on the throne of the Russian Empire, and generously leave Russia. The "renaissance" follows. Culture and church life can bloom, and so on and so forth. What morons they are.

I wish I could fall asleep and remain asleep until the good times are back, but it's impossible, that's life.

19 OCTOBER 1941

There is a new issue of the paper. They took Odessa, after having spent three months trying. Here, in town, though, they say Moscow has already been captured.

Regarding potatoes: now, my fellow citizens, we have to live without potatoes. In civilized countries, or the countries where German culture has already begun to function, it is not the proper thing to eat potatoes. Or bread. Or bacon. It's not a pretty sight, a man who sits and eats a piece of bread and a slice of bacon. It just doesn't look good. It's not proper for a man to sit and eat. Besides, in the countries where German culture has spread, people have bad teeth because of eating too much sweet stuff (saccharine and such). The teeth they have are more often false teeth, though. And as the false teeth are unemployed, they rest on shelves. Occasionally, they chew on some water and saccharine and then get back onto their shelf. All this is done because it is trendy. Today's fashion is to wear the belt tight, not to exceed 10 centimeters in diameter. That's the review of the latest trends. Oops! I began writing about potatoes.

24 OCTOBER 1941

We are now getting 250 grams of bread instead of 300. So far one can survive.

They say that a ghetto for Jews will be established in Kremenets. They are in panic. The rumors have it that they can take only clothes, beds, and linens with them. They have done the right thing: selling everything and trading it for food. It's the end for them.

At school—no changes.

The progress at the front is most likely just as poor. Moscow residents are being evacuated—according to our little paper, that is.

27 OCTOBER 1941

Our little Kremenets paper was busted yesterday. Its staff, all 42 people, were "caught, arrested, and imprisoned." They say that Tkachuk, its editor-in-chief, managed to escape. Well, in any case, he has really nowhere to run now. He can't go to Moscow, can he?

The POWs worked in the stream. All, without exception, are wounded. I spoke to one. They are fed thus: one beet a day and occasionally 100 grams of bread. I asked where he was from, and it turned out "from Siberia, from Eastern Siberia."

30 October 1941

Yesterday they arrested the head of the militia. Our principal's home was searched. Of course they could not find anything incriminating; this one is of the kind who cannot be caught red-handed with anything or anywhere, but he will be, he should be caught one day!

What's new at the front? What's with Moscow?

I brought home three volumes of Marx's *Das Kapital*. Could use them one day. Today in school they told us to turn in all Soviet books of political nature. No way!

It is interesting how quickly Soviet upbringing manages to affect kids' attitudes. One of our acquaintances' son attends the fourth grade. The first day of school, when the boy came home, his mother asked him about the day. "Well, they were telling us fairy tales during the first lesson," he answered.

"Who was?" she asked.

"A priest," he replied.

Poor priest.

Naturally, the author didn't then consider himself among the children that had been subjected to the Soviet re-education, but he also was absorbing like a sponge the new ideology that seemed so beautiful on its surface! The road to realization of the difference between theory and practice would be a long and painful one, and not only for him. And the process is irreversible.

When it comes to the diary per se, I feel that its reading can be tiring, so further on, I'll shorten those entries that, in my view, could be shortened painlessly. As I wrote earlier, I hold its typewritten copy. I am in good relations with the staff of the Kremenets District Museum where the original is kept. Every time visiting my place of birth, I visit the museum as well, and they arrange something like a media briefing every time I'm there. In this briefing, I'm considered as a representative of Russia, but my request to take the diary and make a photocopy of it was denied; I was told it was an exhibit; it was not permitted. I have my own opinion about the reasons for this denial.

6 November 1941

November is here. Winter will be here soon, but meanwhile it rains and snows simultaneously. Time flows routinely, no changes whatsoever. There is no local paper any more, but I saw an issue of the Rovno paper: battles continue in the Crimea, and Simferopol has been captured.

What will be the end to all this? I continuously ask myself this question, every day and every hour.

7 NOVEMBER 1941

It's 7 November. Twenty-four years since the Revolution. They have survived twenty-four years, but what will happen on the twenty-fifth anniversary I sure don't know. I'm not sure about anything, or rather, I'm more confident about negative things than positive ones. I wonder how this holiday is observed in Moscow? Most likely they do it differently this year from last year.

10 NOVEMBER 1941

I was on my way to school. I saw a group of armed men coming toward me, led by four *Gestapo* men, and followed by our militia men. This surprised me; I hadn't seen processions similar to this one before. I spent all the usual time in school, was on my way back home, accompanied by the sound of the requiem concerto inside my stomach from the only 250 or so grams of bread. Then on Shirokaya I see a sea of *haydamaks,* and in front of the houses marked with stars there were carts standing in addition to the *haydamaks.* The carts were filled with things: mattresses, pillows, suitcases, and other stuff. I couldn't understand what was happening.

When I got home, I—actually my overcoat and boots—were met as if I had risen from the dead. It turned out that the Jews in the town were being "cleansed" so that they wouldn't feel themselves too free. The part played by the *haydamaks* was to help assure that the German public wealth (that is, Jewish personal wealth) didn't get lost. Excitedly they took attractive boots off some people who happened to be walking along the street. That was why I was greeted with so much joy when I made it home safe and sound.

12 NOVEMBER 1941

A person whose information could be considered very credible told Dad that in Kremenets people who the Commissioner trusts have radios in their apartments. This gentleman, let's name him X, is on good terms with one such radio owner, and visits him. X listened to Stalin's speech on 7 November, during the Revolution holidays, broadcast from Moscow. X related the following with such a sincere horror that we had every reason to believe him. According to X, Stalin's speech was something like the following:

"Yes, it is absolutely true that our forces retreat, but this retreat follows our, rather than German, plans. If they have advanced for two thousand kilometers, then there are ten thousand kilometers left, and two and a half thousand to the Urals. If, according to the German information, our losses were five million people, then, according to our information, their losses were four million, which in comparison with the total population figures, is not to the advantage of the Germans. They have used their reserve, while we haven't tapped ours yet. They may be in the sunshine of Yalta," but we threw them 200 kilometers away from the city of Lenin and they are as far from Moscow, where they will break more of their teeth than they did taking Kiev."

That's what X told us. I cheered up.

Now I would suppose that the mysterious X heard the speech as retold by Y, who had learned about it from Z, a *Gebietskommissar*'s (district commissioner) trusted friend. As a result only the bottom line of the speech was preserved: the unshaken faith in the victory that sounded in that speech. This explained the "sincere horror" of the narrator. We didn't get the now-classic words, "Our cause is right, and victory will be ours!" then, but albeit distorted, this information nonetheless carried along their meaning.

18 NOVEMBER 1941

Yesterday one of our acquaintances came by, fresh from Kiev. He says that generally Kiev didn't get destroyed much, but is being destroyed now. On the fourth day following the German takeover, the Kreshchatik [Kiev's main boulevard, *Ed.*] began exploding, one house after another. A lot of Germans died. They pulled a pipe all the way to the Dnieper to stop the fire because the city water system doesn't work. Unidentified men cut the city pipes in four places. In response to this, the Germans massacred 170,000 Jews. Explosions and fires continue. [Modern research has shown that during the German occupation of Kiev some 100,000 persons, mostly Jews but also Russians and Ukrainians, were taken to a ravine called Babi Yar and executed. The peak of the killings was 29–30 September 1941, when about 34,000 Jewish civilians were murdered at Babi Yar. This two-day massacre was one of the largest single mass killings during the Holocaust. *Ed.*]

Our acquaintance said that the Germans have already reached the minefields that surround Moscow. According to them, Moscow is protected by fortifications like they had never seen before.

He also spoke about events in Rovno. They massacred 7,000 Jews there. Having ordered them to take all valuables with them, they were all marched out of the city and told to completely undress. Then taking them to already-prepared pits, they were thrown down, followed by grenades and machine-gun bursts. The earth with which the pits were covered moved for a long while after that.

22 NOVEMBER 1941

Our school is over. The Commissioner's decree justifies this by pointing at the risk of spreading typhoid and other diseases. They promise to open the schools again in spring. We'll see. In the meanwhile, I'm an unoccupied individual. The atmosphere in local "circles" is funereal. I can't write any longer; it's frigging cold here, in the attic.

26 November 1941

The town is filled with continuously circulating rumors. When the paper resumes its publication, it will be announced that all privately owned houses will be turned into state property and will be nationalized. The Germans promote Bolshevism very well. Now even the staunchest anti-communists admit that it was better under Bolshevik rule.

Regarding the situation at the front. In this respect the angle of my chin has risen by some 45 degrees. It is clear now that the Germans will have to spend the winter here, and what will the outcome of this winter stay be? We'll live and see. It is late November now, and the temperature is -13 degrees Centigrade. That is here, but what about some 2,000 kilometers toward the east?

Flyers are posted about openings for students at a technical school. Now it's clear that the schools were not closed because of disease epidemics. Most likely the secondary comprehensive schools like the one I was in will not exist whatsoever.

5 December 1941

I'm writing, sitting in the attic; it's −6 degrees Centigrade in here. I put a coat and gloves on, and keep writing because there are things to write about.

First of all, regarding Rostov. The rumors have circulated for a while now that there was quite a mess there, in which the Germans were well knocked about, and after that, they departed quickly from Rostov. Yesterday I read a note in the paper, something like, "An event without precedents during this war." With an outrage, it informs that when the glorious German army entered Rostov, the armed local population attacked it from the rear. As a result of this treacherous attack, the German divisions had to leave Rostov. I can only imagine what really happened there if even the Germans had to tell us this much about what had occurred. As a result, the German command ordered to open fire against the civilians.

It was indeed an event that happened in that war for the first time: it was our first major victory, the first major city liberated, and the first time German divisions were dangerously surrounded. We didn't know any of these facts then as Hitler's propaganda downsized it all to the "treacherous attack of the armed local population," and this was the first attempt at explaining losses of the *Wehrmacht* in the east.

5 DECEMBER 1941 (CONTINUED)

This is not all, however. The other day a proclamation by the *Gebietskom-missar* was published in which he announced that he "was forced to issue a strict, but fair, new decree and order in the Pochaevsky District." As a result of this, 80 people were executed for Communist activities. Today huge posters were pasted everywhere in town. Their contents read approximately as follows, "those individuals who will turn in enemies or saboteurs of the German public economy and Ukraine will be awarded a bonus of 1,000 rubles. Optionally, the bonus could be issued in products. The last name of the informer will be kept in strict confidence." What Ukraine has to do with it, I don't know, but they surely know how to deal with local scoundrels, who would turn in their parents in exchange for a kilogram of sugar.

Since yesterday, I've been attending math and physics lessons. That seems to be all. It's frigging cold in here!

9 DECEMBER 1941

That's quite some news! Last night, there was an urgent issue of the paper: "Churchill and Roosevelt achieved what they wanted," and so on. So some-one has attacked someone else, and now we have a new war. Nothing is mentioned about a "treacherous evil attack" [by the Americans], which must mean that Japan was the attacker.

What would be the outcome of this new war? The navies of England, America, Australia, and Holland are on one side, while Japan is on the other. Furthermore, hostile naval bases surround Japan. Besides, it is deeply involved in its war in China.

The natural question: how this will affect the course of war between the USSR and Germany? I think, rather negatively than positively. If there has been some assistance from America before, now this assistance will disap-pear. On the other hand, since this assistance was more in words than in deeds, perhaps the new war will hardly alter the situation. That's it. (*Never-ending applause*)

13 DECEMBER 1941

A new dispatch: Germany and Italy have declared war against America. What does it mean? Nothing really. Until now this war has been fought in white gloves; now it'll be fought openly. That's all. According to the papers, the Japanese started their war well; they are hitting hard at the English and Americans; and are attacking Hong Kong and Singapore, with paratroops landing in the Philippines.

No news from the Soviet front.

Now the "public opinion" is concerned with another issue—whether there will be a war between the USSR and Japan. I personally think that neither of the parties has any real reason to start such a war. The USSR is way too busy in the west, and it would mean total encirclement for Japan.

In one of the November issues of the paper I saw an article on the topic of the five months of the war in the east, "The world will see that Bolshevism was practically destroyed in the course of five months of fighting."

18 December 1941

It is quiet on the Soviet front.

In our town a Jewish militia has been formed. Its responsibility is to make sure that Jews are not loafing around. Their uniforms are quite interesting with a yellow V-shaped angle (starting from, pardon my French, the rear end and going up the back to the shoulders). One could see them a mile away.

I heard from a reliable source that the Germans quietly closed all "Prosvita" societies that had appeared like mushrooms after rain. Our nationalists are as mad as rabid dogs whose tails are pulled in the midday sun. That's all.

[*Prosvita* (enlightenment) societies were public societies instituted by nationalistic organizations prior to and during WWII, for encouraging the promotion of the Ukrainian culture and education. *Trans.*]

22 December 1941

The situation has changed. Those in panic exchange marks for rubles. Again the Germans have gotten a beating at the front. Even our local, lousy, paper placed a brief article about how because of heavy and strong frosts the command had to change the tactics of the war and to *straighten the front lines* in some locations. Rumor has it that Kharkov, Orel, Kursk, and many other cities and towns have been retaken, but I don't believe too much in this part. There is some heavy fighting on the approaches to Sevastopol.

A new decree was published in the town: to turn in all and any maps of any nature, as well as any political books and images. We have plenty of this stuff—I myself added Marx to our library—but there are no fools to hand them in.

24 December 1941

First of all, I forgot: 22 December marked six months since the war began. The second half a year begins on a more consoling note than the first one, but what will be the end to it?

It is still rather warm around here, but according to the rumors, there are nipping frosts along the front lines. Full echelons of frostbitten and wounded Germans are pulled out from there. There are rumors that the Polish army is fighting together with the Soviets and does it quite successfully. I don't know where the rumor came from though. In any case, all local Poles cheered up and became avid supporters of Communism. They certainly have fleeting emotions.

I go visit one family that feels approximately the same way about things as I do. Some Soviet POWs come there from the hospital, two lieutenants—one senior, the other junior—and a private. Their interactions are rather interesting. When the private wants to go somewhere he addresses the second lieutenant, who then addresses the first lieutenant. If the first lieutenant permits it, the private leaves, if not, he obeys without any complaint. Even in captivity they preserve their discipline, and this is very encouraging to see.

3 JANUARY 1942

Here is the New Year, then. The mood is not very good, but there are no reasons for being totally depressed. Most likely it is quiet on the Eastern Front—or the Germans are being beaten, since the little paper keeps silent.

The partners in Africa—Rommel and the Italians—are being beaten to death. So, indeed, I suppose there is no reason for weeping. On 31 December I saw my lieutenants again and gave 100 rubles to one of them, Nikolay Oksanych. That's why I consider that I ended my 1941 well.

That New Year

"My lieutenants." That was the last time I ever saw them. I had a conversation with the one whose name was Nikolay Oksanych just before their departure.

"We're going home," Nikolay had said. "Time is up. Soon all this will be over."

"All this" was a small hospital and a camp where approximately a hundred POWs were kept. It had its own medical staff, but the medications were those that they could get from local residents and food was coming from the same source. There was only one advantage to all this—a relatively easy regimen for those who could walk around. They provided the supplies, and so far the guards were lax regarding these "provision scouting expeditions."

Pretty close to the camp there was a house where two local girls lived: Katya and Zhenya. For some reason, the lieutenants began paying visits there rather frequently.

Zhenya was my classmate back in the Soviet school. Zhenya was pretty and flirty; older boys surrounded her at school and she mostly ignored "babies" of her own age. Mostly.

I shared a desk with Frida and sometimes I would notice Zhenya glancing at me. She would stare at me intently without looking away, making me blush and feel uncomfortable behind my desk.

The German-Soviet war began. Again we were in the same class, in the so-called *gymnasium* that existed for only a few weeks and was later closed by the Germans. Frida was no longer sitting next to me. Once I got a note that had traveled from desk to desk and reached me. "Come visit us in the evening. It will be interesting. Zhenya."

Thus, I met the lieutenants.

Later Zhenya said, "I wanted to win you over from that little Jewess."

Actually, she didn't have to win me over. Frida virtually disappeared in late summer, when various Draconian decrees and orders started to be issued and posted about wearing yellow patches on the chest and on the back and not walking on the pavement. Frida's Jewish Orthodox parents had always treated me with reserved enthusiasm, and my visits, becoming less and less frequent, were accompanied with an increasing alienation. Later, much later, I realized that Frida's pride was a big reason for the alienation. Having found herself in the position of a despised "slave of Germany," she didn't wish to accept my friendship as a charity, as if now I was unwillingly obligated into it by our pre-war relationship.

Later, much later, I found out, that in the most difficult times, my father went to Frida's parents with an offer to take the girl away and hide her. Frida declined his offer, though. She refused to leave her family in distress behind and she remained all the way with them, until the very end.

That's why Zhenya's victory was in fact relatively easy.

In gloomy winter evenings quite a diverse company was getting together in the girls' home. Zhenya was in one room, together with the lieutenants and me, plus a half-insane poet, whose one creation, devoid of any apparent meaning, I remember well:

Golden plates with dates,
Macaronis by the ton,
Standing, watching by the gates
Is Pharaoh Agamemnon.

In the pre-war Warsaw *gymnasium* we studied ancient history with passion, and that "Pharaoh Agamemnon" of his made me shudder. The poet, who was older than me, had the most obvious crush on Zhenya, but Zhenya quite skillfully managed the escort of her admirers, not allowing fights or deserting. The lieutenants were playing guitar and singing quietly, "it was spring, with lilacs in bloom, and little birds a-singing" or another song, about a skating Baltic sailor. The private went out and returned with packages and bundles, packing things up in his duffel bag, and going back to the camp. I could never outstay the poet, who lived next door; I had to leave as the curfew approached because our home was at the other end of town.

In another room, Katya, Zhenya's older sister, was entertaining her admirer. He was a German soldier. Well, Kurt was actually from Vienna, but at that time neither Austria, nor any Austrians existed. The *Alpengau,* the Alpine Region of Germany, existed then instead of Austria. [As a result of the *Anschluss,* the German annexation of Austria, the country was initially called *Ostmark,* which in 1942 also was abolished. Henceforth, the formerly Austrian territory was known as the *Donau-und Alpenreichsgaue* within Germany. *Ed.*]

The German from Vienna was friendly. He was staying at a nearby health resort where he was recovering. The Germans established that *Erholungsheim* (convalescent home) in the building of the former Lyceum, having strengthened the stone wall, putting in the portholes, and setting up concrete machine-gun nests. That winter the health resort was packed with frostbitten Germans.

Kurt brought food—canned foods, bacon, sausage, and bread. I knew that part of those goodies ended up in the lieutenant's duffel bag. That was one of the reasons why we all got along so well in the Nepritsky's home. The lieutenants and the German seemed not to notice each other.

They didn't have parents in the house. Being former small landlords, in 1940 they were deported to the east, to Kazakhstan. Then the word "deportation" was whispered only, and it became more and more frequently used as we were getting closer to the summer of 1941. The sisters were not touched— "The children are not responsible for their parents."

Kurt had the most serious intentions toward Katya. In the fall of 1943, having liberated Kiev, our troops reached Zhitomir in one fast breakthrough and were suddenly very close—which caused panic among the Germans that were securely cantoned in Kremenets. Kurt appeared from somewhere, putting the sisters in a car and taking them away to the west, to his Vienna, under the care of his mom. I learned about it from a hastily scribbled note from Zhenya, the second and last one I got from her.

The sisters are still living somewhere in the west, quite well, once in a while letting Kremenets know about themselves. A Kremenetsian remains Kremenetsian, even if in America.

In the first winter of the occupation I visited that home frequently. The memory from those days that really stands out for its clarity is New Year.

It is twilight—and it is cold. A pine tree branch with the melted remains of a candle. The poet covered up in a scarf is pacing the room from corner to corner, mumbling something. Zhenya is sitting on the couch, with her legs tucked underneath her and covered with her little fur coat. Her moist eyes shine and she is laughing at something, throwing her head back. Her teeth are white and straight. The lieutenants are by her side, at her feet. The guitar resonates.

Nikolay told me the day before, "We're going home. If you can, get us a hundred rubles. Heading back without any money at all just won't do it." The front was some 1,500 kilometers away, if one went straight.

I told my Dad in that New Year's night, "Dad, I need one hundred rubles, badly."

"Why?" Dad raised his eyebrows.

"Well, I need them real bad, know what I mean?"

I also asked Mama for a piece of bacon from our meager home reserves along with half a loaf of a round farmer's bread, and I got some tobacco from Rostislav. Then one could still trade food and homegrown tobacco for clothes.

"Are you going anywhere?" father asked me.

"No. Not me."

In our family, we trusted and respected each other.

"We'll leave soon," Nikolay said. "We have some fighting left to do. If I survive, I'll find you. You're good kids."

He never found us.

He was Nikolay Oksanych, a true Siberian. Perhaps, someone knows about him?

3 JANUARY 1942 (CONTINUED)

Yesterday the temperature hit a record low. It was -28 degrees Centigrade.

The other day there was a new decree by the Commissioner to hand over all warm Soviet-manufactured things—felt boots, cotton felt jackets, fur hats. Special groups walk from house to house taking clothes away. There is a certain quota set up for the town: 150 long fur jackets, 150 short jackets, and so on. If the town doesn't meet the required number, then gendarmes will go from house to house. Local "free citizens" (including us) shake in fear at the thought of such visits.

It is -15 degrees Centigrade in the attic, I can't write there. That's why I'm now writing in my room, and I'm brief.

12 JANUARY 1942

Yesterday the paper published new decrees by *Reichskommissar* Koch himself. From now on we cannot stay outside later than 8 PM, which is an hour earlier than before. There is a decree about sabotage, hidden weapons, Soviet POWs—to turn everybody and everything in, including those who escape.

Following the "collection of warm winter clothes" the Kremenets Germans now sport Soviet-manufactured felt boots, which makes me laugh out loud seeing it all. [Until recently the very same Germans said everything Soviet was bad and they wouldn't have dreamed of wearing Soviet clothes. *Ed.*]

14 JANUARY 1942

Quite a story, I am telling you! Today's paper had an article titled, "The Soviets Have Established Guards Regiments." Wow! Can you imagine, "Comrade Stalin's First Armored Guards Regiment." Well, let's suppose I believe it. In that case—on one hand I rejoice from hearing this, but on the other hand I'm saddened. I rejoice because if they are capable of thinking about Guards regiments, then obviously the situation can't be so bad. I am saddened, though, because this demonstrates their departure from principal ideas, a return to old things that they fought and defeated only to return to in a peaceful manner. Damn it!

Now, a few more facts from my life. I study—German, algebra, geometry, physics, and every other important discipline. Due to the school's unavailability, however, I stroll along the streets as an unemployed and unoccupied element. That's the entire essence of my life. Recently I wanted to read something by the poet Mayakovsky. Right. I won't be able to read any of his works anytime soon. When? This is all covered in the darkness of unknown. I think never. My father and I have switched positions now: early in the war I was filled with jingoistic spirits while he was full of skepticism. Now, it's otherwise.

21 JANUARY 1942

The farmers are being robbed to their bare bones. The Germans raid villages, taking away the livestock, and everything that they can get hold of. They drive herds of cows through the town all day long. The peasants are forbidden to enter the town without a special Commissioner's permit. This most likely has to do with the decree on "free trade."

The streets that the Ukrainian nationalists had renamed with the German occupation into the streets of Mazepa, Petlyura, Bogun, and the like from now on will be named in German, like Ritterstrasse, and so on. I can only imagine the mood of our respected "national patriots" and I am amused.

The Hungarians and Slovaks have been cantoned in Kremenets for a few days now. The Germans treat them approximately the way they do the local population. In the school where they are staying there is no heating. They get 15 rubles a day, which should allow them to sustain themselves somehow. They all hate the Germans, and wish them to be defeated. They only dream of going back home. Recently in the street, one Hungarian punched a German in his face, saying a lot of "nice" things, for which he was arrested and taken away to be punished. His words met with great approval by the crowd that gathered at the scene. This also proves something.

I think that some 80 percent of the population is now for the Soviets and their rule. The moods and preferences are so fleeting, really.

The Germans treat local gatherings very interestingly, too. They communicate physically, in particular by applying their hands against the locals' faces, a quite simple and rather effective method.

31 JANUARY 1942

Our Commissioner welcomes guests from Rovno [where the German military government of the Ukrainian-occupied territories was situated, *Ed.*]. Yesterday he threw a ball for them.

The *ghetto* is the big news of the day. The Jews were ordered to move from ten streets where there are also Germans residents. This should be done no later than 14 February. A closed ghetto will be established in the town over the following six weeks. Going downtown has become nauseating, seeing those unbelievable scenes. People silently leave all their worldly belongings. The dirtiest, most crowded streets were allocated for them.

There are 10,000 Jews in the town. If they are all packed into these tiny streets, one thing can be said for sure: typhoid. All trading and sales are banned in Kremenets because of the typhoid. Where it is? Who knows? This is obviously a very convenient thing for the Germans, and you can blame anything on it.

Another thing about riding horses and using horse-driven carriages: it is now banned not only in town, but also throughout the whole area. Well, walk around on your two feet and no horses will be needlessly troubled.

A priest we know stopped to visit us and spoke about interesting things going on in his village. On a holy day, he put on his robes and set off to officiate the service. So he came to the church, but it was empty. A red poster was pasted on the building of a local school, "Long live the parachutists!" Then the "militia" came, began investigating, but nobody turned in the perpetrators, and so they left with nothing. I don't believe too much in this story, but I would rather record it. The priest would not have a reason to lie, would he? According to him, there are many parachutists hiding in villages and in particular throughout Dubenshchina, as well as Soviet army servicemen, and generally speaking, other dangerous "elements."

6 FEBRUARY 1942

Today I am in no mood for writing. I will limit myself to facts only. Starting 4 February we've been getting 200 grams of bread. Starting the very same day I stopped attending my German classes; my tutor had to relocate to the ghetto.

As far as the ghetto is concerned, Jews have until 28 February to relocate from all over the place to the three streets designated for their residence—Kravezkaya, Gornaya, and Levinson. The locals call Jewish

militiamen "cherubims," "seraphims," and "archangels"—they have yellow
crossing lines on their chest and backs.

The very latest news: today's paper had a new decree by the Commissioner. All young people born from 1925 to 1928 are subject to compulsory
registration at the *Arbeitsamt* (labor registry office). The deadline for the registration is 20 February. What is this all about? We'll see.

13 FEBRUARY 1942

The relocation into the ghetto continues. The Jews are moving absolutely
everything, which is what surprises me. The Jews trade things for food without any problem, and this is even more surprising. I suppose there is only
one satisfactory explanation to all this: our Commissioner knows the value
of money. You have to catch an opportunity while it presents itself, and he is
not the one to miss it.

Because of establishing the ghetto, all Jewish men have to shave their
heads and women must get short haircuts. I can imagine how an ancient
rabbi feels about parting with his beard. Yesterday I witnessed a sad scene
at the hairdresser's: a rather intelligent-looking Jewish woman came in with
a wonderful thick, long braid. When the hairdresser cut it off, the woman
went hysterical.

Another thing: Jewish girls are getting married "in bulk." The Commissioner requested the Jewish community to provide sixty unmarried females
for a German brothel. Now they have twenty girls, while the rest have gotten
married. I don't know how the Commissioner will respond to that. Again, the
"shekels" will perhaps play a critical role in it.

Now, the world news: there is some kind of total mess in Africa. The Germans and the English chase each other from one end to the other and there
is no end to it. In the Pacific, the mess is as bad, but seems like the Japanese keep kicking the other parties.

No news from the eastern front.

Another piece of news: the Polish community representatives were called
in to the Commissioner and he announced that if the Poles did not stop
Communist propaganda, they would be either locked up into a separate
ghetto or deported to the west. This was published in the paper. Since then,
all rumors have ceased, in an instant.

22 FEBRUARY 1942

I'm writing in my bed, in the middle of the night; have no other appropriate
time for it. Starting 16 February I began working at the comb-making factory.
The work is very bad; there is so much dust that I walk out of there looking
like a bakery assistant. Besides, it is all accompanied with horrible screeching and noises. Well, I guess I'll be OK, though.

My Working Debut

The requirement to be registered at the *Arbeitsamt,* mentioned above, meant that one soon was employed by the Germans. Our neighbor, Modest Grigorievich, helped me get the job at the *Kammfabrik,* which in fact was located on our Stream Street in an old residential house that had previously been nationalized by the Soviets.

I have to tell more about this comb-making factory as it was my first working experience.

Modest Grigorievich was the director there; Seva and Kolya were the master workmen; and Styopka and I were apprentices. Also on the payroll was Taras Ostapovich, an accountant. Thus, with my starting to work at the factory the working class made up two-thirds of the total personnel, with one third represented by the administration.

In the office, above Taras Ostapovich's desk there was a big colorful portrait of a grand man with a piercing and wise look in his eye, accompanied with an explanatory sign, "Hitler, the Liberator." Another picture of positive contents was decorating the office. It exhibited a tiny figure of a Bolshevik who was scared to death, half-naked and barefoot, running away to the east, along the lands of Ukraine, rich with golden wheat fields. A huge and noble-looking German soldier in a helmet was in the forefront of the picture with a machine gun, completely armed, and was addressing the on-lookers with the words, "What else are you waiting for? Now is your time to work!" So we followed the appeal.

In their past lives, Modest Grigorievich, Seva, and Kolya had been shoemakers working in their homes for the shoe factory of Margulis. In their yards leather was soaking all the time, in barrels standing under the drainpipes, and the frequent sound of hammers was heard continuously from their open windows. From morning until night these shoe masters skillfully put straight rows of wooden pins into soles, pulling the pins from their mouths. The head-spinning smell of leather was everywhere in their homes: from raw material and cut leather pieces; from shoetrees and forms; and even from low stool seats upholstered with worn and polished leather.

Modest, Seva, and Kolya worked together frequently; it was more fun and besides they were some kind of cousins, or second cousins. When occasionally their mouths were freed from pins—wooden nails—conversations sparked on various topics. I loved all of this in my childhood: skillful hand movements, the clop-clop of the hammers, the smell of leather, and comfortable, almost toy-like, stools. I observed with awe and envy how, with a few movements of their hands, the pieces of shiny chrome leather that gripped the shoe form took the shape of a delicate lady's dress shoe. The shape of the shoe was then enhanced with a lining, sole, and a heel. The slanting knife cut through uneven spots like butter and gradually the shoe became more perfect and more finished. The black wax was then melted and covered bottoms of soles and heels, making them shiny and smooth.

"Romka! Dinner time!" my mother called out from our porch, and I didn't want to leave, so exciting was this supreme show of handwork.

"Under the Soviets" Kolya and Seva continued their work in a workmen's cooperative association named in honor of the pilot-hero Chkalov. Modest Grigorievich at first worked in the Revolutionary Committee and then in the City Council. The respectful, friendly, and neighborly relationship between Modest and my father never changed, in spite of my father's dark reputation as a former Czarist officer. I was happy about it—and happy for Modest.

Then the war began. Modest was gone. A month later he reappeared, though, somehow unnoticed by the new authorities. The sound of hammers was again heard from his window; shoes always need repair and not least in times of war. Evidently even the extremely smoothly working German occupation mechanism was faulty, for Modest was not bothered for a long time. Somehow he even became the director of the above-mentioned enterprise, Kammfabrik, as its sign read. It was clear that the staff was selected on the principles of nepotism. In my case I was there because of ties of friendship with my family. Working at the factory, Styopka remained a part-time acolyte at the nearby Church of Exaltation of the Cross. The job of an acolyte didn't qualify for a labor card, and thus didn't guarantee protection against trouble from the *Arbeitsamt,* though. And the troubles seemed to be in the air.

Taras Ostapovich, the accountant, was old, gray haired, and wore a Cossack-style forelock and moustache, and a single leg. The piece of wood that he used instead of the missing leg made a distinctive "clack-clickety, clack-clickety" sound when he was walked. This was important, too. In his youth Taras Ostapovich had served the Ukrainian nationalist leader Petlyura loyally, and lost his leg in a bloody Cavalry battle with the Reds. For the rest of his life he maintained his loyalty to anti-Semitism, militaristic nationalism, topped with an antipathy toward the Reds, and a firm belief in the liberating mission of the Germans, because he didn't have anything better to believe in. He made sure that inappropriate conversations were not held in the state factory and that the state language was used at all times. Fortunately, the clacking of Taras Ostapovich's wooden leg announced his approach beforehand, so by the time he arrived, everything was always tip-top.

As more and more draconian orders and decrees were issued, along with growing oppressions against Jews and Christians alike, accompanied by signs that the "statehood" was evaporating, Taras Ostapovich's mood was getting gloomier with every day. On top of that, we, the working class, did our share to steer the accountant in a better direction.

During a smoking break in the little office, without addressing anyone in particular, master workman Seva announced into the air, "This morning they searched women again. The gendarmes. They caught one man, with a Cossack-style moustache and forelock, and began whipping him on his back. That's right, no need to violate orders. The Germans like order. God bless them, that they'll teach it to us all."

Taras Ostapovich gloomily rustled his papers and pretended not to hear him.

Silly Styopka then joined in, "Right! And on Ritterstrasse two Germans made a mess out of a policeman's face, and then kicked him with their feet. He hadn't barked *Heil Hitler* properly at them. Hadn't learned well, that cop. Bah! Taras Ostapovich, you know him; it was Mikolka Savchuk. He is not your relative, is he?"

"Right," Seva supported. "Our *Führer* was offended, God bless him."

In that manner they "worked" with the accountant. Of course they didn't like him much, but nonetheless their attitude toward him was humorous. With the exception of Taras Ostapovich, there was a complete accord among the staff in the principal issue: everybody wished the Germans a speedy defeat and they shared thoughts about this openly with one another.

Ah yes, the production. Between smoke breaks, the factory produced two-sided combs, very popular in those days, called "lice-killers," and the remaining material was made into cigarette-holding mouthpieces. These production tasks were solved on two primitive machines—one per each workman—with a circular saw, and polishing and abrasive wheels. The workshop air was thick with dust.

The raw material—horns and hooves—came from the slaughterhouse. Yes, horns and hooves. Styopka and I worked in the sooty basement. For hours we boiled horns and hooves in a huge barrel; then we cut the softened material, split it, took out the core, which was used for cigarette holders. Then we pressed the "unfolded" horn or hoof with a manual pressing machine. When cooling off, under the press, the material was turned into sheets that were then moved upstairs, to the master workmen.

The work in the basement was difficult. Moreover, in its interior, the underground looked like a torture chamber with the corresponding equipment, and I associated the word "stench" with that place from then on.

Workman Seva didn't mention the marketplace accidentally. The major part of our produce was sold there—with much success—by the workmen. The profits were shared based on position held—with the exclusion of Taras

Ostapovich, who was naturally unaware of these trade operations. The director took a part of the produce to the *Industriezentrale* as evidence of a properly functioning enterprise.

Occasionally, Modest's daughter would stop by the factory. She was some two years younger than I and came to get my advice on solving math problems. I was called up from the underground and transformed from apprentice to teacher; I sat down at the desk and began doing her problems. The girl breathed into my ear, looking over my shoulder. That was why the comb-making factory was not always a torture.

Any ideal situation has its end, though. The *Gestapo* came for Modest.

No one else learned in what, beside lice-killers and cigarette holders, Modest Grigorievich had been involved.

After the war, having finished medical school, Modest's daughter, Tamara, remained in her hometown, and she saw my father, Yuri, Mama, and Rostislav to their final resting place—for both formal and friendly reasons.

In that emptied house behind the hill she remains a good friend.

22 FEBRUARY 1942 (CONTINUED)

The paper published an article about establishing three schools: one for trade, one vocational, and one for construction studies. It is, of course, too optimistic to be sure that you can get into one of the three (I'd prefer, the construction one), but you cannot be pessimistic all the time.

The paper also published an order of the General Commissioner not to help and not to provide shelter to strangers. They are all called "Stalin's bandits." This is what they do: "Stalin's bandits rob peasants, take away their living stock, and some clothes" (literally). Normal bandits (non-Stalinist) catch a man, get all his clothes, and let him walk naked. Stalin's bandits, however, are decent people; they do not take everything, but only "some clothes"—well, pants or perhaps a jacket, if there is one, and a hat. Naturally, boots, or perhaps felt boots. Most likely, though, these kind souls leave underpants on, and socks, perhaps saying, "Well, at least you'll get home looking decent." We have here yet another sort of bandits that are taking away all clothes. By the way, I could name them, but perhaps I shouldn't.

Our former Shirokaya Street, later Mazepa, and now Ritterstrasse begins to look odd. One side is alive with restaurants and drunk and noisy militia; the other side is assigned to the ghetto—windows and doors all boarded up, dead and disgusting. All of the streets and alleys of the ghetto are closed off with fences; it seems that the only point of entry is from the side of the burnt synagogue. There are people who enjoy this new look of the town

About the brothel: the Jews managed to keep from sending girls to it by paying 60,000 rubles—a thousand per girl.

1 MARCH 1942

Yesterday at 4 PM the ghetto was closed. Now one can't leave or enter it without a special permit. These permits are issued only to those who work at the enterprises in the town. The final steps for a complete separation of the Jews are being taken: all doors and windows facing "Christian" streets get boarded up.

I submitted my application to the technical school. On 3 March the tests will be held.

It's cold! (I'm back to writing in the attic.) For two days we had warmth and thaw—a real spring! The snow melted. Now, although it is not frost, the wind is very strong, and reminds me of fall.

3 MARCH 1942

Today there was nothing of particular interest with an exception, perhaps, of the fact that spring is finally outdoors. The sun is warming up things so well that I just want to jump up onto the roof (because I'm inside the attic now.)

I took tests in written Ukrainian and math. A piece of cake. Tomorrow there will be oral testing, and if I pass that, too, then it will be all right. The classes will start 5 March. Darn, what a time to start the academic year! It is spring now, after all—little birdies chirp, and all that—and alongside all this there will be seven hours of math weekly!

By the way, cats have begun their screaming outside already. I need to remember the date.

Perhaps I should write something about politics, but it is so nice outside that I don't want to touch this topic, as it just doesn't correspond to my mood right now. That's all. The notebook is almost over, too. My handwriting is getting noticeably smaller; I don't know where I'll get a new book.

12 MARCH 1942

The most unreliable March weather is outside. Just now the sun was shining brightly, and again it is snowing—at such a rate that you can barely see anything.

The spirits are so-so—I attend school and so on.

The "Militia" has relieved all second-hand and pawn shops, which have appeared in abundance recently, of all goods as well as their windows.

All alleys leading to Ritterstrasse are crossed with road barricades. The same kind of barricade has been placed at the entries into the town. Soon, it looks like they will start putting up a wall, something like a defense line supplied with pillboxes to protect the civilian population from . . . life. They seem to want to make absolutely sure that we be able to starve to death quietly. I wonder whether we shall ever live again? And what will the former

Shirokaya Street, formerly Mazepa Street, formerly Ritterstrasse be called then?

16 MARCH 1942

Today there are a couple of theories about the front, based on some seemingly insignificant words in the paper: "10 Soviet divisions were defeated to the west of Kursk." The thing is that the previous articles, when talking about Kursk, spoke of dozens and hundreds of the Soviet divisions defeated to the *east* of Kursk. And now—to the west! Got it? The conclusion is that the Soviets are advancing successfully at the Central front. Yes!

23 MARCH 1942

The latest issues of our paper again contain not a single word about the Eastern Front. This is good. I remember some time ago that I wrote about the Soviet POWs kept here in the hospital; tomorrow they all will be moved to a camp in Brest-Litovsk. This makes me recall Lieutenant Nikolay Oksanych. . . .

25 MARCH 1942

Now, comrades, the holy Easter and the Lord's Day is approaching, and I'm fasting because of this. God forbid you may think I have become one of those holy old men. No, it is just that in our school, besides all the special subjects, they also worry about saving our souls and eternal lives, amen! The confessions of sins that burden our soul are compulsory. Whether you wish it or not, you have to get saved! One scoundrel, Soyko, from theologians of the closed-down seminary, is in charge of all this at the school. Most likely he dreams of getting into God's heaven, and joining the saints for saving poor lost souls. And we'll have communion, too!

3 APRIL 1942

Yesterday it stormed for the first time. I was happy; this was definitely and finally springtime. Now, not so soon! Today it is only two above zero, and the rain is mixed with snow. The school let us off for Easter break, and that's why I'm now in the attic and eating nuts. I found them, even though Mama had hidden them well from me. The paper has not a single word from the front. Obviously there is some heavy fighting going on there.

9 APRIL 1942

I'm so busy that I cannot take even a ten-minute break. School lasts until 2 PM, and then more classes follow from 4 to 6.

My head is absolutely empty; I just wrote two sentences and that's precisely all I could offer. The gray-colored, boring life.

By the way, another detail from the lives of our free Cossacks: the obligation to provide labor has been introduced among them. They send a note from town to the warden of a village telling him to allocate this many cartloads of food per week to the such-and-such institution, factory or a peat plant. So the warden takes a reserve of bread and bacon (they really have plenty of this, unlike us), and goes to serve his labor duties to his German "motherland." If somebody tries not to go, a couple of days later a German punitive squad will come to the village and make some order.

13 APRIL 1942

New orders were issued by the authorities—the kind of orders that shock and puzzle. Now we have to black out the windows—based on what, I wonder? We seem to be living here in peace, building a new life, and so on, and so forth. They also tell us that the honored Commissioner seems to have noticed recently that the population has failed to follow his ordered blackout. There was no such order until now!

The second order bans talking to Jews, on penalty of incarceration.

The third one, which also makes you wonder, is about turning in weapons. It is the third time they order this, which most likely means there have been no results from the previous two.

"Militia" raided the marketplace again and the market was closed. Soon the militia is bound to start raiding homes—and closing them.

As a matter of fact, the Germans have published an *"Aufruf,"* in which local youth are conscripted for work in Germany. They promise all possible benefits, the German culture, and 130 rubles a month paid to your parents. The local youth respond to this with silence.

So what do the German authorities do? They send *SS* squads, which come secretly to towns—as it has already happened in Rovno and Dubno—and start raiding streets and churches. Young people who are caught are sent "voluntarily" away to work. Such a detachment has recently arrived in Kremenets; that is why I predict that there soon will appear such a "movement."

Children under 14 years of age now receive 100 grams of bread. We still get the usual 200 grams.

21 APRIL 1942

It is warm, sunny; it is spring. We had two days off because of Hitler's birthday. Today we had to be at mass in the church because of this occasion, too. For the very same reason today we received 200 grams of bread more than the standard ration. In his address, our principal shouted a lot about what Hitler has given us. If you ask me, these 200 grams of bread above the standard ration are it.

During the principal's speech, some other students spoke out about some of the things that I, too, had been thinking, but had never said out loud. This only proved how foolish they were; they put themselves under suspicion; they became enemies in the eyes of the principal, and they will be watched from now on. I'm not watched, so far, and I think I therefore am a more valuable enemy of him and his kind.

My wife, Lyudmila Ivanovna, who helps me invaluably by proofing the text as I enter it into the word processor, commented on this diary entry, saying, "You were a cautious young man." I can't help but agree with her; that was the way that I was. I can't make the image look better today by juggling the text written some half a century ago. The only thing I would like to add is that two years later, soon after liberation, holding a paper entitled "exempted" in my hand, I nonetheless went to the military commissioner's office and didn't show that paper there. I became an active participant of the events that followed. I will write about that in due time, however.

In those years my wife-to-be and other kids were happily and loudly reciting on stage, "Thank you, Comrade Stalin, for our happy childhood!" while her father was somewhere in Vorkuta, on a "vacation" provided by Article 58 of the Criminal Code of the Russian Soviet Federative Socialist Republic. [Article 58 was used in sentencing on grounds of "counter-revolutionary" anti-Soviet activities, actual or alleged, followed by sending to a (labor) camp or execution. *Ed.*] Fortunately, they had a chance to get to know each other all over again, because the Lord granted her father another thirty years to live.

The upbringing then required that one who happened to end up in the zone of occupation, at least to resist and fight back. Like Zoya. [Zoya Kosmodemyanskaya, an eighteen-year-old schoolgirl from Moscow, voluntarily joined a partisan detachment in 1941, participated in a number of actions against the Nazi occupants, was captured, and executed by the Germans. *Ed.*] The photos were everywhere showing her half-naked body in the snow, a noose around the neck, and a beautiful face, . . . but I was cautious.

24 APRIL 1942

Nothing of significance except the fact what I had predicted earlier: they have started catching people in the streets to make them part of German culture. I'm absolutely out of the mood for writing, and so I stop writing here.

25 APRIL 1942

I spent the whole day at home. Most likely I will have to stay home and be bored tomorrow and the day after tomorrow as well. The reason for all this remains the same: they are hunting and catching the servants of God and sending them to hell.

In Rovno, approximately a month ago they opened special courses for all those who hadn't finished elementary school. A few days ago, all these students were caught in full, and sent away to an unknown destination.

The principal slightly hinted to us that we should not hang around too much in the streets because the certificates they issued us are not of any particular value. I don't know how he must have felt saying this; it was a wonderful illustration to contradict his speech on Hitler's birthday about all the things that the German authorities give us. On Monday, I will take two changes of clothes with me to school and some dried biscuits. I'm kidding, of course; I'm not going to go to school on Monday, damn them all.

What a life! A person is afraid to step into the street and if he does, he stealthily moves along the fences, like a beaten dog. At the same time as all this they have enough audacity to talk of some new Europe, about Hitler, the "great European" man who supposedly came to liberate us. Even on his portraits, which are now innumerable, it says, "Hitler, the Liberator!" He indeed has liberated us from our lives and awarded us eternal fear. Enemies and rogues are everywhere. Here is an example from school. The principal picked on one student, a Polish boy, because he was talking to his friends at school in Polish. At this moment one of the so-called "patriots" gets up from the back row and announces, "We also have here those who speak Moscovian." [Moscovian is a derogatory name for Russian by the Ukrainian nationalists. *Trans.*] This referred to a few of my other Russian friends and me; we occupy a separate corner in the classroom. That's what today's school is like.

It is hard to live, oh, so hard.

28 APRIL 1942

That's what things are like here, I am even afraid to lean out of the window.

Our principal went to the *Arbeitsamt* (labor office) to find out the policy regarding school children. He was naturally told that the school children would not be rounded up for work, he shouldn't worry, and so on. This was true, on that particular day.

An order reaches a village (take for example, the village of Kuliki, with the information provided by a reliable source) which entails the obligation to provide 45 volunteers. The unimaginable lament begins in the village with packing and getting the "chosen" ready to leave. This is how it works in a village. On that day the town is only filled with rumors. Here is a scene that I witnessed myself yesterday, though. A major group of Jews, escorted by "archangels" returning home from work, some 400 people. At the entrance to the ghetto, the "militia," headed by a gendarme in a helmet, stopped them. Swearing and cursing, the gendarme pulls some ten victims out of the crowd. Screaming and noises followed. The victims are surrounded by the "militia" and are taken away. That's all. They will never be back. Last night 300 people were taken out from the ghetto, and they were also taken away. These events caused so much panic that the others having completed their shift remained overnight at the workplace; they were afraid to return home.

This is not all, however. It is a common knowledge that the Germans, after having tried some novelty on Jews, instantly extend it to the rest of the "free" population.

It began today. At a vocational school in Kremenets, where the students hadn't even completed the fifth grade yet, the whole school was put on trucks and taken away. Motorization. I'm waiting for our turn to come.

Let's switch to other matters that I already have dealt with once.

The rules of our school read (in Ukrainian, naturally), "In school and other public places the students can speak Ukrainian only or, as an exception, German." I had a very pleasant talk today with our Soyko, the school's Administrator, regarding this regulation. I was called to the principal's office.

"Close the door." Soyko was in front of me, darker than a cloud.

"I was informed that you openly demonstrate your use of the Russian language in the school yard (this was stated in a rather calm manner). There is no Moscow rule here—and there will never be! (Obviously becoming hysterical.) I won't allow any demonstrations on the school premises!" (He crushed his fist on the desk.) Then the storm slowly subsided. Of course, he promised to kick me out of the school. I kept silent all of the time. I was wondering who had "informed" him so well. Then he began citing an article from the school rules: one can speak Ukrainian only, or German as an exception. "If your knowledge permits," the latter he said with contempt and obvious mockery.

I could not help but answer, "Indeed."

He rolled his eyes, but withheld his rage saying only, "May God help you then."

I wanted to respond, "May He help you, too," but didn't.

Now our gang abuses the German language in school and other public places.

Contacts

Some still ask me, with a tinge of suspicion, "How did you ever come to speak German so well?"

The inference of the question is clear—you must have had a lot of contact with them during the occupation.

Yes, I had.

One evening I was running home from Zhenya's place. There were only fifteen minutes left to the curfew and I knew my family was worried about me at home.

By then Ritterstrasse was empty except for a couple strolling slowly ahead of me, a German and a girl wearing a light-colored summer dress.

Running past them, I accidentally slightly touched the German with my hand.

A few seconds later I heard, *"Halt!"* coming from behind.

I knew the meaning of that word well. I realized it was addressed to me. I knew I couldn't disobey. I stopped and turned around. The German and the girl were standing a few steps away from me.

The German slowly motioned with his finger for me to come up, *"Komm!"*

I knew I couldn't disobey. I started walking toward the German and the girl and only one desperate thought was pounding inside my head—the curfew hour! Everybody at home is waiting for me and worried. Now I will be late.

The German and the girl stood some two steps apart from each other. The girl looked at me with a confused half-smile. I knew this girl; she went out with the Germans.

The German slowly put on his leather glove. I realized that he didn't want to get his hand dirty from slapping my face. He wanted to demonstrate his German superiority to the girl, and my inferiority. The German was young and tall, and was wearing the uniform of a *Luftwaffe* non-commissioned officer. I realized he was from the health resort.

The German was standing with his feet slightly apart. His boots were polished. His left hand with the glove in it was resting with its thumb on the belt. His right hand in glove was held down.

I stopped three steps away.

The German slightly raised his gloved hand and again motioned for me with his finger to approach him.

I made two more steps and mumbled, *"Verzeihung."* (I'm sorry).

The German slowly began moving away his gloved hand.

I said, *"Polizeistunde. Verzeihung. Polizeistunde."* (The curfew.)

The gloved hand stopped. The German let go of the belt and glanced at his watch. His watch was white with a white metal bracelet. I knew the time was ten minutes till the hour.

The German hesitated and then said, *"Gut."* (Good.) He brushed me away with a contemptuous gesture, motioning ahead, away from himself and added, *"Weg!"* (On your way.)

All movements were slow. Like in a theater. I remember thinking then that it was exactly like in a play.

I caught the girl's glance filled with relief, mumbled, *"Danke!"* (Thank you.) turned around and ran off.

The German's loyalty to punctuality and order saved me from slaps in the face. There were no grounds for arresting me—the curfew hour had not started yet. Besides, when organizing the arrest, the German would have wasted the time he had assigned for the date with the girl, which most likely was limited as well. Although another possible explanation cannot be excluded today. Perhaps the German didn't want to slap my face at all, but he was supposed to demonstrate his racial superiority. He didn't have the right *not* to demonstrate it.

Although it seemed to me that the incident in the street lasted forever, I entered our house when the clock on the wall was chiming.

So I had opportunities to communicate in German. It seems amazing, but throughout all those dark years I *never* had a chance to talk to any of them like a human being. We were separate from them. Although there were *humans* among them as well.

Fortunately through the long years of forced time out of schooling I studied not only German, and not only foreign languages, but other subjects as well, and this was my saving grace. If I would have studied only German, that would have been suspicious.

The desire to learn German well was, however, explained by the previously mentioned need for information. Thick Berlin magazines and journals were displayed on a stand on Ritterstrasse. They had a whole page dedicated to the events at the front. I had to learn to understand what was written and I learned it. Moreover, I learned how to get through to the meaning that lay between the lines. By the end of the occupation I was even able to grasp some meaning of the broadcasts from London that were preceded by the *tum-tum* drum rolls, *"tum-tum-tum-tum . . . tum-tum-tum-tum. . . ."*

My knowledge of German was polished later, in another era—during the occupation of Germany.

28 APRIL 1942 (CONTINUED)

Another last minute addition: today approximately 400 people were taken out of the town, mostly craftsmen. I am not even counting how many peasants and farmers were taken away. They were put on trucks today all day long and taken toward Dubno.

That'll be all! I was prolific today, though my style was very weak.

1 MAY 1942

I don't have much joy on this holiday now, but perhaps nobody rejoices today about it, even in the Soviet Union.

We are done with our last reserves of oil and fats; haven't managed without them before, but will now try. By the way, eggs have 11 percent fat. This makes me very happy since a "factory" is right here with our hens.

They register everyone aged 16 to 45 now in the town for labor. The mood is close to panic.

5 MAY 1942

The town slowly calms down after the worst fears. The rounding up of people is now done in a more organized and quiet manner as they no longer catch people in the streets. The results of "voluntary removal": all drivers in the town were taken away, as well as brick-layers, carpenters, and other craftsmen. Also, many Jews were taken away.

There seems to be a serious file on our gang in school, almost blaming us for the organization of the anti-government underground. I found out about this from my teacher, the Pole named Baupret. I promised to keep it in total confidence, but I suppose I can put it down into my diary, because if it ever gets into the unwanted hands, it already has enough material to be sent into the stratosphere.

8 MAY 1942

On Wednesday, 6 May, at 9 AM (the information is precise) there was an air raid on the Dubno station; 12 bombers were in the raid.

Again rumors are circulating about the schools closing. By the way, the Commissioner banned teaching God's law in schools. That was a good one! As a farewell, the priest told us a tale of God creating the world in 6 days.

14 MAY 1942

Today a new train—12 cars with laborers—left for Germany. They stop people in the streets and check their documents. If a fellow cannot present proof that he is employed somewhere, he "gets employed" instantly. People are getting more or less used to this by now.

No news from the front. The paper comes out rather irregularly. By the way, the English have taken over Madagascar. If this step was taken for some reason, it must have been a diversion. So, not a very great victory.

I don't have anything else to write about, and I don't feel like writing really. The "writing" mood comes over me in waves.

16 MAY 1942

The only remaining wall of the synagogue collapsed today burying 130 people under its ruins. The wall collapsed rather unexpectedly, that's a fact. As far as the number of casualties goes, it was slightly exaggerated if you ask me.

I haven't seen the paper in a week now, and again various unbelievable rumors appear and circulate. They say that negotiations are being held in America between representatives of the Axis countries on the one hand, and the USA and Britain on the other, on making peace.

I'm very curious about the German advance on the Eastern Front planned for this spring. They have been hailing it so much in all the papers that it should have started by now. Even Hitler in his stormy speeches is always mentioning it, "Soon we'll deliver the final and devastating blow!" "This will be our last and most critical battle!" and so on. All this should have started long ago because the regrouping was completed during the winter, so why do they procrastinate? A thought, which is too good to be true, comes to mind—perhaps the advance started . . . and is already over? The Germans are still too powerful; they could not have weakened that much over one winter. I don't understand it. I sure would like to know what the Soviet command is thinking about all this.

According to the new decree the blackout commences at 9 PM now; those who violate the order "aid the aiming work of enemy aircraft and will be court-martialed." This means that air raids are not imaginary. They do take place and even the *Gebietskommissar* has to admit it.

21 MAY 1942

Quite a lot of material has accumulated. For two days I was taking notes of separate events but my notes were written with so many abbreviations (for the fear that somebody may stumble across and read them), that I can't now decipher them myself.

Regarding the collapsed wall incident: just as I expected, the information on the number of casualties turned out to be extremely exaggerated after having gone through many hands and ears. In fact there were only thirty people injured, and only three were killed.

Now back to rumors: Roosevelt didn't host the above-mentioned delegation of the Axis states that had approached with a proposal of peace talks, and now they are off to London. This is all rubbish. I have to put it down nonetheless, so that one day (under a different rule) I can get a laugh. The Germans are not the kind to beg for mercy out of charity. If during the first war they managed to hang on for four years, and under much worse conditions, then now they are closer to victory than ever before.

Starting today we will be getting 150 grams of bread per person, and children under the age of 10 will get 75 grams of bread each. Recently there has been an article in the paper saying that in the Soviet Union people starve and get 150 grams of bread a day only. Then, what could be said about us? We prosper.

There is another news item, this time a military one. The recent issue of the paper reports that a Soviet group of parachutists had been defeated; it was in the size of a full brigade that landed on the Arctic Ocean coast. It was stated rather vaguely; the Arctic coast is pretty extensive. This vagueness tickles me; if a brigade had indeed been defeated, they would have leaped at the opportunity and named the exact location where it happened. The Soviet troops must have landed in Norway and now act from there. As far as I understand strategies, nobody would send a brigade of paratroopers to enemy-occupied territories without carefully studying the situation first. In such instances they would have landed a small unit, which would then prepare conditions for a bigger one to follow. All this leads me to believe that the situation over there is not as good as presented by our journalists. What a strategist I am!

26 MAY 1942

I'm counting the pages left till the end of the book, and I see that I should be able to fit a complete year in—through July 1942, unless some really important events happen. I mean advances at the front. Of course if the German side initiates these, I won't write especially much; the gentlemen from *Vöelkischer Beobachter* would cover it. [*Vöelkischer Beobachter* was one of the leading German national-socialist newspapers. *Ed.*] If the other scenario comes true I'll be writing very patriotically, with many a hurrah.

A few days ago another column with laborers left Kremenets; it is the largest one so far, according to some of those who had been mobilized earlier, but who managed to get away. The first day they got some decent food—bread and sausage—but this was on the first day only. Then the train stopped at some rural station in Germany; local farmer women stood on the platform and picked laborers for their farming needs. Everybody was driven out of the cars, put in lines, and the examination began. They were touched, probed, their mouths and teeth were inspected. If a workhorse (laborer) met the requirements, then he or she was taken away. This reminded me of the slave markets in ancient times. In fact, all this trumpeted and glorified German culture that is now the foundation for the building of a "New Europe" reminds me a lot of the Middle Ages. There is no Holy Inquisition, but there is *Gestapo, SS,* and other similar institutions.

28 MAY 1942

A brief news item in the paper: "The supreme headquarters informs that on 23 May the German, Romanian, and Hungarian divisions began their counter-advance along the full front line." No word so far of their victories. The Germans use the following tactics: they inform about their victories only when they are certain that nobody will ask them to step back. After 23 May the Soviet air force bombed the railroad line Slavuta-Shepetovka and Shepetovka itself heavily. Today a few powerful explosions were distinctly heard toward the east.

30 May 1942

On the situation near Kharkov—the events that are unfolding there have been attracting my attention for two weeks now. Quite a lot of news is coming from that portion of the front. German reports used to start with the words, "to the east of Kharkov," then it was "in the area of Kharkov," and now "near Kharkov." I suppose Kharkov was under the Soviets until recently. Now after the German advance began, however, the situation there seems to have gotten worse and some major Soviet divisions got surrounded there. The news now starts with the words "to the south of Kharkov." The situation there is worse than in other places.

The central section of the front—the news from here purports that a lot of places have been overrun, but their names are not given. I suppose the reason for this is as follows: if the Germans announced the names of the same locations that they had taken during the first advance a year ago, it would make it obvious that they had been thrown back far to the west. Generally speaking, for some reason there was not much heard about this section of the front throughout the whole winter.

Leningrad—here there are signs of success. Some two months ago there were only occasional stories about attempts to break into the city. Then, there was news about Leningrad being bombed by heavy artillery and from the air only. For about a month now there has not been a single word about Leningrad. This is quite comforting.

About the final section of the front, which once was called "near Murmansk" and now is called "Lapland." I was extremely delighted by what I saw on the map. All of northern Finland is called Lapland, and it also extends into northern Sweden. Only Lapland's final letter "d" is in the Soviet Union. The result of my analysis: on 23 May, the German troops began their advancing along the full length of the front line, but the advance ended only in a partial success near Kharkov. It failed along the rest of the front (no less than 2,000 km).

[The initial total length of Operation BARBAROSSA's frontline was 2,768 km, and 1,320 km of that was along the main front. In 1942, during the peak of the German advance, it was 3,058 km long totally, full 2,052 km on the main front. Ed.]

30 MAY 1942 (CONTINUED)

I would like to add that all of what I write is the result of my personal observations, which are not always totally unbiased. At times I have embellished something and at other times I have kept silent about something, but generally speaking, things are not so bad. The advance is not over yet, however, and the near future can bring a lot of surprises that could debunk all of my conclusions.

For some reason we expected that again everything would be in a state of uproar that the whole front of 2,000 kilometers would come alive the way it had the previous summer. At that time we simply couldn't know that Hitler no longer had enough resources to throw his forces ahead along the full front line; the "storming" speeches of the *Führer* had created another impression. That's why when the name of long-suffering Kharkov was heard, at first this looked like a local success of the *Wehrmacht,* and almost as a failure in their general offensive. In fact, however, the forces of the enemy were again picking up strength in the Kharkov battles. The avalanche was breaking through and accelerating—now on its way to the Don, the Volga, and the Caucasus. This time it was only happening in the southern section of the gigantic front, though. That wasn't making things easier for the Red Army, however. The Soviets seemed unprepared in spite of the fact that the Germans no longer had the element of surprise.

The mere thought of another defeat, following the clear victories of the winter months was bitter indeed, and gradually grew into a strong feeling of despair.

My pessimism in that period was counterbalanced by my father's optimism. The latter knew Germans well. He had spent World War I in the trenches fighting them. (For many years a *Pickelhaube,* a German officer's parade helmet with a golden eagle and "spike" on its top, my father's war trophy, had been displayed on an oak armoire in our library. In the first days of the invasion we buried it deeply in the yard, just so to be on the safe side.) My father was confident. The Germans had bitten off way too much: they didn't have any secured rear, their communications were in continuous danger, and their defeat was inevitable.

3 JUNE 1942

Again there is no news from the front except for "successful actions near Kharkov." There is nothing to write about, or rather, I'm not in the mood for writing. I noticed long ago that I try to avoid writing down the news that is personally unpleasant to me. In this particular instance the German victory near Kharkov is such an unpleasant thing for me, it may be exaggerated, but it is obvious enough.

This morning's event is among the local developments worth noting. It clearly demonstrates just how nervous the local population is. A car and truck convoy arrived in town and a few trucks pulled into the school's yard because parking was unavailable elsewhere. Braver kids started jumping out of the windows and ran for their lives. An incredible lament ensued from the less brave kids who thus tried to save their lives. Rumors spread throughout town that now the schools were being loaded into trucks and taken away. All kind of details were added to the story. Things calmed down only when the trucks left the unfortunate schoolyard. Weeping moms were in our school, too, trying to save their children. Frankly, I myself was about to skip the final lessons and run away for my life.

5 JUNE 1942

Yesterday I turned 16. Didn't consider it necessary to mark this date, as it feels so gloomy this time. Last year it was really a happy birthday; I hoped and dreamed. And what now? What can I dream about now? Perhaps of 200 grams of bread instead of 150 grams; my dreams cannot fly any higher than that, otherwise they might be considered insanity. Last year my heart and soul were filled with light and happiness; the exams were over and long summer months with all their pleasures and joys were ahead of me. My dreams flew high. I would finish tenth grade, enter university and would work for the sake of some ideal. All this was crushed within a few days, and with such a bang!

I read all I just wrote and I think that this dark melancholy is silly and results from my temporarily bad mood.

Today a squadron flew above the town at low altitude—nine dive-bombers. The event was most unusual; for many months German military planes of this kind and in such numbers haven't been seen.

10 JUNE 1942

A few days ago, a mine exploded under a car in the village of Dunayev. The explosion was not big, but the fact remains a fact.

Traffic has significantly increased over here: a station of the Stralo German military transportation organization has been established in Kremenets, and now multi-ton trucks move continuously through it in different directions.

The school year will be over in three weeks and I'm curious whether they have plans to take us on a "bonus" tour to see "the happy life in Germany." In that case I will have to flee from town.

I wanted to write something else down, but I can't recall what now. My memory, comrades, has grown lousy, from malnutrition.

12 JUNE 1942

There is some bad news that has not been confirmed yet. It seems that German radio has announced that they have seized Sevastopol. This is a horrible blow and one cannot understate it. The capture of Sevastopol means that the Soviet Navy has lost its main and most convenient base by the Black Sea, and along with that, lost a very serious section of the front, thus freeing enemy forces to be employed on other fronts.

Following a rather quiet period after Kharkov, the news again reports of heavy fighting in the southern section of the front.

13 JUNE 1942

Discard the dispatches about the seizure of Sevastopol! I can't remember being as happy as I am now, and I try to calm myself down. I shouldn't rejoice too early. From today's paper it is clear that some heavy fighting is still unfolding there.

A local development: beginning 14 June we can be outdoors in June and July until 10 PM. At least this is good; I can go out and have some fun.

Some three weeks ago some unidentified "bandits" tried to assassinate Heydrich, the precious Czech protector. Then they reported that his life was not in immediate danger. The danger was indeed not immediate and that was why a few days ago he succeeded in presenting his soul to the devil. Looks like he was (and I'm pleased to apply the past tense here) one incredible bastard, judging by the biography included in his obituary—when he wasn't the head of the secret police division, he was the head of the *Gestapo, SS,* and the like. This characterizes him well enough.

[Reinhard Heydrich (1904–1942), was the head of the *Sicherheitsdienst (SD),* the NSDAP Security Service, and then the Bavarian Political Police within the *SS.* In 1941 Hitler made him *Reich* Protector of Bohemia-Moravia, today's Czech Republic. *Ed.*]

17 JUNE 1942

Today *Reichskommissar* Koch "himself" visited us in Kremenets. I don't know what the hell he wanted here. A delegation was sent from our school to greet him, dressed in national costumes (or at least they called them that way)—embroidered shirts, sweat pants. One of the delegates wore a fabulous belt, some three yards long, glittering in all colors and embroidered with gold. It seemed glamorous from a distance. Once you looked closer and more carefully, though, you could see it was only a decorative ribbon from the ceremonial Red [Soviet] Banner! I wish the *Reichskommissar* had realized this!

Today at a literature class, the Ukrainian national hero Mazepa was added to the list of saints while Pushkin was called a gendarme. Our inimitable Vesselovsky performed these transfigurations. Just imagine the angry face, with moustache, yet dressed in silvery robes and a halo over his head: the holy man *Hetman* Ivan Mazepa. Sounds rather saintly! Poor Alexander Sergeyevich Pushkin, dressed in a gendarme's uniform seemed to know one thing only: how to torture poor and suffering Ukrainians.

Thus I complete my first notebook. It covers events from 11 July 1941 through 17 June 1942—almost one full year. Many things were missing, and many were recorded inaccurately. I now regret that I didn't start writing on the very first day of the war. It would have contained material of supreme interest. One can't undo things that are done, though, and even less the things that were never done.

I hope that I won't make the same mistakes in this new notebook: when the explosions will burst above our heads again, I will write down everything, if I survive.

I counted the pages in my new book; it has 178 pages, and it is a squared notebook. I wish it will be completed in a shorter period of time, and if not its beginning then at least the end of the story will be about the joys of freedom.

My Secret Diary
2nd Notebook, 1942-1944

The division of the diary into sections was caused by practical reasons only. It was a mere coincidence that the second book of the diary started on 22 June. The one was over, and I had to start working on a new one—that was all. In those days one still had to purchase thick notebooks with calico binding to attend regular—Soviet—school. Regular schools were closed, and so I got some extra notebooks.

Speaking of schools, some readers may be surprised—enemy occupation and functioning schools? Local "enthusiasts" viewed schools as an integral component of the statehood that had been given to them by Hitler and which Vesselovsky and other Ukrainian "stars" of the diary praised so eagerly.

At first there was the *gymnasium,* which lasted a few weeks only. Obviously a very harsh policy soon thereafter was conceived: middle school deemed to be a first stage in forming a class of intellectuals, which was not desirable, regardless of its political "color." Moreover, it was even considered to be something harmful. "Culture," to the extent that would be necessary, would be supplied by Germany, and the Germans would be the carriers of culture. The purpose of the local population was to execute and obey the will of the representatives of the superior race. To realize this role, basic literacy and technical skills would be considered more than adequate. This was probably the reason permission was granted to establish elementary, vocational, and trade schools in Kremenets. These also lasted only a few months, however. By the fall of 1942, when the pretense of independence had ceased, this form of education, too, was terminated. Further to the west, however, in the lands of former Galicia—which, during World War I, was a part of the Austro-Hungarian Empire and now was incorporated by Hitler within the borders of *Grossdeutschland*—the schools operated well and regularly. Anti-Russian feelings were strong there, fuelled particularly by the Uniate Church, and the local cadre there were raised in such an atmosphere to become useful in the future Nazi management of more "eastern lands." [The Ukrainian Uniate Church—an Eastern Rite Church. Like other Uniate churches, the Ukrainian Uniate Church maintains allegiance to the Roman Catholic Church, and can be said to be a "western" church, as opposed to the Russian Orthodox Church. *Ed.*]

The only thing left for us was self-tuition. It is a well-documented fact that underground universities operated in Nazi-occupied Poland and they even issued graduation certificates! Studying despite the invasion became a form of resistance. Kleonovsky, our math teacher, and Baupret, our chemistry teacher, mentioned in the diary continued their noble work through the years of occupation.

22 JUNE 1942

I'm not reading any papers, I'm not interested in anything, and I don't want anything. It's that kind of day today. I wonder if it's observed on the other side, too, and I wonder how it is observed there. I don't know. I suppose I have to spend a week without taking a look in here, or something special must happen that will help me come out of this apathy.

29 JUNE 1942

I'm writing with a pencil because I lost my pen somewhere. Now on to the things that are more important: I have also lost my bike, but that was thanks to *Herr Gebietskommissar.* Yesterday the paper published an announcement on registration of all bicycles. Thanks to the amiable attitude of our "favorite" authorities our people treat these registrations with much suspicion. That is why the bikes brought to the registration post were, if I may say so, rather "naked." For instance a man came in carrying a wheel in one hand and with the other he was pushing the bike's frame on the other wheel. When put together it could be a bike, but one would have difficulty riding this one. At the post, the owners of bikes received papers and they could go home then, relieved of their bikes. This is called "the power built on the trust of people." Soon they may start registering us as well.

2 JULY 1942

Today marks one year since the Germans entered Kremenets. It's been the most difficult year of my short life.

I remember it all very clearly. It was a stiflingly hot day. It was unusually quiet after a bomb exploded in Shirokaya Street at midnight. Around eleven in the morning we perceived a sound of approaching motorcycles in the street, followed by another moment of silence. Everything had been quite obvious by then and the feeling was so heavy. It was all unbearably difficult; now everything was lost and life was over.

I began to hear the noise of heavy boots stomping the street, followed by the noise of an approaching transport train. I went up the hill to see. Carts rolled along the street in two rows. Huge horses, blonde people wearing unfamiliar gray uniforms. Their speech was foreign and not understandable. The soldiers looked at local residents gloomily and with no trust.

The endless two-row motion of the Germans lasted for many more days. It became clear why they won: the movement of the Soviet troops lasted a day or two and then streets went dead. It was clear that in the beginning of the war, the Germans had not only quality but also a quantity advantage. Well, that's enough about those days.

New currency has been introduced—10, 20, 50, and 100 "karbovantsi." The notes are printed in German and Ukrainian. They have a sign saying "the Ukraine Central Bank." Judging by the structure of the phrase, it is the name of the bank, the Ukraine Bank. That's an odd name. It is not very likely a typo, the document is of a too serious kind for that. Most likely it's a trick. The word "Ukraine" is there, but it stands for the bank rather than for the country.

Today, a plane flew by at high altitude above the clouds. I glimpsed it only once, sparkling in the sun, and my heart skipped a beat—it sparkled of silver! The German planes are all colored in dark colors, and this one was silvery, which means it was Soviet! Also, why would the German plane hide beyond the clouds, it was clearly ours! (Perhaps it actually wasn't, but I convinced myself of this, and I feel much better.) My hopes having been sparked recently began to subside. Now I sustain them any way I can.

7 July 1942

Sevastopol is captured. I had expected something like this to happen so I took the news rather well. They won't win the war! Bearing this in mind, does it really matter whether we have one more city or one less?

A town more or less was not irrelevant. Even one life more or less matters. And this was Sevastopol!

There was a book in my father's library, a big one, adorned by St. George's ribbons on a brightly-colored, somewhat tacky cover, *The Sevastopol Defense*. The book was about that very first defense (during the Crimean War and the Siege of Sevastopol from 1854 to 1855). It had numerous pictures, hundreds of portraits and sketches. I had flipped through the book in early childhood, browsing through the illustrations, then I began reading it and it was an absorbing read. Admirals Nakhimov, Kornilov, Istomin, General Totleben, a sailor named Koshka, and Dasha Sevastopolskaya. I knew those names and was proud of them. I was attracted and drawn to that city, and I encountered it numerous times. There is a notion, "a symbol of faith." Sevastopol, the "Magnificent City," and its history seemed to me to be such a symbol.

7 July 1942 (continued)

Even with the loss of Sevastopol I didn't lose my hope. It's not the same as in the summer of the previous year. The situation has changed, and not in the favor of Germany.

In an August issue of the daily *"Volhyn"* there was an article about the Washington conference of Churchill and Roosevelt. It said, "the parties reached the conclusion that at this particular moment they were much closer to victory than in August or December the previous year." You bet!

Yesterday I read an interesting document—a letter from a girl, our neighbor, from Magdeburg where she "went to work."

"When we had crossed Peremyshl, we encountered major misfortune, which I will never forget it, for as long as I live," she said. She also said, "I don't want to jump up in the middle of the night and run down to the cellar for beer. Everybody runs here. You don't have to run for beer because you don't have any."

What beer was she talking about, what was all that really about? The hidden meaning lay in that beer was something very English, and must have come by airmail straight from England, just like those "dots" in Peremyshl. You get it? [Beer and "dots" referred to bombing. *Ed.*]

The British are really doing a very good job, though. Magdeburg is the center of Germany, and Peremyshl is in Poland. Based on that letter I can judge the actions of British aviation ten times better than based on the German papers, although even there it occasionally becomes transparent to a certain degree.

Local developments: now they take horses from our villages and send them to the east. They also take scythes and sickles. This is all in preparation for gathering the harvest.

The following conversation demonstrates how the population relates to all this (they were talking so loudly, I couldn't help but overhear it): "Oh, our poor villages tolerate this all patiently, but then one day we will arm ourselves with pitchforks and chase them out." Most likely in some places that's what is already happening because more and more notices appear about fighting "bandits," sabotage, and so on.

9 JULY 1942

My spirits are low because they are closely related to the tense situation at the front. I think something will happen in the near future.

I've got a lot of interesting materials in my "archive" in the form of German propaganda posters. Some day it will be interesting to open them up and laugh with relief. I have "Hitler, the Liberator" and many similar ones.

10 JULY 1942

My premonitions turned out to be prophetic: there was a German breakthrough to the north of Kharkov. Voronezh has been occupied. What will come next?

In their turn, the Bolsheviks made an offensive to the south of Orel, perhaps as a deception. Based on the information that I have deduced from the paper, the Germans haven't responded to the offensive yet. Besides, according to the paper, the German advances have begun in the southern and central sections of the front. Just begun! There is no victorious news from the central stretch. Which means they were stopped there.

Today's paper published an article by a German military correspondent about Sevastopol. The bottom line of the article was that Sevastopol exists as a name on the map only, but the city no longer exists. When I read the article, my hair stood on its end. I can say but one thing: Sevastopol sustained its name with pride, and even more impressively than in the years 1854 to 1855 of the Crimean campaign. I salute Sevastopol!

A few words on local developments: now we are about to have a nine-hour workday. When they arrived, the Germans spoke a lot about the advantages of their eight-hour workday.

15 JULY 1942

"Voluntary trips" to Germany of considerable duration have once again become an everyday occurrence.

Militia and gendarmes are so kind; they go as far as to stop by the home of those destined for these tours and sometimes even in the middle of the night. To make it an even more pleasant surprise, they stop people in the street or an automobile comes and picks them up as if they were some bankers—only, the automobile is, in fact, a truck—and it takes them to the station.

I'm in a disgusted mood today.

The fighting at the front continues in the area of the German breakthrough near Voronezh and of the Soviet breakthrough near Orel.

18 JULY 1942

Today we received our report cards for the past half a year and now we are free from school for one month and ten days. My grades are pretty good—no Cs, but a B in behavior—for the first time in my life.

19 JULY 1942

All farmland in the town was registered in order to limit an issue of bread ration cards. I wonder what will happen to this year's harvest and what percent of it will be actually seen by the local population.

There are rumors that Voroshilovgrad has been occupied. This is not good; the Soviet troops will then have to leave Donbass. Rumors are only rumors, however. We'll see what kind of news the future will bring us.

20 JULY 1942

Now for a few days in a row I've been regularly getting down to my note-book. The reason for that is that I'm finally back in my attic. Nobody bothers me here and I can do whatever I want.

The Germans are going to start conscripting here. It is already known that battalions are being formed—out of young people who were conscript-ed as if to serve in the militia—and sent to the east. If it's true, the German situation is bad, and our situation is even worse.

I have to finish now—it's getting dark, and my eyes hurt. From 1 August we have to blackout at 9 PM, which means days are getting shorter. It is not nice on the one hand, yet on the other hand it is somewhat good; fall is on its way, along with winter, with it comes the hope that it will be over with the Germans soon.

The other day Danzig and Gdynya got a lot of fire from the British. The latter are reaching so far that in a couple of weeks they will bomb German positions on the Eastern Front. The English are really something; when the war was announced in 1939 their aviation wasn't worth anything. During the fighting in France, the Germans were undoubtedly the kings of the skies. Now, the English are on top! I remember reading in one Soviet magazine back in 1940 about a claim of the English defense minister that the English aviation will be equal in strength to the German aviation in 1942. This promise was kept.

Again the Jews are feeling the pressure. They were ordered to turn in 300 Communist Jews. I think it will all end the same way as in Rovno where currently there are no Jews left at all, with the exception of a few dozen spe-cialists who until now have been kept alive.

27 JULY 1942

I haven't written for a few days now because of my terrible mood. In their breakthrough near Kharkov, the Germans, having seen the resistance in the east, moved their forces to the south. Now not only Voroshilovgrad, but also Rostov-on-Don has been taken. I don't even want to mention this front sec-tion; it has no news of comfort.

The recent local developments have been primarily focused on the Jewish issue. The Jews are persecuted more with each day; there's panic in the ghetto, and everybody's expecting a pogrom. Last night two Jewish men were shot dead when they tried to get into the ghetto—they had been out somewhere in search for food. It is impossible to describe all crimes that the Germans are instigating toward Jews.

It was Sunday yesterday and I went on to the river. A wonderful company gathered there: officers, the *Gebietskommissar*'s deputy with his lover, beer and a phonograph. I was sick just from looking at the way they behaved themselves. The lady was changing into her bathing suit. Don't you even suppose for a minute she would go at least into some bushes to do so? She was doing it in front of everybody. Her "husband" was covering her with some shawl, having left a peeking gap for himself, and it was so wide that half of those on the beach had an opportunity to enjoy the view. When he was changing clothes, however, nobody held the shawl for him. Having taken everything off, he spent a couple of moments enjoying the sun stark naked. This is all their "culture." "Oh, God, it's the twentieth century and you are still full of prejudices. You find it sinful? Not so! That is all a bygone." I will have to join a nudist's club in the near future.

[The Communist Russia had a very brief period of free love just after the October Revolution of 1917 but under Stalin the Soviet society soon became indeed very anti-sex. *Ed.*]

30 JULY 1942

Today there was a lot of news; all was from abroad and all of it was interesting. The most important news came from yesterday's military bulletin from Moscow! I heard it from a person whom I trust completely, and the news seems to be quite credible at that. In the area of Rostov-on-Don heavy fighting is now taking place inside the city limits, and they fight for every building and for every step. The situation is the same around Voronezh. There is some heavy fighting on the Leningrad front, too. Much attention is paid to the actions of partisan units, and now all regions to the west of the front are said to be involved in the partisan war, all the way to Polesskaya Region. Kronstadt is under heavy air raids. The news was filled with figures and numbers just like the German bulletins: numbers of planes shot down, tanks destroyed, and troops taken prisoners. The report also debunked the report by the German radio that German POWs were executed in the Crimea; according to the official announcement they died from friendly fire of the German artillery as they were to be transported. The reports from abroad spoke of some heavy air raids on Hamburg.

Now on to the news from unofficial sources: again about partisans and paratroopers, and the developments in Lutsk. As a result of the bread policy that is being implemented by the Germans, a lot of farmers, and in particular young people, leave for the forests and start fighting the Germans. They attack mills and bread transport trains. The activities of the paratroopers have increased as well.

America offered Finland a way out from the war. The Finns declined the offer (that is, the Germans would not let them exit).

The partisan war is on in Yugoslavia, too, and a brief report about it was even published in our lousy little paper.

Bloody August

4 AUGUST 1942
There is really nothing to write about. I will limit myself to a few sentences only. They say that the results of a medical examination that was held in the ghetto showed that two thousand people were swollen as a result of starvation and a thousand were not capable of working.

6 AUGUST 1942
I'm not going to write a lot; I'm not in the mood. Voroshilovsk was taken. This is close to the Caucasus. It would be a disaster if they get to Grozny and Baku; it is already too bad that Donbass is in German hands. Wherever you go, whomever you meet, the topic is one and the same: German military advances.

Starting from today all shops that have been distributing bread will be closed. There is no need to keep them open any longer. They will be distributing flour, but only to those who are employed.

A few days ago *Gestapo* paid a brief visit to the town. The execution of 150 people in the prison marked their stay.

I don't want to think about anything. I'm just writing down facts, and that's all. If one starts thinking, one can easily go insane—and I still desire to live.

The Serbs are doing great! Out of all nations occupied by Germany, they are the only ones who stood up together. I admire them!

8 AUGUST 1942
Today, the German *Deutsche Ukraine Zeitung* gave me at least one piece of news to cheer me up. The paper, of course, didn't intend to bring me any joy; it just happened that way, accidentally, having slipped through. Among the reports of 6 August, among other, not so pleasant things, there was the following piece: "and today near Rzhev, in interaction with heavy armored units, the enemy continued its advance, expanding it to the nearby sections of the front. Heavy fighting continues." When the Soviet advances started near Kharkov, the reports were similar to this one.

Finally the partisan movement is reaching our area, too. From the eastern regions it extends on to Polessye and from there it branches off into all directions. Partisans are in Belovezhye forests; they have started working very near Kremenets. On 6 August a truck left for Dubno from a butter factory, loaded with butter (naturally, intended not for us, the mortals). It left the factory, but it never made it to Dubno.

Our town is expecting a Jewish pogrom. All information available points that it will happen in very near future. There are six trucks in the town assigned to the *Gebietskommissar.* High board frames were set up on their backs. The *Gestapo* is back in town; they borrowed some hundred spades and shovels from local enterprises. You get the picture, right?

8 AUGUST 1942 (IN THE EVENING)

Something similar to a state of siege was declared in the town. One can be outside no later than 6 PM.

I went downtown today. You can't walk along our main street, Ritterstrasse; it was full of militia. They open fire the moment somebody from the ghetto looks out of the window or comes out in the street. According to some information, this morning they took out some 1,500 people—doctors, engineers, and workers. Most likely they removed those whom they were not going to shoot for the time being. They say that there are weapons in the ghetto and somebody even shot back and supposedly they even killed one gendarme. I wish they had killed more than one.

The shooting that somewhat subsided during the daytime now increased again. What will happen during the night I wonder?

These bastards are brazen enough to call themselves Christians. They even have the saying, *"Gott mit uns"* on their belt buckles—"God is with us." If he exists, then how good is the God that watches all this indifferently?

I heard machine guns. What do people doomed for death feel when hiding in the corners of their homes? The silence is horrendous. The clicking of revolvers is heard clearly along with short bursts of machine-gun fire and heavy crack of the *Schutzman's* rifles. It is going to be one difficult night. If the Jews decided to defend themselves, this could go on the whole week, trying to get them out of all cellars in those dirty ghetto quarters, full of alleys and nooks.

I keep my notebook under my pillow; I'll write later at night—I don't want to miss or forget anything.

Perhaps one day also my notes can be added to all those evidences against those monsters and their chief, Hitler—"the liberator."

[A *Schutzman* was a member of *Schutzmannschaft der Ordnungspolizei* (Auxiliary Unit of the German Police). The members of these units were local recruits or volunteers who were often former soldiers or policemen. There were numerous *Schutzmann*, or *Schuma*, units in both *Reichskommissariat Ukraine* and *Reichskommissariat Ostland. Ed.*]

11 AUGUST 1942

The final act of the tragedy in our town is about to end. I'm writing about the events of yesterday that I pieced together from several witnesses to whom I've talked. I couldn't do it last night; I couldn't find enough strength in myself to do it.

Approximately 5,000 people were shot and killed yesterday.

Outside town there is an old trench, about a mile long. This was a trench of the Yakutsky Regiment that was encamped by Kremenets in the Czarist times. Yesterday's execution was held there.

They began taking people out of the ghetto at approximately 3 AM and it lasted until late at night.

The scene was horrible! The ghetto gates were wide open, and a line of the doomed began from there, in rows of two. A truck pulled up, and the line slowly and silently moved onto the truck. The first pairs got down on the bottom of the truck, those following got on top of the first, and so on, in human layers. It was all done in total silence: no talking, no screaming, and no crying. The *Schutzmänner,* who were absolutely drunk, were using rifle butts to hurry people who were late or slow, and used them to ram people who were already at the back of the truck. The truck pulled off, sped up, and left town.

Similar trucks with high-boarded sides returned to town loaded with clothes. A "militiaman" was riding one of them, sitting atop the pile of clothes, with a happy look on his face. He was playing with a ladies umbrella. His contented looks could be explained easily: he has pocketfuls of watches, five pens, and he left a few suits and an astrakhan fur coat on the way here, in a safe place. Moreover, he must have drunk a liter of vodka.

Once outside of town, the truck sped toward the trench. From time to time four *Schutzmänner* standing in the corners of the back of the truck, swore and hit those who were lying down on their backs with rifle butts. Thus finally they reached the destination.

The truck stopped and the doomed people slowly got off it. Taking their clothes off right there, the men and women proceeded to the ditch one by one. The ditch was already filled with bodies of people and chloride lime had been sprinkled on them. Two *Gestapo* men, naked down to their waists, sat on the top of the mound holding guns in their hands.

People got down into the ditch and laid down on the dead bodies. Gunshots followed. It was all over. Next!

I don't know what a person might feel in his or her last moment; I don't even want to think about it. One could go insane.

There were some who tried to resist, who didn't want to take their clothes off, who didn't want to get down into the ditch. They were executed on the spot and thrown into the pit.

When the pit was filled full, the militia covered the bodies with ground.

The line moved on to another pit; there was plenty of room for everyone.

Now one person, naked, set off running across the field. The *Gestapo* men just sneered, watching him. He crossed some 200 yards when the *Gestapo* calmly aimed and began shooting at him. A few minutes later his body was thrown into the pit as well.

There was a man who was chewing on a piece of bread while walking to the pit.

The militiamen who were the only witnesses of this horror sobered up after a few minutes there. They were fuelled with a new dose of alcohol.

The *Gestapo* men did not need alcohol.

It was not their first time.

They threw hand grenades on people who were still alive in the pits of Rovno, and then they watched how the earth moved under the pressure of moving and agonizing bodies, and this never affected them. They shot endless rows of people lining up the road ditches in Kiev. Prior to the pogrom in Dubno they had removed all professionals and offered them to pick one child out of their families, and then were enraged when these poor people refused to work and begged to be shot together with their families.

The trucks rolled one after another. It was evening, and they were not as full—women, young girls and children sat at the bottom. One girl smiled a meaningless smile. Another straightened her shawl on her head. In ten minutes you will be killed. Do you understand it? Why don't you fight back? No.

The victims were filled with apathy; all they wanted is for this terror to end soon, as soon as possible. That was the effect of starvation and beatings.

Here was Arek Z., a friend of mine, going on a truck. He sat at the end, his head hanging out of the side of the truck and he watched the cobblestones of the pavement flickering under the wheels. Every stone brought him closer to his final destination; it brought a person who hasn't lived closer to the end of his life. I will never forget his face; the face of someone who knew that in a few minutes he would be dead, and in an hour his body decomposing with lime, would be covered by another layer of dead human bodies. One would have to be in these people's shoes to feel everything that they felt—at least those of them that were still able to feel and think.

Fifteen hundred people who were taken the day before yesterday out to Belokrinitsa were also killed. They were killed because they attempted to reach some kind of deal. Setting terms to the superior German race! They were supposed to come out today and work like they would normally do at 7 AM, and they said that they would do so only if their families were spared and returned to them. That "if" killed them all. Rumor has it that only 250 people survived—those who agreed to work.

The horror comes to an end. One still cannot walk along Shirokaya Street; occasional shots are heard and occasional trucks run outside of the town where the last ones are being executed. They are the last ones who have been hiding in basements hoping to save their lives. They will have one advantage only—their bodies will be buried closer to the surface.

Now anarchic robbery is unfolding in the ghetto. The "militia" robs the place along with anybody who is under its protection. In a few days they will start destroying the ghetto. A few months later the place where 7,000 people lived and suffered will be a flat spot.

Yesterday the Jews from Berezhtsy were massacred. Today the *Gestapo* left for Pochaev and Vishnevets. Today they have the same thing going on as we had yesterday.

14 AUGUST 1942

From 10 August through today there were no more killings because the main executioners—the *Gestapo*—were getting around the area.

Last night they were back in town. That's why today was marked with killing another 1,500 people. They had been found over the three days—hiding in cellars and basements. Once the darkness fell on the town, the shooting resumed—these poor people tried to escape under the cover of the night. They shoot everyone. There is a horrid cadaverous stench coming from dead bodies lying in the center of the town, across from the ghetto. It is horrible. Last night the shooting went on for two hours, non-stop, just like in June last year.

People tell what's going on inside the ghetto. There is a pit dug out. A gendarme standing above it gorges himself on a bun. People come up carrying a stretcher with a wounded person on it. The gendarme continues talking to someone he knows, then he pulls out his gun, and shoots the wounded person in the head. The body is thrown into the pit. Another person is brought on a stretcher and the scene repeats, and so on. What a peaceful scene! Lighters, silver spoons are scattered everywhere on the ground and nobody pays any attention to them. The militia has stolen so much that if they'd wanted to, they just couldn't take any more. That's why now the proclamation is issued that death punishment will follow any new cases of robbery in the ghetto.

Many tried to escape. Today there were three dead bodies lying in the middle of the street and nobody cared to remove them. Some children who saw a woman while she was asleep when hiding in the Jewish cemetery turned her in. How can people stoop so low, especially after they have seen so much blood?

Today it seems to be the end.

The situation at the front is of the kind that I don't even want to think about it. The Germans are getting closer to Vladikavkaz and to Grozny. The loss of Grozny would mean the loss of fuel for the aviation, and they keep retreating! I feel like swearing and cursing the Caucasus command. The Bolsheviks keep pressing the enemy near Rzhev and Voronezh but this pressure could hardly be compared to the German one. Ah!

17 AUGUST 1942

The extermination is almost over. Yesterday they took out two more truck-loads of people, now mostly women and children. They must have been found hiding in cellars. A few dozen people were left in the ghetto, and their task is to bury the dead. I don't know what they are hoping for by completing their assignment.

Under Soviet rule the town of Kremenets reached its highest level of development, and here are some statistics:

1939—28,000 residents (Polish figures)

1941—approximately 40,000 residents

1942—24,000 residents (they say there are that many, but I doubt it.)

After massacring 8,200 Jews there will be only 15,000 residents left in town.

It used to be the town of Kremenets and now it will be a settlement called Kremenets.

This transfiguration was not an outcome of military actions, which just rolled through town, but a result of the actions of our wise German rulers.

18 AUGUST 1942

Finally something happened that reminded me of the existence of the Soviet Union. Today a group of our paratroopers landed in the mountains. A worker from the power plant who witnessed the landing told us about it. They were on a lunch break when one of the workers noticed descending sky-blue parachutes. The paratroopers landed on the slope, one after the other, and disappeared into the forest outside the town limits. A few minutes later a truck with Germans appeared. They jumped out of it looking pretty brave and rushed toward the woods. The closer they got to openings in the forest, however, the slower their steps became. Then the Germans stopped. Having discussed something for a few moments in agitated voices, they turned back, approached the group of workers, and suggested the latter to go catch the parachutists. The workers refused, saying that they were not armed. The Germans left. This was just the beginning. Now the Germans moved some 200 people there, primarily Slovaks. Two hundred people against nine parachutists.

I can't understand the meaning of these airdrops, though.

It is also interesting that the plane that dropped them off was neither seen nor heard.

19 AUGUST 1942
Today they took away F.

I can't really explain what I feel now. I feel awful and ashamed. I feel shame for those people who watch all this with indifference or who gloat. "What, he feels sorry for Yids? What an idiot!"

How is F. inferior to you? She is ten times better than you are together with all your friends, in any respect!

She was the only girl with whom I've always been open and sincere and it was so wonderful to have a friend who understood and agreed with you. She was a good and brave girl. She was taken away on a truck, standing proudly, with her head held high.

This happened half an hour ago, at 6:35, on 19 August 1942. And I'm certain she won't lower her head even when dying.

F., I want you to know that I remember you, I won't forget you, and some-day I will avenge you!

My "first love," who has left the most bright emotions and memories behind. She was my ideal.

A final good-bye to you from Romka!

I was sitting on our hill, my knees pulled up to my chin, embracing them with my arms. Our glances met as the truck passed. When standing she could see the roof of our house through the treetops. Most likely she asked a *Schutzman* to let her stand. They were all supposed to be lying face down, but she was standing facing the front of the truck and she was looking toward our hill.

She had fair hair and dark serious eyes. In school back in 1941 she was about to get braids. Now she had a short haircut, but her hair was nonetheless blowing in the wind.

Our eyes met.

She could have said, "Bye, Romka," or simply could have waved at me, and then perhaps there would have been two dead bodies instead of one, but she looked in silence. She saved me.

She is no more. And I, with this living image of her in my mind, live. live, live. . . .

I might not have been sitting on our mound during those days. The days when trucks with high boards were constantly passing by, I might not have been sitting there, but I was.

And waited for as long as it took.

Dad was digging around the apple tree in the garden. He had a good look at me, put aside his shovel, walked up to me and said, "What?"

"They just took Frida away."

He understood why I kept sitting on the hill.

In my diary, half an hour later I had not very eloquently written, *"I won't forget you, and someday I will avenge you."* I had a dream: to survive until our guys got back, become a soldier myself, get a submachine gun, and head westward with them. Our forces weren't moving westward, however. They were still busy retreating, somewhere there, on the Volga, in the Caucasus. It was a vague promise I had made to myself—to "sometime, someday. . . ."

19 AUGUST 1942 (CONTINUED)

They were being taken to the prison, a few trucks a day. These were the people who were found hiding in cellars.

This morning there was a dead woman lying on Shirokaya Street. She had tried to save herself and thus only had sped up her end. She paid for her desire to live!

As I'm writing I hear shots coming from the prison. Another one! Perhaps this one was aimed at F.? In that case, she is better off now. No, she is neither better nor worse off then.

I can't imagine—F., naked, with her body covered in lime. Wounds. Lying under a pile of similar bodies.

Such horror, such abominable horror!

That woman lying on Shirokaya Street was also naked covered with some rags only. She obviously had worn a nice dress.

21 AUGUST 1942

Yesterday they executed everyone they had crammed into the prison. A five-ton truck that pulled out of the prison, filled with shoes all the way to the brim is the only thing that lets one estimate the number of the massacred.

So F. died yesterday.

Today only a few single shots were heard from Dubenskaya.

I heard that German radio seems to have broadcast a report that an English division has landed on the French coast. Following a 24-hour battle, the Brits fled to the sea. [Indeed, on 19 August 1942 a Canadian-British force made an amphibious assault on the French town of Dieppe. After heavy losses the survivors withdrew by sea. *Ed.*]

Maybe that meant the second front? In that case, you're bastards, you fine Englishmen. Your ally is losing millions of people and you keep playing games. I ought to curse you and your mothers here.

Now it's about time to figure out some things about the situation at the front. Precisely why did the Germans choose the southern front for their advance?

First of all, it should be noted that they have chosen to strike not alongside the whole front line as they did in 1941; the German forces wouldn't be able to tackle such a task now.

After the recent failed Soviet offensive on this front, the Soviet forces were shaken up and the Soviets couldn't rearrange themselves properly. That is the first probable reason why the Germans chose to attack in this particular sector. Second, one should choose to attack the adversary's most sensitive places and the southern front meets this criteria particularly well—here is Donbass, the major Soviet coal reserve, and if we look further, there's Krasnodar, Maikop, Grozny, and Baku. This is the direction of the forthcoming German strikes—toward the major oil reserves. The first attack was successful. Having cut off the Caucasus, the Germans attempted to deprive the Soviet Union of its major oil resources. Now one can expect three strikes: toward Stalingrad (I suppose this one has already taken place, although I don't have any information on that); toward Baku and Batumi, with the objective to cut off the whole shoreline of the Black Sea and leave the Soviet navy without its harbor. We'll see whether it is so.

When I start thinking about all this, it becomes so unbearably difficult. About a month and a half ago I was full of hope, and now my feeling is the total opposite. Now there is no use in trying to console myself—the prospects are utterly grim. An extreme amount of energy and strength is needed and the Red Army is doing its very best now. Nonetheless, that is just not enough. I recall the first days of the war, how confident we were in the Red Army's victory, in its power, and how bitterly we were disappointed later. I want to live in full, and feel myself a human being again. I can't express the feelings I have accumulated in my heart. It is unbearably hard. They announce rewards for those who help catch the parachutists that landed near town. Of course, the biggest reward today is the increased food ration.

More troops have been brought into the town, armed with submachine guns. They most likely think that those paratroopers are a vanguard and will be followed by much stronger forces. They say that a radio transmitter was found in the ghetto and that the paratroopers were sent to organize a riot in the ghetto. I don't believe that. In any case the paratroopers arrived too late. And who decided about their landing in broad daylight, at noon? I don't understand how they can waste so many people.

31 AUGUST 1942

I will start from the event that is the most pleasant to me: a report from Moscow. All attention is now centered on Rzhev; a 150-kilometer-wide breakthrough was made on the front near Rzhev. In the course of the battle fourteen German divisions were destroyed, along with hundreds of planes and tanks. The advance, at the cost of huge losses, continues. The radio didn't say anything about battles near Stalingrad or the Caucasus, which means that most likely the situation there is not precisely splendid. It's certainly a good thing, though, that at least in one location things are more or less looking good. The objective of this breakthrough is perhaps to pull the German forces away from the menacing southern front. Oh, I hope they don't blow it!

The cities in Poland and eastern Prussia are under heavy bombing. As a result of this, a new decree was issued to blackout immediately after the sunset. Why in the world would one want to light a candle when the sun is still out? Idiots!

Parachutists keep landing and landing. Now each village is hiding a few of them. You may wonder, "What? Villages are hiding them? But only a year ago. . . ." Well, whatever was a year ago is no longer the case. Now the following words are typical, "Should they walk in here, I won't eat butter myself, but will give it to them!" Now, sharing butter with anyone is the greatest deed of Christian spirit.

Psychological warfare is obviously the main objective of the parachutists, and one could say that they are successful; the mood and atmosphere here are now ideal. Another significant thing is that not a single one of them has been captured yet.

Some 600 people have been found in the ghetto since the last executions; they were put into prison. Today at 5 AM it all started again, *Pow, pow! Rat-a-at-at! Pow! Rat-a-tat.* . . . It lasted for two hours.

The decree that threatened those who would rob the ghetto with execution turned out to be insufficient. Now they issued another one, in which they say that any person met in the ghetto without a special permit allowing them to be there will be shot dead on the spot. The headline reads "shooting decree."

I have been by those trenches where most of the killed were buried. Now this place looks like a flat white surface—white because of all the chalk. The days have been hot and bodies decompose fast, swelling, with arms and legs re-surfacing; stray dogs pull them around the area. The stench is horrid.

2 SEPTEMBER 1942

Last night the ghetto was set on fire.

By 3:00 in the morning some 400 houses had burned down, leaving less than a quarter of the ghetto standing. The fire engine pump has been working continuously since early morning, pumping the water up all the way from the stream. What could be done with one pump, though? The fire engines came all the way from Dubno, and even, they say, from Rovno, but they can't do anything either. The arson was caused quite obviously by the ghetto residents themselves and was thought over carefully, with weather today being the most appropriate for this.

Yesterday an unusually strong eastern wind started blowing under completely clear sky. The ghetto was set on fire unexpectedly, the fire picked up at the front row of the buildings, and all the easternmost houses caught on fire instantly. Looks like some fuel had been spilt. Intense shooting started in the area of the fire. Most likely the militia spotted some commotion inside the ghetto and began firing. This happened around 1:00 in the morning. I woke up hearing shots—and was surprised by them, because for a week, it had been quiet now at night. The fire followed the shooting, the sky was lit up by the blaze, and heavy clouds of smoke were everywhere.

In the morning I had a chance to observe the results of the six-hour "work" of the fire. The lonely chimneys sticking out among the ruins now make up the entire eastern part of the ghetto. The fire was still not extinguished. The firemen fussed around. Germans helped the firemen. The head of the militia was scurrying observers with his stick to work the pump. Public Inspector Windrat yelled at the head of the fire engine crew that they were not trying hard enough to save Ukrainian property. Now, that was the moment it became Ukrainian.

In the southwest, the fire leaped across the fence, burned down the city hall and a few houses that belonged to the "Aryans." I'm very happy, that was their punishment. Now under the bright sunlight the fire is not noticeable as much, and there is less smoke. Perhaps they have managed to bridle the blaze at least partially.

In the middle of the "military action" some 300 people were led out through the burned-down gates of the ghetto. Some of them had red armbands. Some say that the armbands identified those who were left to clean up the ghetto. Others—that this was a demonstration. I'm more inclined to believe in the former. In any case these *last ones* will not die unnoticed. Perhaps the parachutists started the fire. Nothing is known for certain. I'll write down any details once I know them.

Now our little town presents a miserable sight. Most of the houses were destroyed, some intentionally, although against the wish of the Germans, the others—also intentionally, though "legally." The town looks as if it's been under heavy bombing.

It's quite a time now; these are extraordinary days. I have to write everything down, or otherwise if I recall this some day, I may not believe myself.

The pump is working hard and smoke is again increasing. The blaze has moved considerably to the west. If they don't stop the fire by tonight, there will be a spectacle right in front of my nose.

4 SEPTEMBER 1942

The atmosphere in town is filled with anxiety and expectation of something about to happen. Flyers in Polish were posted everywhere, calling the Poles to resist. They could have been posted by Polish parachutists or . . . the other day many *Gestapo*-men arrived in town, in plain clothes, and they might just as well have posted the flyers. It is expected that Poles will follow the Jews in their footsteps. The Commissioner had some kind of meeting today. It lasted the whole day and nobody was allowed into the *Gebiets-kommissariat*. The tension gets worse also due to the fact that yesterday the total registration of residents aged 15 to 50 was announced, under the pretense of sorting out the food and housing issues. After the memorable "registration" of the bicycles, however, we stay alert.

The burnt part of the ghetto is still smoking. Out of the whole ghetto—some 500 houses—only a few dozen remain. Burnt remains of poles hang from wires, torn pieces of some clothes and a smell of smoke and fume is everywhere.

I'm back to school again. The school break was short—only a month and a half. I compare my moods then and now. Then, the "nationalists" chanted, "Arise, Taras! Wake up!" [calling on the memory of Taras Shevchenko, a nineteenth-century Ukrainian poet who was a major inspiration of the Ukrainian nationalists, *Ed.*] "Ukraine is up again" and other highly melodious songs along the same theme. They cast their unfriendly glances at me. Now, they chant no more, and shake my hand with so much energy and emotion. If you happen to spend some time with any of them alone, they start with pausing, followed by a sigh, and then curse the Germans.

If you could only hear *Pan* Vesselovsky now! You would faint! Here is what he said yesterday, "Now I can see that our nation is not ready for independent statehood. It needs a couple of centuries more to be beaten and abused." And so on. He ended with the statement that under the Czar we had freedoms like no other country had: one could live a long life, and nobody would ever be asked for his or her passport or other IDs.

Unbelievable! Is he simply choosing the more appropriate stance now? He spoke the above having just observed a scene of his "nation" equipped with sacks, pillowcases and bed sheets, using the opportunity of fire and chaos to get inside the ghetto through windows and across fences to thieve what could still be found there.

7 SEPTEMBER 1942

They are shooting again. Where do they find these people? They say that 4,000 more people were shot than had been registered, that is, approximately 12,000 total. People are found in huge cellars that make up a whole underground system and where the militia is afraid of entering.

At night a squadron of Soviet airplanes flew above the city at a very high altitude. They seemed to be en route to Lvov, because they returned back in about an hour and a half. It is simply amazing how such an event can lift the spirits! There, a mile above you, there are free Soviet people who haven't experienced life under the "German liberators."

I totally forgot that 1 September was the third anniversary of World War II. The editorials in the German papers were titled, "Three years of victories." To a certain extent it is true. Everybody who had to face the German forces, broke down and collapsed under their blows. The Soviet Union has been the only exception so far; it only bent down under these blows. The trouble is that it still can't straighten up—but we have to hope!

Warsaw has been bombed again. Rumor has it that it is on fire. Poor Warsaw. It has never had a break in this war. What is now left of the magnificent sight that it was prior to September 1939? It is nice to be sitting in such a rotten place as ours where there are no decent objects of attraction. I wouldn't wish to be in Warsaw now.

There is fighting going on around Stalingrad, twenty-five kilometers away from the city, in its suburbs, in its vicinity! I can't believe they will occupy Stalingrad! Or perhaps it is already in German hands? The steppe is on fire, but even the fire doesn't stop them. What kind of power do they have? Are they really invincible? The bravery of the Red Army soldiers is such that they keep shooting and fighting when their clothes are on fire. Patriots keep fighting; they know what they are burning alive for. They are so different from guys like me.

9 SEPTEMBER 1942

Yesterday I listened to the radio, a broadcast from Moscow! I tried to tune up for three hours. Now "The International" is played at ten, which is eleven o'clock in Moscow. ["The International" (*L'Internationale*), the official Communist song which from 1918 to 1944 was the national anthem of the Soviet Union. *Ed.*] I remember when the war began, the end of radio broadcasts was moved from midnight to eleven o'clock. I didn't hear any news bulletins—only reports by military correspondents from the frontlines. In addition there was plenty of music: opera and romances. The front reports were just like the German ones, except that they were the other way around.

Three days ago the Germans captured Novorossiysk, with 8,000 prisoners of war taken there. They repeated this enormous number figure a couple of times. The fighting near Stalingrad continues. Looks like the situation there is going bad, and Moscow is keeping very silent about Stalingrad.

I will have an opportunity to listen to this receiver occasionally. I have to note, though, that what I heard yesterday from Moscow didn't significantly enhance my mood, as I had hoped and expected.

The defensive fighting near Stalingrad would last until 19 November 1942. On 10 September, the Soviet troops left a major part of Novorossiysk. Until November the advances of the charging enemy continued in the Northern Caucasus. The coil gets tighter and tighter . . . and in the meanwhile . . . in the meanwhile, *"what I heard yesterday from Moscow didn't significantly enhance my mood the way I had hoped and expected."*

News from Stalingrad

The Volosevich family had a radio. It was a powerful seven-valve super-heterodyne model. The Volosevich family lived next door. With the arrival of the Soviets in September 1939, they were gone and their house was nationalized. They returned when the Germans returned, and they got their house back, too.

Such one-family houses with little yards, orchards, and vegetable lots constituted the greater part of old Kremenets. It seemed that a life of its own was unfolding in each of these houses, separated from the neighbors by little fences, walls of greenery, or brick. Well, it was indeed that way, to a certain extent. The lives went on here for decades, however, from generation to generation, and that was how an exact and sometimes very detailed perception of every home and every neighbor was formed, regardless of all and any fences and walls. There was no need for questionnaires and biographical records: neighbors knew everything about one another, including the slightest shades of their political coloring.

"If shoemaker Modest Grigorievich was pinkish back under Polish rule, why wouldn't he be red under the Soviets and what would his color be under German rule? What do you think?"

"If Yuri Kravchenko punched a German in his face because the latter had made some advances to Lyda, Yuri's girl, and the German started reaching for his gun, do you suppose Yuri will adore the Germans? And you should just ignore even the fact that his dad is a former Czarist officer. They have Marshal Shaposhnikov now who used to be a colonel of the General Staff and High Command when Nicholas ruled; with aiguillettes and all. Now he is one of those who command the Red Army! No, don't tell me—I know it myself: Yuri's dad had troubles with the Soviets in June, at the Dubenskaya? So what? Anybody can have trouble. Isn't he alive? So was that really trouble? No, I know. . . ."

The range of political preferences and views in that area was extremely wide. Ukrainians, Jews, Poles, Russians, Czechs, and Germans lived there. Those were not just Ukrainians, Poles, or Russians, but independence supporters: OUNists; Prosvita liberals; internationalists; Pilsudchiks; PSPers

(Polish Socialist Party) and PWPers (Polish Workers' Party); monarchists; Anglo- and Francophiles; and Reds. There were, of course, also those among all the nationalities whose main criteria for judging the current order was the availability of basic goods and products in the stores, stability of prices, and a good night's sleep, that is, not being awakened by someone breaking down your front door.

Neighbors knew everything about one another.

Frequent changes in rulers had taught people certain mutual tolerance: if one day I betray my neighbor who lives to the left of me, then the following day my neighbor on the right could just as well betray me.

The Voloseviches were known as nationalists and independence supporters claiming to be both theoretical and ideological leaders. The "old man" Volosevich held positions in the local administration established by the occupiers, and won their trust and favors. The superheterodyne model was one such symbol of the trust between the Germans and Volosevich.

Our father was known as a Russophile, in favor of the "united and undivided" and, simultaneously he had a "pink hue"—he had never made a secret of his satisfaction with the growing power and influence of the new Soviet state. He even recognized something from the old-time monarchs in the role played by Stalin. A seemingly clear picture was somewhat darkened by the fact of my father's arrest in the first days of the German-Soviet war. Did his opinions change after this? If so, then how did they change?

Then one day in the early fall of 1942, Yaroslav, the Voloseviches' boy, saw me in Ritterstrasse across the street from the burnt-down ghetto and asked, "Would you like to listen to the radio?"

"Yes, I would," I replied without a second of hesitation.

"So stop by in the evening."

A family council was held at home that day. I was certainly going to be tested. Dad said, "It's okay, you're no baby any more. Don't say anything extra, don't demonstrate your curiosity too much. Don't tune up to the Moscow channel. Unless by accident. If they treat you, eat. No drinking!"

Indeed they sat me down to have dinner with them.

The smell of sausages fried up with bacon stupefied me.

Then a bowl filled with dumplings in sour cream and bacon bits was set on the table.

The "old man" Volosevich walked out from his study. "The young man has a healthy appetite," he said in a friendly way.

I only nodded—my mouth was stuffed with food.

Then we had some real coffee.

"It's mocha," Madam Volosevich said. "It was brought from Berlin to *Pan Stabsleiter* [head of staff]. He treated us with some."

Pan Volosevich then asked me, "So, how is your father doing? We live next door, but don't see each other very often."

"He's alright," I said. "He works, in the chalk factory, as an accountant."

"I know. How was it there, in prison, at the Dubenskaya? Did they beat or torture him there?"

"No. They didn't manage to. The *Wehrmacht* soon arrived. They let him out."

"They let him out," *Pan* Volosevich repeated vaguely. "They let him out very conveniently. I can see that you speak our language rather fluently. Have you learned it fully because you kept talking Moscovian all the time?"

"I always could. To some I speak in Ukrainian, to some I speak in Polish, and to some I speak in Russian."

"And to some you speak in Yiddish." *Pan* Volosevich seemed to be very well informed of my heart matters.

"Yiddish resembles German a lot, though, as it is easy to understand," I responded diplomatically. "*Tisch—tysch; Fisch—fysch; Brot—broit.* You must understand it, too. In Kremenets everybody understands it a little." [*Tisch – tysch, Fisch – fysch, Brot – broit,* are German and Yiddish words for table, fish, and bread. *Trans.*]

"Well, well, so you can speak German, too?"

"I study. Dad knows German well, from that war with . . . the Austrians. He speaks French and English, too. He knows Latin. I began studying back in the *gymnasium.* Now I read papers, polishing my knowledge."

"Today it is very important to know German. And your father is an accountant. Don't the Germans hold that war against him? He fought on their enemy's side."

"No. They respect old officers. When he started working, they called him in. '*Herr Hauptmann,*' they said. '*Pan* Captain'."

"The war will be over, and you will go to your Muscovy, right?"

"Well, it's not over. And why would we go there? Our home is here."

"Well," said *Pan* Volosevich. "If there is anything you need, tell father to stop by. We are neighbors. Tell him so."

"Thank you, I will. Thank you for the meal."

"Would you like to listen to the radio?" Yaroslav asked me.

"May I?"

"You may, if you're careful," *Pan* Volosevich smirked.

"Well, come along."

So they left me in their living room, all by myself, along with a wonderful Telefunken receiver. I quickly tuned in to "*Deutschlandsender,*" and listened to the announcer's cheery metallic voice for a long time and with veneration.

"What's new?" The "old man" Volosevich called out to me from the door.

"There is fighting in Stalingrad. They can see the Volga already. They say a flag has been planted on top of Mount Elbrus, by mountain infantry under the 'Edelweiss'." [It was the 1st Mountain Infantry Division of the German Army. *Ed.*]

"So it used to be Stalingrad, and now it will be Hitlerstadt?" *Pan* Volosevich commented as if asking, and walked out of the room.

I didn't say anything, but kept tuning the radio. On long frequency channels where Warsaw was, it was all German; RF-9, where Kiev used to be, German news was broadcast as well. Russian words occasionally came through where RF-1 was. I turned the sound down, and for a moment I returned to that frequency. They were reading letters from the front.

I put down into the diary then, "Yesterday I listened to the radio, a broadcast from Moscow! I tried to tune up for three hours." Perhaps it was less than three hours. I could only tune in to the Moscow frequency for some moments, but nevertheless managed to pull out the things that I later wrote down. It was not much, but it was "so nice, to hear the voices from the homeland."

They told me, "You may come again. You listen to the radio, practice your German," hence the record in the diary, "I will have an opportunity to listen to this radio occasionally."

Pan Volosevich didn't exclude possible alternative outcomes and didn't want to burn any bridges. He played his game as if it were chess, carefully considering every possible future move. The Eastern Front advances, moreover, started to slow down. And in Kremenets, neighbors knew one another's thoughts well.

An actual collaborator was quite different from the literary image of them that evolved later. The real ones didn't constantly run off and report matters to the *Gestapo*. Even back then, in the fall of 1942, he would reflect on his own future, and take necessary steps for it.

As for me, after that first night at the Volosevich's, I suffered from bad stomachache; I had gotten unaccustomed to eating plenty of food. Future visits didn't have any such consequences—they didn't invite me to dinner any more, and I went straight to the Telefunken in a business-like manner: to practice my German.

Then the power plant simply stopped supplying power. The power became *"Nur fuer Deutsche"*—for Germans only. We had to recall the treasure that we had buried in our garden, but I'll write about that later.

In the early spring of 1944 this family disappeared for the second time, but was it for good? "For good" or "never" are terms too categorical for actual life. Today it is quite possible that some descendant or heir of "old man" Volosevich might turn up in Kremenets; their house was one of the best and it is still standing where it has always stood. I know this because I return once in a while to tend to the graves of loved ones, although they are now situated in a foreign state, and no one is hindered from going there.

10 SEPTEMBER 1942

It was half past one at night. I wasn't sleeping at all. Suddenly I heard a strange and growing roar—planes! Then everything went quiet again. Some fifteen minutes later, the roar resumed and a plane was above us some-where close, then again all was quiet. Then a machine gun began firing. A few shots were heard from the ghetto, too. There was another attempt of arson there. The weather now is damp and there is no wind, however, so the fire didn't spread and it all ended with clouds of smoke coming out into Shirokaya Street. The firemen were busy there the whole day.

18 SEPTEMBER 1942

The situation at the front has deteriorated, with the exception of Stalingrad, which was not taken, at least as of the day before yesterday. Other sectors of the front report only about the repulsion of Soviet attacks.

The other night I listened to the radio, but didn't manage to pick up any news from Moscow. They were reading letters from the front. It is clear from these letters that the struggle is serious and deadly. There were two inter-esting expressions—"Guards Tank Division" and "Anti-tank Rifle Company." So the existence of the Guards in the USSR was not a German rumor. The anti-tank rifles? I haven't heard of such before. They are most likely one of those "technological surprises" of which the Germans once wrote.

It is so nice to hear voices from the homeland.

Farmers keep bringing in supplies. They must turn in all wheat and rye and can only keep barley and buckwheat for themselves. I can easily imag-ine how they feel; they don't need to get any more "red" than that.

21 SEPTEMBER 1942

The massacre of the Jews has been going on now for over a month and a half. Since early this morning again I can hear the firing of machine guns and occasional rifle shots coming from the side of the prison. They say there are approximately 200 people who are still in prison—craftsmen and profes-sional workers.

Heavy street fighting continues in Stalingrad. German radio announced that the Bolsheviks had some successes near Rzhev, but these don't justify the number of casualties involved. If the Germans have to admit the suc-cesses of their enemy, then things are going well.

As we know, Byelorussia is now the center of the partisan movement. The most fantastic rumors are heard about this movement. They say that recently proclamations calling for mobilization were posted in all villages and that they were signed by the Sovnarkom of the USSR! [Sovnarkom, the Council of the People's Commissars, the revolutionary and later Communist government of the Soviet Union. *Ed.*] Partisans hold whole villages there. They even have armored vehicles, planes with ammunition supplies fly freely in there, and generally speaking everything is rather organized there. I wouldn't be surprised if they even have socialist competition. [Socialist competition, an economic program adopted in the Soviet Union and used to spur workers to higher levels of accomplishment. *Ed.*]

22 SEPTEMBER 1942
Yesterday Stalingrad has not yet been taken.

28 SEPTEMBER 1942
Stalingrad still has not been taken!

The issue of what to eat: I can surely say that the situation is now worse than ever. It was announced in the villages that farmers are strictly forbidden to consume any products using flour. The only exception I think is barley and something else. Everything else belongs to the German people!

Last night a house in the ghetto was burning, but now it was clear that the Jews had nothing to do with it. The real perpetrators were exclusively from "our people" who simply can't rest while so many goods are out there. They enter the ghetto in the middle of the night, with candles, and after that the fires start. And the *Gebietskommissar* has to express his appreciation to the firefighters for their selfless work.

I study English and am making pretty good progress with it. I do hope my diligence will last.

1 OCTOBER 1942
So, October is here. Usually it brings disgusting rain that drizzles for weeks, but this year we have true summer in October.

The news coming from the front is not quite comforting for the Germans. Bolsheviks attack them everywhere. Such weather is the perfect opportunity for the Germans to attack, but instead they are just standing, petrified, fighting off Soviet blows.

More and more houses are being set on fire for the third night in a row. The militia does nothing, however, which leads to the conclusion that this is the work of the militia itself.

3 OCTOBER 1942
A decree was issued and distributed throughout schools to stop all classes until 12 October. All students have to go to villages to help with the potato

harvest. I'm going to the village of Novostav to a friend of mine. I will stay there for about a week. I'll take a small notebook with me.

9 OCTOBER 1942

Here I am, back. Due to unforeseen circumstances I returned home on 5 October, and ever since I've been in bed with the flu.

I accumulated a lot of material since then, too.

After the extermination of the Jews, the town quieted down, but yet again "the storm is in the air"—all rumors stopped, and here the Poles are the ones who mostly spread them. Now they are silent and wait. Most likely the Germans plan to direct the next step of repression against Poles. Father I. is the most respected among them in town. He was arrested over a week ago now, along with a few other influential people of their community.

At noon Saturday, a group of twelve parachutists landed in a field some four kilometers outside of town. The workers of a tobacco factory who were having lunch saw it all. The farmers who worked out in the field where the parachutists landed say that they didn't notice anything until a man jumped down from above right into their midst, his parachute falling after him. Without paying any attention to those working in the field (and this proved that they are well aware of trends and preferences currently prevailing among rural residents), he pulled out two colored flags and waved above his head. Then the farmers looked up, too. One can imagine their surprise when they saw eleven more men, going down at different altitudes to the very same field. Having landed one after another, the men pulled up their parachutes and calmly set off toward the nearest village. That's all. The Germans who arrived some time later couldn't get anything out of the farmers.

Generally speaking the attitude in the countryside could be described as follows, "Well, you know, the Bolsheviks were this and that, yet it was better under their rule, and it would be good if they were back. We wish that the devil would take the Germans away." A multitude of flyers is flooding the countryside, calling for disobedience, failure to deliver supplies, and so on. They are signed F.N.R., and are in Ukrainian. I have no idea what F.N.R. stands for.

There is another interesting rumor coming all the way from abroad: Romania demanded from Germany a part of Ukraine into its eternal possession—all Podolye and a part of Volhyn—otherwise threatening to withdraw its troops from the front. If they reach an agreement, we may find ourselves under Romanian rule. Who hasn't ruled here yet, over our poor souls? We get used to it.

The fighting in Stalingrad continues. There are no German reports from the Caucasus about which I was so much concerned, and this seems to be a good sign.

Today it is some kind of church holiday. That's why a lot of women from villages nearby set off to Pochaev for praying. They were stopped by gendarmes and transferred to the *Arbeitsamt* as unemployed—if they have time to hang around churches, it means they have nothing else to do. So much for the freedom of religion praised by the Germans as a contradiction to the Soviet attitude. Indeed, the difference is immense; then a woman could spend her whole day in the church and nobody would ever bother her.

Again I would like to draw the reader's attention that the text of the diary is reduced in part. The only purpose of these reductions is in making the text more readable. I was careful not to change the tone of the text or add a different coloring to the author's views—even if they differ from the views of the same author who is by six decades older now, and who has gone through thick and thin. One example of repetitions, which I would like to avoid, is the statement about Poles as the ones who spread most of rumors; this statement could just as well have been another rumor. At the same time this rumor could have been started by the very same Germans; the Poles were not too much inclined to collaborate with the occupiers and it could be just another German idea to keep them in tense expectation of repression.

12 October 1942

Recently a general mobilization to work in Germany has been announced. It is being carried out primarily among the young people in villages, and as the result, young people go into hiding in the forests, where they join partisans. Nobody goes to Germany. The consequences are difficult to describe, however.

The *Landwirts* [the local German head of agriculture in the occupied territories], together with a special execution squad, come to villages that have failed to provide a defined number of people by the deadline. Having arrived in the village and not getting enough attention, they get all the attention they want by setting the village on fire.

The majority of cases so far took place in the Lanovetsky District where the local *Landwirt* is notoriously ruthless. These are so-called physical consequences, but there are also moral ones, and unlike the former, the latter are positive. The German actions enhance farmers' hatred toward them, and they enhance and strengthen partisan units that use every opportunity to harm the Germans. In their actions, Germans pay absolutely no attention to human psychology, and this is their major mistake, which will soon hit them in their rear ends. Let us hope that this will further weaken the Germans and, in the long run, bring about their defeat.

Ninety percent of the population now thinks about Bolsheviks as an actual force that can bring them relief and salvation. There are some, however, who still hope for some mythical dear Father Czar, and these make up some 9.9 percent. There is also a 0.1 percent—those who got everything when the Germans came, and who will lose everything, their lives included, when they leave. They don't like Germans, they don't want them here, they even hate them, and yet they cling on to them with all their might as their only salvation. I know some of them.

Another characteristic thing is that people who had expected that Germans would bring some mythical Ukraine along with them have stopped pinning their hopes onto that as well—their disappointment was much too great! They stopped believing in their own young people (that is, in their infamous *Schutzmänner*) who blindly serve Germans and turn in their own people so that the Germans don't hurt them. This "militia" was organized with the arrival of the Germans. They were going to fight for the independent Ukraine, "beat Yids," and so on. The Germans then took them over, and made whatever they wanted out of them.

Now they are being sent to the front [to fight for the Germans, *Ed.*]. . . . Oh, they don't feel like going there at all. And they have to fight against Germans now because the latter do not allow them to spend days lazily, leaving them out of it.

13 OCTOBER 1942

The villages that surround the town are now on fire, and partisan movement keeps extending. More paratroopers landed in the district yesterday and today. Even passive resistance enrages the Germans. What would happen if the resistance becomes active? The Germans take out food supplies, and factory equipment, one echelon after another. What does all this mean? Who knows?

19 OCTOBER 1942

Taking people to work in Germany has been the biggest drama in recent days. They send away everyone who is not registered as working. Even housewives get summons. The atmosphere at home is dreary because Mama and I are in danger of getting "cards." I could get it as a student of the school that no longer exists, and Mama as a housewife.

The use of millstones is forbidden under the threat of strictest possible penalty.

The paratroopers began acting. In one location they burned a bridge, and in another they destroyed a small German ordnance unit.

Regarding changes in the Red Army: they say it looks like its political commanders and commissars are being replaced again.

[Often, as a result of the text being written in diary format, the author's observations don't always relate to each other, but are presented here as they were written. *Ed.*]

20 OCTOBER 1942

This day is very significant in my life. On this great day I finished my education and I finished it with excellence! To put it simply: the need for field help was only the excuse to close the school down. Now a grain delivery central is established there. I wonder what I will do some four years after the war is over. Most likely I will be a clerk with an incomplete school education. What a terrific career!

I will be back to the comb-making factory again. There I could be secured against going to Germany because I'll be registered as a "master worker" and they don't touch this category, at least for the time being.

One hundred sixty members of the *Schutzman* battalion in Belokrinitsa ran away last night. Of course, it is not the first time that men run away, but this is the first in such large numbers. Now Germans raid the area, which, of course, brings no results whatsoever. The *Schutzmänner* that stayed behind obviously seem to approve the actions of their friends because when asked, they say, "Of course, they preferred to go join partisans and have a nice meal at least once a week; we are always hungry here." The reasoning is correct and dictated by "stomach logic."

Recently the amount of mail from those who were taken to Germany has decreased dramatically. The most recent letters are very similar in their contents to "Expect no more letters from me. You'll see me when you see our grandparents." The grandparents have long been gone to heaven. The people who return—escapees or those who have been sent back because of their illness (the latter are more fortunate)—tell horror stories of people dying from starvation. I can only hope that the world will learn one day about these atrocities and the villains will be punished the way they deserve.

22 OCTOBER 1942

I'm back to working at the factory. I got registered in the *Arbeitsamt* and have an *Ausweiss* (identification paper) now. Everything seems to be in order finally, but I'm edgy nonetheless. I heard that the cards were issued for all of our school a few days ago and they would be sent out soon. So my spirits are as low as they can be. Getting the card is similar to getting a death penalty.

At this point the readers may lose their patience: "why do you keep sitting in that attic of yours? Couldn't you go to the forest and join the partisans?"

Perhaps I could have, but the partisans in the forests of Western Ukraine were of a different kind. When in early spring of 1944 the Red Army avalanched to the west, the partisans in my area did not support it but instead turned against it, attacking the Soviet troops from behind.

26 OCTOBER 1942

Today they began selling the "manufactured produce," that is, clothes of the murdered Jews. There are people who actually buy it!—they are rather numerous, and have to stand in line.

No changes at the front—according to German reports. After a few days of silence the reports resumed about fighting near Stalingrad. The Germans in the Caucasus complain of bad weather. That serves you right!

29 OCTOBER 1942

Yesterday I again listened to the Moscow broadcasts. I heard a news brief that also covered Stalingrad. After I listen to Soviet military reports, I feel so much better. As if there is some balance inside of me, with one side of the scale filled with German reports and the other with Soviet ones. Now it is well balanced. And the news from the Soviet side is much joy for me. Now a major campaign is on in the USSR for storing food supplies for winter, "The rear area helping the front to defeat the enemy!"

And now I'll be praising England!

Well, that's England! Frankly, I didn't expect such a development from them; they are advancing in Africa now! In today's paper it was reported that the British began the general advance that had been expected by the German high command. One hundred forty tanks of the enemy have been destroyed, but the fighting goes on. The latter surprised me. I thought that the British had been defeated, but what do you know? The fighting goes on! All this is written under the title: "German Victories in Northern Africa." How great is human stupidity! It would be so nice to hear about the general advance of the Red Army, too. That would be just perfect!

2 NOVEMBER 1942

My holiday—7 November—is approaching. I wish I could hear the Moscow broadcasts then.

[The Russian Bolshevik Revolution took place on 7 November 1917. Nonetheless, it is called the October Revolution because the actual date fell on 25 October, according to the Julian calendar, which was in use in Russia prior to

1918. The Julian calendar was later substituted with the Gregorian calendar in which the date fell on 7 November. *Ed.*]

4 NOVEMBER 1942

Persistent rumors have it that the Germans offered a truce to the Bolsheviks. I didn't believe this, but now I do, and this is why. Today's issue of *Volhyn* published the following contradiction by the German command: "The English radio informed that the German high command addressed the Soviet government through the Red Cross with the request of a four-day truce in the area of Stalingrad and that the Soviet government denied them this request. We would like to state that this is all a lie, the purpose of which is to justify the upcoming fall of Stalingrad."

Can you believe such a contradiction? I know contradictions well—I've got the feel of them. Let's recall the contradiction by TASS that there were no troops concentrated at the Soviet-German border, and this was all just another lie. [TASS, the Telegraphic Agency of the Soviet Union, the official news agency of the Soviet Union. *Ed.*]

They must be having a really hard time there since they wanted a truce, S.O.B.s! And they are brazen enough to speak about the upcoming fall of Stalingrad! Are they completely nuts? They have been fooling around there for a month now, and are brazen and stupid enough to still state something like that.

7 NOVEMBER 1942

This is the second October Revolution anniversary that I celebrate all by myself, but my mood is extremely festive. In the morning I went to work as usual, but after my lunch break I called in sick with a fake headache and stayed at home. I went up into the attic and played all the Soviet records I had. Today they bring so much sadness that I just want to cry. The phonograph was playing quietly, under the blanket; it is way too dangerous to openly be playing these records.

In the meanwhile, my dear comrades, I congratulate you on the twenty-fifth anniversary of the Great October Socialist Revolution!

I believe that older family members had clearer memories of the loud knocking on the door at dawn on the second day of the war, as well as the figures wearing the uniforms of the NKVD, and the pencil checkmarks in the house register. My more pro-Soviet leanings was why the author of the diary celebrated the anniversary of the October Revolution all by himself. Tolerance, however, has always been the fundamental law in my family. Besides, everyone was unanimous in longing for Hitler's defeat and death. That was paramount.

11 NOVEMBER 1942

A forest ranger working in a forest not far from town told me the following story. It demonstrates how frightened and unnerved the Germans are by the partisan movement.

Two rangers were shooting their hunting rifles at a dog in the forest. Suddenly four mounted Germans appeared in an opening from approximately the same direction. The rangers got scared because they could be beaten simply for having fired the rifles. The Germans jumped off their horses, one after another. The rangers braced themselves, getting ready for the worst, but what was happening? The Germans had thrown something into the grass, stuck their hands up in the air, and set off toward the rangers. The latter got very embarrassed, not so much for themselves as for the Germans—hearing shots, the Germans had decided their end was near and went forward to surrender! One of the rangers ran up to their horses, picked up the dropped revolvers and handed them over to the Germans. The Germans were surprised, but happy. One pulled out 100 marks, threw the money at the rangers, then they all ran toward the horses, mounted, and flew away. I wonder what they feel now looking into each other's eyes?

Another small and funny fact—farmers spotted a new road sign at the crossroads, for some reason pointing to the nearby forest. It read, "Whoever is tired of German rule, come join us!'

Outside town, cars and trucks get shot at more and more frequently. Drivers are unnerved and don't want to go anywhere.

The very latest development is a German poster pasted everywhere on the town's outskirts, "Partisans!" Then there follows an appeal full of Christian compassion along lines like: "You poor souls will be cold there in the forest in winter. You'd be better off by going over to us. We'll forgive you, warm you, and give you food," and so on. Unbelievable! As a result of this appeal, however, the next day, someone whispered into my ear that somewhere on the outskirts of town a man was spotted who was wrapped in an impossible number of machine-gun belts, with a dozen hand grenades stuck into his belt, brandishing a submachine gun—a partisan!

The partisan movement that is represented rather weakly in our parts has spread extraordinarily in Byelorussia. People coming from over there say that partisans virtually have complete control of the area. There are Poles and Jews among them, as well as German deserters, and even those who have been *Schutzmänner,* but the majority is Communist. They all attack cars, trucks, burn warehouses, grain stores, and are on rather friendly terms among themselves.

Larger English paratrooper units have landed in Morocco and Algeria, in the Germans' rear. France presented England with an official note of protest regarding this, but England just ignored it.

14 NOVEMBER 1942

There was a brief report in our paper: in response to the American troops taking over Northern Africa, Hitler ordered his troops to take over the unoccupied part of France with the consent of the French government and with the objective of its protection against forthcoming enemy landings.

23 NOVEMBER 1942

The reports from the Eastern Front speak only of repelled Soviet attacks. I wonder what the result of the winter war months will be. I hope it will be positive.

On 23 November 1942, the encirclement of the military groups of the enemy in the Stalingrad area was complete. The Hitlerite information service kept mum about it.

28 NOVEMBER 1942

Last night in the "Crimea" restaurant two Germans were shot dead. Confusion reigns in the German colony. They are afraid of coming out into the streets and most likely wish they were not here. I could comfort them by saying that few places would be much safer for them—because of the shooting we are now allowed to be outside no later than 6:00 PM.

A German driver, who stays not far from us, lives in a house separate from the other buildings. Every evening he comes outside and fires his rifle in the air. "To scare them off," he explains.

The most unbelievable rumors appear among the population. They're so fantastic that there is no need to repeat them here. If real events keep developing the way they do now, however, then soon enough, no matter what is said, it won't be an exaggeration.

The Soviet troops advance along the whole front. Some major advance was made in the area to the south of Stalingrad and on the Don branch. Its general direction is toward Rostov. It would be such a breakthrough if the Red Army managed to reach Rostov, but I doubt it.

In general, pressure is increasing throughout the front, and this is very important. I would like to think that there could be a huge change on the Eastern Front by the end of the winter, to our advantage.

1 December 1942

I listened yesterday to a Moscow broadcast for quite some time. I didn't manage to hear the news, and yet I heard a lot.

All programs mention the advances around Stalingrad and on the Central Front. The atmosphere is elevated. One could feel that the nation tries its best in helping the front. Everything else now is second priority. Wives work at factories and plants instead of their husbands, who are off to the front. The country pulls together every effort to win—and it will win! I feel sorry I can't contribute to this great cause.

A German report of 28 November said, "The Bolsheviks managed to break through our positions in a few locations, but we stopped them from extending these breakthroughs and our defense selflessly repels furious blows of the enemy." If the Bolsheviks managed to keep on with this advance and attack toward Rostov, it would be wonderful.

The taking of Rostov meant cutting off the whole German Southern Front (the Caucasus group of armies) from the main forces. The author, being a "strategist," considered this possibility as very important.

My Family

I find it a pity that the diary contains so little regarding the life of the family—above all it was the family's "soil" in which the author's personality formed and developed. Now it is not easy to recreate the atmosphere of the time, I mean not the global one, of which he was so concerned, but rather his own home's atmosphere. It was at that time, in late 1942, that a new face appeared in our home. It was Boris Petrovich Tarasevich, born in Kupyansk, a veterinarian, who had escaped from a POW camp in Vladimir Volhynsky and somehow found Kremenets. Thanks to his saved graduation certificate he was appointed as an assistant to the sanitary doctor at a local slaughterhouse.

Even today the sanitary doctor's position is not unimportant. And in those days, oh my! For us another thing mattered, though. The doctor was a very good person.

I don't remember exactly the circumstances under which Boris Petrovich came to our place for the first time, but soon it became very clear; he was brought in by the household spirits and assigned by our family's guardian angel.

In the early spring of 1943, when Kharkov was liberated and the front line leapt on to Dniepropetrovsk and Poltava, Boris Petrovich left for the east, to join our troops. Alas, the military success of that year turned out to be unsteady, and the Red Army had to retreat and leave Kharkov. The road back to our troops was a long one.

Throughout the earlier winter months, however, Boris Petrovich was a constant and daily guest at our home. He used to come in the evening and pull out beef bones from under his military shirt. Those were real bones, though without a trace of meat on them. Wonderful broth was cooked out of them, and a stunning meaty smell would fill the house. The flavorful taste of a well-boiled bone lasted for a long time. It seemed as if we were eating meat!

Such was the effect of Boris Petrovich's visit to our home, in the sense of daily bread. The food for our minds turned out to be of larger significance, however. After finishing a broth with dumplings made out of home-ground flour, followed by mashed potatoes mixed with onions fried up in oil, we sat down to talk—or at least to listen to what the older members of the family talked and argued about, taking turns in agreeing with one or the other.

"Ivan the Terrible," my father said, "ruling the country with his ruthless iron fist, tried to consolidate the State of Russia. How could all the things that happened a few years ago be explained, though? The elimination of the military leadership, of the state officials? [Here the mass liquidations in 1937 and 1938 of Soviet top-ranking officers and party members are implied. *Ed.*] Weren't these actions the reason for the obvious weakness and unpreparedness when the enemy attacked? You speak about the communal mind. How does it demonstrate itself?"

"It demonstrates itself," Boris Petrovich responded, "at least in that all of that is over now, or in the process of coming to an end. Many have been brought back. You already know the name of General Rokossovsky? [Konstantin Konstantinovich Rokossovsky (1896–1968), a Soviet military commander particularly known for his role in the Stalingrad battle (1942–43). *Ed.*] This war will promote many absolutely new names. The historians will later call them great military commanders. As for recent years. . . . The country was encircled. We were probed and tried now and then, both from inside and outside. In such circumstances the nerves could fail even the best of people. No need to justify those actions, but we should try at least to understand them. This war is a great trial for the whole nation. Everything will be different once it's over. The political idea that we have is wonderful."

"I don't argue with you on that point. The idea is truly wonderful," father disputed, "but is it permissible to try and strive for the implementation of an idea—even the idea of happiness in the future for the whole human race—by applying methods of ruthless oppression when both the guilty (often guilty of only having disagreed) and the innocent suffer alike? The families were dispossessed, but what was the fault of the children? Was it in that they might take the place of their fathers, and also become *kulaks*? [A *kulak,* in Russia, a rural land owner, farmer. *Trans.*] And where is the guarantee that somebody else might not take their place one day? You keep telling me yourself that we walk an unknown path."

Boris Petrovich retorted, "Are you capable of giving an example of the triumph of humane ideas that was achieved by 'clean' methods? Take your Christianity. What could be more humane? Weren't the flags of Christianity above rivers of shed blood? Crusaders, warrior knights, the inquisition, the burning of religious heretics. No. The past ways always try to resist. You can't manage without violence in that stage. That would be utopian. Nothing new can be built without getting your hands dirty."

"The past ways? It is not that easy to determine what is past," my father replied. "Some time will pass, and then it will become clear that something isn't old at all. Meanwhile rivers of blood have already been shed. A plan is one thing—putting it into life is a totally different matter. Colonel Vengrinovsky used to live here; he was a very old man, so was his wife, well over seventy. I don't want to judge on the degree of his participation in the "White" movement. He probably would have faced a trial if he had been actively involved. They were deported last spring, though. He was sent to the north while she had to go to Kazakhstan. Why was this done? Such cruelty."

"The policy is implemented through the hands of people." Boris Petrovich responded, "and these people have their own individual advantages and defects, their own level of culture and morality. The actual implementation of policy cannot be freed from such problems. And they were 'Whites'. This is all still fresh and clear in memory. Again, I don't justify anyone. I try to find explanations,"

"So it turns out that it's not the policy that's ruthless, but those who implement it are. I can hardly believe it is so," my father answered. "This 'White' fellow we just mentioned, had he been here today, he would have felt the same way as we do. He was a Russian patriot, and in these times of an enemy's invasion, he would have walked our way, as an ally. Instead he was treated as an enemy. At the same time, thousands of true enemies were here, welcoming the Germans with their arms wide open. Now that we are already discussing the subject, they are the ones who should have been neutralized before it was too late. And old Russian officers hadn't studied the fundamentals of Marxism and Leninism. In addition the revolution proclaimed the dictatorship of the proletariat, which was not a majority of the Russian population. One minority group's power was to be traded for the power of another minority? This was enough to get thoroughly confused."

Boris Petrovich answered back, "The point is not about who holds the power; the point is the purpose of the power. Our power is for the people, for the majority. And you can see how it fights!"

"Well, we may also recall that in the world war, the First World War, we also fought bravely and didn't surrender such vast Russian territories to the enemy. Russia, together with its allies, was on the verge of victory. The military power of Russia was exploded from inside. Surrender was unnecessary since the enemy was almost befallen and starved. Surrender provided the enemy with the strategic resources of Russia, which resulted in a prolonged war. That most shameful Brest peace agreement," my father asserted.

"All the industrial force of Europe has now been thrown against us; and the Germans have only one front, the Eastern Front. We can't even compare the two wars," Boris Petrovich insisted.

"Nonetheless we fought well. Just recall the Brusilov breakthrough. We were fighting in the enemy's own land, not in ours," my father responded.

"Just you wait, we'll be fighting in the enemy's own land, too."

Such were the conversations that went on during the long winter evenings.

"To the defeat!" Boris Petrovich raised his samogon shot on the New Year's eve. [Samogon, home-made vodka (strong alcohol beverage), a type of moonshine. *Trans.*] "To the defeat of Adolf Hitler and all of his pack!"

"To the defeat!"

The flame flickered and smoked above the lamp glass, filled with a mixture of sunflower oil and gasoline instead of kerosene. Our family ensemble performed: father played the guitar, Yuri played the balalaika, and I played the mandolin. Mama sang in a beautiful soprano.

"Shining weapons in the sun,
And the tunes of brave trumpet players.
Regiments of mustached hussars,
Passing through the street, raising dust in the air.
And there, barely moving a curtain,
They are watched by a pair of beautiful blue eyes . . ."

It was a brave and cheerful march—about a beautiful and carefree life.

"This was a good one!" Boris Petrovich sighed. "Now let's sing one of ours, a Soviet one."

We sang "Suliko," a favorite song of Stalin's, in half whisper, accompanied by the guitar. The heaviness returned, pushing out an illusionary fantasy world and bringing back the actual world with all of its despair.

"Yes," Boris Petrovich resumed his talk. "The revolution, any revolution at all, should be able to defend itself. Or else."

"Not to the extent, however, when it destroys its own cadre, its own people," Father replied, meeting the challenge. And the lesson in political awareness resumed. I butted in occasionally, but my arguments were totally opposite: either "Stalin didn't know anything," or "Stalin knew more and thus there were more reasons." I felt painfully sorry about the Vengrinovskys, however. They had soon died far from each other, and the news from there had reached us before the war.

Boris Petrovich Tarasevich was the first person with a Communist outlook, with whom we had an opportunity to communicate regularly. His confidence was not doubted. Especially under those circumstances.

My understanding of issues was better for having listened to these discussions, therefore my writings in my diary were of a higher level than a boy my age might normally have done.

Boris Petrovich returned back to the Red Army somewhere there, beyond the Dnieper. We received letters from the front. The last one was mailed from near Jassi, in other words from foreign soil. Then there were no more letters. [Jassi was a place in Romania, later a target in the Soviet Jassi-Kishinev operation that started on 20 August 1944. *Trans.*]

4 DECEMBER 1942

Our glorious *Kremenets Courier* was attacked! Here are the details according to an account by one of the printers. It happened at about 10 PM. Five sleighs with bells stopped in front of the building, with two men in each sleigh. Two stayed at the door while others wearing masks and carrying submachine guns entered the building. All workers were driven down to the basement and threatened that if anybody reported the incident to the gendarmerie before dawn, they would be punished. The attackers carried out all light equipment in half an hour, and damaged the heavy machines seriously, after which they left.

Nobody noticed anything until the morning when the printers finally decided to call the gendarmes. For such a delay the gendarmes now threaten to execute them all. Trachuk, the chief editor, is already in prison.

The attackers wore masks, which lead me to think that they were locals and nationalists rather than parachutists. The former finally have realized what the Germans are up to and have decided to act at their own risk, not relying on any major powers.

Parachutists keep landing. The shooting goes on in the forests. Gendarmes and militia (with gendarmes, of course, letting the militia lead the way) come to the edge of the forest and keep firing the whole day toward the woods, and return home in the evening. This is their new military tactic. I sure don't recognize the German "superheroes" that we see in the German press in any of the Germans that we have around here. I'm kind of disappointed!

Half a year ago, one of our neighbors enlisted with the Germans. He says that "on a train from Germany one can ride peacefully to Brest-Litovsk only, further on any train is being shot at along the way. I was in Vyazma, and had to escape from there, we were completely cut off. Now every German studies the map, trying to figure out which road will be the shorter one to get home."

One local pro-active lady returned home from her trip to the east, and then she told an intimate company about her adventures. It is a fact, however, that no matter how intimate the company is, there is always someone who spills the beans. So now the entire town knows about it, and she stays home and trembles with fear. She said that in all the places she'd visited, public executions had been introduced. This is definitely a step toward the introduction of European culture in our dark and ignorant lands.

The rumors have it that a *German army has been surrounded near Stalingrad* and it maintains contact with other divisions and units now by air only.

10 DECEMBER 1942

They say that Soviet prisoners of war get retrained in the German camps, receive uniforms, and are assigned to serve in auxiliary duties, such as convoy guards with transports, as militia, and so on. In accordance with this I am reminded about rumors of a Soviet decree which states that all soldiers of the Red Army who surrender are considered traitors to the homeland and will be punished as such. Yes, those who now serve Germany could indeed be considered traitors of the state. There are also many of those, however, who got imprisoned beyond their control, being wounded and such. How will they be treated?

[According to the latest Russian estimate, up to one million Soviet citizens were voluntary or involuntary soldiers of the German armed forces from 1941 to 1945. The survivors that were caught by the Red Army were sent to filtration camps from which they were either released or sent to the execution squad or to work camps. *Ed.*]

10 DECEMBER 1942 (CONTINUED)

Partisans are bothering the Germans more and more. Yesterday they blew up the railroad bridge not far from Dubno. The traffic hasn't resumed yet. A very important transport line goes along that bridge and it was the only one that until recently had been considered a safe one.

One more brief piece of news: as a result of the partisan threat, the *Landwirt* in Shumsk has insured himself with 7,000 human lives—his life against theirs—while the *Landwirt* in Katerburg insured his with 4,000. I'm speechless. I would call them swine, but that wouldn't be sufficiently strong, and I really don't like to curse.

There is talk about serious paratrooper landings near Rostov, and even that a part of the very city is in Soviet hands. Whatever is really going on there, I feel sorry for the city; it used to be so beautiful. Now there are so many places like that—Smolensk, Sevastopol, Voronezh, Stalingrad, Kharkov, and those are the major ones. There are dozens of smaller towns that have been washed away with the war's tide.

24 DECEMBER 1942

Today they let us go home from work after lunch because of Christmas. *Pan Gebietskommissar* treated us royally on the occasion of the holiday, giving a half a kilo of ox meat to each of us, but I refuse to bless him for it!

Today, my friends, I'm in good spirits, and I feel festive—every cloud has a silver lining! I have lived to hear a German military bulletin about the "regular retreat of our divisions to earlier prepared positions." Wonderful, eh?

The Soviet advance continues all along the front line, and it is more or less quiet only in the northern section of the front. Last summer, when the Soviets were pushed back so much, I didn't believe I would witness this moment. I hope I will witness when the Germans flee from here, but I don't think we'll live to see that.

I have very little time now. I come back from work so exhausted that I don't want to move a finger.

It is so hard! And these are the best years of my life! Now I ought to be studying and studying! The one who is to blame is a raving madman, who started it all. He deserves punishment for everything he's done, and if one day he is tried, we'll testify at this trial, as victims.

1 JANUARY 1943

Happy New Year to you, my dear comrades!

The spirits are not very high—I ought to be happier when celebrating the New Year.

The situation is such that hope is no longer considered to be silly, as a Polish proverb says, *"nadzieja—matka glupich"* (hope is the mother of the stupid). The initiative at the front is now steadily in Soviet hands. In the south, according to the recent German reports, the Bolsheviks advance in major force. Especially interesting are the following words, "the cargo aviation magnificently deals with the task of providing supplies and ammunition to divisions that stand on the defensive." If there is a need to use cargo aviation, then it means that the ground supplies are hard to get through or otherwise totally impossible to deliver. Does it mean that the army has been cut off? That's what I'm driving at! Well, such theories are supported by rumors originating from the local Germans that their *Sixth Army, operating by the Caucasus, is under threat of encirclement. Wow!*

They are telling horror stories about how the Germans retreat. The Soviet radio supposedly has reported that in the areas that are currently being taken over, everything has been destroyed. There is not a living human or a surviving building. They say in Moscow a special commission was established that includes representatives of the allied countries, dealing with the issue of how to prevent such behavior on the part of the Germans. Major air attacks on Germany are planned. You know, though, self comes first; and I'm more concerned about the annihilation of Soviet citizens.

Beasts! They tried to pull this Colossus down—and achieved nothing. Now they try to cause the maximum damage so that the threat in the future would be smaller. Most likely they have let their longing for destruction and blood run free—if you can't defeat the enemy who is opposing you, then kill the weak and, most importantly, make sure that the blood is running, a river of blood!

4 JANUARY 1943

In their magazines, the Germans have placed pictures of living quarters that they have prepared for the upcoming winter: wonderful, warm dugouts with beds, and so on. I wonder how they are feeling now that they have been forced to leave these apartments and look for new ones, somewhat less convenient, amidst the wide open fields, amidst blizzards and snow storms? Don't you feel shitty, *Kameraden?*

In accordance with the changed situation at the front, the following joke is now quite popular: Hitler fell in love with a rather pretty actress. The feeling was not mutual, however. The friends wonder why she doesn't try to "seize the opportunity" and why she doesn't like the *Führer.* "His hollow eyes and sleek hair. How can one like such an appearance?" she replied. Her friends didn't give up, though, "Don't you worry. Spring will come, his eyes will bug, and his hair will stand on its end!" Such jokes are our history.

14 JANUARY 1943

There is nothing newsworthy to write about, so I write just for the sake of the holiday. We celebrate today, you know, the "old style" New Year, in accordance with the Julian calendar. We may have had little of anything recently, but definitely not holidays; we had the "new style" Christmas, New Year, then the "old style" Christmas, and yet another New Year; it's not a simple life, but endless festivities! I've turned so religious, don't laugh or I'll punch you!

Another holiday's coming up and the Germans ordered us to work this time. Then I become agitated; after all, mind you, we are Orthodox Christians, we cannot stand such a desecration of our most elevated feelings, and so on and so forth. We sin if we should work on a holiday, while all our thoughts should be turned to. . . . So we got together, closed our comb-making factory, and went observing the holiday. Because it is better to be observant than work for these *SS* (stupid scoundrels). [In Russian this is slightly "better" as the abbreviation for *sukinykh synov* (sons of bitches) is *SS. Trans.*]

All German military reports of these days have been limited to the words, "Heavy defensive fighting with large forces of enemy infantry and armor in this or that section of the front." They speak of Velikiye Luki as "an extremely advanced defensive position" that is fully supplied by cargo aviation.

16 JANUARY 1943

Attention! Attention! Starting from today I will have a bunch of accurate Soviet reports daily. Cannot explain anything else in more detail right now. Perhaps I will explain it at some point later. In any case, everything that does not start with "they say that . . ." will be a most accurate fact.

Our Secret Radio

"Perhaps I will explain it at some point later..."

The vagueness is understandable; I was writing about the clandestine radio receiver. The one we had set up in our basement. The directions of the occupiers were clear in this respect: the detection of a radio receiver or any radio parts inside anyone's house resulted in the execution of all residents and burning the house down. Nonetheless, ensured by the awareness and consent of everyone in the family, the receiver was put together, although the task was not an easy one.

We remembered about the radio parts that were buried in the garden in the first days of the invasion. Under the darkness of the night, Yuri got the bundle out of the secret hiding spot.

Why did it happen exactly then, in January 1943, though?

It was then that the desire to know exactly what was going on there—at the front—was the strongest. The Red Army advances were unfolding, and the irreversibility of the course of action was becoming more obvious. I wanted to know—and wanted to calculate when it would happen, when. . . .

With the *Wehrmacht* advancing in 1941 and 1942, there was a need to hide, to turn away from all of this, to escape from the reality, and to know nothing—only more and more hopeless news was coming.

Now we wanted to hear and know, and to share whatever we heard. Starting with the almost sacred words, "they say that . . ." and slightly exaggerating, made the news sound more credible.

We couldn't put together a superheterodyne radio receiver; it required getting a superstructure and needed equipment plugged into an electric outlet. There was no power at all at any time in outlets then.

Yuri decided to get a simple straight receiver circuit. Faded Soviet Radiofront brochures were pulled out that earlier had been moved as a safety measure from the library shelf into a dark corner of the attic. The necessary circuit was found.

First and above all, the samogon was needed. The premium strength moonshine. The technology had been perfected for the occasion of Yuri and Lyda's wedding, so the task was resolved rather easily. The pre-war spirit stove was filled with the samogon. The samogon was used to heat the soldering tool, because how can you put it all together without a soldering tool.

An issue of secrecy was considered carefully. How could we minimize the risk of being discovered? Where could we store the radio?

Jars of various sizes and shapes were overflowing the shelf above the stove in the kitchen, as well as boxes, cartons, and bottles that once had been used to contain spices, coffees, teas, and seasonings. Day by day the contents diminished, but the containers were still filling the shelves. Mama gave us an idea: to put the receiver inside a wooden box that once contained tea and keep it up in the open, on the shelf, as always. Who would think of going through the kitchen supplies?

The logic was perhaps naïve—if somebody wanted to earnestly search, they would have. Everybody liked Mama's suggestion, though, and the receiver fit inside the "Polish" box with a foreign label that read: Coimco Tea—Ceylon, brightly green palm trees, very blue ocean, and a beautiful girl with chocolate-colored skin. Had I been in the shoes of *Schutzman* houseraiders, I would first grab the half-naked beauty painted on the box.

The household gods never left the house by the hill, however, and didn't leave us unprotected. Not once did a *Schutzman* step through its door.

The receiver was put together. Under the lid with the Ceylon girl there was a panel with three tuning knobs, a socket for the antenna, a socket for the headphones, and a socket for the power outlet. A minor problem was left—to find a source of power for the other end of the wire, and preferably into an anode battery.

So we did, later, in November 1943 when the German units were hastily retreating across Kremenets (the panic was caused by the Soviet breakthrough by Zhitomir, after Kiev had been liberated.) We then stole an anode battery from a communications officer who stayed overnight in our place. In the morning when a car came to pick up the *Hauptmann* and his orderly was hurriedly packing and loading things, acting brazenly and in perfect coordination, we stashed away the battery. The Germans departed without missing the loss. The battery then served us faithfully for four months, until our boys took over the town. After the departure of the *Hauptmann* (Captain), actually a rather polite person, we found out that in the haste his orderly had packed and loaded our family icon—in silver setting and all. So basically, nobody lost more than the other. Speaking in today's terms, we paid our dues by barter.

I suppose that was the only visit of the Germans into our home. No, there was one more instance that happened earlier in 1943. . . .

In January 1943, the problem of power supply for the radio receiver had to be resolved by our own means. There was only one possible solution—a galvanic battery. *The Big Encyclopedia* published in the early twentieth century by the *Prosveschenie* (Enlightenment) Society contained all the necessary information under the title of "Electrical Batteries" in its twentieth volume, with articles ranging from "pulmonary consumption" to the letter "V." What a wide variety of batteries there were in existence then—the Wollaston copper and zinc battery, Gravais, Daniel, Meidinger, Siemens-Remak, Bunsen, and Leclanche cells. Yet at that time it was easier to get pulmonary consumption than a battery—they all were complex and impossible to get. We solved our problem using a simple school lab experiment: a saline solution, copper plates, carbon rods pulled out from used batteries that for some reason had not been thrown away. We collected bottles and smartly transformed them into cylindrical glasses: the bottle was wrapped with woolen thread to the necessary height; the thread was soaked in the same old samogon and set on fire. The bottleneck would fall off. We needed a lot of bottles. The receiver wouldn't come alive no matter what we tried. An unpleasant suspicion crept in that over the years that Yuri had forgotten everything he knew about radios and mixed things up in his memory. Then eventually we heard a noise in the headphones, followed by barely audible speech and far-away tones of music.

We didn't want the music, though, we wanted to hear words, Russian words, so we kept getting bottles and enhancing the battery. The cumbersome construction was put on the porch, with a wire extended to my bed where a lamp could be lit by the battery. Nothing dangerous in that construction; it looked like a rather innocent boyish invention.

The major secret wire extended down to the basement under the porch, and it was connected to the battery when in the evening I would go downstairs with the tea box. On the lid of the trap door, leading down, the family would put a rug, a light garden table, and a wicker chair. Downstairs, in the light of a smoking lamp, I set up the radio, put the headphones on, took a pencil and a sheet of paper, and for ten minutes I surfed the short airwaves. (That was all the power that the battery could provide.) "From the Soviet Information Agency . . ." thundered the announcer, Yuri Levitan's, voice coming through the rustling and whistling, and I tried quickly to put down the names of places that had been liberated from the invaders, in abbreviations. [Yuri Levitan was a well-known announcer on the Soviet radio and later TV. During the years of WWII he announced the official reports of the TASS, and his voice for many Soviet people is particularly associated with the official government information. Levitan's importance to the Soviet people can be compared to the significance of Walter Cronkite to Americans. *Ed.*]

The skills of that shorthand came very handy a decade later when I was in college. My note-taking skills were the envy of the class.

The voice of the announcer faded in the distance, yet the tiny bits of information were picked up successfully.

Sometimes the barely audible tum-tum sounds of the drums from London were heard across the airwaves. The English talked more about their own news: air raids on Germany, Northern Africa, than about Pantelleria and Lampedusa, Sicily, Italy. . . . Sometimes I could hear emotionless, neutral Russian speech from Stockholm. Those were ten or fifteen minutes a day of words heard from the other side, from the world, free from the brown plague of Nazism.

The Alexandrov ensemble sang songs about an olive-skinned girl and I soaked in the cheerful and lively tune, forgetting about the dark reality that was surrounding us then. Then a march would roar, "Get up, the country vast and strong, stand up in deadly fight, . . ." and goosebumps covered my skin. Now I carried it all inside me, constantly, and I couldn't share it with anybody—how could I?

The battery lost voltage; then even vague noises disappeared in the headphones. I shut the box, hid the antenna wire that was connected with the "clothes line" in the garden, and put the headphones away to the secret hiding place. I knocked on the trap door quietly and heard the noise of the furniture being moved.

Then followed the political information sessions.

Doctor Boris Petrovich was the only outsider who knew about the radio. Using the information picked from the basement, the doctor figured out the suitable moment for his departure to the east, to his division.

There was another illegal object in our home. It was a detailed administrative map of the Ukrainian SSR (Soviet Socialist Republic), a major map with details down to every little district. Out of the very same reasons of secrecy, no notes and marks were made on the map. A tracing paper sheet that was placed over the map was used for the marks and notes. The dashed section of the map was steadily growing in its direction toward the west. When taken off the map, the sheet seemed a meaningless scribble.

Alexander Vassilievich Kravchenko-Berezhnoy, my father, in his Russian Army field uniform during WWI, circa 1916. In this photograph he has the rank of a 1st lieutenant.

The wedding portrait of my parents, Yuliya Yakovlevna and Alexander Vassilievich. They were wed in September 1917, that is, on the very eve of the October Bolshevik revolution in Russia.

Two of my father's WWI service medals awarded for valor. From the left, the Cross of St. George and to the right, the Order of St. Anne with Swords. Both can be equated to German Iron Crosses of different classes.

My father's parade dagger with the words "For Bravery" engraved on the hilt. The dagger is placed now on the wall of our flat in the Russian Arctic. I made this small exhibition of the family relics after my parents were gone. For my children to be proud of their forefathers, as I was always of my father.

My brother, Yuri, and mother, Yuliya Yakovlevna, taken in 1922. Yuri died in the age of 59: sepsis after peritonitis. I had the same disease, but our northern doctors proved to be more skillful.

This picture of me in my school uniform was taken in 1935. The bands around my cap are black and orange—the colors of the cross of Saint George. My father liked the bands as they reminded him of his military past.

"The house by the hillock" around 1937. At the time it was situated in Poland.

Without having moved an inch "the house by the hillock" is today situated in independent Ukraine.

This picture was taken in 1942, during the time I was writing my occupation diaries.

An illustration from an official Red Army instruction manual depicting an infantry scout in winter camouflage armed with a PPSh-41 submachine gun, the weapon I used. This is what I looked like at times in the final battles on German soil. (LG)

ГІТЛЕР ВИЗВОЛИТЕЛЬ

A German poster for Ukraine. It says "Hitler the Liberator" in Ukrainian.

My two top Red Army decorations for my participation in WWII. From left: the Order of the Patriotic War (2nd class), which was awarded after the war "for personal bravery, staunchness and courage," and a "For Bravery" medal which was awarded for concrete displays of "personal courage and valor."(LG)

I was a sergeant when this photo was taken.

Two army friends and me (center), in Bernau, Germany in 1946. The lilac flowers on the uniforms denote the first post-war spring.

This picture of me was taken in Bernau, Germany, in 1947.

An accidental snapshot that I made. There were Americans in the Jeep and they did not like being photographed. They bent down when they noticed being photographed by a Russian. The photo was taken at the Soviet monument near Brandenburg Gate, in western sector of Berlin, probably in 1946. Had the "cold war" already begun?

Western colleagues preparing a coffin. They belong to the inter-Allied group with which I worked in 1946 and 1947. Our main mission was to dig up the remains of Allied pilots who had been buried in makeshift German graves and send them to their home countries for reburial.

Captain Gorodetsky, the
Russian-French aristocrat that
I worked with in Germany, is
shown making notes in a
German graveyard during an
exhumation operation in
which we were involved.
Photo taken circa 1946–47

In 1948, for the first time
after 4 years service, I
received as incentive a leave
and thus could visit my folks
and spend 10 days in my
home town of Kremenets.
My brother, Yuri, made this
photo.

This was taken around 1949 after I was promoted to *starshina*, the highest NCO rank. I did not become an officer during my six-and-half years of service, a benefit that I became aware of later. There were many such benefits in my life.

Here I am in 1949 with Guards Lieutenant-Colonel (later Colonel) Murachyov, the Soviet military commandant of the district of Bernau bei Berlin. During the last battles of the war Murachyov was the head of a motorcycle-borne reconnaissance battalion within the 2nd Tank Army. After the war I served as a military interpreter in the Commandant's office in Bernau.

In home at Apatity, the county of Murmansk, Russia, 2005. (Natalia Isaeva)

Alexander Nevsky (1220–1263) is a saint of the Russian Orthodox Church. He was a count in ancient Russia and became famous because of his victories over Swedes (Neva combat, 1240) and German knights (Ice slaughter, 1242), and because of his clever politics toward the Tatar yoke. My father (also Alexander) considered Saint Alexander Nevsky as his patron. He had this icon with him during all four years of being in combat during WWI. The icon now decorates our northern flat.

Now we knew about the situation at the front and the records in the diary became more and more scarce. Gradually the need for guessing was gone.

In the final months of the occupation when we got totally used to having the radio and the captured anode battery allowed me to spend a long time in the headphones, traveling along the airwaves and picking up more news reports or just listening to music, our vigilance got somewhat low.

I was getting cold in the basement, so we moved the receiver to a little walk-in closet next to the kitchen, the warmest place in the house. I sat there in my headphones, sometimes even during the day. Sounds in the air, a live and close voice of Kiev broadcasts solidly isolated me from the surroundings. Having heard something of interest, I would make a relevant comment right there, out of my doghouse.

One day when I was sitting with the headphones on, and Mama and Lyda were in the kitchen, the door opened and a German walked in. He wore a helmet and was armed with a submachine gun.

Having looked around, the German said, *"Wasser. Bitte."*

Mama filled a glass with water and gave him.

He drank it, paused and said, *"Noch bitte."*

Mama refilled his glass. The German slowly emptied the second glass. He put it down, paused again, then took another look around and said, *"Warm, schön"* (warm, nice). Then he clicked his heels and added, *"Danke."*

Then he left, closing the door carefully behind him.

Had he made two more steps inside the house, or had I, not suspecting anything, spoken up from my secret place, nobody would have known about the diary but the *Gestapo,* and these recollections wouldn't have appeared.

All residents would have been shot dead and the house would have been burnt down, in accordance with the respective decree.

The Germans were accurate in executing their orders.

Though the guardian angel was unseen, it was present, and that was why the story of the house and its residents continued. As a consequence, however, the "radio operator" had to return to the basement.

Again the diary records were filled with references to German sources. The secrecy in the author's understanding didn't allow him to mention the receiver—he was the only one responsible for the diary while the whole family was responsible for the radio.

16 JANUARY 1943 (CONTINUED)

German radio reported that recently there was a meeting of the Politburo in the Kremlin where the bill for the restoration of the old order in the Red Army was drafted, with the Army now being called the Russian Army. [The Politburo (Political Bureau) in Soviet history was the supreme policy-making body of the Communist Party of the Soviet Union and, in effect, the cabinet of the Soviet government. *Ed.*]

The old order includes the re-introduction of shoulder boards, officer ranks, orderlies, and so on. At the same time they provided for the design of the uniform and banners for separate regiments. As it was mentioned in the report, the plans are to remove Jews from the army because they are not respected by the soldiers (?) and to form separate divisions out of them.

If this is true, then I'm in the opposition to it because I don't approve of all these decisions. I remain true to myself. I don't want Jews to be persecuted or officers and shoulder boards reinstated. What would Vladimir Ilyich [Lenin] have said had he seen how his idea was being implemented, the idea for which so much blood was shed? Everything was done in the name of the revolution, equality, and international brotherhood. And now—the "Russian Army"!

Among the important developments in the life of the army and navy was the transfer to the new military uniform and re-introduction in early 1943 of more prominent distinctions of rank as was used before the Soviets came to power—shoulder boards. The reinstatement of the shoulder boards in the Red Army and the Navy emphasized the "continuity of the best traditions of the Russian military." That's how that event is interpreted in the *History of the Great Patriotic War, 1941–1945,* vol. 3 (p. 224).

It is obvious that the words were the same, yet their interpretation was totally contradicting. The war went on, not only on the military battlefields, but in propaganda sources as well.

24 JANUARY 1943
I haven't written for a while, but there are new developments, of course. Both good and bad. I will begin with the situation at the front.

The Germans report that in the area of Leningrad, "to the south of Lake Ladoga" there was a breakthrough. I don't know the details, but at least no one speaks about the encirclement of Leningrad any more.

The siege was over!

24 JANUARY 1943 (CONTINUED)
Velikiye Luki. Various rumors regarding the situation at this section of the front were demonstrated in full in the German report of 10 January: "The garrison of the bridgehead fortification of Velikiye Luki got through to the major forces following the order of the Supreme Command." So the rumor about the German divisions being surrounded there proved true. Now a new

question arose: if Velikiye Luki is already in the Red Army's rear, then where are its forward divisions? According to the rumors the Germans set Vilna on fire and left it.

There is another front of which people speak a lot—Stalingrad. The situation there is not clear, however, according to the rumors and semi-official reports about an "island, floating amidst the raging Bolshevik sea." They are also surrounded there, but in much larger numbers. Yesterday a German news report spoke of "our brave soldiers who defend against the enemy— highly superior Bolshevik forces that are better adapted to heavy fighting and the weather." As Comrade Zoshchenko would say, "Look how they are blatantly lying!" Now it looks like the badly armed and less disciplined Soviet soldiers are better adapted to combat than the Germans! No, really.

The other day the head of the Berezhetzky district was killed. Today he is being buried, with all military honors. That's one scumbag less in the world.

Some kind of headquarters is moving here; they say an aviation staff and command. If they set up an airfield here, we'll get visits by Soviet aviation.

A new quota for laborers to be sent to Germany has been assigned: 700,000 people from the Commissariats of Volhyn and Podolye!

29 JANUARY 1943

The news from the front is amazing and pushes everything else toward the distant background. The German report of 26 January was a clear funereal requiem: "The Soviet advances in some areas of the Eastern Front continued yesterday with new strength. In heavy defensive fighting against the enemy's highly superior forces, the German divisions face the threat of breakthroughs and encirclements." Then a report about the defense of Stalingrad followed where Romanian and Croatian divisions were mentioned. It said that their own generals are commanding the troops. It was said perhaps to counter the Soviet report that the German cargo aviation was now engaged in getting out the generals from the surrounded divisions. "The troops fight on a narrow blade of earth, completely surrounded by the enemy." Further on, "the fighting continues in the area of the Kuban and Manych. The movement to reduce the front line extension continues gradually. Heavy fighting also continues on the Don and in the area of the Donets River."

The conclusion is as follows: the Red Army advances from the north, east, and south on to Rostov; their objective is to cut off the Caucasian army, to eliminate the front there, and, of course, to keep driving them out further to the west. Finally, this long awaited phrase: to the west!

Even the German papers now admit that their divisions in Stalingrad have been surrounded. They write about horrible conditions in which they are living now: hunger, cold, complete exhaustion. At the same time, new Soviet forces seem to appear every day.

30 JANUARY 1943
The German military briefs speak about their retreat from the Caucasus, the straightening of the front line to the west of Voronezh, and heroic defense of Stalingrad. Please note that I don't put quotes around the word "heroic." Judging by the German reports they are indeed fighting desperately there. The following relevant headlines and mottoes have appeared in the papers: "The fate of Europe is in Stalingrad," "The will of the Sixth Army in Stalingrad to stand fast expresses the will of European nations to fight," and so on. The tone of all this is such that Stalingrad cannot be surrendered by any means, but then it should be surrendered because of the course of the fighting. The German army is encircled, 200 kilometers away from the major forces, and no matter how it struggles back, it will have to surrender.

For those readers who find this surprising, the term 'the defense of Stalingrad' was used both in Soviet and German literature. The Soviet army was pushed toward the Volga, and kept fighting in Stalingrad, even after the German armies and their allies had surrounded them. In both instances it was defense, with the only difference being that the Red Army was defending its own home, while the invaders, closed off in a mousetrap thousands of kilometers away from their home and the main front, had only two options: to continue defending or to surrender. An attempt to release the encircled group of units was fought back by the Red Army. Hitler didn't let them try to break out toward the west as that would mean retreat and failure to complete the task that he'd set for them—to seize Stalingrad. The *Führer* preferred to sacrifice his elite Sixth Army, giving the loss of hundreds of thousands of soldiers on the Volga a heroic halo. The propaganda trick worked, as we can judge by the author of the diary.

My colleagues ask me what I read. One is supposed to read, isn't it one of the musts of life? I joke, saying: always being short of time to write, where then could I possibly find time to read? Yet I do read. Now I have a book in front of me that I have just finished reading from cover to cover, 351 pages entitled *Stalingrad* by Theodore Plievier. [Berkeley Edition, 1967.] The book was translated from English into German and constitutes the complete history of the encirclement and annihilation of the Stalingrad group of the invader, dissected to the least available detail—from its first to its last day. This book, which I consider to be an extremely honest and masochistically naturalistic account, contains everything but the term "heroic." Undoubtedly, the German "Stalingrad men from the other side" who managed to survive and return home have written several books about their experience and the assessments in them will differ. I don't know whether the book by Plievier has been translated into Russian, but I haven't yet come across a more serious accusation toward Hitler and Hitlerism, including genocide against his own soldiers, in German literature. One believes this book.

30 January 1943 (continued)

Ah, there is more! I forgot that today is a "public" holiday. It is a decade since the day when Hitler I ascended to the throne. The Germans drink and carouse in the streets. An address by Hitler is expected.

3 February 1943

Finally, Stalingrad has surrendered! The Germans reported this on 1 February. Now a blow should follow! I think that the fall of Stalingrad will have a major effect on the further course of the war.

In connection with the celebrations of the decade of Hitlerite rule, Hitler and Göring addressed the people. They say that Hitler's speech was overflowing with such exclamations as, "We cannot even speak about the surrendering!" and so on. Well, if you are mentioning that word, then your state of affairs is . . . well, . . .

The universal conscription of men aged sixteen to sixty-five and women aged seventeen to forty-five was announced in Germany. That's some news!

Yes. There is certainly a difference between this advance of the Red Army and the one last year!

10 February 1943

Everything that could be expected has been done: the Germans reported about the fall of the Sixth Army, announced three days of mourning (3–5 February), trumpeted their "heroism, loyalty, and sense of commitment" in the papers. "They stood until the very end because they knew that the state of the whole front, the safety of their fatherland depended on them. Now they have fallen, though." Six Soviet armies that operated there are now free in their actions and most likely keep operating further since the "planned campaigns" are unfolding now throughout all of the southern front. They perished, honor and glory to them, but they didn't change the situation.

The Germans compared Stalingrad to Thermopylae, but there was a major difference. The people who defended the actual Thermopylae were protecting their homeland. The Germans at Stalingrad were very far from their homeland.

Just like modern-day researchers digging the remains of Troy or other ancient battlefields find the traces of battles in helmets, swords, and bones, some 3,000 years from now at the place where in 1942 there stood a tractor factory, among the ruins, they will find remains of tanks, rifles, machine guns, and thousands of metal helmets with the remains of eagles on them. And they will try to explain the purpose of these objects.

As fate will have it, in my life there will be numerous encounters with Germany. Now, my reader, we are in the middle of the first and quite extended one. Yet the glimpse of light was already in sight. There will be more encounters later, and they continue until this day. Germany changed and so did I. It would be appropriate to here study a snapshot very much related to Stalingrad, that took place in 1975.

1975: An Encounter in Stalingrad/Volgograd

I have visited Volgograd, as Stalingrad was renamed in 1961, more than once. Twenty years after the Victory and then again on the thirtieth anniversary of the Victory.

This city is grand and quite beautiful. Superficially not that much remains of the war. The shot-up buildings are long since gone. The scrap metal of war has been melted down long ago and it was done at that very same tractor-building plant, resurrected on its old location. Only the turrets of T-34 tanks protruding from concrete foundations remind of the line where the Stalingrad men, the heroes of the 62d Army, fought to the death.

Going through some color slides from my visits there, I came across some shots taken in the "Hall of the Military Glory," a memorial to those who took part in the defense of Stalingrad. The centerpiece of the Hall is a statue in the shape of a gigantic hand that grasps a torch with an eternal flame. The hand extends from under the ground and makes an awesome impression on visitors. The entire hall promotes an atmosphere of remembrance and reverance.

Another picture: an endless flow of people that walk up a slanting spiral alongside the cylindrical wall of the hall. The wall lists names, names, and more names. . . .

Another one: the change of honorary guards. Tall soldiers in parade dress and bayoneted short rifles held vertically in their hands. Their pace, as steady as the ticking of a metronome, can be guessed even from the picture.

Another picture: A close-up of a young flaxen-haired man in the crowd. I remember that he was tall—taller than the rest of the crowd by half a head. His blond curly hair ran down to his shoulders. He wore an unbuttoned corduroy jacket and had a lit cigarette in the corner of his mouth. His eyes. . . .

People obsessed with some idea have just that kind of expression about their eyes, I had seen it before. He had come from far away to *see* for himself. Perhaps he had received the last message from his father from here. Standing in this hall, which is sacred to every Russian, he called on his feelings of hatred and aversion to foster contempt for the ceremonial changing of the guard.

Then the click of my camera made him wince and look back. The confusion flashed in his eyes, as if he was caught in some wrongdoing.

I said quietly, *"Man soll hier nicht rauchen."* (One shouldn't be smoking here.)

We studied each other intently.

He paused. Without looking down, he took the cigarette out of his mouth and said in a hoarse voice, *"Ich sehe keine Anweisungen."* (I don't see any notices.)

"In der Kirche gibt es auch keine." (There are no notices in church either), I retorted.

He crushed the cigarette butt under his heel and asked, *"Warum haben Sie mich aufgenommen?"* (Why did you take a picture of me?)

"Zum Andenken." (As a keepsake.) *"Habe seit dreissig Jahren keinen Nazi gesehen."* (I haven't seen a Nazi for thirty years.) *"Und Sie? Was wollen Sie hier?"* (And you? What do you want here?)

He made an abrupt turn and made his way through the crowd toward the exit and we joined the human river ascending the spiraling slope by the wall with thousands of names on it.

The hand with the torch is in the middle of the hall. The eternal flame shines as if a relay—from them and from then to us, the living, and to those who will come after us, in a hundred, two hundred, and a thousand years from now.

10 FEBRUARY 1943 (CONTINUED)

The Moscow radio reported on the reactions of the British papers, "The grand victory by Stalingrad bears witness to the fighting capability and excellent military qualities of the Russian army."

Now on to other developments. Germany has declared it as a total war. Everything that has nothing to do with defense industries and the war is closed down. The entire nation is being reassigned to the military authorities, and all efforts will be directed to the war. Obviously Germany's situation is very serious if they have to resort to measures they have never employed before. The most recent appeal by Hitler is "The one who does nothing, should be annihilated!" If applied to us, it could bring on the most unpleasant results.

15 FEBRUARY 1943

A group of strangers enter a village and step into the homestead closest to the edge. "Are you the owner?" one of them asks.

"I am," the scared man responds.

"You have to slaughter a pig in a day from now. We'll come and pick up the meat. If you tell anyone, we'll burn the house down." Nothing can be done, so he slaughters the pig and waits for them to return.

They come and pick it up. Hardly has the door closed behind them when a new groups walks in. "Hello, squire. Feed us," one of the new visitors say.

At this point the man loses his temper. "Are you crazy? You have taken the whole pig moments ago and you ask for food again?"

"Who took the pig? Where are they?" the partisan asks.

"They just left," the man responds.

"Come on, go with us."

They put the man in their sleigh and chase after the first group.

"Is it them?" they ask, seeing a sleigh of men up ahead.

They stop the first group.

"Who are you?" the leader of the real partisans asks.

A member of the other group responds, "Partisans."

"Of which unit or formation?"

"What formation? We are partisans and that's all."

"Now, get off your sleigh. Keep your hands off your rifles!"

The real partisans put the bandit partisans along the road and execute them right there. They tell the man that he should know by now how to tell partisans from bandits. "We are organized formations and do not have the right to hurt the local population. So take your pig and go home."

My story is not embellished with any literary merits, yet more importantly, it is a true story.

18 FEBRUARY 1943

According to German military reports, Rostov and Voroshilovgrad have fallen, and there is street fighting in Kharkov. I was not extremely impressed by these reports since I had prior knowledge of both the liberation of Kharkov and Lozovaya. Now the question is whether the Dnieper will be reached before the ice breaks up, and if not, whether this year they will manage to conduct a forced crossing of the Dnieper at all. I don't believe that this advance can go on until the complete and total victory. It will be brought to a stop, and the Germans will advance again. And yet, *victory will be ours!*

The editorials in German papers speak of the threat that is now hanging above Europe (that's how they put it now!). In addition, in Spain, Franco is actively engaged in preparing the defenses. Quite some perspectives!

20 February 1943

Today at 3 o'clock in the morning a group of heavily armed men on bikes and horses attacked the prison. Prior to the attack they had cut off the wiring and set up watch patrols with machine guns. At this time the streets were filled with wagons carrying supplies of huge logs to the station. The wagons were toppled; the logs were scattered across the street. The guards at the gates were instantly and quietly disarmed, a part of the group approached the prison, the gates were closed and on the outside everything looked ordinary. The shift of *Schutzmänner* that was resting was caught off guard and they were all locked up in one of the cells. The prisoners were taken to the back wall of the prison where a ladder was set up, which they climbed, then jumped down on an extended canvas cloth. That's all.

Now about the look of these partisans. According to witnesses, the men wore similarly looking greatcoats (yet at night any garment may seem the same) and spoke Russian. Many believe that they were Soviet partisans. The prisoners they freed, however, were local nationalists.

What was the point for Soviet partisans to conduct an operation to release the nationalists? There could be none. Thus the suggestion about Soviet partisans reflects the narrator's sympathies toward the Soviets. I think it was a gang of nationalists and it is pretty unpleasant to conclude that they were so properly organized. The fact that they spoke Russian could simply be a trick.

There will be a price to pay for this, I'm certain of that.

23 February 1943

People were arrested across town and consequently the situation is extremely tense. The people who were arrested today do not have anything in common with each other. They are all very different in social status, behavior, and convictions. The tension is even stronger since it became known that yesterday pits were dug in the prison courtyard.

In the evening shots are heard coming from the direction of the prison.

24 February 1943

All the arrested, approximately 60 people, were shot dead last night. The execution was held in the prison courtyard and people living next door witnessed the action.

The arrested were ordered to get undressed—the way it was done when the Jews were killed. There were a few women among the doomed. There was Dr. R. with his wife, who was also a doctor. She was forced to get undressed, too. The doctor charged a *Gestapo* man, grabbed his revolver and hit him on the head with the butt of the gun. At that moment, though, another *Gestapo* man shot at his back and killed him. Horrible screaming accompanied the execution.

The town is in despair. Not a soul is outside and lights are not seen from a single crack. Everybody is waiting for his or her turn. . . .

Now everyone, even the strongest opponents of Bolshevism, is sustained by a single hope—to survive until the Bolsheviks' arrival. The Bolshevik redeemers. How can one survive, though? The closer the front gets, the worse the atrocities will get. They say that in the places from which the Germans are retreating, not a single living soul is found. And we won't be an exception.

Many nationalists, who at the time of Soviet rule were among its worst opponents, now wish they had been sent off to exile in Kazakhstan. I'm certain, though, that had they now been in Kazakhstan, they would have waited impatiently for the Germans to come. That's human nature.

I haven't lived at all yet. I have only dreamed of living—to graduate from a university, become a construction engineer, and work somewhere in Magnitogorsk. If until now I have written as a grown up, in my dreams I do not get over my actual sixteen years of age.

10 MARCH 1943

The situation at the front got worse and I don't even feel like writing about it.

Everybody in town is anticipating mass deportation, under the general motto of "defending our joint homeland of Europe against the Bolshevik flood."

Some headquarters staff have moved in here from Kiev, with a multitude of officers and automobiles. They seize apartments and at the same time they destroy houses. The town looks like one huge ruin. Where the ghetto used to be, not more than a dozen houses are left and even those are being destroyed now. The only things left everywhere are the posters with attractive sounding offers and stories of the heavenly life in Germany.

The other day all residents of the Home for the Disabled were taken out, both the elderly and invalids. Trucks arrived early in the morning before sunrise. Everybody was herded onto them and taken away. Rumors say they were all killed. An entirely justified measure from the German standpoint—they were consuming bread while being of no use. The proclamations are published so frequently, not least of which are the ones authored by their supreme leader: "We won't spare the lives of others when ours are in danger, and when precious German blood is being shed."

Well, my dear fellow citizens, correspondingly the mood is not at all good! What a fool I was when I started hoping! The Red Army was getting so close to the Dnieper! I feel like crying. . . .

17 MARCH 1943

The days are colored by forced deportation to Germany. So far, however, the volume of deportation has not been as bad as it was expected—350 people were taken out of the Pochaevsky district and 1,100 people from the Shumsky District. More people were taken out of the Shumsky District because the other day the head of the local gendarmerie was killed there along with four *Schutzmänner*. They were lured into the forest on some pretense and partisans killed them there. In response, the punitive squads were sent into the district and real fighting ensued, with even more casualties, but the partisan units slipped away to the forests of eastern Ukraine. Now almost everyone in the village where it all started has been deported. They are first brought into a prison which had been "cleansed" in preparation (the "surplus" had been thrown into the pits), and there they expect their departure in a column.

23 MARCH 1943

On 21 March the partisans burned down three sawmills, killing a few Germans in the process. Repression followed suit and hundreds of people were sent to the pits. On 19 March, most likely following the order by some nationalist organization, the *Schutzmänner* in Rovno, Dubno, and in our Kremenets ran away. It is clear that there is some strong organization behind this.

Last night the *Landwirt's* house in Berezhtsy was attacked. The *Landwirt* himself was burnt alive in the cellar where he'd hidden. Also a few Germans were killed, as well as the "head" of the district. When in the morning, completely unaware, I went downtown and was surprised by all the commotion in the street—semi-armored vehicles were rushing on, one after another, filled with Germans armed with submachine guns and light machine guns. The Germans were clearly agitated and yelled in excitement.

Panic ensued in the evening, though, when churches had to suspend their services and it was announced that because of an uneasy situation, we were allowed to walk outside no later than 6 PM. Everybody hurried home.

Oh, what will happen to us when our Commissioner is wasted? It is not surprising that the partisan forces and their power grow. The Germans encourage it by their constant persecutions in the villages. It is clear that everybody who can leaves for the forest. It is not at all clear, however, what "color" they are.

Will I witness the end to it all? My own end, most likely. I only wish that my records might serve as yet another prosecution document against the Germans.

24 MARCH 1943

A state of emergency has been declared in town. It is forbidden to be outside from 7 PM to 5 AM and violators will be shot. [These times are not consistent with times previously noted, but this should not be surprising in a diary written under wartime stress. *Ed.*] One cannot be outside without some business or purpose; it is forbidden to stop and talk, or to gather in houses, and so on. All violations are punished by execution. Cinema, restaurants, and churches are closed (poor God-fearing old ladies), and so on and so forth. All Germans are now authorized to shoot any local resident they encounter later than seven in the evening.

I went outside into our yard, under danger of being executed. Not a single rustle or a single beam of light from houses. One hears only the dogs barking, which seems even more menacing, affecting the already weak nerves.

One of these days they are going to bury the frail remains of the seven Germans and four locals burnt in Berezhtsy. Now their remains are in the hospital where out of a pile of bones and ashes they try to put together some likeness of the *Gebietslandwirt* and his followers.

1 APRIL 1943

Nothing of interest either on the local or on the global fronts.

Punitive expeditions are sent one after another to our district. Partisans, that is, bandits, are touring the villages, killing Poles and ravaging barns. Yesterday they seized some alcohol from the distillery's storage facility. The Commissioner stays inside his home, which has been turned into a fortress.

The state of emergency is still maintained in town; and one is confined to one's home and this absolute inactivity results in family quarrels. Frankly, not a very intriguing pastime.

10 APRIL 1943

Total war has started here. Anybody who wants to do so burns down villages and beats people up.

1 MAY 1943

I don't feel like thinking or writing. When I come from work I sit down with some silly novel.

Today I forced myself to take a pencil and write. The only motivation for that was the holiday, although the mood does not call for festivities. Total apathy! I have even stopped caring for myself!

The villages burn like bonfires. People are forced from their homes. They are shot at and burned by pseudo-partisans, Germans, punitive squads. In their turn, partisans kill Germans, burn sawmills, and blow up bridges. The "partisans" kill Poles and Russians; rob farmers; and also set on fire anything that can burn. There are almost no nights that are not lit up by a blaze of fire and with no machine-gun bursts heard.

The "partisans" obviously view annihilation of the Poles as the first stage in their "rebuilding of Ukraine." The Poles are right now the partisans' most defenseless enemy; one can annihilate them and stay a hundred percent unpunished. The Polish farmers are burned, stabbed, and shot in the most vicious manner. As a result of this, all Polish residents are leaving the countryside and coming to town seeking the protection of the "law." And the "law" took them under its protection—a few villages were evacuated under German supervision. The farmers were brought here and were immediately placed in a camp. All their cattle was taken away from them and sent to the slaughterhouse. Then a commission selected anyone capable of labor to be sent to Germany. The rest were told that they could immediately return to their villages. Poor people!

7 May 1943

Last night they killed some agricultural manager for hiding a Jewish woman and the woman was killed, too. His body was left outside in the street, and hers was taken to the Jewish cemetery and thrown there, so that "she didn't spoil the air in town." A common occurrence.

A more unusual thing happened in the morning: Alexis, the Ukrainian Metropolitan [a leader in the Orthodox church. *Ed.*], was killed on his way from Kremenets to Lutsk.

10 May 1943

Speaking about the killing: in the announcement posted throughout town, Germans accuse "those who are your bandits—nationalists and your *Schutzmänner* who deserted" and threaten them with consequences. This is the first German proclamation in which Ukrainians are addressed as a *hostile* nation. It's obvious: *your* bandits and *your* deserters. The report about the assassination on the radio said that the "Yid Communists" did this, and this was the first contradiction. That's why I lean toward the common opinion that the killing was done by the Germans, but then, too, I don't care much for this religious fuss.

The Poles, scared of the terror, sign up for labor in Germany. In this instance the bandits assist the Germans. It is terrifying to look at this caravan of carts and wagons with various possessions, crying children, and gloomy mothers—tired, hungry, indifferent to life. Only one man is to be blamed for it; the one who started this horrendous war and who is doomed to lose it.

14 MAY 1943

Now we are turning to the news from abroad, as Olga Vyssotskaya used to say, that pleasant-sounding announcer of the RF-1 "Comintern" station.

The end is in sight in Tunisia. A part of the German and Italian army surrendered, and another part has been thrown back to the south, where they fight until the very last bullet, according to German reports.

At the same time the fighting progresses at sea, where the Italian navy is being beaten. The heavy bombing of Italy and, in particular, Sicily is obviously in preparation for a massive landing.

Now one more advance is needed here, on our front, and the war would be over. Are the Bolsheviks capable of launching an offensive such as the one they launched during the winter, before the promised German summer offensive? That would be the final one.

"When the sun is at its highest, you'll again see the invincible German Army advancing," Göring said in one of his speeches while the invincible German army was retreating. The Red Army has had three months of rest, and the losses were not as huge as earlier in the war. Now all our tanks that were shot up by the Germans are in Soviet control they can be refurbished and sent back to battle. When we were on the retreat, these fell into enemy hands.

Smart people are sitting in the supreme headquarters of the Red Army, though; they know what they are doing as well as what the Germans are up to, and I know nothing.

16 MAY 1943

Yesterday they announced total mobilization for labor in Germany for those born in 1923, 1924, and 1925. This was the first group. Those who go can be considered dead. I was lucky, being born in 1926. I will most probably get into the second group, however.

What should I do? Go join the partisans? But where are they to be found around here? There are only bandits burning villages and killing people. I don't want to start my life's path like that.

18 MAY 1943

Today was the deadline for everyone who is subject to conscription to report to the authorities. Sixty people turned up over the day; forty of them being immediately released because they were unfit.

The town turns out to be in a state of siege; all roads are cut off. Almost all cars and trucks are getting shot at and the hospital is full of wounded. Now cars and trucks do not move alone; they get together in a convoy: a mail truck, a truck full of gendarmes, other cars, with an armored vehicle guarding all of it. Nonetheless they get shot at.

19 May 1943

Tomorrow the first transport with those that have been conscripted for work departs. I wonder how the partisans will treat it. There ought to be some kind of fireworks because of the occasion.

Today another convoy of cars and trucks was shot at and people were wounded. One car was captured by the partisans and it was the very car in which a new head for the gendarmes was riding—the one who was coming to replace the killed one. This place is full of bad luck for gendarmerie commanders, poor fellows. I wonder whether they will find anyone else to fill this frequently available vacancy.

20 May 1943

The train with conscripts didn't leave today! Last night a freight train was blown up. The tracks were seriously damaged so the departure was delayed.

I looked through my recent records and came to the sad conclusion that I will never make it as a writer. Now I will have to urgently find some other occupation. I'll sweep the streets or something similar.

4 June 1943

I turned seventeen. If not for the war I would be finishing high school, but what now?

Beside this event, there is nothing happening on either the local or world fronts. The fact that somewhere out there fifteen gendarmes were killed again, a village was burned down, and so on cannot be of any interest: this has become a commonplace thing.

13 June 1943

Finally the English allies pulled themselves together and took over two silly little islands not far from Italy: Pantelleria and Lampedusa. They have obviously decided to knock on Italy to force it to surrender.
The air raids on Sicily become more frequent, and it will most likely become the next stage, but when? If it took them a month to prepare for taking over those tiny ones, this time they will need at least two months to put things together.

Well, we'll see—no use slandering.

The front is still quiet and I can't understand the reasons for it.

22 JUNE 1943

The second anniversary of the war with Germany and there is nothing to write about. Everywhere things seem to be quiet and in order. I have been sitting for half an hour thinking of what else to write, but can't think of anything. So I leave it as is, although it is a shame that I don't have anything but a few lines to write on such an anniversary. It's like those English and those little islands.

11 JULY 1943

[The author here describes momentous events in the summer of 1943 when the Germans launched their final, major offensive of the war on the Eastern Front, Operation ZITADELLE, which quickly foundered against a strong Soviet defense in depth. The Soviets immediately responded with their own, long-prepared counteroffensive, Operation KUTUZOV, followed closely by Operations RUMIANTSEV and SUVOROV. *Ed.*]

FINALLY!

A very intense battle is taking place in the Orel-Belgorod section. The Germans rendered the first blow, which, however, didn't turn out to be much of a surprise for the Red Army. According to the German military report, "to counterattack the Bolsheviks threw in a reserve shock army throughout the whole length of the front." Now very heavy fighting goes on there, and according to all available sources, it is concentrated in one area. What will be the outcome of this latest attempt of the Germans to raise the morale in their country? The government promises them "we'll take care of the Bolsheviks, and then it's time for the English to pay." It seems that it is a bit tricky, however, to finish off the Bolsheviks, although the *Führer* promised, when starting it all, to take Moscow in two months.

16 JULY 1943

At the Belgorod-Kursk section the Germans do all they can to push the Bolsheviks at least somewhat. They are failing, though, and the fighting goes on along the frontal fortification line. From their offensive line our boys may even start advancing, and this could end pitifully for the Germans. We'll see!

The landing in Sicily finally turns out to have taken place. The assault troops occupied all of the southeastern section of the island, and they advance forward steadily.

Last night and today arrests were made in town. They say that up to two hundred people were arrested. It seems as if some organization was disclosed. Or, most likely this is just an intentional way of decreasing the population. The *Gestapo* that appeared here not long ago, approximately a hundred of them, made the arrests. Many of the *Gestapo*-men speak a most fluent Russian. People suppose that these men have been recruited among the POWs. What scoundrels! The things people are willing to do for some good food!

20 JULY 1943

They report about a major Soviet advance along the Orel-Sukhinichi section of the front. The Germans write about heavy defensive fighting. The Bolsheviks, they say, gathered their last, their definitely very last, forces and try to break through the front. Take that, huh! And where is the German summer advance? Nowhere.

You most likely have noticed that earlier I used to write about every blown-up bridge, and now pay very little attention to local events. People are so fed up with them, that they stopped mentioning them at all. They just note, in between other matters, in passing, "Have you heard that yesterday the village of Shpykolossy was burned down, and those who fled were shot, while those who were caught were put in a barn and burned alive?" The other person says, "Yes? And the other day the village of Verba, held by partisans, was bombed. Did you hear?" After such an exchange each person gets on his way, attending his own matters. All that really matters now is the nutritional issue.

All the Germans who live in various parts of town are quickly moving to the southern part, where they entrench. The house of the *Gebietskommissar* looks really interesting, with its walled-up windows and five rows of barbed wire around it. They set up fences everywhere, extra openings in the walls get boarded, and the guards walk around with grenades. It makes one think that the front is not 800 but 100 kilometers from here.

I don't know what the state of the German army is right now, but the way things are looking here in the rear, the future doesn't look very promising for the Germans.

26 JULY 1943

Well, Italy has definitely been affected. Yesterday Mussolini, "one of two pillars on which the new Europe is being built," fell. Seeing that he couldn't sort out the mess in which he had put Italy, he decided to run away before they come after him. They have already started killing party fascists—"the Black Shirts." Marshal Badoglio was appointed in his place [of course, not as the *"duce"* (leader)—Italy seems to have had enough of them for a while, but as the prime minister only.]. He began his rule with a number of decrees to calm down the rebelling nation and the statement that the "fight goes on." He didn't add the typical phrase, however, "until the victorious end."

8 AUGUST 1943

Comrades, Hurray! The breakthrough on the Eastern Front is complete! I jump with joy. The reports of the recent days spoke about furious fighting throughout the whole Southern Front and shook the remaining nerves. I realized that they are breaking through the German positions where they have concentrated their best *SS* divisions, where their "tigers" are, where everybody is armed with a submachine gun. Every day I had been asking myself whether it had happened yet? The answer was no. And today the answer is yes, now! I have lived to hear a German military report with the wonderful words, "as a result of reducing the front line, we left the city of Orel. Heavy defensive fighting continues."

This was according to German sources. According to non-German ones I knew yesterday that Belgorod was taken back, and today, Graivoron, which is 50 kilometers to the west of Belgorod. That means that the breakthrough is in full swing and the Germans retreat. They say that as a result of capturing Orel and Belgorod, the martial law in Moscow was lifted.

Today, on the occasion of the breakthrough at the front, we are having tea with sugar.

1 SEPTEMBER 1943

Again, for a whole month, my writing's been "stagnant." I even wonder how I made myself write something today. So many various world events have accumulated over this time, though, that I have at least to mention them with a word or two.

The Soviet advance develops and progresses with relentless continuity. They took Kharkov back and the Germans were seriously broken by the Miuss River.

The story with Sicily has long been over and the next step seems to be in progress, that is, Italy.

Boris, the Czar of Bulgaria, died with God's help. Perhaps there was some human help, too, but we were not informed of that.

There have been serious disturbances in Denmark that the Germans calmed down with the help of divisions called in from Norway.

Berlin was evacuated, and it is half-ruined with all the bombing.

"When will they come to the Dnieper?" Soon, fellow citizens, soon!

The most important thing that is related to this day is that today is the *fourth anniversary of World War Two!* Even if on this day last year the Germans clearly had the initiative and the successes, now they lack both.

The Germans have come to the conclusion that the partisan movement in our area has grown to an unacceptable size and decided it is time, once and for all, to annihilate them. A whole army has been assembled here: *SD* units; field gendarmerie; Ukrainian, Polish and Lithuanian *Schutzmänner;* as well as units of the notorious *ROA* (Russian Army of Liberation). Three airplanes specially assigned to the action were circling above the town. Nearby villages were set on fire, but no further than fifteen kilometers from town, because it's scary to go any further! In the daytime, the planes bomb forests; at night all armies start firing to scare the enemy and sustain their martial spirit.

The Germans thought that the partisan activity was all over, yet another bridge was blown sky high, so they decided to approach the matter more seriously. It was known that in one village (I forget the name) there was a partisan base, so obviously, the attack should strike straight into the enemy's heart! The Germans just "attacked" the village and kicked the partisans out of it—took over the village, encamped there, and waited. They don't even dare go out into the yards, however, because everywhere there are hills, covered with forests, and partisans fill those forests! Once they stick their heads out, submachine-gun chatter greets them.

The planes circle above those forests, dropping bombs and something else. Leaflets! The text reads as follows: "Valid for Passing. The person presenting this pass and reporting to the post of the gendarmerie or *Schutzmanschaft* [the basic *Schutzman* unit. *Ed.*] will neither be arrested nor deported to Germany (as you can see, the meanings are analogous), and may be employed wherever this person may desire."

Having dropped an adequate amount of the leaflets, the planes departed with dignity. Some three days later, the German ground units followed. The singing of partisan submachine guns accompanied them. End of story. I had the honor of being your storyteller!

Today announcements were posted in town that on 3 September, all youths aged fourteen to eighteen must report in the square next to the convent. Another announcement says that starting 6 September, all Polish refugees must report in the very same square to be deported to Germany. Can you tell how similar these two announcements are? The square is, well, square, and fenced off by buildings on two sides and stone walls on the other two sides. In view of this, my persona will be absent from there; it will be sitting in the attic.

3 SEPTEMBER 1943

Well, it's absolutely clear now. The youth assembled. A band arrived; a German in a superb uniform appeared. The moment he started speaking, *Schutzmänner* quietly materialized at the exit. The speech was emotional: "We are not Barbarians, we do not force anyone, and we know that you're conscientious young people, ready to build the new Europe. So, *bitte,* children under sixteen years of age can leave while we thank the older ones that they agree to voluntarily go to Germany." This is when it all began— screaming, noises, and a general mess.

Eventually the *Schutzmänner* pushed out all the ineligible, and approximately 180 guys were retained in the square. They were immediately sent via a side road to the prison. Along the way fifty of the energetic ones escaped—all they got were bruises from rifle butts on their bottoms. The rest were put in prison.

4 SEPTEMBER 1943

Today the boys from the prison were taken to the station and they were put onto the train. A crowd of parents rushed in and they managed to get approximately thirty more out. Yet a hundred was sent away. During the brawl the *Schutzmänner* and gendarmes were firing in the air. They didn't dare fire at people, otherwise they would have been torn into pieces.

Another development—the Allies landed in southern Italy and see almost no obstacles and opposition in their advance forward. The Italians surrender en masse.

9 SEPTEMBER 1943

This is the news: Italy surrendered. On the radio the Germans are cursing in a most uncivilized way. Had the Allies been faster than the Germans, taken northern Italy, and advanced into southern Germany, the end of the war could be expected in the next couple of months. They won't do it, though, they are basically slack. What will happen now to the German troops in Italy? According to German reports, "the high command has taken all the necessary measures in order to avoid the fate planned for the German divisions by the traitor Badoglio." Further on the reports said that the Italian army turned in weapons without any opposition, and in Germany, a new Italian fascist government was established, which has decided to continue the war.

On the Soviet front, the Red Army has made further progress in the Donbass; Stalino was taken and the Donbass is almost cleansed of the Germans.

Stalino was liberated the day before, on 8 September. The author of the diary more and more frequently violates the rules of secrecy. The only way to find out about the successes of the Red Army in the Donbass was to listen to Levitan and his reports from Moscow, as was the case with the successes at other fronts, too.

9 September 1943 (continued)

The next region is the area of Sumy, Bakhmach, from where the advance proceeds toward Chernigov, Nezhin, and Kiev. There the advance is also rather fast. The Red Army is approximately eighty kilometers from Chernigov, 130 or 140 from Kiev. In about a month and a half they will reach the whole length of the Dnieper.

In two months the Red Army could be here, and I finally could stop keeping this silly diary. I'm pretty fed up with it.

I decided on keeping it "from departure to arrival" [of the Red Army, *Ed.*] and the day when I am able to write the final words "The End" will be the happiest of my life.

That was the second to last entry in my diary, after which a break of three months followed.

Help from an Angry German

The work activity went on at the chalk factory where my father worked as an accountant. The workers—some thirty men—crushed chalk in a quarry and took it in wheelbarrows to the mill. The ground chalk precipitated, dried in settling collectors, then it was ground all over again and packed into sacks to be shipped, naturally, to Germany.

All of this was done without haste.

A German with an odd surname, Vatter, was in charge of the factory. His name could be interpreted as "Father." He was bandy-legged from his birth, lame from World War One, gray-haired and loud-mouthed. His all-time favorite word was *Scheisse* (crap). He screamed constantly, obviously thinking that this way he would attain the maximum working efficiency. When particularly agitated, he would storm into the office, grab a war-trophy rifle, and begin firing in the air. As a result of his screaming and firing, he was known far and wide as a menacing and dangerous German.

Not a "real" German, Vatter was a Sudeten German from the late state of Czechoslovakia. Thanks to his familiarity with the Czech language, he was able to use certain commonly understood Slavic words, richly peppered with "crap" in his administrative yelling sessions at the factory. This ensured the so-much-needed direct contact with the working class.

Gradually it became clear that this German never went beyond screaming. In fact, he turned out to be a nice, helpful man. By visiting some German institution he was able to stop "his" workers from being deported to Germany. Sometimes he added and personally distributed some extra food rations.

A huge full-length portrait of Hitler was hanging in the office, above the German's desk. One day in February 1943, after the mournful reports about Stalingrad, the portrait on the wall was gone. Having caught a surprised look on my father's face, the German yelled, "Ah, *Scheisse!*" and ran out of the office, slamming the door behind him.

Vatter even showed some kind of respect toward my father. Perhaps this had to do with the difference in their officer ranks: father ended World War I as a staff captain [a junior captain] of the Russian army, and the German ended it as a non-commissioned lieutenant of the Austro-Hungarian army. Both remained at those levels, yet even under the changed circumstances, the subordination remained, and in moments of benevolence, the German addressed Father as *Herr Hauptmann* (Mister Captain).

Once, in the fall of 1943, the German said, "*Herr Hauptmann,* and what is it really that your younger son is doing at that crappy comb-making factory?"

Father shrugged his shoulders and said, "Working."

"Crap. I think it would be better for him to work here. I strongly advise it. Naturally, it is all crap here, too, but, . . . and better, as soon as possible."

Thus I ended up in the chalk factory. Yuri worked in a mine, where the brown coal was mined in small amounts, and Rostyu worked there as well. The deportation to Germany was not a danger there yet.

By then I had almost stopped keeping the diary. I had other things to attend to. The front was approaching the Dnieper and the situation got tense. I could barely find the time to write down all the names of the locations that were listed in the reports from the Soviet Information Agency. They got closer and closer, all those cities and villages liberated by the Red Army. In conversations with an occasionally encountered acquaintance, I could indifferently precede my diary entry by "they say that" and list a few names.

A few days after I had transferred to the chalk factory, a decree was posted regarding the next mobilization to Germany. The chalk factory, where there was a *"Führer"* of its own, however, didn't let its workers go.

That was the first time I got lucky with a German. Come to think of it, it was the second time. The first incident was with that junior officer of the *Luftwaffe* who could have slapped my face with his black leather glove. He could have, but didn't.

Naturally those Germans must have come from somewhere, those who, starting in May 1945 cleared away the ruins of the Hitlerite *Reich* to build something human in its place. Among the re-builders there definitely were some of those who had come to our land wearing field-gray uniform. They were all so much the same and, at the same time, they were all somewhat different. Perhaps returning home from captivity, the men of the new age were joined by Vatter who in 1943 dared to take down the *Führer*'s portrait from the wall and put it away behind the cabinet, accompanying it all with a dangerous comment. Who knows?

The short period of my employment at the chalk factory had to do with an episode of my transformation from an observer and recorder of events to a participant.

An ancient Remington typewriter stood on Vatter's desk, with Latin letters. The German would occasionally—moaning and continuously mentioning "crap"—use the old typewriter to type work reports, applications, and letters addressed to German authorities.

The retreat was now progressing on all fronts. Roar and thunder wasn't heard from the east quite yet, but the "local" Germans were behaving themselves in a markedly more nervous way. Some military units briefly appeared and then left, and Kremenets once again had the look of a town not far from the front line. The ruins enhanced this and empty spaces added to the landscape we had come to live in as a result of three years of "new order" in action.

Now I can't recall whose idea it was to type a pamphlet addressed to the Germans on that very same Remington. The temptation was huge, and at his fifty years of age my father retained a youthful inclination to risky ventures. Typing the pamphlet on a typewriter with Latin characters was total insanity because the number of such typewriters didn't exceed a dozen or two in the whole town. Just as insane was to paste those pamphlets under a pall of darkness along the Ritterstrasse, mostly close to home—the curfew was becoming more restricting and the Germans had begun firing without warning. Mailing those pamphlets to German institutions, including *Pan Gebietskommissar,* showed the utmost audacity—but we so much wanted to tickle their nerves.

We wrote the text together. Taking advantage of Vatter's absence, I typed the pamphlet in low-case letters and with carbon copying paper while father was watching guard. Then we solemnly burned the carbon paper. We pasted the pamphlets together with Yuri, late at night, when the barking of dogs was the only thing that disturbed the tense silence.

In the morning I took a stroll along Shirokaya Street enjoying the results of our work. The sheets of white paper with the German text on them were seen on all poles along the street, and they were torn down by the evening.

I don't remember the contents of the pamphlet. Mostly, it was abusive, though we wouldn't go as low as *Scheisse.* The bottom-line was, of course, the advice to head back home, *nach Vaterland,* while they were still safe and sound.

That was one of those memorable episodes in our life. We had no one to gain advice from, and acted out of our own understanding of things.

The diary didn't mention the radio receiver or those leaflets. The author steadily maintained the rule not to put his family into his diary affair. He naively believed that had the diary been discovered, he would have been the only one to be punished.

Most likely it was the growing confusion of the final stage of the occupation that prevented the *Gestapo* from establishing which typewriter was used and who typed this first invective leaflet. It also prevented them from finding out about another sheet of paper, this one including details of the actual situation on the Eastern Front (based on the Soviet Information Agency reports). At the same time, they could have discovered the full-size portrait of the *Führer* covered with dust behind the cabinet in the factory's office, and an almost ownerless rifle. They could have acted accordingly then.

In fact, right before the very escape of Vatter to the west, however, the German typewriter was abused once more. I typed the following in German, "Notice. This house and its residents are under the protection of the *Waffen-SS*. It is strictly forbidden to enter the house. *Hauptsturmführer* (signed illegibly)." The notice was stamped with a round seal with an eagle on it. When Vatter was out of breath packing and preparing to leave, we stamped the paper, slightly twisting it so that the German inscription around the eagle reading, "The Chalk Factory of Kremenets" became illegible, too.

Now the important thing was to choose the right moment for putting the notice on the entrance door to our house. It had to be done neither too early nor too late.

Even more important was not to be late with removing the paper. The Red Army could have people who were insufficiently endowed with a sense of humor.

In fact, neither party saw the notice.

Everything worked out without it.

The Red Army forced and crossed the Dnieper, liberating the capital of Ukraine, and advanced far to the west. There were 200 kilometers straight from Zhitomir to Kremenets. The Soviet tank units crossed the 150 kilometers separating Zhitomir from Kiev in six days. The Kremenets Germans, too, figured that out and fled. The *Gebietskommissar* fled, along with the *Gestapo* and their collaborators. In November 1943 there was anarchy in Kremenets. The local residents began inspecting German warehouses. Shirokaya Street was covered with spilled grain, and people with sacks and bags moved here and there in a business-like manner.

Having considered the situation based on my handwritten reports from the Soviet Information Agency brought up from the basement, father said, "No, they won't reach here. It is too narrow of a wedge. The flanks are much too extended. The Germans can strike back from the north or south. The flanks should be strengthened; to advance further is impermissible. The fact that Germans are in panic, though, is wonderful! The Germans are no longer the same. Yet they can be back."

In anticipation of the Germans returning, the family council made a decision to build a shelter promptly. It was not far from home, in a side of our hill covered with thick hazel. The spot was noted a long time before. The four of us worked through the night—my father, Rostislav, Yuri, and I—and by dawn everything was ready. The bars brought from home enhanced the ceiling and the entrance was covered with a shield of wood and masked with turf.

Father proved right. The Germans concentrated their strength and cut off the tip of the wedge near Zhitomir, advancing a few dozen kilometers to the east, toward Kiev.

They came back to Kremenets, too. Then there was no time for the diary.

Flames danced from nocturnal fires. Sporadic shooting was heard here and there. People were caught in the streets and their Ausweiss, of whatever type it was, did them no good.

I neither understand nor can explain why and how all this could just pass by the house by the hill. We lived in hunger, having no opportunity to go scouting for food. We kept vigils through the nights, always ready to leave the house and run for the shelter. The house seemed abandoned. So did the one next door. The deserted town seemed to have lost its very last residents.

Then in late December the advance of the armies of the First Ukrainian Front began from the Kiev base of operations.

On the eve of the New Year of 1944 Zhitomir was liberated once again, and this time for good. In the second week of 1944 I wrote my very last diary entry.

11 JANUARY 1944

I haven't written for a long time; didn't have time.

Today the front is exactly 150 kilometers away from us. The evacuation is going on here.

I'm getting ready to flee to the forest and am going to bury the diary now. I will be happy if one day I'll have to dig it out.

Hello, Comrades!

Death to the German Occupiers!

For many months now I have been regularly—on a daily basis—listening to Moscow, and I'm well informed of everything that's going on at the front.

Fight these beasts to the very last one, for they wanted to annihilate our motherland.

Never before in its history has Russia stood as high as it does now, but after the war, the USSR will stand even higher!

I wish to survive and see it all.

The Return

It was early spring 1944. Our boys were back in town, marching on the mud-covered cobblestones of Shirokaya Street. The soldiers of the Red Army were heading west.

Back in July 1941, young boys were going east; they wore well-made uniforms and helmets. They held semiautomatic SVT rifles and had grenades. They weren't numerous and they had passed our town in a few hours only. Wagons and carts rattled down the street, followed by a few trucks and a few tanks. That was all.

And now they were going toward the west along the very same cobblestone street. They were dressed in various kinds of greatcoats and jackets; some had legs wrapped up in rags, others had boots; some wore helmets and some wore caps. They didn't march abreast and even seemed not to keep any kind of military order—some walked on the road, some on the sidewalk. The most important thing, though, was that they were going west! The majority of them had submachine guns, some carried them on their chest and some on their shoulders, with barrels pointing down. Pairs of soldiers carried long guns, PTR anti-tank rifles. A guy who stopped to straighten up his gaiter explained to me. That was some explanation. He seemed to be my age, a little bit shorter than I was, with two bars on his shoulder board. He wore a green greatcoat, made of quality cloth.

"The second front," he said. [The Russians commonly referred to the Western front of the Allied forces as "the Second Front." *Ed.*]

"What's the second front?"

"The greatcoat, see, comes from the second front. The Allies gave it to us—Churchill sent it to us, instead of the second front. Get it?" he explained.

"Ah, I see. Cool!" I replied.

"Not so cool perhaps, but at least something. You're Russian, aren't you? You jabber away like one of ours. Which year?"

"Which year what?" I asked.

"I mean how old you are?"

"Ah! Born in 1926, I soon will be eighteen."

"Well, you will soon go, too."

"And you, which year were you born?"

"1925. Soon it will be a year I've been fighting," he said.

"In this . . . drum magazine . . . how many rounds are in it?" I asked.

"They'll tell you everything, don't you worry."

We were by now walking side by side; he was catching up with his squad.

"Would you like to smoke?" I offered. "The cigarettes, I don't need them."

"Kraut cigarettes? What? They were supplying you with cigarettes here or what?" He glanced at me sourly, then took the pack from my extended (and how else?) hand and walked away without looking back at me.

Young and old soldiers walked by, some had moustaches, some needed a shave; some examined us all over and exchanged remarks. A feeling that I could not shake off slowly grew within me—I was a stranger to them. They saw me as a spectator, a loiterer, while they tended to business. They walked along the cobbled street, in their soaking wet and crumpled trench coats, tired, and perhaps hungry. They were walking to wherever they were told and I was standing on a sidewalk, standing aside.

Thus, gradually, a heavy feeling grew inside me—like shame—for those cigarettes and for being a mere spectator. Perhaps there was some envy, too? Those were the winners marching on, they were the ones who had the right to say "our cause is right, the victory will be ours." [A classic Soviet wartime phrase. The Soviet medal "For Victory Over Germany in the Great Patriotic War of 1941–1945" carries the following text: "Our cause was right—we were victorious." *Ed.*] Their ashen faces, sprinkled with mud, showed no fire in their eyes, yet they were walking on, to the west, steadily pushing that seemingly infallible machine away from their country. From the Caucasus, from Stalingrad, God knows from where else, but they kept pushing it on. And the process was picking up speed all the time.

Certainly, when the war started, we stayed behind not by choice. We were not accepted as a *part of them.* Dad's arrest and everything that followed happened so fast then, in the first days of the war . . . but now? One just had to walk along with those soldiers, along the street, to have the right to be angry, to be proud, and to carry one of those submachine guns.

And what about Mama and Dad? Just leaving them was scary to consider, but then Dad went to the previous war as a volunteer when he was nineteen. He had always been proud of this and of his wounds, of the St. George's cross (a rarity on officers' tunics) along with other decorations, and of his "Honorary Weapon."

He was proud of the fact that he had served Russia, although later no one thanked him for that.

Then, back in 1941, our school's military instructor was an expert marksman. Perhaps he managed to fire at least one bullet out of our school's smallbore rifle, and kill at least one enemy. Thus he, too, had brought this day in March 1944 closer. On this day I had to quickly make up my mind whether I should wait until others avenged everything that had been brought down upon our land during all those years, or go join up and go west myself, carrying one of those submachine guns.

It would be very hard on my parents. In his heart, though, wouldn't my father approve of it and be proud of me? Then, back in 1914, he was almost my age and perhaps was reflecting the same way as I was at that moment, although I couldn't see him ever having been my age. Why was that so?

Some infantrymen lingered along the curbs, and then moved over onto the sidewalk completely. A transport of trucks and cars overcame them, six-wheeled trucks with strange roundish hoods, small agile off-road vehicles, with four people sitting inside and two more on the fenders with their feet hanging in the air. I gazed at officers with fine leather belts and star-spangled shoulder boards. A hand appeared on my shoulder. Father was standing next to me. We briefly exchanged glances. We watched the troops, our army that was going west. To the west! There the war roared.

Father knew what I was contemplating, and I knew that he knew that I had to go there, with a submachine gun in my hands.

———◦◦◦———

Two weeks later, Yuri and I were taken on by the *Komsomol* (Young Communists' League). They called us in, saying, "We know about you, we know that you haven't blemished yourself with any wrongdoings," and told us that we were admitted to the *Komsomol*. They didn't issue us any membership books then, however, since they didn't have any forms yet, but we both received "warrants." [During the years of the German-Soviet war, a number of civilians were issued "warrants" that relieved them from being enlisted during the universal draft. Such warrants, for example, were given to those with professional skills necessary to effectively work at the defense plants, or highly-qualified professionals in certain field, scientists, engineers, and so on. *Ed.*] Yuri was "sent to work with the communications," and he was engaged in it for another thirty-five years, until the last day of his life.

As for me, a few days later, just like all other boys of my age, I received a summons. I went to the Military Commissioner's Office with my "warrant" in my pocket, yet I didn't present it. Thus I was drafted.

Father taught me how to wrap puttees and foot wraps and how to roll up the greatcoat, as well as many other things. [Puttee: a wrap from ankle to knee. Traditionally Russian soldiers do not wear socks, but foot wraps. *Ed.*]

If asked today about the most difficult moment of my life, I would most certainly recall more than one. Among those was the moment they took Father away and how he made the sign of the cross toward me from the truck as I stood in Shirokaya Street, behind the hillock, opposite our house; the moment when my eyes met with Frida's at almost the very same spot as she was being taken away; and the moment when we, newly-drafted recruits, walked bravely along Shirokaya Street and two figures, those of my father and mom, growing smaller and smaller, followed our column along the sidewalk. I had an acute feeling of guilt toward them for all the pain I was causing them. I couldn't stay home after everything that had happened, though, after my life of separation from my motherland, after that long, long night of occupation.

Having seen me off, Father himself went to the Military Commissioner's Office, but he was sent back home. They told him it was no longer the situation of 1941, and that no more levies en masse were formed. They suggested he get busy with restoration, by setting up a park on the ruins of the former ghetto, the ruins of the town that had never really seen any military action in that war, a mere two bombs back in 1939. Today there is a big impressive park where the ghetto once used to stand. Come visit and see it. You would never believe that there are cellars and bones underneath the park, . . . but then, I invite you there as if today it was not situated in a foreign country for many, including myself. My memory has preserved all kinds of different things about that town, where my family members now rest in peace.

In June 1941, my friend, Gogi Gedjadze, had come running to me to say good-bye. He brought me a fragrant letter from another classmate that read, "My mom and I are leaving. I don't think we'll meet again. I will remember you. I will write to you in Kremenets, after the war, if that's ok? Lyusia." This was the first letter of that kind addressed to me and it was from the girl who used to sit at the front desk in our class and continuously weave the tips of her blonde braids with her slim fingers. For some reason it was clear both to them and to us that they had to leave, get evacuated, while we had to stay behind. Their respective fathers were Soviet officers.

In the early spring of 1944 I was leaving as well, and now for many reasons. Already with the duffel bag on my back, I asked Father, "If there comes a letter, would you send it to me, to the field post office at the front?" He promised, but the letter never came.

For the rest of my life my memory preserved the desperate look in my father's eyes, "Try to survive and come back." My father was in the army for a long time—he was constantly reminded of his military past and eventually, in 1954, it probably killed him, through a heart attack. Yet I consider it a major happiness to be able to die in one's own home, surrounded by one's dear ones. My father was given that kind of happiness.

———————◦∞◦———————

Back to the diary—so that I don't have to return to the topic of it. Then, leaving the family home, I hid my diary in the very same favorite spot, in the attic, instead of burying it the way I wrote in my final record. Something had hindered me. When I joined the fighting army, I instantly realized that I could be killed, and then the labor of the chronicler wouldn't be known to anyone, so I sent a letter to my family. The diary was retrieved from the hiding place and was read. Then the only one right decision was made, which was to submit those notebooks to the Special State Commission on Establishing and Investigating the Atrocities and Crimes of the Nazi German Occupiers. Thus my diary made its way to Moscow and was included in the materials of the Soviet Prosecution at the Nuremberg Trials where the major Nazi war criminals were charged. In 1946 the notebooks were returned to Kremenets with an accompanying letter from the Secretariat of the State Commission (registered as document C-840, of 2 July 1946):

The town of Kremenets, 'Ternopolskaya Region
Municipal Council
To Comrade A. V. Kravchenko-Berezhnoy
The delay in return of the diary to you was caused by the circum-
stances related to the Nuremberg Trials.
It is with gratitude that we are returning the diary of your son to you.
Enc. the diary.
The Executive Secretary of the Special State Commission (P.
Bogoyavlensky)

Then my father gave the notebooks to the local museum, where they have been put on display ever since, to be seen by anyone, including the author.

In 1958 the diary made its second journey to Moscow when its original was requested by the Central State Archive of the October Revolution and Social-ist Construction (*TsGAOR*) following my meeting with the militia major that I described earlier in the book. The diary was requested with the purpose of excluding, with the author's assistance, ambiguities and correcting errors in the text of a typewritten copy that had been kept in the *TsGAOR*—even back in the years of his youth the author couldn't boast of having legible and neat handwriting. Once again, the notebooks were returned to Kremenets with an accompanying letter which, in particular, said:

This diary played a significant part in the unveiling of Nazi German
crimes not only on the territory of Kremenets, but also on the territory
of the Soviet Union in general, and was used at the Nuremberg Trial.
Once again we would like to express our gratitude to the Kremenets
District Museum for forwarding to us the diary of R. A. Kravchenko-
Berezhnoy.

Enc. two notebooks, 276 pages, and maps, 3 pages. Signed: Captain Illeritskaya, Head of the Department of the TsGAOR of the USSR.

I think that Captain Illeritskaya, a very nice lady, somewhat exaggerated the part played by the diary "in the unveiling," and yet it is pleasant to know that the young author's hard work there, in the attic, wasn't useless.

In any instance, she gave a copy of the diary to the author. Otherwise this book wouldn't have existed.

Enough said about the diary. I didn't continue the diary during my military service. We weren't allowed to for security reasons, but even if we had been, who would have had the time to do it? For that reason, my experiences in the Red Army are based on my memory rather than a diary.

SERVICE
IN THE RED ARMY

The Troop Train

The wheels kept knocking and clattering, slowly and out of sync, and our troop train kept crawling somewhere toward the northeast. The remains of railroad ties laid along the railroad tracks. In order to turn the intact ties into such crumbled pieces during their retreat, the Germans had designed a special "plough." It was attached to the last car of the train going to the west, and it smashed the ties while retreating. Then the Soviets fixed the tracks "on the go" to keep up the flow of supplies to the fighting Red Army, resulting in fragments of rails of various lengths to be put together, wheels clattering on them—as long as it worked! Suddenly an echo resonated from a burned carcass of a car lying near the tracks, and from the smoking chipped remains of a brick wall. The traces of war are everywhere.

We rode the train going toward the northeast. Soon, hopefully, it would head west? Our train made long stops at some forlorn little stations. Clear girls' voices could be heard from an oncoming train singing a verse from a heart-rending song, "Farewell, my beloved city. . . ." Freight cars flew by noisily, carrying tanks, tanks, and more tanks, then guns. Then more freight cars passed carrying soldiers, but with wide open doors so that another verse from the song was heard.

The bond connecting us with home and family was still felt strongly. At night, the feelings of loneliness and yearning built up inside my chest, leaving me breathless. It was easier in the morning. In the morning I saw sunshine and spring. The bright outside world pushed away and suppressed all that was inside me. Seen through the doorway of our car, the earth moved on and kept turning—patches of some fresh greenery were seen intermittently between unusually spacious black masses of fields. Again I saw ruins, a stack of chimneys above them, an oddly positioned wing from an airplane and a pile of helmets by the side of the road. A cow was tied up and a blonde girl was next to it, wearing something so ancient, worn, and faded. She waved at us and we waved back at her. A bunch of girls standing by the railroad tracks shouted something at us and also waved as if inviting us, and we shouted back. We were real men. *I'll come back from the war, wearing a faded field blouse, medals for bravery tinkling on my chest, my arm in a sling,* I thought, *and one of them, smiling, will come up to me. . . .*

The station was a mess, steam engines wheezed, and the oncoming train began its motion with much clatter and noise. Weathered faces, worn boots, field blouses with open collars, no belts, many medals. Battle-seasoned. "New recruits? Soon you'll be there, too, and will get to fight some." "We'll fight all right!" "All aboard!" The spring sun caressed us gently, the air was filled with smells of coal dust, tar, and steam-engine smoke. We saw the awakening earth, the barely-open, sticky, birch tree leaves. A small forest flew by, all transparent and tender as if the war was not out there, as if spring was the only thing that was happening out there in the whole wide world.

The troop train crawled like a snail, still heading northeast. Far ahead, the steam engine puffed heavily and unsteadily; at times, its puffing grew frequent and at times it slowed down and the train skidded. There seems to be no end to this hill, the train slowed down, and wheels clattered less frequently. The doors of all cars were wide open; those who managed to get a spot in the doorway sat on the edge with their feet dangling in the air. They sat on the floor getting warm under the mild, gentle sunshine. Those who were not so quick stood behind them, leaning on the crossbars. There was more room on the bunks, where those boys who didn't get enough sleep last night could catch up on it. We were singing, contesting the neighboring car in who could sing the loudest. A song, out of sync, was heard from the train, "and a Cossack goes with her, taking his horses down to water. . . ."

The steam engine eventually choked, and the train stopped, unable to conquer the hill. The green sides of the railroad mound were immediately filled with people. It didn't look like we would go on soon, and there were so very many of us on the train.

It was indeed pleasant to stretch out on tender sprouting grass, to inhale the smell of thyme. This was the kind of smell of the hillock at my home, where we used to send kites flying in the blue sky. We had put only about 200 kilometers behind us, and yet home was now so far away. How were they doing now? I couldn't let go of the stinging feeling of pity and guilt. Mama, my mom, who had spent all of her life by Father's protective side, had rushed along, through the front-bordering landscape, had hitched rides on some vehicles passing by so that she could see me once again and give me a can of meat she had managed to get somewhere.

My thoughts flowed slowly, half-asleep, and melted together. Then they were pushed away by something new, something alarming . . . a noise that roared dully and deeply somewhere out in the blue. Voices went quiet. Everybody looked up to watch a small silvery toy beautifully colored by the setting sun. It was a reconnaissance plane or a "frame" as our boys called it. [The aircraft in question was probably a German Focke Wulf Fw 189 reconnaissance plane, which indeed looked like a flying frame. *Ed.*] It seemed harmless and almost stationary there, in the heights. Somebody came back to his senses, "A-a-a-i-r-r-a-i-d!" and an order came from the head of the train, "All aboard!" but it seems to be late. The silvery two-tailed little craft slowly floated away melting into the sunshine. Beautiful.

The train stood for a long time. They said another steam engine is coming. I got into my bunk, on the upper level, toward the little window. Slumber crawled over me.

I woke up in the middle of the night. It was silent in the carriage, yet nobody was asleep, alerted breathing and whispering was heard. It was dark, and I could hear the roar of engines. It was the well-known sound of a Junkers 88, a medium-range bomber plane. The deep, moaning roar faded and then grew louder. The plane was circling somewhere in the dark sky above the quiet, hiding troop train. The "frame" was not glittering in the rays of the setting sun just for the sake of beauty—this Junkers wanted *us*. It was looking for us. It was looking for *me*, me again. . . .

And I was unarmed and helpless. I was not even a soldier yet; only about to become one. I was supposed to have become one. I tried not to breathe; my heart pounded like a hammer in every cell of my body. It was raw fear. Fright numbed the body and froze the thinking. My mind, hiding somewhere deep, deep inside, tried feebly to resist despising myself—a miserable crouching bundle—by trying to alert feelings of pride. A will to do what, though? I was unarmed. I was a warm, fragile, little world that was about to be turned into bits of smoking flesh. Was it worthwhile to get out and try to prove something to myself and others?

The roar grew, powerful and steady. Now the Junkers led a whole pack. A sigh was heard throughout the carriage. A ruthless, ghastly light from illumination rockets launched by the Junkers briefly shone upon the faces looking up at it.

During the night we traveled some more. The doors of our carriage were still wide open.

We were blinded by the white walls of buildings at the Grechany station, with a bright field stretching out to the unsteady darkness. Where we were the light had no shadows to spare. It seemed that there was not a single corner or nook left with life-saving darkness. Blinding lights hung in the sky, immediately followed by the crazy, choking roar of antiaircraft guns and threads of machine-gun bursts, which meant we were not forsaken and not helpless. Even from our train, somewhere very near us, guns fired in frequent bursts, and the carriage started to shake. The thick and continuous roar of engines covered it all. It would begin any moment now. . . . Then, with the air-splitting sound of the first falling bombs, people rushed out of the carriages, the desperate figures of people hurrying toward the distant hazy darkness. People fell, covering up the field.

"Our Father, who art in heaven," somebody started praying next to me, switching to hysterical screaming. I stayed down, covering my head with my hands. I was tempted to join in, to seek salvation from the series of explosions that shook the carriage and seemed to shake the whole world. An explosion went off far away, then closer, and closer . . . the following one would go off right where I was. . . .

"Give us our daily bread!" The voice next to me was exasperated. A crazy thought crossed my mind, "Which bread? What bread is he talking about?"

"He is not there! He's not! You're an idiot!" I screamed with all strength in my lungs, trying to cover the sounds of the hell that surrounded us with my screaming, thus depriving myself of the hope of being rescued by some power from there, from above. Then Dad's final word of advice flashed up somewhere in the deep corner of my darkened mind, *"if they bomb you, get under the carriage."* I shook the guy who had prayed when we were bombed earlier. "Get up! Under the car! Wheels and rails will protect us!"

We fell out of the car together and pressed onto the oil-covered ground, under the protection of the train wheels.

The plane roar went quiet. Heat emanated from a carriage nearby that was on fire, and ammunition exploded somewhere. Antiaircraft guns kept firing. *"The guys didn't stop firing during the hellish bombing, didn't bend, and didn't run off. They covered me. And what about me? What did I do to help out? This was the very first time, though, . . . not considering two bombs in 1939 that were meant for the President. These bombs, meant for us, kicked up earth right next to us to make sure we would never reach the front, and would never get weapons in our hands. . . ."*

Then for the first time ever, albeit feebly, a feeling of satisfaction appeared—it was the first, although small, victory over myself. I didn't go crazy, and I helped a fellow next to me.

Many years later, together with my son, I was sitting in an international-class carriage of the Prague–Moscow express. Respectable-looking foreigners were smiling ingratiatingly, looking at Vassily's mischievous face. In order to somehow neutralize, at least for a moment, his urge to act and to destroy everything, I pointed out of the window and said, "Here I once was bombed."

The carriage was softly clicking on the passing track points of the Grechany station. That was the very same station we stopped by on our way to Proskurov.

"How were you bombed?" Vassily asked excitedly.

"Properly bombed. Seriously," I replied, and didn't have anything else to add.

"Where are the craters?" He asked, wanting proof.

There were no craters. Only beautiful, peaceful, first-rate earth was turning and swirling outside the window.

"Is it true," Vassily started, as always, without any obvious link to the previous conversation, "that when we have Communism, everybody will have his own little power plant?" I thought peevishly about what they must be teaching at the day-care centers if now the kids crave personal power plants!

Moscow

Going further toward the northeast, the troop train brought us to the capital. The Moscow of 1944 seemed gray, strict, sparsely populated. Perhaps it was not that way at all, yet that was the way I saw it in those few hours I spent in the city.

The captain in charge of our team of recent recruits took me along with him to the city. The troop train, weathered by the bombings near Proskurov and in Fastov, filled with lice and somewhat-starved boys—our food had consisted of whatever we had secured at home—stopped in Likhobory to let us get cleaned, washed, and receive a hot meal.

It was our first hot meal in two weeks!

Then we were led to a delightful and spacious *banya* (traditional Russian steam and vapor bath) that smelled of carpentry.

We cleaned ourselves and changed our underwear, then some of the others smoked self-made cigarettes while waiting for the command to line up for dinner. The captain, who during the trip had become our mentor and teacher, called me up and asked, "Would you like to see Moscow instead of the dinner and movie?"

I was stunned, "Is this Moscow?"

"Not exactly, but it is not far from here."

"May I? Shall we have time? I would love to."

"We'll be stationed here through the evening. We'll have time," the captain said, and as if justifying himself, added, "I have a younger sister here. Her husband went missing back in the summer of 1941. It is hard for her. I have to see her."

"Maybe we should take a food ration to her?"

"We will receive our next rations at our destination only, but then, not much longer is left. I will take mine. You decide for yourself. We'll soon part. They will teach you some stuff, give you a uniform, and send you off to the west. I have to go back to the rear again."

The captain walked with a limp. He was burdened by a wound, and by not being allowed to serve in a combat duty. He openly envied those who were at the front. During the trip he told us about Stalingrad, about the Kursk battle. There, near Prokhorovka, his front life ended. Now all he had were memories . . . as well as wound stripes. . . . and military decorations—it was the first time I saw any Soviet decorations that close.

"I will take my ration, too." I said. "If we are close to our destination, then it doesn't matter."

"All right, rush to the carriage, and pick up my duffel bag, too, will you?" The Captain replied. "I will go to the commandant in the meanwhile. Things are strictly regulated here."

Half an hour later we were riding some hitched truck, he in the cabin and I in the back. The road was battered and the truck jumped badly on it. Squatting in the corner of the back of the truck and holding tight onto the sides, I looked at the shabby suburbs that hadn't known repairs for a long while now, with unfamiliar signs—*"Grore"* (Grocery Store), *"Indoes"* (Industrial Goods), and so on—that seemed to be in Russian. I hadn't had the chance to see any signs in Russian yet, excluding those near the combat front, reading things such as "No mines."

Two days before, when our train passed Khutor Mikhailovsky, the captain had said, "Here is Russia." Nothing particularly Russian could be seen from the open doors of our train carriage, however, only fields and small woods still in winter slumber, dilapidated constructions, piles of rusted military scrap along the tracks, and ruins, ruins everywhere. Oncoming trains filled with new, green military machines and guns were rattling on parallel tracks. Somewhere or other all these arms were being manufactured. In Moscow? Beyond Moscow?

Now I was in Moscow. The years of German occupation in Kremenets were behind me. The next day I would become a soldier. I would go to the front and meet the enemy face to face. I would have a chance to pay them back for everything—for Frida, for Kremenets, for all the ruins and trenches filled with bodies, for the lost years—for everything.

We rode an old clattering streetcar. People were scarce; they were definitely not smiling; they look concerned. Buildings with traces of camouflaging flow by. There is a little park, and there are children in it. They haven't seen any occupation. These gloomy people haven't known occupation, either. The Germans didn't come here—didn't manage to get through! These very same people made it possible to stop that huge machine and turn it back. These people, they seem so simple, so commonplace. Just like the captain. His leg doesn't bend.

"Comrade Captain! Why are people so . . . gloomy?" I asked.

"They are tired. They work hard. You cannot imagine how hard they work."

Then we walked along Sadovaya Street. The captain told me, "Stay with me all of the time. You don't have any papers. They can easily take you for a deserter. It's all very strict here."

We were walking across Moscow.

The captain limped. I walked trying to keep next to him and walk in step. We always used to walk that way: Father, Yuri, and I. Father used to say, "An old habit." It became my new habit. The duffel bag pulled my shoulder downward. We walked across Moscow and everything around us was commonplace. The military patrols would look at us carefully, and then saluted at us. The captain saluted back. I pulled in my stomach and tried to keep pace with him.

Then captain said, "Here we are."

We turned into a dark alley, crossed the cobbled yard covered with remains of asphalt, and walked up some screeching stairs. I was surprised by a dozen buttons on a rusty, red doorpost. The captain found the one he needed and pressed it twice. Somewhere in the depth of the apartment a bell dully rang. Light footsteps approached the door, something clanked, and the door screeched open.

"Kolya!"

We had tea in a room with a very high ceiling and peeled-off stucco ornaments where the windows were twice as big as I was. Through the windows I saw roofs and onion domes of churches, and silhouettes in the distant mist that one could mistake for the towers of the Kremlin. Nina Pavlovna told me, however, that one couldn't see the Kremlin from there.

"Look from the other side," the captain told me. "Go out, take a walk. You must be tired from sitting in that carriage. Don't step outside the yard, though. They will arrest you. We'll go back in an hour. I will call you."

Closer to the evening, when we were going back, there were more people in the streets. The captain explained, "Their shift at the factories is over." Teenagers, young girls, women, elderly men wearing kerchiefs, jerseys, caps, fur hats with earflaps. Their faces were tired and their hands were oily. They spoke unusually quickly. The girls standing on the landing of the streetcar car whispered something, and kept glancing toward us. Something in my looks made them laugh. Perhaps it was my knitted cap with tassel—they didn't seem to wear anything like this here. I was like a foreigner among them, not yet one of them. I moved around and tried to hide behind the captain.

The girls also moved somehow and again I caught their mischievous glances at me. Nina Pavlovna came out to see us to the streetcar. She was very pretty, too. She touched my hair with her palm as if by accident, "Your mother must love you. The war has scattered you far and wide. . . ."

Then she hurried off to work. Moscow worked 24 hours a day.

At night back on the train, when the wheels again clickety-clacked in the now so familiar fashion, I couldn't fall asleep for a long time. Everything that seemed commonplace and gray during that long day now turned bright, tangible, and significant. I wanted to bask in my recollections of this day again

and again: streets, streetcars, straight silhouettes of bell towers, girls' glancing, Nina Pavlovna's face and hands, the bookcases in her room, the dusky
and confusing hallway, and her kitchen with all those camping stoves on the
tables. There were a dozen light bulbs in the bathroom, each with its own
wiring. Every flat in that enormous apartment had its own switch for the bathroom. What had happened to the idea of collectivism? I fell asleep to the
irregular clicking sound of the wheels, and my thoughts buzzed in my head,
getting transformed into vague, fantastic images. In my dream I was also
yearning for food.

Closer to the evening we got off the train in Vyshny Volochek. I said good-
bye to the captain.

"Thank you, Nikolay Pavlovich, for taking me to Moscow."

"Why Pavlovich?" The captain was surprised. "I have been a Semenovich
all my life since my early childhood."

Now it was my turn to be surprised, "But Nina . . . ." And then I shut up.

Our new commander, a sergeant with wound stripes, yelled at us, "Has an
order been given? An order has been given! That's all you need know!"

I have learned that brilliant formula, simple in its universality, and applied
it for the rest of my life. *Has an order been given? That's all you need know!*

The First Step

There was a brief stay with a training regiment where we got "class three"
meals. A fish called *vobla* (Caspian roach)—a rare delicacy today and much
adored by beer lovers—was the staple there. It was meant to substitute for
meat. We consumed it in its air-dried form as well as boiled. The main topic
of conversations during our free time was, therefore, recollections of various
home-cooked meals that had been consumed in enormous quantities back
then, in our earlier lives. At the same time, being busy and training from 6 AM
until the order to retire at 11 PM, we learned the basics of the military art at
the level of a regular infantryman in a rifle unit. There was marching drill,
exhausting endless forced marches, and hours spent at the firing range. All
that time one wanted to eat. . . .

Even though we were still only in training, I almost died. There was a
forced march when we had to carry every field gear item, except that there
was a brick in my duffel bag instead of combat rations, and in my right hand
I had a rifle with a fixed bayonet instead of a submachine gun. We were training in close combat and were charging straw dummies of the enemy with
these bayonets. Generally we were supposed to become submachine gunners,
but a bayonet could not be affixed to the PPSh submachine gun so they taught
us the basics of close combat using the rifle; nobody knew what kind of

battles we would see. In one place a well-trodden forest path crossed a trench some two and a half meters deep. We had to cross that obstacle, in a flash, and continue with the speed-march. Just like everybody else I jumped into the trench, but the heavy rifle went ahead of me, a split second earlier, landed upright, and the fixed bayonet scraped my cheek, stroking by a millimeter my right temple, pulling off my cap. I still shudder when I recall that incident— had the bayonet been a little bit off to the left, it would have spiked my head through to the very brain. The bayonet was off to the right, however. Many years later, having shaken off my superficial atheism, I put that incident into the list of events of my life where interference from above was apparent and essential. That snapshot was preserved in my memory for the rest of my life, along with the feel of the clay in that earthen trench in the spring of 1944, the many square tents that formed the training regiment, and the forests not far from the town of Vyshny Volochek.

There was a *banya* (Russian sauna) and a complete change of uniform; before that we were wearing "second hand" uniforms—we could only guess who had worn them prior to us. The very same night we were put on a troop train again. Now we were called "a marching company" and received meals of category #2. Trying to compensate for still missing calories, at some burned-down station in Byelorussia, I bought a pot of clotted milk. Finishing it in one gulp, I pulled something hard and difficult to chew from my mouth —it was a frog's leg. I was instantly relieved of the milk that I had just drunk, and of an earlier consumed meal category #2. That reckless thing I did only increased my appetite and served as additional proof of my complete immaturity as a soldier. Consequently, when I finally arrived in the forward military zone and reached the regiment's kitchen with meals of category #1, I overindulged mindlessly. This, of course, led to my suffering from an acute intestinal problem.

It was in connection with this incident that my first encounter with my mentor, godfather, and guardian took place. He was the *starshina* (master sergeant) of the submachine-gun company that would become my new home. As Odysseus had to endure many obstacles on his way home, however, my road also entailed plenty of obstacles.

After arriving at my new unit, the company's sanitary instructor diagnosed me vaguely saying, "You have either dysentery or a simple case of diarrhea" and that was when the *starshina* first appeared in front of me.

"Well?" He asked.

"Actually," I started a speech in my defense.

"Actually?" The *starshina* spat his words out. "Actually, now you get your-self on the double to the sanitary battalion, otherwise, you'll crap all over us, you, Mr. Intellectual!"

Usually, the rule was that only those with wounds or contusions from battle got to the sanitary medical battalion, but I got there in the above manner.

I was assigned to the infectious disease division, set up in the forest, far from the "regular" wounded. I received my personal diet: a mug of tea and a dry biscuit three times a day. In a spacious ward I was the only one; no more soldiers in the whole division were suffering of my ailment.

I laid down on fragrant pine branches and watched how the tent cloth let the yellowish light through, and how the shadows of tree branches were crawling all over. The feeling of hunger dulled all higher thoughts and there was no energy left even for self-reproach.

Then a tempting demon appeared before me, in the form of a major of the military medical service. Having noticed a little book in English, *Little Lord Fauntleroy*, in my hands—a keepsake from home, my tempter said, "Listen, kid, stay with us. I won't release you prior to the advance, and then we'll enlist you as a paramedic. You'll survive. You'll go back to school. Think of it."

While I was thinking, my friend, that guy who started praying next to me during the bombing, was sent to me to counteract the tempter. He came to visit me and told me that later that day the guys were issued weapons and equipment: brand-new PPSh submachine guns, still in grease, as well as six magazines in a cartridge pouch and three hundred cartridges, close-combat knives, hand grenades, small entrenching tools, and a combined raincoat/shelter-half. The advance was about to start.

I ran to the Major. He listened to me and let me go, regretfully telling me, "You are a fool. They will kill you for nothing." They didn't kill me, though.

Later my son, Vassily, asked, "How did you survive?"

I replied, "At war, it is always like that—some survive, and some do not."

"Why was it that you survived?"

I didn't know how to respond to that.

On the Art of War

When it was bedtime for my children and I came over to them—to touch their foreheads or to wish them good night—they always asked me, "Sit with us. Tell us something."

Everything seemed to have been told, and more than once, but they persistently wanted more stories about the war. They wanted to know exactly and precisely how many tanks I had shot up and set on fire, how many planes I had brought down, how many fascists I had killed, and how I survived. They wanted to know the truth and nothing but the truth. As a result I produced the following autobiographical tales on the art of the war, as they call it. Perhaps I had been ironic about myself when I was younger and exaggerated some points. The lessons of eloquence as taught by our *starshina* were showing and will keep showing.

The *Starshina*

At the end of my prolonged active military service (which I still frequently dream of at night!) from the spring of 1944 through the end of 1950 I was promoted to the rank of *starshina*. To the rank, but not the function. After the war my job was that of a military translator and interpreter, at one of the military commandant's offices in Germany. The residents of the town in question, Bernau bei Berlin, addressed me with a lot of respect as *Herr Dolmetscher* (Mr. Translator) and even *Herr Leutnant* (Mr. Lieutenant) in attempts perhaps to flatter my vanity. Zhora, our colonel's private chauffeur, however, addressed me patronizingly as *"starshinka"* (little *starshina*).

A true company *starshina* is quite a character. He has to earn this position, although the way up, including mine, was not paved with rose petals. My path to it all started with a horse—or rather, a steed—and with a pig. This all was happening when we were in the Baltic region, since by the fall of 1944 we had been transferred there from Byelorussia.

There was (or perhaps still is) a very commonly applied formula in the military: "If you don't know how, we'll teach you, and if you don't want to, we'll make you." It was in its application to me that this formula failed.

The *starshina* of our company of submachine gunners didn't show any respect toward me. In his eyes, I was a worthless person. When during one night in a barn a pig chewed at one of my foot wraps, the *starshina* stated, "You won't make a soldier. Why would it pick your foot wrap and not anybody else's? Because it can smell Mr. Intellectual!"

The *starshina* assigned that shameful nickname (today in certain circles it might be substituted with a no less contemptuous "Mr. Democrat!") to me on the second day of my stay in the company. It stuck to me permanently, and I gradually got used to withstanding and bearing all blows of fate as if they were fair and natural consequences of my worthlessness.

Although that pig didn't really devour my foot wrap, it chewed on it, spit it out, and didn't even touch the other one. For some reason it obviously did not like the taste of them.

At the time we were advancing from Pskov to Riga along the highway. I still remember the names of all those little Latvian places—Ale, Vireci, Cesis. For some reason you remember them better when you have foot-marched through them, and even run through them in short stretches, crouching and occasionally pressing the trigger of your submachine gun.

Many years later my wife and I drove along the same route in a new Volga, which had been one of my highest desires to acquire. (I almost had to go to war to get this car in 1960, but that's a separate—no less dramatic—story, because of the cost and effort involved in getting it). I used to tell her things like, "Now Ligatne will be ahead of us. Or Sigulda." Every time she was surprised and every time I had to explain, "I went along this entire road on foot, all of it. Slowly. Stopping along the way. Sometimes the stops were necessary when we had to wait for artillery units to pull up and knock down the opposition ahead of us. Sometimes those stops were planned, when the soldiers needed to get a night's sleep."

That was the case in the episode I just mentioned with the pig. Our platoon was housed for the night in a well-built barn with fragrant straw and they allowed us to take our boots off. The surrounding situation was favorable as we were part of the second wave of troops to arrive.

I unwrapped my foot wraps and hung them over a little fencing in the corner—to let them dry and to let my feet rest. A big pink pig lived on the other side of the fencing. It was asleep and our noisy arrival didn't bother it whatsoever.

When the reveille was screamed at dawn, only one foot wrap was hanging on the fencing. Not far from the pig that was still asleep there was a bundle of cloth, covered with gooey mucus and looking absolutely disgusting.

By then I hadn't completely lost the squeamishness that I had brought from home, so I just put the second shoe on my bare foot. By the next night my foot sole had turned into a piece of worn flesh and I had to be given a rest from the marching company.

That was something that the *starshina* couldn't forgive me—and he was right. In war a soldier should be removed from the frontline only due to military reasons: following an order, as a result of wounds, contusion, or when killed. If it is not a wound, but a self-inflicted injury, the soldier is no longer one, he is a deserter and should be court-martialed. If the reason is sore feet or diarrhea, the soldier is not one yet, but still a mommy's ninny. This soldier cannot yet be relied upon in any serious situations.

I had a very kind mother and was still under the influence of *that* life. My transfer to a new status was just too shocking.

In his attempts to forcefully accelerate the process of my turning into a soldier, the *starshina* reached amazing heights of eloquence. It seemed unbelievable that a person of a seemingly plain and simple-minded appearance could generate such amazing comments and observations. In the war, however, I learned to pay less attention to looks and more to the awards and decorations on someone's chest and symbols on the shoulder boards—they would clearly testify what this particular person was worth in combat. Our *starshina* was worth a lot and in spite of all his sarcasm and criticism I felt that he didn't lose hope of making a soldier out of me. Which was exactly what I wanted to be myself.

He was fair, and never called me a coward. Everything else could be endured. Moreover his highly artistic comments addressed to me brought much enjoyment to my comrades—and are there many pleasures available to soldiers at war? The *starshina* exaggerated any given situation incredibly, outlining my true and imagined flaws with rich brush strokes, as a result depicting me as an extraordinary goofball. That was me. My friends got immense pleasure from our amazing bard, and the subject of his talented ranting ably supplied the necessary ingredients. Actually, it was no coincidence that I had been chosen.

On the Art of Carrying Water in Buckets

One day our wagon boy was killed so the *starshina* ordered me to harness a horse. My attempts to explain that I hadn't had any experience doing that were suppressed by the very same military formula I quoted earlier. As I turned to the left, the *starshina* commented, "You have learned to do an about face in the army? So you will learn how to harness, too," I set off to tackle the task.

The animal was standing by its wagon chewing hay. Most likely, it was finishing on the soft driver's seat that had been used by his late master. The horse was friendly and even kindly to me. It allowed me to get a grip on its bridle and readily followed me to the end of the wagon where the shafts were. The challenge, however, was that I had to make the horse step back between the shafts until it stood close enough to the wagon to allow me to harness it. It was at this stage that our mutual understanding ended. The horse totally ignored any and all attempts I undertook to make it step back. At one point I even thought it went to sleep. I let go of the bridle in order to contemplate what I should do next, and at that moment the horse sorted out the situation in its own manner. It took a few steps forward and stuck its head into the unfinished meal to complete whatever it had been doing until I interrupted. At the same time the horse securely bordered itself with the shafts from both fronts, thus becoming totally inaccessible for me. It stopped paying any attention to me whatsoever. I tried pulling the wagon away from it, but it calmly and steadily kept following the wagon and continued to munch. The horse felt that the wagon belonged to it, and I suppose it believed that the hay was its own, too. I didn't risk pulling it by its tail for fear of being kicked.

The *starshina* found us amidst these exercises. I felt his stare at the back of my neck. I looked back and there he was, standing with his legs wide apart and his hands on his sides as if in a cartoon. I turned to face him, straightened my belt, pulled down my uniform shirt and put my arms along my sides, "Comrade *Starshina*, this horse. . . ."

"There are no horses in the military. Every military horse is a steed!"

The *starshina* kept looking beyond me, at the wagon. Hearing some noise there, I looked back. The horse slowly stepped back, then turned around, stepped a few steps back again, and assumed the so-very-sought-after position, between the shafts. Its face bore an expression of utter innocence and purity of heart regarding the whole event.

"You got it?" The *starshina* asked me.

"Yes, sir," that was all I could respond, totally flabbergasted.

"Proceed to the kitchen. Report to the cook that I sent you to carry water. Can you carry water, in buckets? 'This *horse* . . .' " he hissed at me as I left.

Thus the object of the application of the *starshina*'s educational talents was chosen well.

I remember him very well, our *starshina*. That was not surprising—if even horses instantly obeyed his mere glance, shouldn't a man? If the *starshina* played not the supreme role, he certainly played a determining role in my whole life.

That assignment as a water bearer was the prelude to new incidents in my life, rich in encounters and emotions, successes and failures.

My ambition to show at any price how well I could carry water—although I had no experience whatsoever of this—resulted in yours truly immediately getting lost in search of the well. And the very first night on my own just about converted me into one of the *Tolstovtsy* [the spiritual and religious movement in Russia following in the steps of Leo Tolstoy, organizing communes, and so on. *Ed.*]

I didn't have great eyesight even then. I used to carry a pair of glasses with one cracked glass in my pocket, but tried not to wear them, having enough reasons for being mocked even without them.

On that particular night I had left them in my duffel bag, though, and thus I got confused and lost on my way. In the course of my nocturnal wandering in search of water I experienced an amazing adventure.

I came across an estate home hidden away in the middle of the forest. I knocked on the door, and it immediately opened for me. I was taken into a big parlor barely lit with oil lamps, filled with books and people. A battle was progressing not far away and the owners of the house, a large family, were very upset, sitting together restlessly at this late hour. An old man with a long gray beard was the head of the household; he wore an ancient *kossovorotka* with a woven thread instead of a belt (although I had never seen a *kossovorotka* before, I recognized it from the famous picture of Lev Nikolayevich Tolstoy walking across a field). [*Kossovorotka,* a Russian traditional shirt, with the collar fastening at the side. *Trans.*] My appearance at their doorstep, with the submachine gun on my chest and buckets in my hands was sudden and scary, but the old man addressed me calmly and in fluent Russian. He said he welcomed my appearance, as I was the first liberating soldier in this house amidst the wilderness. They sat me down at their table (being confused I had left my buckets and the gun at the door), and they treated me to milk, homemade rye bread, and honey. The women sighed over me, being so young, and asked me about my mother. And there was interest, shyness, and traces of a smile in the glance of a girl my age. I didn't feel even the remains of that inferiority complex to which I had become accustomed.

Then the old man took me into a nearby room also crammed with books and with a heavy old desk by the window. He showed me letters from Tolstoy, addressed to him, and the writer's autographed portrait. He told me of his encounters with Tolstoy in the early years of the century (before the First World War!). He talked of loving thy neighbor, about vegetarianism, non-resistance to evil, . . . which reminded me of the submachine gun I had left lying atop the buckets next to the door. Notwithstanding my Komsomol orthodoxy and intolerance, the old man, his family and his ancient home provoked in me only feelings of trust, empathy and peace. It smelled like home . . . and that felt good.

With these feelings I wandered back toward my company and my *starshina.* They accompanied me, helping me carry the buckets filled with water, and then bid me farewell once our field kitchen could be glimpsed through the trees.

The old man kept his promise and wrote to my family about that encounter. He kept corresponding with my father, and then, in the post-war years they started planning for a meeting. My father later used to forward the long and wise letters of the old man to me in Germany.

Some years later he died, but the image of that fleeting meeting in the dark forest, the obscure room, with golden spines of ancient books along the walls, faces both young and old, the feeling of trust toward people—will live on in my memory and warm my heart.

Twenty years later together with my wife we set off on a trip "along the sites of military glory"—that expression was in common use then. I tried to find that house, too, but I couldn't. It was gone, and now survives only in my mind. To think of all the things my mind is preserving. . . .

When I stopped by the company's kitchen with full buckets of water and with my submachine gun on my back, the *starshina,* of course, materialized in front of me. This time he was pretty brief (perhaps as a result of our late encounter and lack of an audience.) He said, "So, you changed your mind, eh?"

"Changed my mind about what, Comrade *Starshina*?"

"Change your mind about deserting?"

That was the first instance I got really mad at him. So I retorted, "Yes, I changed my mind, Comrade *Starshina*. I'll endure some more."

"What will you endure?" he asked me menacingly.

"Endure you, Comrade S*tarshina*."

He suddenly starts laughing and he asks me almost in a friendly manner, "Have you at least brought water?"

"Yes, sir."

"You've been searching for it too long. Should have worn your glasses. Come on, then, let's wash ourselves down to our waists with this water. We are moving out in an hour."

Meeting Death

It had been raining for days. My mind had accepted this as the normal and everlasting condition: water falling from above, as if through some sieve, and swampy slosh dough under our feet.

We walked along a forest path, generously overfilled with rain and now also treated by tens of thousands of feet and pressed with a thousand wheels. A large bore howitzer leaned on the side, with wheels so deep into the mud that the hubs weren't visible. Nor could one see the towing vehicle. Its service crew sat around, waiting for the help to arrive, sheltering from the rain. A T-34 tank roared and skidded in a pit it had made itself, and was veiled by gray exhaust smoke; clumps of mud flew everywhere, along with roots. Horses were grubbing away, getting exhausted. They got the worst jobs and they couldn't relieve their hearts by saying a harsh word. They simply collapsed, silently.

We walked along a road leading to the very front.

Perhaps, once, here, there used to be a regular clearing in the forest. One of those that split the forest into neat and accurate squares reminding of the presence of a man—a good and nurturing landowner. Perhaps, once there was a winding path running along the clearing, barely seen, from the bushes and young trees independently spreading along the clearance. This would not have been the environment for these young forest sprouts to be growing among the thick rows of the mature pine trees—there was neither space, nor sunshine. Both were available in the clearing, yet here the life and spreading processes of forest greenery were carefully controlled by men. That was why the clearance was maintained. The path was maintained due to irregular walkers—a forest ranger, a hunter, a kid attending some herd, a mushroom gatherer, or a girl carrying a jar of milk in her hands. All together—the forest, this clearing, the men, the path and the audacious and lively green underbrush—had maintained this balance for years and decades. That was, until this fall offensive.

Somebody drew a bold line along the dotted marking of this clearance on a large-scale map, assigned a number of units, and decided the order and procedure for their advance. Somebody else wrote the word "Approved" across the corner of that map and signed it.

Following that order, soldiers came to the clearing, and began applying their axes. Saws squawked. Mature trees fell with their heads rustling, covering the expanding clearance with their trunks. Thus the military road appeared. The troops set off along it, pushing, pressing the logged covering into soft forest ground.

That was when the mind-numbing fall rains started.

The logs soon stood on their ends, covered with shiny mud, under the weight of all those wheels. The logs that made up the road surface crawled away in all directions and finally drowned in the muddy ground. The artillery fire and bombings didn't exactly improve the state. The road was turning into a heavy torrent.

Trying to help horses on the verge of collapse, soldiers helped skidding vehicles to get out of the mud by shoving anything they could find into the road whirlpool—and again they turned to the same woods for help. The forest receded and got thinner and thinner along the clearing.

By the time it was our turn to move along the forest path, it was a picture of primeval chaos, an anteroom to hell. A sinner's final path must look that way—impassable, but also inevitable.

At the end of this road was the distinct roar of war.

Somewhere there, near the horizon, beyond the wide forest valley, everything animate and inanimate that the road managed to let through was ground into pieces and consumed with a rumbling. The advance itself was skidding and drowning in the fall slush.

Now the flow of people, carts, and vehicles was getting thinner, yet the forest on both sides of the tract was filling up with sounds of life—exclamations, axes chopping away, neighing horses, and rattling engines. Smoke ascended from temporary quarters and field kitchens. The troops were accumulating in the forest; a military coil was again contracting, to get ready, set, and give new thrust to the offensive at the appropriate moment.

What seemed chaotic in fact had been planned.

Our column, thin and marching out of sync, was now a part of the plan. Each of us carried the usual load: a submachine gun, magazine pouches, and an entrenching tool that keeps hitting the thigh. Our pockets and pouches were crammed with loose hand-grenades and cartridges. A kettle dangled under the duffel bag. The spoon was tucked behind a leg wrap. We didn't have helmets—they seemed to be a deficit here. Soldiers didn't like helmets anyway: all that extra weight and no real use.

Soaked through, and covered with mud up to our eyebrows, we didn't jabber, we were on a march.

Somebody knew our goal. Somebody knew the purpose and the time when we had to reach our destination.

Those in the forest had at least some kind of shelter above their heads—huts and dugouts—yet we had to go on.

Heavy artillery shells exploded somewhere ahead, not too far away, with a methodic and infamous regularity.

We had been marching since early morning. I lost track of how many days we'd been on the march. Regrouping, that's what they said we're doing.

Our "waterproof" raincoat–*cum*–shelter halves had long stopped protecting us from getting wet. The greatcoats and sailor jackets were soaked wet, and so were boots and puttees. The sticky mud had turned our boots into shapeless blocks of lead and the task of lifting them from the ground should have been entrusted to some machines, not to human beings. So we went on, one step after another.

And although we seemed to be crawling, barely moving our feet, sounds of war, dull and distant in the morning, were getting clearer and closer.

All thoughts were absent. The only, overpowering, feeling was that of annoying hunger and ultimate fatigue.

One phrase kept playing in my half-awake, gluey mind, "I remember the wonderful tunes of a waltz. . . ."

No further lyrics came to mind, but that particular part of the song kept spinning in my head. I could even identify the voices of individual musical instruments in my head. Then again, the velvety throaty mezzo-soprano, "I remember the wonderful tunes of a waltz. . . ." Was it "wonderful" or "beautiful"? I don't really remember. The singer sang it equally well both ways. I didn't have either the strength or desire to shake off this annoying melody. It originated and repeated from somewhere deep inside, regardless of my will, living independently. Most likely I simply had nothing with which to push it away. All thoughts had abandoned me—only brief fragments remained. They were shapeless pieces, wordless thoughts, thoughts that were more like images, like the image of that house I recently stumbled upon in the forest, or of my hometown.

"I remember the wonderful. . . ." A major blow hit the end of the column with a short roaring sound. "It's on the road. Half a kilometer away, caliber— one hundred fifty. It is the first explosion behind us during the whole day, which means there are some ten kilometers left until the vanguard area. If we head there now, we'll arrive before night." All this went through my brain automatically, without words. If words were needed, it would have probably sounded the way I just wrote. My ear detected another shot fired from the enemy's howitzer amidst all other sounds of the war, some fifteen seconds after the explosion. "Right ahead of us. The clearing ends somewhere there, some twelve kilometers away, going right into this gun, into the battery. It has been set up at an intersection of the road to prevent us from advancing. From such a position they will only be adjusting their range. Laterally their aim was just about perfect." These were some of the not-fully-developed thoughts in my head that translated into an urgent sense of danger. Perhaps an animal would detect danger in a similar fashion, through sensed images. When alarmed and all ears, it makes its body tight, ready to flee at any moment.

We could not flee, though. If that was not a single shot just to unnerve us, however, and if the enemy artillery observers had spotted our column and noted the impact, then we'd better start. There was no order, though, and automatically our feet continued their monotonous trod. "I hear the wonderful. . . ." My foot slipped into a slot between the boards, I lost my balance and fell into soft mush, my wrist burned from a bad scrape. I hurt my elbow falling and the cold muddy juice leaked inside my sleeve. An explosion rocked my world, the second round going off. This one was also behind us, but much closer now, much too close. Shrapnel whizzed by. A horse left on the road neighed wildly, trying to get out of its harness. "Now it's just short. . . ." The order "Spread out!" was shouted and there was another explosion, now right ahead of us, some two hundred meters away. "Well, here comes the end."

My legs freed themselves with insane speed from the clinging bog and threw my body away, to the side, towards the forest, the trees. In mere seconds the next, . . . but the forest was now so far, endlessly far away, and suddenly the clearing had become so wide, and the shelter from the trees so insufficient. . . .

I fell into a gap amid some tree roots, behind a thick trunk. At the very same instant the first series of rounds exploded, explosions both on the road and here among us who were alive, warm, and weak. Metal whizzed around. Branches, roots, and clumps of earth rained on our heads, followed by a cut tree crown that crashed down. I stayed down, pressing my body into pine tree needles, and smelling putrid foliage, such a peaceful smell of fall forest. Earth moved as if alive, sliced deep and shattered with explosions. A few seconds of silence, then I heard the scream of a wounded soldier, and another series of rounds. . . . That's it, now this is it. "I remember the wonderful. . . ." Something hit me on the back. It was a different kind of a blow, a tree, a root, just a piece of wood. Again a few seconds of silence when all I wanted to do was to jump up and run crouching, anywhere, just not stay here—to run like a deer, rabbit, or a moose would—not looking back and overcoming all obstacles with ease. To run for one's life! But, no, I mustn't. Running now meant death. The only rescue now was next to the ground, in the ground, next to the tree trunk. It covered my head, my chest; it could take and swallow the shrapnel, the one that's targeting me. I didn't care about my legs. The head, I needed to cover my head. To press myself in, to become invisible. "The wonderful tunes of a waltz. . . ." Nothing alive had survived—it could not possibly have survived. The forest no longer existed; it was a desert, a primeval chaos all around, a chaos that was sliced through every second. Which order did he give over there, in his own language? "Battery, four rounds, quick fire. . . ." Or was it six?

The sound of stomping feet, a hissing breath—somewhere close, above my head. And an explosion—hitting the brain, ears, the entire body! Tree roots moved with a screeching sound, and an unbelievably heavy weight was pressing me into the ground. This was it.

Then silence, interrupted only by some of those dull sounds of the war, but this was as good as silence.

Something thick and warm was running down my face, my neck. I didn't feel any pain. Why didn't I feel any pain? Why? This was it, wasn't it? When you're killed, almost killed—you don't feel what's happening to you. It seems alright, and, in fact, it's the end.

The sour smell of explosives. I heard voices as if from behind some wall. Living voices. "Here are two more. Just look at them. . . ."

I tried to move.

"He's alive. Come on, guys. . . ."

Some shuffling and motion took place above me. The heavy weight was moved away, it was gone. They helped me up.

My face was covered in blood, my rain cape was bloody, and my hands were in blood, but I was on my feet. The forest surrounded me. It was there, it hadn't been destroyed, and it hadn't been annihilated. It lived on. My sheltering tree had been mutilated, half a trunk and a crown that had landed next to my hiding spot.

"Just look at him. . . ." Another soldier was lying at my feet. He had no face. Instead of a face he had. . . . It was his blood that was all over me.

"He covered you up. Already dead, he covered you."

A crater was some five meters away. As a result of it a soldier was thrown on top of me. He was thrown, together with all the metal that ripped and tore his body apart, with clumps of earth, and roots. . . .

"Ok, guys, let's go."

"We should bury him."

"They will. We have to go on. We have to be there by night."

We got back to the clearing. We carried out the wounded and injured. We formed some sort of column again.

Our numbers did not even seem to be depleted.

"Forward, march!"

The feet resumed their work.

"The waltz, that beautiful waltz," the final verse of the refrain suddenly came into my head. "That explosion sure shook you all over!"

The forest was all the same. It stood aside, letting us through. We would leave, and it would gradually return. The clearing would be narrow as would be the path. And a girl with a jar of milk in her hands would. . . .

The artillery fire was increasing ahead of us.

"One-hundred-fifty-caliber. They are wrecking that railway station. Vainede."

The *starshina* was walking next to me. He didn't carry that much on him, though. Well, that was a commander's privilege.

"Are we going toward that?" I asked.

"What, you don't feel like it?" he replied

"I just wish we could reach some place, take a rest, get dry. We are about to rot."

"Better to rot marching than in the ground," the *starshina* observed philosophically. "Come on, cheer up."

We'd been shuffling on the road since dawn, and there was no news about a rest stop ahead. My stomach was empty and as if glued to my spine.

"I wish we had some grub," I said.

"You, Kravchenko, have begun to express yourself in a most uncivilized manner. Want to sound as if you were born in the streets? Afraid of missing something? If I now would let you rush to the kitchen, you will surely just end up in the sanitary battalion again."

He could not forget my debut in his company.

"Now I'm experienced," I replied.

"I once read in a very smart book that if you feel hungry, take a few slow sips of water. It is important that you do it slowly, though, not hastily, enjoying every drop. In half an hour you won't feel hungry again," he suggested.

"Thank you for the valuable advice, Comrade *Starshina*."

"Yes, that's better."

Wooden roofs could be seen beyond the treetops. We walked along the edge of a village, while the shells kept exploding somewhere out there. Again we turned to the forest haven.

In the darkness we relieved a unit on the frontline, crawling inside warm trench shelters. Now the Germans were the only ones ahead of us.

Were we really going to attack over this bog?

Under the Cover of a Smoke Screen

The rain slowed down.

The soil was loamy and the dugout I made turned out neatly. Under the cover of the breastwork I set up smoke pots in a row, put my submachine gun in a convenient position and began waiting for the morning. Our trench extended behind me, along the crest of a riverbank.

Beyond that there were meadows and a forest—where our service troops were. In front of me there was a field—and somewhere out there, by its edge, some 200 to 300 meters away, there were enemy positions. Occasionally a clap would be heard coming from that direction, and there would be an illumination flare hanging from the sky. In the morning, after the preliminary artillery bombardment and under the cover of the smoke screen to mask their movements, our units would advance. Why we would be here, otherwise, on these outposts with these smoke pots? I didn't know whether we would just attack here—or perhaps in other places, too. I only knew my assignment— once the preliminary bombardment ended, the artillery fire would be concentrated deep into the enemy's position. After a flare appeared in the sky, it was my task to create a smoke screen. The wind was toward the enemy's position, everything was right.

At dawn, however, the racket of guns and roar of six-barreled mortars unexpectedly came from *that* side. I was lying low, pressing my body into the bottom of my small trench, and clay clumps were raining down on me. After one particularly close explosion, one of the smoke pots fell on me from the breastwork and I decided that it was a direct hit. There was one, indeed, but only somewhat later when a round opening suddenly appeared in the rear smooth side of the dugout. All this went on forever, but the initial changes in the situation didn't become clear to me at first. The earth stopped falling inside my dugout and there were no more nearby explosions. I looked out of my shelter and saw tanks and infantry advancing against our positions along the field. I looked back and saw little figures running back toward the forest. Not so long ago our battalion had received some new recruits that had never seen any kind of fighting before. . . .

I lit the fuses on the remaining pots, grabbed my submachine gun and thrust myself back toward our trench. It was empty. I rolled down the hill to the creek, crossed it by leaping, and fled across the meadow toward the shelter of the forest. I was alone in the whole wide world. I was running and could feel with my spine the Germans taking over our trench, and slowly getting ready to aim and fire at me, like they would shoot a rabbit thrashing around in an open field.

And yet I reached the forest, collapsing at the edge of the meadow, tripping over a strap of somebody's rifle. I heard voices not far away—they were digging out new trenches. Having taken over the position by the river, the Germans calmed down. Indeed it wouldn't be much fun going against them across that meadow. Everything was in plain view, as I, myself, had verified.

As I found out years later from historical publications, the Kurland group of the enemy remained trapped on the peninsula until May 1945 and surrendered at the end of the war. [The Kurland Peninsula in Latvia had one of the last large concentrations of German forces when the Third Reich surrendered on 8–9 May 1945. *Ed.*] Soon we were transferred to fight toward the Vistula, near Warsaw, the direction of the main thrust. There, starting in January 1945, the most dramatic and fateful events of the war in Europe were unfolding.

The *starshina* appeared in front of me when I was sitting on a little tree stump and studied the flaps of my greatcoat with blunt wonder, looking at the torn holes in them.

"You are a lucky one," he said. "What have you armed yourself for?"

"No, I found this rifle, Comrade *Starshina*. Where do I take it?" I asked.

"You went for a stroll and you found it, eh? Give me that rifle; I'll see that it is put to good use. Where are the smoke pots?"

"The pots are there," I replied. "They were used for erecting the smoke screen after the preliminary bombardment, in accordance with the order."

"What about the green flare signal?" he asked me acidly, sitting down and pulling his tobacco pouch out.

"There was no signal, that's for sure. I acted according to the new situation. I retreated under the cover of the smoke screen and followed everybody else. The trench was empty."

"You, Mr. Intellectual! You have invented something new in the art of war. 'A bug-out under cover of smoke screen.' Or 'a smoke pot used as an individual soldier's personal weapon.' The Germans must have been pretty surprised!"

"They must have been, since I made it out alive." I responded. "They must have thought we used poisonous gas as they started putting on gas masks. They are disciplined. *Ordnung muss sein* (order is necessary). Otherwise, I wouldn't have made it to the forest. See, how my greatcoat got torn."

"Yes, what's the point of issuing you new uniforms?" he retorted. "Well, now you have one tried and heroic greatcoat. Did you figure out how to erect the screen?"

"I don't know, Comrade *Starshina*. I must have thought that you would punish me for abandoning military ammunition. In fact, I didn't think much at all. Their tanks were too close, and our guys were already by the forest. The other guys were so fast! So I set off those pots and headed back to our lines."

Knowing I wasn't a smoker, the *starshina* teased, "And you're the one who doesn't even smoke, aren't you?" Then, noticing my mood, he asked, "Why are you so gloomy?"

"It's depressing to bug out, Comrade *Starshina*."

"Oh, it depresses you, does it?" he said. "You should have been around in 1941, then you would have known what a real depression was. Retreating some three hundred meters, big deal. Our entire force here is made up of one lousy trench. We thought of advancing, but you can see for yourself. . . . Had we had some tanks, reinforcements, and supporting artillery, we wouldn't have needed your smoke screen. See how things progress at the other fronts. Oh well. Go eat something. The kitchen has arrived. We'll keep fighting."

<hr>

Many years ago I visited Vainede together with my wife. We walked all day long through the surrounding fragrant green valleys; we found that little river and the remains of the trench on the loamy side of the river. I said to my wife, "Here is where I retreated, running." We walked through the area around that little town, lost among the forests, and came out to the railroad, leading to the station that had been bombarded. A steam engine with a protruding chimney overtook us. It was pulling a train of charming little wooden cars. The engine man on the old train did a really sweet thing: first, he blew the whistle in our honor and then, coming up close to us, he looked out of his cabin and gave us a genuinely friendly smile. It seemed that if I'd asked, he'd have stopped and let us take a ride. The cars were obviously an inheritance from the former Latvian Railways. Had they had an exit outside of each compartment and shining brass handles along the pot-bellied sides of the cars—as well as a wide board along which the stately-looking fare-collector would deftly get from one compartment to another—they would have looked just like the cars from my Warsaw childhood.

We brought flowers to the memorial to Soviet soldiers, next to their imposing common graves. In the evening we invited our Latvian hotel hostess to join us and share a drink in memory of those killed.

I will never again be in those parts and visit those graves; I'm not that strong anymore. State borders separate us now, with all the different visas and invitations required. Who will invite me there since the Latvians now see Soviets as "occupiers"? I thought we were the liberators. Those, resting in the mass graves, who are they?

An Encounter

The months of my war passed by. I became a real soldier. Then, providence acting in an amazing manner, I was sent to Warsaw.

I walked from one end of Warsaw to the other, through the ruins of the elegant city of my childhood. Had it been so long ago, my childhood? Warsaw of the 1930s with its horse-drawn wagons and gas street lights. Although, of course, there were taxis, automobiles, and electric lights, too. We lived at that transition time when one thing pushed out another. Memory tends to preserve the oldest things. I used to follow a lamplighter. He had a long and neat ladder that he would hang on to a streetlight post; he climbed it skillfully and lit the light. The streetlight in use made a slight hissing sound. In the morning the lamplighter put the lights out with a special little hood set on a long pole. Warsaw. Its residents liked to call it Little Paris. Everybody wants to be like Paris, even if only a little one.

Had it been so long ago, my childhood? It had been less than six years since we left Warsaw, and then a stunning kaleidoscope of events began swirling around that brought me back there again, but now as a soldier of the Red Army.

In My Old Neighborhood

Having learned that I was a former Warsaw resident, the commander gave me a three-hour leave. I walked along familiar streets and was surrounded by dead, empty sandlots. I searched for familiar houses and found walls with empty openings instead of windows. I crossed a pontoon bridge over the Vistula to its eastern side and went to Praga, where my first school was, with *Panna* Javorska, Jozek Puchalski, Tadek Vrona. . . . Praga had been liberated during the fall, so there was less destruction in this part of the city. The school was in its place, too, but there was no babbling of children's voices heard. Now the building housed a military hospital. That was all right, too; the school remained a school. We were not like the Nazis; it was we, the liberators, who had arrived.

There was no house where a thirteen-year-old girl by the name of Tanya lived on the second floor, in the far right windows. Instead of the house there were remains of its walls and an ugly pile of rubble and bricks, already covered with some bushes. It was her resting place. I took my hat off and stood there for a minute. For some reason the words of a prayer came into my head: *Lord, let the soul of your deceased servant rest. . . .*

The house where I grew up was standing. On the second floor I knocked on the door. My hand felt a familiar scratch on the brass handle. I had once made that scratch on the surface polished by long use. It was the time I turned up without a key and sat next to the door waiting for Mama to arrive. Being bored, I had played around with a piece of metal file that I had picked up in the yard. This was a thousand years ago, in another life.

Now some strange people opened the door and I spent a few moments in an unfamiliar setting of the apartment that was familiar to me down to the smallest crack in the wall. Here in the corner, Father Ignatius used to sit in our old wingback sofa with carved decorations. He smoked and coughed and his rare comments were the first seeds of doubt in the inviolability of the current world. That world was gone, was crushed. Were we happy then, in that apartment? Perhaps, when parting, childhood itself leaves behind a barely sensed aroma of happiness. . . . I had to hurry, and I sat down at the table with the new residents of that home for only a moment. We each had a swig of moonshine—there was not more anyway—to *our* victory. Decades have passed and the opinions of contemporary Poles and Russians on the victory of 1945 have transformed greatly.

Then I went running to where our troops were taking their rest because I had to be back in time.

Forward, to the West!

The worst thing you can do is to try and catch up with a tank army enjoying the freedom of operational movement. We marched for twenty hours, had a hot meal, and slept for four hours only. Sometimes there was no hot meal, but a dry ration. Again another twenty hours of marching. We could sleep as we marched, especially if we could hold onto something. You were asleep while your feet kept marching on. Or one could reflect while marching. Or recall things. It was much easier to recall things in the first hours of the march when the mind wasn't yet so foggy.

My hand held onto a cart as my feet kept marching. My head was filled with images of the past and pictures from my childhood. There were horses in those images, too. The cart was transformed into a wagon and there was

Dad in a Panama hat. The air smelled of the wheel grease and of horses. Invisible bees kept buzzing. Their buzzing got louder and louder. . . . Then explosions followed—one, two, three—slicing through the air, hitting the ears. Random shooting and then machine-gun fire. "Cover!" My legs threw my body to the right, into the roadside gutter, prior to awakening the brain. A *Messerschmitt* flew by at a low level, then turned around, climbed straight up, moved ahead, aimed, and dived at us again. Somebody screamed "Air!" although it was already clear. "Target the plane! Fire!" The fighter plane flew over us again and disappeared beyond the forest treetops. A wounded horse in agony thrashed around on the road, screaming wildly. We got out of the gutters and shook off some dirt. "Fall in!" Everybody seemed to be all right. We set off. I avoided walking close to the prostrate horse, and tried not to meet its stare. We were fine—and the horse? A gunshot was fired behind my back; somebody felt pity for it.

The Loudspeaker

After Warsaw, somewhere in the west of Poland, an unfamiliar lieutenant walked up to our fire and asked us to fill his flask with tea. While I burned my fingers holding the hot flask, he asked me who I was, where I came from, and whether I had studied anywhere. Finding out that I understood German and a bit of English, he instantly tested that knowledge of mine. My comrades, witnessing the conversation, for the first time, as it seemed, abstained from joking at my expense. The lieutenant wrote down my name and my company affiliation. Then he left, thanking us for the tea. He never appeared in my life again because soon afterward he was killed. Somebody must have opened up his little notebook, however, and paid attention to the record about a German-speaking private named Kravchenko of a Submachine Gun Company within the 356th Rifle Division. That somebody sent an order to send Private Kravchenko to the regimental headquarters.

"Most likely they will send you to a continuation course," the *starshina* commented when he received the order. He left it to me to guess whether it would be for advancing in the art of horse harnessing or water carrying or perhaps in making smoke screens.

My thoughts then were basically, "I'll be going to where mines don't explode and where people aren't suddenly ripped apart in front of your eyes, just like I could be. Well, what can a soldier really know about his fate when there is a war going on?"

I set off to regimental headquarters in the rear, located some three kilometers away. At first I moved by leaps and bounds, then walked upright. Little did I expect that only a few hours later I would not only not be in the rear, but instead find myself in no-man's land.

The Germans were holding a farmstead. Their retreat venues had long since been cut off. Well armed and sustained by mortar fire, however, they used *Panzerfausts* to stubbornly hold their ground and block our advance. [The *Panzerfaust* was the first effective individual soldier's anti-tank rocket launcher. *Ed.*]

At Regimental Headquarters I reported, as ordered, to the Second Deputy Staff Commander, who was the regiment's intelligence officer. And so I reported, "Comrade Guards Captain," (the captain wore a Guards badge on his chest though we were not a Guards unit) "Private Kravchenko has appeared, according to your order!"

"Appeared, huh?" The Guards Captain repeated, and added acidly, "Christ appeared before the people! You *report* in the military, and do not appear, do you understand?" Following that, he scrutinized me with a doubtful look, "Have you been in the military for long?"

"Soon it will be a year, Comrade Captain."

"How old are you?" he asked.

"I'm eighteen. Turning nineteen."

"What, they drafted you at seventeen, did they?"

"I asked to," I replied. "To be with everybody else."

For some reason the Captain sighed and paused for a moment. Then he added, this time without spitefulness, "Oh well, then. You are certainly aware of the farmstead situation. We need to get rid of the enemy in this farmstead by the morning. We have received the order from above. They say you can read in German? Now, read this. Read loudly. With emotion and meaning, and try to convince the listeners!"

The text was a message to the German garrison, explaining the current situation and exhorting them to capitulate.

"That's all right," the Captain summarized, having heard my performance. "You just about convinced me that I must surrender. So then, our boys dug out a full-size trench last night, some 100 to 150 meters from the farmstead. When it gets dark our scouts will take you there. You take this." A huge tin loudspeaker stood in the corner of the room. "You'll set this thing on the breastwork, toward the enemy, not to the sky. At first light, you start your broadcast. Just keep your head low. Our guys will be near, and won't let the Germans get to you. Take a few hand-grenades, just in case. If need be, we'll cover you with fire. We have to try and convince the Germans. It may well work—they are not as they used to be anymore. Thus we'll save lives. If they don't listen to us, then we'll storm the place. You understand your assignment? Well, then proceed."

In the night we belly-crawled to the trench with the loudspeaker covered in a cloak, so as not to make any noise.

I spent a few hours, by far not among the best of my life, in my hole. I stood in the darkness, listening intently to the strange night sounds, and each of them seemed to forebode danger.

Finally dawn began to arrive. It was time to start. I assumed an appropriate position in the trench, turned the loudspeaker toward the farmstead and shouted, "German soldiers! You are completely surrounded and your situation is hopeless. Surrender now voluntarily. The Soviet command guarantees to save your lives, to provide you with food of our own soldiers' standard and after the war to let you return to. . . ."

At first there was machine-gun fire, then mortars joined in. A brief howl and racket, then more and more explosions, right by my side.

I pressed my body to the side of the trench. Clumps of earth filled the air. They even entered the loudspeaker as if it were some filter and flew straight into my mouth. I spit them out. The loudspeaker jerked from heavy pounding. "Now a mortar shell will hit me right on the head," I thought. "That's just my luck—now they're honoring me personally." Something barks unexpectedly from behind me, and then again and again. It was our battery covering me as the Captain told me they would.

It got quiet.

"German soldiers!" I continued. "If you don't surrender, you'll be killed, and the farmstead will be destroyed by aviation and artillery fire. . . ."

Our side fired at the other edge of the farmstead. Heavier guns also pounded from somewhere and a wave of explosions slowly approached the farmstead from behind. "They must be doing that so as not to hurt us—me and those that are somewhere near." The rate of explosions close to my trench became less frequent; most likely our guys knocked out their battery. A few minutes passed.

"German soldiers!" I began again.

I didn't notice how suddenly everything got quiet and then a voice right above my head said, "Enough yelling. The Germans are surrendering. You've convinced them!"

I peeked over the breastwork; a field-gray column moved straight at us, with a white flag in the front. Guys from the reconnaissance unit next to me helped me up and out of my trench, patted me on the back, and said, "Good boy!" I picked up the hand grenades, stuffed them into my pockets, and hung my submachine gun on my shoulder.

"Don't leave your instrument here," they added, reminding me about the loudspeaker. "It's military property, and you may still have some use of it!"

The captured Germans passed me. They looked at my "weapon" and me, and I looked back at them. They could have killed me minutes ago. Now it was all over, and they were still among the living, having done their share of fighting.

A scout squad was sent to check out the farmstead. I picked up the loud-speaker and strolled back to our side. An incredible fatigue came over me and my legs trembled; I didn't have any energy left to be glad, but I didn't feel depressed, either. Now the *starshina* would have said something like "Why so gloomy then?"

Guards Captain Vlassov, the head of the intelligence section, was having breakfast. Somehow, I had to report.

"Comrade Guards Captain! Private Kravchenko appears after the completion of his military . . . after the completion of his mission!"

"Here you go again! Really!" he replied. "You have to report as follows, 'Private Kravchenko has arrived after the successful completion of his combat mission!' You understand me, professor? Sit down, have a drink!"

The alcohol clasped my throat and gagged me. I quickly started to chew on something. My head was instantly filled with fog and my ears began to ring. All by itself, my mouth decided to put on a silly smile that I couldn't wipe off my face. I could see funny sparks in the Captain's eyes and heard him as if through some muffling cotton, "Go to the scouts, eat something hot, and get some sleep. Hero!"

I got up, saluted, turned around, and marched toward the door. There the loudspeaker stood where I had left it. I made a motion to pick it up and then remembered that I didn't need it any more as it had been given to me just to complete the mission.

Waking up in the evening I found out that I didn't have to return to my company anymore. I was reassigned to the reconnaissance platoon, with an interpreter's duties—taking the place of that killed lieutenant, where I would serve until the victorious end of the war.

That wasn't the end of my acquaintanceship with the *starshina*, however. We were to meet at least twice more. He would present me with gifts and I will speak about them more ahead. The *starshina* had a capability, or rather, I would say, a mysterious talent—to turn up in front of me at certain moments, as if marking milestones in my military career. I wish I met him later, in my civilian life. I met others that were like him and reminded me of him, though. How else could it be? Life without them would be dull.

Gifts Differ

One colleague of mine, knowing about my continuous interest for everything related to World War II, gave me a German road atlas published in the years of the Third Reich, around 1937. In those maps, Germany's outlines reminded one of those of a wolf's head that had its mouth and fangs pointing east. Her father brought home the atlas in 1945 as a war trophy. Decades passed. Going through her father's papers, she came across that worn brochure. It was a trace, an echo of the war.

The atlas was a plain-looking edition, on gray paper, small scale. The pages were all covered with names of towns and villages and a dense red grid of roads. Once I was looking at the page with the territory east of Berlin, which I knew very well, and then a word suddenly came up in my mind. I didn't even comprehend at that moment its meaning or from where it appeared. Yes! It was a name of a place, of a little place, and I recalled the well-built farmers' houses lining its streets. I promptly armed myself with a magnifying glass and began studying the blue line of that year's border between Germany and Poland and I found it. There it was! Mellentin, of course!

Mellentin

Guards Captain Vlassov entered the properly-built barn where the scouts were having a rest, and shook wet snow off his coat.

He opened up his mapboard, pointed, and said, "Here, guys, is a river we crossed five kilometers ago, do you know its name?"

The guys kept silent.

"The Netze. Or the Notec in Polish. Got it? Look over here. Poland ended at the Netze. Germany started at the Netze. The border of 1939. We are in the enemy's den. Are you getting it? *In the den!* What's the date today?"

The guys were still silent. Then a faltering voice, "I think, . . ."

" 'I think, I think. . . .' It's 1 February. You ignorant people. You don't know crap. Forgot the calendar." The Captain was obviously in a good mood. "You must remember this date! On 1 February 1945 we entered the enemy's den. Now we'll fight him in his *own* land. Got it now, guys? Schönlanke is seven kilometers ahead of us. That's it. Germany! As you well know, the enemy hasn't been observed ahead. Looks like he has fled, and in haste. We have an order to move ahead until contact, in the direction of Schönlanke and Mellentin. Here along this country road," he said, pointing to the map. "The highway Schneidemühl-Landsberg-Berlin is beyond Mellentin. Berlin! Do you feel it, guys? Schneidemühl is here, twenty-five kilometers to the right, a major location. Our neighbors are already working there. We set off at midnight. Rifle battalions will follow us in marching columns. Our immediate mission is to check out Schönlanke and the road toward Mellentin. If we are not stopped, we reconnoiter the place and the situation to the west of it. We take over the highway and stay put until the rifle battalions arrive. Yes, there are none of ours ahead of us. Earlier we have been covered by tanks all of the time. Now the enemy alone is ahead. Since we shook them up well there is no continuous line of defense. So that is why we shall go through one of the gaps until contact. Keep in mind, anything is possible out there. He's on home turf now and knows everything here."

This was the first time Guards Captain Vlassov gave such a long speech to his scouts.

The guys had indeed only a vague notion of the calendar at this time. On the dawn of 14 January, after heavy preliminary artillery bombardment we had started from the Vistula, from near Magnusew off to the northwest. In a day we seized Pilitsa, and in another day, riding the tanks of the Second Guards we were on the southwestern outskirts of Warsaw. We took a little rest and turned to the west. Since then we had been on forced march. Two weeks? More? It had been a chase after an armored avalanche, until that very day. Yes, two weeks it was. Now the tanks had turned toward somewhere else and there were none of our guys ahead.

We entered a quiet farmstead in the snow-covered forest and found properly-built stone buildings with tiled roofs. Guns roared somewhere in the north, near Schneidemühl, but it was quiet here. Cows mooed as if there was no war. There were no residents either, however. None. They were all gone.

So it had been two weeks with no rest. We "unlearned" to use the calendar. The Germans had a new weapon—the *Panzerfaust*. We took over a whole storage room filled with them, and armed ourselves. They had Fausts and so did we. It was a serious threat to tanks. They were fleeing so fast that they had left everything behind there, in Pilitsa, including this arms and ammo depot. It was amazing how we were advancing. When they were not far from Moscow and Stalingrad, we fought for every meter, and fought a long while. Here in a mere two weeks' time we must have crossed some five hundred kilometers. The Captain said that we were covering sixty kilometers a day, all by foot.

Beyond Mellentin is the highway to Berlin. We could almost see the goal now. At last.

In the morning a Messerschmitt flew low and didn't open fire, I thought. Most likely it was going back—and empty. Yes, we had pushed them back well. Would we go for Berlin? So in a month or two it would be all over?

"Do you understand the mission? the Captain asked. "The reconnaissance platoon sets off on sleighs; we've got a few here. The logistics people are getting them ready now. I'll go with you. Now catch some sleep. We are moving out at midnight. We have to get on the Berlin highway in the morning."

It seemed as if I was awakened, however, the moment I fell asleep.

"Report to the Guards Captain, in the headquarters. On the double!" I was told by some stern voice.

I reported to headquarters. "Here," said Guards Captain Vlassov, "are some local residents, Germans. Fascists."

An old couple was sitting on a bench in the corner. They looked neat and had gray hair. They were sitting, clinging close to each other, like newlyweds.

"You call yourselves scouts? 'Nobody's here, everybody's gone!' Well here they are—they were found hiding under the bed, in the gatehouse. Ask them why they didn't flee with the rest?"

I interpreted.

The old man said, *"Unsinn.* (No use.) *Sowieso Schluss.* (It's the end, in any case.) *Wir sind hier geboren. Wir wollten hier bleiben. Sowieso Schluss.* (We were born here, and we wanted to stay here. It's the end.)"

The Captain asked, "What's the end?"

For the first time the old man looked up. *"Alles kaputt. Deutschland. Menschen. Kinder. Alles."* (Everything is over), he replied.

"Why *Kinder?* Which children then?" The annoyed Captain interrupted.

"Unsere Kinder," the old man said. *"Zwei Söhne gefallen."*

"Your sons? Where did they die?"

"Demyansk. Stalingrad," he answered.

"We didn't invite them there," the Captain said.

I interpreted. The old man nodded.

"Did you fight yourself?" the Captain asked.

"Jawohl. Im ersten Weltkrieg. In the First World War."

"I see, *Jawohl,* huh? You got an Iron Cross?"

"Jawohl," the German answered.

"War-lovers. Is there anybody else in the farmstead?"

Here I hesitated.

"What?"

"I don't know the word 'farmstead', Comrade Captain."

"Damn it, say 'here'! *Wer ist hier noch?"* For some reason the Captain was mad.

"Wir sind allein. (We are the only ones.) *Alle geflohen.* (Everybody ran away.)" the old man replied.

"Okay," the Captain finally said. "Take them away. Damn them! Take them to that gatehouse, near the clearing. Make sure they stay there and don't get in our way!"

I straightened up and hung my submachine gun on my shoulder. As if by some command the old couple stood up, still holding hands.

The old man turned to me, *"Was sagte der Offizier? Wollen sie uns erschiessen?"*

"What?" Captain Vlassov clinched his fists. *"Erschiessen?* We are not Hitler's men, to kill old people! Tell this old Fascist. . . ."

The old woman was pulling her man to the door, but he asked, *"Warum Faschisten? Faschisten-Italien. Mussolini."*

"Fascists, in Italy? And here?" the Captain asked.

"Hitler. *NSDAP.* Nazis," the German replied.

The Guard Captain said, "What do you know? There seems to be a difference. Don't worry, though. We'll hang Mussolini, and then we'll hang Hitler."

"Ah, *Scheisse,*" the German said.

"What?"

I interpreted, "Crap." I remembered that word well, from *those days* at the chalk factory. The old man reminded me somewhat of our shouting Vatter.

"All right. Take them away. Make sure they don't get in our way. I don't have people to guard them—warn them—and somebody may not know the difference. Yes, ask them, are there any troops in Schönlanke?"

"I don't know," I interpreted the old man's response. "Yesterday everybody ran away from there. We stayed behind. I don't know."

"Okay, take them away," the Captain said.

Then the German told me near the house, "It seems to be empty in Schönlanke. Everybody ran away. They said that you would kill everyone, children, old people, and women. Everybody."

"The soldiers, they ran away, too?" I asked.

"Seems to be empty," the old man repeated. "Everybody's gone."

The old woman pulled him by the hand inside the house, saying nothing.

"And in . . . Mellentin?" I asked.

"Mellentin? It's a small place. Why? Yes, there are roads, crossroads there."

"Sollst nicht klatschen," the woman mumbled.

I didn't know the verb *klatschen.*

"Warum. Genug Leichen. (Enough of killing.) I don't know for sure about Mellentin, but there are roads there, crossroads."

"You must sit here! Don't come out! Do you understand?"

The door closed shut.

Going back to the scouts in the barn I thought of how I needed a dictionary, "I need a dictionary. *Klatschen.* . . ."

Heavy German horses refused to trot—either they were not trained to or just didn't understand Russian. They paced in a lively step. The spacious sleighs screeched and knocked on the bumps of the road. The wet snow kept falling.

We were sitting along the sides, legs hanging out and submachine guns in the ready position. No talking, no smoking. If something went wrong, we would jump out into the road ditches and open fire. The assumption was that the Germans wouldn't immediately be able to figure out what was going on; it was twilight, then sleighs and people in them. Who knew on whose side they were? They weren't yet used to having enemies in their own land. For us, though, a word would have been enough. Two more sleighs followed us, at some distance. Each of them had a squad.

Finally we didn't have to walk.

"Comrade Guards Captain," I whispered quietly.

"No talking!"

"There, by the house, I didn't get one word. . . ."

The Captain moved over. "What is it?"

"I asked the old man about Mellentin. The old woman mumbled something to him, 'don't . . .' and I didn't get the rest. And then he said, 'Enough killing' and that there are roads and a crossroads in Mellentin, and that was all. He didn't say plainly that there were no troops in Mellentin. He was very vague."

"Well, the Fascists remain Fascists. Our mission is to scout the area. We'll get there, and we'll find out. Is that all?"

"Yes, sir."

"Okay." Then he paused. "You need a dictionary. You spent three years with them, and couldn't learn the language properly."

I got his joke, but thought, *And had I learned it to perfection you would have asked me, "How? Must have spent a lot of time socializing with them there." You never know what is worse. Now, though, it is worse that I didn't understand* Klatschen.

Captain Vlassov was assigned to our rifle regiment following recovery from wounds for the umpteenth time. Prior to that he had served in some Guards unit. He cherished his right to be addressed with the Guards title and to continue to wear the badge on his chest. He didn't request to be returned to the Guards, however, saying, "Never mind! We, too, can fight Guards-style with guys like you, right?"

The guys really respected the Guards Captain.

The road to Schönlanke had not been repaired in a while, and potholes could be felt everywhere, even under thick layers of snow. Our sleighs were shaking and on top of it all we were in Germany. The road bumps plus a feeling of imminent danger, which had dulled in the days of our tank-covered march, now awoke again and took drowsiness away. At the same time, being well-fed and unexpectedly comfortable as we sat on soft and fragrant hay, the advance "to the west" seemed to be happening as if by itself. This had a relaxing effect on us, as did strolling through perfectly still snow-covered forests.

Everything imaginable and unimaginable was left behind on the roads after our tank columns had passed by—crushed people and horses; helmets and guns; carts; wagons; field kitchens; motorcycles and their riders; vehicles with passengers of high ranks. It turned out that the pressed "cakes" lying on that road consisted of the above. We zigzagged along and tried not to notice that frozen bloody mess. During night marches through Germany when the smooth road surface suddenly changed into a chaotic and invisible obstacle course, however, it didn't take us long to guess the origin of those remains. The inevitable torrent of our revenge was rolling all the way to the west. Everything that stood in its way was doomed.

Yet now, on that night road in the forest, the potholes under the sleigh runners were just regular potholes, and were not supposed to bring on any feeling of nausea.

The old man had said, *"Genug Leichen"* (enough killing). The cows on the farmstead mooed; there was no one left to milk them. They were milked every day, always, morning and evening. Then suddenly nobody came, and nobody would come. The war also brought along our guys, however, who started to milk the cows. The milk was warm and fresh-drawn, like the sort I drank in my childhood when visiting my grandma, Anna Danilovna, in the village of Kushlino. It was a hundred years ago. In this mood I realized that a farmstead in German was *Vorwerk. Das Vorwerk.* And then I remembered. Of course! *Klatschen. . . .*

The old man had spoken the truth—there were no Germans in Schönlanke. Nobody was there. Only silhouettes of buildings, darkness, and silence. The place was dead, empty. There was not even any mooing heard; the remaining cows must have exhausted themselves, and fallen asleep. Or perhaps they had all been evacuated?

We went through the village, leaving scouts at its entrance and exit. Then we went back into the forest. In the north, to our right the artillery roar didn't stop for a moment; the battle continued there, by Schneidemühl.

The dim dawn was upon us.

The forest gradually got thinner. We could make out some wide-open space through the trees ahead of us—fields. In the distance, some two kilometers away, there was a dark, dense group of buildings, with a church spire in the center of the group. The panorama that opened up to us in the dawn twilight seemed surprisingly symmetrical. There was something about it that reminded me of a theatrical setting.

The snowfall finally stopped.

It was a wide, semi-lit stage. The show must either be over—or it hadn't started yet.

"Finished smoking, guys?" The Guards Captain asked us. "Now listen to my order. The first and second squads will move ahead to reconnaissance the place. We follow them on the sleighs, with an interval of 500 meters. With this snow and on foot it'll be difficult to disperse. If the enemy opens fire, the second squad will return to its initial position. Together with the first squad I'll act according to the situation. The squad commander will take the third squad and will scout the forest adjacent to the road. The advance of the lead battalion should be stopped here, until I give a signal to go on with a green flare. The lead units will be here approximately in an hour. Any questions?"

"Comrade Guards Captain," said the platoon commander. "Perhaps the platoon should advance as one, together? Artillery is with us, *Fausts*. . . ."

"Have we opened up some kind of parliament here?" the Captain retorted. "We are not going to storm the place, but to reconnoiter it. That's all. Off you go."

The sleigh pulled out into the open and unprotected space. The sheltering edge of the forest was getting further away, while the walls of buildings and the church spire were getting closer and closer.

An irrigation ditch ran in the center of the field, crossing it from one edge to the other—it was straight as if made along some ruler. We crossed a bridge. Now we were walking behind the sleigh, scattered along the road. If the enemy was there, he had us in clear view.

The second sleigh was looming somewhere behind.

"This is where it might hit us," the Captain said. "It is the distance of aimed fire."

The buildings spread aside, and the road ended at the church.

Mellentin was silent.

Barns with cattle yards surrounded the scouts; they were of stone and solidly built, with dim attic windows. The village stifled us with its silence. Even cows and their desperate mooing were not heard anywhere.

"Why?" the Captain wondered aloud. "Why have they taken the cattle out? Were they getting ready for a battle? Huh?"

A village street was running perpendicular to the road, taking a detour around the church. It was lined with residential houses, hiding behind low brick fences. Drawn blinds, closed shutters. The road continued beyond the church toward the Berlin highway. That's what the map said.

The second squad arrived. We put the sleighs in the yard of a house next door to the church. The Captain sent groups of scouts to go through the village and, in particular, to check out the farm buildings that faced the field with their little windows.

The house next door to the church wasn't locked. We could still feel the warmth inside it. The cinders were still hot in the kitchen stove. The linen was still in the chest and the clothes remained in the closet. Its spacious basement with white, tile-lined walls was filled with built-in shelves. They were lined with glass jars filled with homemade preserves. The glass lid had an indentation in the center of it, a red rubber lining with a ring, and a metal spring lock. If you took the lock off and pulled the ring, the air was sucked in and the lid came open. There were hundreds of jars, with canned meat, vegetables, and fruit preserves.

"Not bad, guys, huh? They are on the eve of losing this war. These bastards have robbed the entire continent. Be careful—they could have poisoned the food, but then, they were in a hurry."

Shouldn't the scouts be . . . scouting, however? We quenched our hunger and felt no side effects.

Having found two linen towels that could be used accordingly, I changed my dirty old foot wraps for them.

The Captain said, "Let's go check out the church. We will get up into its bell tower and look around from its top, and from there we'll send up that flare."

The church was locked up. It had two massive doors of dark wood that were iron-sided. Nail tops were wide, a size of a quarter.

"Come on, shoot the lock off," ordered the Captain. As I raised my submachine gun the Captain shouted, "Get down!"

A grenade with a long wooden handle landed next to the steps, rolled away, and exploded.

We hid in a deep door bay, then a machine gun went off somewhere from above.

"Comrade Captain! There, in the field!"

A column of our infantrymen was moving toward Mellentin, crawling out of the forest and going along the road. The head of the column had already reached the irrigation canal.

The machine gun in the bell tower began firing at the column on the road. The column began falling apart; figures in greatcoats, dark against the snow, scattered; they were running and crawling away to the sides, hiding in the ditch, with the tail of the column crawling back into the forest. Then, as if following some order, German machine guns opened fire from the flanks, from where the ends of the irrigation ditch entered the forest. Their tank guns opened up fire from the northern flank.

The machine gun in the bell tower went silent for a second and a grenade flew from above. The ledge in the middle part of the tower obstructed his view, so the German soldier was throwing grenades at random. Pressing ourselves into the church porch we waited for another explosion to be over. Stone crumbs rained on us. The machine gun started firing again, targeting the field and the lead elements of the battalion.

Our soldiers in the field now responded with more fire, but the enemy was invisible.

"To the sleighs!" the captain commanded and we rushed on, crouching under the protection of the building. "The *Faust* cartridges in the sleigh! Quick!"

Other scouts came running toward us, along the cover of structures and fences. We pulled out a long, green box and opened it, inserted fuses, and prepared the *Faust* warheads. The Captain aimed and fired toward the little lancet window of the bell tower. The fired rocket hit the wall, exploded, and made a deep hole in the wall. The machine gun went quiet for a moment and another grenade flew out of the window.

"He's alone there! Fire on the window!"

Covered by submachine-gun fire, the Captain shot *Faust* rockets at the bell tower. It blinked, something rumbled inside the tower, and bits and pieces went flying. The machine gun stopped.

"Everyone here? We'll go back to our guys. Move by bounds!" the Captain shouted. "That son of a bitch battalion commander couldn't wait for our signal! Move out!" Now that we had completed our task, we moved back to rejoin the main force.

We were running back scattered, and occasionally falling flat to the ground. Machine-gun bursts were slicing across the road. We were some two kilometers away, however, from the edges of our troops on our left and right, "in the zone of imprecise fire." Two or three invisible German tank guns were firing toward the forest where our boys were seeking cover. The shells exploded somewhere far inside the forest. Then some responsive claps came, mortar grenades went flying by with their howling vibrations, and started exploding by the northern edge, from where the tank and machine-gun fire originated.

Mellentin, now behind us, was quiet. Its last desperate defender died at his post.

Bundles of gray greatcoats could be seen inside the ditch. They were scattered on the field, here and there, and on the road. They were gray, motionless bundles in white snow. The scouts slowed down by the bundles while running back, but it was too late for help. Completely out of breath, I just fell to the ground as soon as I reached the perimeter. The Guards Captain looked back and ran toward me crouching, but I was already getting up.

"Did they get you?" he asked.

"No, I just tripped badly," I replied.

"Come on, a little more, " he said, encouraging me.

We reached the edge of the forest and lay down under the cover of some pine trees. With snow in my mouth, I hoarsely spoke, "I remember, I remember, Comrade Captain. 'Don't talk,' is what the old woman said. 'Don't talk.' *Sollst nicht klatschen. Klatsch und Tratsch,* gossip, rumor-spreading. . . . 'Don't disclose it,' is what she said."

"What old woman? Are you nuts?" he asked.

"The old woman back at the farmstead. When I asked about Mellentin, she told her old man, 'Don't talk!' but he hinted. He said, 'the road, crossroads'."

"They are fascists," the Guards Captain said. "They are all fascists."

"Comrade Guards Captain, that old man. . . ."

"Enough said about that fascist?"

"No, you see. He *didn't* say the troops *were not* here."

"Whether he said or didn't say—no difference. If not here, we would have come across them further, by the highway. We were to walk on until contact. In any case, we made some twenty kilometers deep inside the country over the night. Inside the den."

"Yet, he kind of warned us. He couldn't know about the ambush; only those in command would have known about it. He definitely knew we'd meet them here, though. He said, 'enough killing', and he was a German. He was a former soldier with an Iron Cross. So it meant he was not so much a fascist, . . ." and again I recalled old Vatter, back there, in occupied Kremenets.

"We didn't have any other way to reconnaissance this Mellentin. We couldn't surround it with the forces of our platoon, could we?" the Guards Captain asked. "Our objective was to establish the position of the enemy and we did. Can you let it go? There's a war going on, you know. Or how does that saying go?"

"*À la guerre comme à la guerre* (War is war), I answered, continuing, "But the guys that remain there, on the field. . . ."

"Listen, Einstein! We'll get you a dictionary."

The invisible tanks continued firing. Shells exploded randomly, here and there.

"Looks like they don't have any fuel," the Guards Captain said. "All right, then. Have you caught your breath, guys? Then get up. Let's go search for our staff headquarters."

The usual front-line life was already emerging in the forest. Soldiers were digging shelters and trenches. Guns were pulled up to the perimeter. Communications were being established. We picked up a pleasant scent from somewhere. The snow was trampled and worn and no longer white. In addition it was subsiding, melting.

We went off deeper into the woods, following the communications line.

"It is about time to scout out the kitchen," someone observed.

"Didn't it cross your mind that this old man could have warned them that we were interested in Mellentin?" The Captain asked me, turning his head. I increased my pace and caught up with him. He continued his thought, "Perhaps he had a walkie-talkie in his outpost house and he was left behind as an agent? Counting that we wouldn't execute him, because of our forgiving, Slavic nature? What do you say to this?"

"No, Comrade Guards Captain." I said. "He said, 'enough killing.' He didn't say this to the old woman or to me. He said it to himself. He was convincing himself. They had been here since the evening, waiting for us, just in case. It was a convenient location: an open field, with a ditch across it, and the road directly to the west, with the bell tower at the cross section of the road, with a far view. They were supposed to ambush us somewhere. When we were walking toward Mellentin across the open field, it felt like someone was watching us. They would have ambushed us somewhere anyway."

"Yes, we have met a tactically well-educated enemy. One who understands psychology. He hoped that we would go forward audaciously and he was right. He counted on us being dizzy with our successes and he attacked us from behind the corner. He bit quite a chunk off us today. He was quiet, and let our scouts get in. He acted very intelligently. What are you going to do after the war is over?" The Captain changed the subject abruptly. "You should qualify for a military college." *Our Guards Captain is a good man,* I thought.

The enemy continued to disturb us by firing on our forest until late night, then withdrew.

At dawn, the light breeze from the east brought an ever-increasing roar of engines to us. Our tanks were rolling in, a multitude of tanks.

The roar was steady, and then it went quieter. Only the noise of cars and truck engines remained—the steady and continuous noise. There, beyond Mellentin, our tank and motor columns were rolling on. Then the wind brought a song, a marching song. We couldn't hear the lyrics—but everybody recognized the melody.

There, on the Berlin highway, our motorized columns were rolling filled with singing infantrymen:

"Our dear Byelorussia and golden Ukraine
Our young happiness will be defended
With our steel bayonets!
Our young happiness . . ."

The Fifth Shock Army was advancing toward Landsberg, toward the Oder.

Later, from historical texts I found out that mobile divisions of the Red Army had reached the Oder in a wide front by that day, 3 February 1945. It was the last waterway obstacle on our way to Berlin. They seized and crossed the Oder and built fortifications on the other bank.

Precisely seventy kilometers were left to reach the capital of the *Reich* that was planned for a thousand of years. Those final dozens of kilometers were very difficult.

"Well?" Guards Captain Vlassov said. "Are you ready? Let's go, guys. The horses and sleighs are still with us, waiting here for our return"

When we were crossing the bridge over the irrigation ditch, back on the familiar road, the very same wind brought sounds of neighing, hungry horses to us. The guys hurried back to Mellentin, to the horses that were left there yesterday. They were hungry and thirsty, poor animals.

What about Mellentin? It was a big deal for us who were there but actually it was just a small episode at the end of the advance from the Vistula to the Oder, on the eve of the larger, gigantic battle, the bloody battle of the Seelow Heights, and then finally the fighting on the streets of Berlin.

The Boots

The *starshina* of our Submachine Gun Company is well preserved in my memory.

For some reason I remember vividly how he presented me with a pair of leather boots.

This happened after Mellentin, somewhere in Eastern Pomerania. Well, somewhere *in the den.*

We were walking along a street in a town that had just been surrendered by the enemy. We were walking, customarily crouching. A house was on fire, glass crackled, and the wind rustled some rags in an empty window opening. There was a body of an old woman lying on a church porch—she was gray haired and shattered. On the curb, almost under my feet I saw a woman's hand—shockingly clean amidst all that chaos. It had groomed nails and a manicure. Most likely a heavy shell or a bomb had just exploded here. War had entered this town, too.

Among the ruins I came across a pile of large cardboard boxes, with many new shoes scattered around. I picked up one box and when I opened it I found a pair of absolutely magnificent German officer boots with smooth and shining bottle-like bootlegs. They were my size. I thought, "A sign of fate." At the very first resting point I pulled on these magnificent examples of the art of shoemaking and I tossed my rubber boots away into the bushes. Previously it was also here in Germany that I had parted with my then-absolutely-worn-out shoes and three-meter-long gaiters when, in an abandoned farmer's house I found and took a pair of rubber boots. The advance from the Vistula had been going on for a few weeks by then. Our rear echelons were hopelessly behind. Besides they used cart traction in our regiment—we were dependent on horses. On top of it all, new uniforms weren't supposed to be issued until a later date, so we looked accordingly. We did not look like beggars—and no doubt were well armed by this time—yet in the movies that were made in the following decades, the look of our victorious army was much more impressive than in actual life.

I was still lovingly gazing at my new acquisitions when a shadow struck their mirror-smooth bootlegs. A pair of dusty, yet also very fine, leather boots appeared in front of me. Naturally, they contained the *starshina* of our Submachine Gun Company, who was standing in them. Who else? After that lengthy separation I even wanted to give him a big hug.

"What's that?" he inquired.

"Good day, Comrade *Starshina*. They are boots, Comrade *Starshina*."

"I figured that. Where from?"

"A little store was bombed down over there, Comrade *Starshina*. They were lying there."

"What a pointy head you are!" The *starshina* scolded me. "Quite a philosopher! In this way, you may finally learn the ropes of life! Let me try them on. Ah, and the foot wraps are in good order as well." He said approvingly as I was taking the boots off. By the way, his wraps turned out to be newer. The *starshina* put the boots on and stood up—he looked like a military monument in knee-high boots come alive. For an instant I visualized myself in his place and was glad it wasn't me wearing those boots. The *starshina,* still looking at the shiny new boots, said, "Now, try mine."

I pulled his boots on.

"Well?"

"They are tight, Comrade *Starshina*. Where my big toe is."

"It's nothing, darn it," the *starshina* summarized gleefully changing his feet. "They will ease on you!"

As always, he was absolutely right because the leather boots had an amazing quality of taking up the shape of their owner's legs and feet. Being worn they embraced the owner's feet with a tenderness and faithfulness worthy of my admiration. In as little as one week, the caps of my first real military boots showed protrusions in the forms of my big toes and those boots served me faithfully until the end of the war, and even a bit longer—may God grant good health to the *starshina*.

As for the *starshina,* it turned out that this time he had made a serious miscalculation. Soon afterward, in accordance with my understanding of global justice, my magnificent trophy was on the legs of a battalion commander. In order to somehow comfort the *starshina*, a few days later a rumor was spread in the company that those same boots were spotted on some high-ranking officer from a higher staff headquarters, In any case, such a story reached our reconnaissance platoon. Jokingly, guys would ask me, "So how are your boots doing?" as if compassionately inquiring about the state of my health. The exchange of my trophy rubber boots for the fine sergeant's leather boots, however, was perceived unanimously as a consequence of having reached soldierly maturity. The leather boots, moreover, were considered part of a proper uniform (while shoes with gaiters seemed more foreign and worn out of necessity only), and nobody could demand these boots off me.

In the very beginning of this book I promised to tell "the truth, only the truth, and nothing but. . . ." As it is easy to notice, however, I was cautious not to promise to tell the entire truth. Besides, I was as cautious in limiting myself to my knowledge of things as a *witness*. I am writing about those things that are preserved in my memory and that I witnessed personally. There lies the origin for my favorite idea of a snapshot.

We came into Germany, which was still a prosperous and wealthy country, yet also shattered by war to a certain degree. We came there from our robbed, poor land. Many of us had personal motives: a burned home, a massacred family. *I personally, though, was never a witness to any single instance of payback or revenge.* I was convinced that when in their country, we shouldn't have, and didn't have the right to act the way they had acted in ours.

Although I don't like talking about some subjects, I think, however, that now is the time to narrate some things that I remember because even at that time they sparked protest within me.

I recall how once I looked back and noticed smoke from a fire rising from a house in the little village we had just passed through. The place could have remained untouched by the war if not for us. I recall another instance, a ghastly smell in a living room of a house abandoned by its owners; somebody had used the piano for a toilet. It was unlikely to have been done by the owners, on the run from us. Once I saw shiny metal tubes that someone must have pulled from a church organ and scattered on the floor—such amazing little tin whistles. One could take them home, for the kids, but we were going in the opposite direction, we were advancing forward, to the West!

I remember being called once to the *SMERSh* officer. [*SMERSh, smert shpionam* (Russian for death to spies), a WWII organization belonging to the NKVD (a predecessor of the KGB). During the war years it worked inside the

Red Army, to ferret out German infiltrators and spies, but also to identify dissident soldiers. *SMERSh* ceased to exist after 1948. *Ed.*] We knew that there was such a mysterious officer in our regiment who, in fact, was not subordinate to the regimental commander, but reported to someone *over there*. The secretive captain was sitting by a table, with a young German woman sitting across from him. She wore something dark, which didn't look neat, and for some reason she had a top hat on her head. There was some food in front of her on the table. I looked into her eyes and I remember thinking that she didn't look normal. Well, the captain said the same thing. From the interrogation, which I interpreted, I remember that she had been captured somewhere by our soldiers who had covered her head up, put her in one of the supply wagons, and during the night stops they took turns raping her. I didn't get to know whether she had that kind of look prior to that or as the result of it. I don't know what happened to her afterward; we went on.

I recall that once the entire regiment was set up in a square. In the center of the square there was a soldier without a cap, shoulder boards, or belt on, with his hands tied up behind his back. An officer read out the verdict of the military tribunal: capital punishment—execution by shooting—for systematic acts of looting. They made the soldier kneel and the officer shot him with a pistol in the back of his head. They said that a sack filled with valuables— gold teeth crowns, and rings, earrings, pendants and bracelets—had been found in the soldier's duffel bag. My memory forever preserved the image of that kneeling soldier, too.

I recall that once in March when we were in Pomerania, Guards Captain Vlassov came to the scouts and said that there had been an order of the Supreme Command that allowed frontline soldiers to send one parcel home each, weighing up to 10 kilograms. The soldiers started running around, pulling various things—mostly cloth and linens—out of their duffel bags and some "secret places." They started sewing sacks for parcels.

The Captain came up to me, "Why are you just sitting around then?"

"I don't have anything," I said.

The Captain watched me closely and ordered, "Hey, guys, give something to fill the parcel of this loser!" Thus my parents received a parcel from Germany.

———◦◦◦◦———

There is still some left to tell of the war itself. Until the very end I lost brothers-in-arms at places like Arnswalde, near Stargard, in Hollnow and Altdamm. We cannot today find these German names on a map, however, as they have been known only by their Polish names since WWII.

Desolation

We reached the Oder. One early morning, when we were on the east bank of the Stettin Bay, Guards Captain Vlassov called me and offered me to take a look through his telescope. Clearly as if on some screen I watched how on the western bank, in Stettin, the town's neighborhoods were being crushed and collapsed in clouds of dust. It was an air raid of American "flying fortresses"; the planes filled the sky in hundreds. They were flying at high altitude, staying in formation, turning around behind our backs, one wave after another. They were so beautifully lit by the sun—and they were so methodical in destroying, wiping this town off the face of the earth. It all looked so commonplace and well directed as if on a parade. It was obvious then, to both sides that the next day, or in a week or two, this town would fall into our hands. Our Western Allies were helping us to capture another set of ruins and rubble.

Looking close into his telescope, all that Guards Captain Sergei Pavlovich Vlassov could say was "Fu . . . hell!"

He was right about it. This method seemed to us somewhat akin to the Nazi way of "waging war": a mass extermination—women, children, old people. That was the most extreme expression of disapproval and rejection for us then.

Soon afterward we were redirected further to the south, to the base in the area of Zeden, which was on the west bank of the Oder. On the right flank of the First Byelorussian Front that was storming Berlin, our units went into battles on their own way along the Hohenzollern Canal, leaving mass graves behind, to finally come to a stop by the Elbe. [*Front,* a Soviet military term for a very large military formation that can be translated into army group, that is, comprised of a group of armies, that each in turn consist of several army corps that are made up of several divisions. *Ed.*] This was in late April 1945.

These names will very soon be a part of ancient history. For me they made some of the deepest impressions of all in my memory. These special moments of mine are not spread out equally throughout my twentieth century and herein lies the difference between these notes and memoirs. Snapshots can be totally different in their significance from the author's and reader's standpoint, but the fact that my main focus is on the few—as seen from today's distant perspective—years of the great war should hopefully be pretty understandable. Yet, each person of my generation has his or her own twentieth century. This is just about how mine turned out.

The war then just . . . ended, quite undramatically, that is, in *my* experience. Not two weeks passed when I was directed to "further military duty" to the staff headquarters of the 1st Byelorussian Front, as it was stated in my assignment orders. There was a demand for servicemen who were fluent in German and my commander, Guards Captain Vlassov, had decided that I was fluent. There would be another instance in my life when somebody decided that I was perfectly fluent in a foreign language. It happened decades later, and in that instance it was English, but I will tell you about that later.

―――――‥∞∘∞‥―――――

I am sometimes asked if I don't have more accounts about how the Red Army behaved itself when it got to Germany. My friend, Swedish journalist Lars Gyllenhaal, gave me a splendid book called *In the Footsteps of Alexander the Great* (BBC Books, 1997). The book was written as an accompanying title for the TV series about Alexander's battles. Its author, Michael Wood, traced every step along the triumphant way of Alexander the Great and his army from Greece to India, his battles, and conquest of the empires of those times. On page 109, in the chapter "Persepolis: Most Hated City in the World," we read, "The city was given over to the Macedonian troops for plunder and horrific sack took place, with looting and rape on an horrendous scale (recalling to us modern atrocities like the Soviet sack of Berlin in May 1945)." The author, a young athletic man whose face can be seen frequently enough in this richly illustrated volume, was obviously born after 1945.

I came to Berlin on 14 May 1945, which means I was there just after the "Soviet sack of Berlin" so well described by Mr. Wood in his book about Alexander the Great. I have to say that I never came across or even heard of any orders in our army to sack cities and to rape. Nor did I see evidence of Soviet atrocities of the scale suggested by writers like Mr. Wood. Michael Wood's comment about the sacking of Berlin simply does not match with what I personally experienced.

I recently happened to read about the museum within the building of the *Reichstag* (parliament). A young guide, demonstrating the images of Berlin in ruins to visitors, quite aggressively commented on "Zhukov's hordes" that had caused all this. I was a part of those "hordes."

I haven't told you *how* I got to Berlin. Well, let me do that now.

The Canteen

Soon after peace broke out they began to scatter us in various directions. Those who were older got to be sent home while we, the young ones, had to stay on in the military, taking the places of the many millions who would never come back. In fact, the draft was suspended for a while, so we, the youngest ones, had to serve more.

So, having received the re-assignment notice to be sent to the staff head-quarters of the Front, I headed to the guys in my company for a last good bye. It was unlikely we would see each other again.

Of course, the first person I met was the *starshina*. He was standing in the middle of a farm, taking a proper look at quality farm buildings. For almost a year now he'd been turning me into a soldier and I was glad to see him now.

"Ah, Mr. Intellectual! What brings you here?" he asked. "I can see that you've been promoted to sergeant's rank? What do you know, a new uniform, and they pinned a medal onto you, too."

"I wanted to say goodbye to the guys, Comrade *Starshina*. I'm being sent away from the unit."

"Must be going to Moscow, huh? To improve on your qualifications."

I said to myself, *Well, now he'll surely remind me of that steed.* Aloud, I said, "To Berlin, Comrade *Starshina*. They say I'll be working with Germans, with the population. Rebuilding."

"Really," said the *starshina*. "All right then, go to the boys, eat something for strength. They are having lunch right now, there, in the mansion." He added as I walked away, "And the horses are grazing out there, on a meadow. Do you recognize your pal? Must have been missing. . . ."

I didn't want to find out who was missing and what was missed.

When it was time for me to leave, he appeared with a trophy aluminum canteen.

"Listen, kid," he began.

Well, it isn't going to get any easier, I thought.

"Here, take it. At first, this canteen will serve you as a key to every door. Most importantly it will open truck doors for you. You'll travel like a count. Although you pointy-heads do not know a darn thing about these things. It contains alcohol, you understand? You don't drink it yourself, but you offer a drink to others."

Alcohol! He could have killed for a hundred grams of the daily allotment of vodka [approximately 3.5 ounces. *Ed.*], and now he was giving me a canteen full of it! I felt like crying! Life can work out so stupidly—you get to know the person at his best at the moment when you part with them for good.

In the meantime the *starshina* was slowly walking away across the wide stone-paved yard—the greatest man of our Submachine Gun Company.

Spring in the World of Ruins

The name of Karlshorst now entered the annals of history. In this German town, our Marshal Zhukov, the Commander of our 1st Byelorussian Front, received the unconditional surrender of Germany on 8 May 1945. The Front's staff headquarters was located here as well.

I hitchhiked to Karlshorst. An hour later all paperwork was in place. I was directed to serve as an interpreter to the military commandant's office in Oranienburg. The major in charge of my paperwork used a pointer to refer to a big map hanging on the wall: Karlshorst was in the lower right corner, and my assigned destination was next to the ceiling. They were separated by some forty kilometers of Berlin ruins.

"Is the assignment clear?" he asked. "All right, you may go."

What else was in store for me?

"You may go" was a familiar thing. Besides, the "key" was gurgling in my duffel bag so everything would be all right.

I stepped out into a world of ruins that were standing as if on parade. The cobblestone was under my feet—it was Berlin, after all. I didn't feel any emotions, as if it was meant to be like it was. I had come here; my war ended here. I could have been one of those millions who had never made it here. I was fortunate, though. I set off and had made it. One day I would have kids and would tell them about that war and about our victory, just like my dad used to tell me about his war. I'd always been proud of him. They would be proud of me, although I had fought only briefly, a little short of a year. I guess I would have fought longer had the Red Army arrived in Kremenets earlier.

Setting off to my war I had walked across the ruins of our Kremenets. During this year I had seen dozens of similarly burned towns and villages. I had walked across the ruins of Warsaw, the city of my childhood, from one end to the other. Everywhere there were corpses, corpses, corpses.

Now I could sum it all up. This past year hadn't been spent in vain, and perhaps some debts had been paid. Was my duty accomplished? During this year in my war I hadn't shot at anyone in particular; that is, I didn't shoot anyone while looking in their eyes. They fired at us, we fired back. Their shells, bombs, and grenades exploded amidst us, just like ours did amidst them. We fell down, and so did they. Of course, during the years of occupation I got to see some of their faces all too well. I could have fired at those fellows while looking them straight into their eyes. I hadn't known the other soldiers, the ones at the front. We were doing our duty. Were they accomplishing their duty as well? Our cause was just. Searching deep in their hearts, could they believe that their cause was just? Yet they fought so ferociously for it! It was all very complicated. I was at the right place at the right time—exactly where I was supposed to be. At the end, it was I who was walking across their capital, with their ruins on parade for me. There was some justice to it, at least personally for me. It was not about gloating.

It was getting dark, and returning back from my contemplation, I noticed that the houses lining the streets were in fact ghosts, with only outer walls remaining. It was very unlikely that somebody was living there. I didn't see any cars either. I could hear noises of engines somewhere in the distance, but where was that busy road and how should I get there? Now only the ruins surrounded me. Soon even this street ended in just a pile of shattered bricks and rubble.

Meanwhile it got completely dark and the only thing left was to search for a place where I could spend the night. In the twilight that came upon me the surrounding houses no longer seemed dead—lights were glimmering here and there, through drawn curtains. The inhabitants, however, were Germans.

A small building standing at the back of one yard seemed more attractive than the others. Of course, like the others, it didn't have any roof, but its front windows had glass and didn't seem empty, with only stars shining through them. In one of the ground floor windows I could see lights. It was a challenge, however, to get across the final few meters of the fence made out of broken bricks and mutilated iron. "I will break my leg here—and it won't even count as a war injury. A wonderful start for a peaceful life."

Having found the door, I knocked on it. I thought how wonderful and easy it felt just to knock on the door, to knock in the normal way, with your finger and not a fist or the butt of your gun or a burst of rifle fire. It was exactly like in old times, back home, when I hadn't been a soldier yet. It had been ages since then.

I heard someone from behind the door, *"Wer ist da?"*

It was a normal and peaceful "Who is it?" and the voice was that of a young man. So what was I to do then? What was I to answer him? It was a German who asked me. I could not say, "Open up!" because the war was over. Then again, I couldn't ask to be invited either.

"Could you open please?" I said. Again I thought that I used the word *"bitte"* here in Germany for the first time. Until now this word that symbolized normal human relationships hadn't been necessary. Now the door was opened for me.

On the other side of the door there was a guy of my age, holding a candle in his hand. Even if he had tried, his eyes couldn't have popped out any farther.

"Good evening. Could I spend the night at your place?" I asked.

He saw a Russian standing in front of him, a Russian who, as a matter of fact, didn't have a gun. Who knew what this Russian might have in his pockets, though? I also had a bayonet dagger attached to my belt—not a bad weapon.

"You should not have opened!" someone whispered from the darkness behind his back. It was the mistress of the house. She must have thought the Russian would not understand. Typical female logic was to blame you for something that can't be undone. Dad used to mock Mama's "you should have" or "you shouldn't have."

"Please come in." The man stepped aside, letting me in. "We have only one room left, everything else here was bombed." As if apologizing for the lack of tact, he added in haste, "The Americans bombed it all." He must have still hoped that the nocturnal phantom would not be satisfied with "just this one room" and would leave. I didn't have anywhere to go at that hour, though, so I entered the room. I could sense that just a moment ago they had felt very cozy here, by the candle, and it all ended in one instant.

While I washed off the road dust over the bucket in the hall, they hastily put up a separating screen in the corner out of a rug, and put linens on the couch. Everything was done in silence. Then I sat on the couch in semi-darkness listening to their whispers, quiet steps, rustling on the other side of the rug. It all lasted for some half an hour. I was hungry. I had a dry ration with me in my bag, but I couldn't start munching here in my corner.

"Excuse me?" she said, deciding to address me directly. How old was she? Seventeen or eighteen? She must have even knocked on the rug; I may have missed it. I had to respond.

"Yes, please," I said. Today was a day full of "please." I was already some kind of master of this corner now.

"We were about to have dinner . . ." (*Prior to this mishap,* I thought.) "and if you don't mind, we would like to offer you a cup of coffee."

How did that social phrase go, darn it? They were beating it into my head back in the *gymnasium,* in Warsaw . . . Yes, *gnädige Frau,* gracious lady.

"Thank you very much, gracious lady. With pleasure."

Oh God, my vocabulary was so poor and even those few words were tucked away somewhere so deep in my memory that I had to search for every word. I needed them all now, but they wouldn't come forth. "Stand up!" "Your papers!" "Regiment!" "Division!" Those were the things I had been saying in German lately. It was one thing to yell something that I was reading from a piece of paper, through the loudspeaker. Now I had to speak without a paper, off the top of my head . . . and they had even assigned me to some new place as a full-time interpreter!

Dinner. *Abendessen*—the evening meal. Evening was here, in fact it was night already. And the food?

The round table was covered with a snow-white cloth, which wasn't there when I entered. The candle stood in the center, the same candle he had held. It had three cross marks with equal intervals of some 3 centimeters each. Each interval stood for a daily norm, as I was later told. The candle was allocated for the entire week. And then? Perhaps the power would be restored. It was a totally wild idea—restored in the midst of this sea of ruins? There were three cups on the table filled with something dark. No coffee aroma. Three pills were on the saucer, which I guessed to be "Saccharine." There was a slice of bread next to each cup, some five millimeters thick. "How did she do it?" It meant that they, in spite of everything, were treating me as a guest in this home.

I addressed the mistress of the house in the most exquisite of expressions I remembered. I asked for her permission to add my reserves to this dinner. I had a loaf of military rye bread, two "Second Front" cans of meat, a bar of lard, sugar, and then the canteen, although the door was opened to me without offering sips from it.

They watched it all breathlessly. Now at the light of the candle I could take a closer look at both of them. He looked more or less ok, but she was small, unbelievably thin and pale as death. Only her eyes were all right. She watched the cans closely. I'm sure she was thinking, "If we make cross marks, they could last for two weeks, three weeks. . . ." Damn it! My dagger quickly took care of all that wealth; I didn't care for the aesthetics of it, just quick! Otherwise they would have grabbed me by my hands and tried to stop me. I poured transparent liquid into elegant glasses. (*It seems not everything was bombed,* I thought.) They mixed it with water, following my directions. (*It's good that there is plenty of water.*)

A moment came when I realized that I was totally happy and had been in that state already for a while, and so were they. That feeling was a joint achievement. They thought that an unwelcome visitor, an enemy was barging into their home and they were wrong. It was just a man coming to visit someone, and together they helped each other.

Little Marika proved to be not at all as quiet as it first seemed. Oh no!

"I saw Rudy by accident in the column of POWs. They were driven along a neighboring street, not far from here. I ran toward him, pushing everyone aside; I hugged him by his neck and started crying. I thought they would shoot us right there, but nobody shot at us. I dragged him out of the column and started shouting that he'd been a soldier for one week only—and this was true!—and that he lived here, in this house, and that we'd been friends since childhood. That we were engaged and I was expecting his baby. I made gestures like this. This was not true, of course, but . . . and you know, your soldier from the convoy, he had a Mongolian face, and held a submachine gun, he waved his hand and shouted, *"Davay, davay!"* Then the column recommenced its march. Yes, yes, everybody had stopped! So the column marched on, and we stayed behind, Rudy and I, and we have been together for a week now. What does *"Davay"* mean in German?"

"Davay!" "Come on!" How should I explain it to them? It's not a spell or a magic word, which makes dreams and wishes come true instantly. In German it's *"Los!"* The *Gestapo* men shouted *"Los!"* when driving people to their death, toward trenches already filled with several layers of dead bodies.

In Poland, at our place, everywhere they came . . . and here the same word in Russian brought happiness. In short, it all depends on the meaning that is put into this word and who is uttering it. And, of course, it all depends on the circumstances. Marika must have shocked that entire column, including its guards. No officer must have been at hand either; he would have touched his gun holster, shouted something, and that would have been it. To finally explain her success I shall use a Russian proverb, if something is not allowed but you need it really, really badly, then you may get it.

I explained all this to them more or less clearly—and they seemed to understand me. Also, it turned out that the canteen "key" had side effects: it eased the search for necessary German words.

They were the first Germans in post-war Germany that fate would have me meet. I was obviously fortunate with them—they seemed happy, they were happy. Their looks, glances they exchanged, their words and gestures spoke about their happiness. We only had to reinforce the feeling, and we went about this very seriously. As a result the canteen got lighter all the time.

He was going to be an architect, I was to be a diplomat. I wouldn't settle for less. The girl watched her Rudy with such adoring eyes that I could only envy him.

All aspects of the postwar peace arrangements were subject to discussion. In this we established extensive mutual understanding. I was a Russian soldier and he was a German who had just been my enemy. We agreed that there should never be any wars again and that all weapons that had been accumulated on the planet should be melted down. We were sincere in thinking so, and we didn't have any feelings of mistrust between us. The cross marks on the candle were gone; it burned down and went out. We slept peacefully until almost noon in that roofless house.

Then they took me across the ruins to the busy road. I waved with my canteen and a truck pulled over to the curb. I got into the truck cab. They waved at me and I waved back. I felt sad, and so did they. The truck rolled on. I settled myself comfortably, because with the canteen I should travel as a count.

Again I passed countless neighborhoods scarred and mutilated by war.

"We should have taken the circular highway," the driver said. "The road there is awesome!"

I knew that highway. We had made sheltered trenches near Stettin by its side and we were hidden well and safe in them; no gun of any caliber could blast that highway. If mines exploded, they left only scratch marks on its surface in the form of scattered rays. Hitler had ordered it to be built so that it would serve for centuries. Well, then he planned his *Reich* for millennia. The *Reich* was dead. The highway would keep serving people, though.

After the night in that house without a roof and after having seriously broken the instruction on using the canteen, I felt drowsy. Again I returned to somewhere in the past when a massive explosion pulled half of my head off. That must have been it.

"Wake up. We've arrived," the driver said.

"What are you, a tanker?" I asked him "You must have missed the lesson about brakes," I added, with a hint of sarcasm.

"Well, you're surely from the infantry," he replied. "You are one heck of a sleeper. I almost fell asleep myself with such a passenger."

I was indeed great at sleeping. If I was able to sleep and march at the same time, then it was only natural when riding in a truck. Why did he have to hit the breaks so hard, though? He almost knocked my head off.

"Here is your Oranienburg," he said.

The same kind of ruins everywhere.

I pulled the canteen out and I found that it was almost empty. I smelled the lid and shrug my shoulders in confusion. "It must have a leak, I guess?"

To comfort the driver at least somewhat, I give him the canteen to keep, together with the meager remains of its contents. It accomplished its mission well, and I arrived comfortably to my destination.

The Accumulation of Wealth

The town commandant studied my assignment order closely, and then he studied me.

"So, what, you really can speak German?" His voice was filled with covert skepticism. *I don't look like the type who . . .* I thought, and silently shrugged my shoulders, not according to regulations, as if saying, "someone higher up sent me here, so someone must have thought so."

"Well, we'll check it all today," he said.

The very same day the military commandant of Oranienburg held a meeting. The representatives of the town council and the town mayors of nearby communities were invited to it.

Many of them were in the Russian commandant's office for the first time and they were not comfortable being there. Fortunately I was already there, so it would only be a matter of time before I would interject a little comic relief.

The day's agenda included issues of food supply for the population. The mayors pointed out the lack of milk. The commandant told me to say that the first priority for daily milk allotment should go to children and women expecting babies.

There was no time for lengthy considerations. The glances of the representatives of the local administration were cast with hope toward me. I didn't fail their hopes: *"Kinder und tragende Frauen sollen jeden Tag Milch erhalten!"* I really liked the phrase as it was well versed stylistically and logically, and it was brief and clear—*kurz und klar.*

For a moment everybody was silent. Then in the corner somebody snorted and total laughter broke out. All the town mayor gentlemen and one town mayor lady guffawed, as did simpler town officials. I didn't laugh. Neither did the commandant. With much curiosity he studied me intently.

The mayor of Oranienburg, a well-dressed gray-haired gentleman, was among the first to calm down.

"Mister interpreter," he said, " *'tragende'* is the word used with relevance to cattle (cows and so on, do you understand me?) In this particular instance you should have used the word *'schwangere'*. Pregnant women, and not . . . ha-ha! My apologies, madam town mayor! . . . and not 'big with young'. Do you understand?"

"Das ist zum Lachen, nicht wahr? That's a hoot," the major said. "The kid (*And how did he know the name given to me by the* starshina?) could hardly have opportunities to study fine differences between the two words at the front. When did you attend school last time?"

"In June 1941," I responded.

"And then?"

"And then there was the Nazi occupation, and they didn't let us study. After the liberation I went to the army."

This was all said in German. For them. Then the silence fell.

"You have to study, do you understand?" I was told, now in Russian.

The meeting went on. The major again completely forgot all his German and I had to sweat it further.

As I found out later Major Zozulya was a Candidate of Philosophical Science. He was a professor in one of the Moscow institutes and volunteered for the people's militia in the fall of 1941. He could judge well, therefore, whether I should study further or not.

Soon afterward I was transferred to the Niederbarnim district commandant's office in Bernau. It seemed that the major was reluctant to let me go. He must have thought I had potential. One had to comply with an order, however. Thanks to such people like the major, for me the years of military service were years of continuous education, which I considered to be years of accumulating wealth. As a result, by the end of my service in Germany I could speak German as if it were my mother tongue. Such wealth, as they joked in the army, didn't weigh down the pockets, and it was never an excess baggage.

Sachsenhausen

I have to linger a bit longer in those most difficult times in the spring of 1945. I just can't move on without making one final stop. I can speak of Sachsenhausen as an eyewitness. In the beginning I promised to tell the truth and nothing but the truth. This is not something that you can be frivolous and carefree about.

In May 1945 thousands of people in striped robes still lived in the Sachsenhausen concentration camp. At the end of the war, the camp was transformed from a place of systematic destruction to a temporary place of residence. Ruins surrounded the camp. It was located on the edge of Oranienburg, which had been destroyed by massive attacks of flying fortresses on the eve of the Red Army's assault on Berlin from the north. There was a major chemical plant in town that belonged to the Auer Company. I was told that uranium was enriched there. At any rate the plant was the target of many air raids. Yet the town got its share as well, which meant that we had a hard time to find a more-or-less complete building on the Berlinerstrasse to house the Soviet military commandant's office.

Following the commandant's order I made for the camp. Gradually the numbers became known. About 200,000 people from almost every European country had been registered as camp inmates. Murdered at this camp: some 35,000. The remainder? Thousands and thousands were still living here in late May, until they were able to walk or ride away to return to the homes from which they had been ruthlessly uprooted. Until then, they were recounting their experiences, in haste and in pain.

I went to Sachsenhausen to serve. My work was to collect testimonies in writing from the former prisoners. The binders were gradually filled with sheets of paper of various sizes and shapes, written in Russian, Polish, Ukrainian, Czech, German, French, Serbian, and so on.

Life gave me yet another opportunity to feel and to perceive in a condensed form that force under which we had existed during three years of occupation. It was an opportunity to personally draw some conclusions.

In my hands I held nice little iron lamps with wicks, intended to light up neat military dugouts on the Eastern Front. I was told that the lamps were filled with oil from melted human bodies. The warehouse shelves were filled with neat bags full of these lamps and short, wide candles of the same origin. [The author adds that, "there were no German officials present who could explain the origin of the product. The former prisoners of the camp made the explanations." Were they misinformed, passing on a false rumor? Already during WWII there were widespread rumors about production of soap made from humans. Research has since uncovered no evidence for mass production of such soap. There is evidence, however, that experiments with human fat were conducted in Danzig. In conclusion then, the above testimony should stimulate new research. *Ed.*]

The warehouse was also stacked with high-quality paper sacks filled with flour made from burnt human bones. The flour was intended to be a field fertilizer. In my intense anger and frustration over all this, I couldn't avoid sarcastic thoughts like, *My, there are over 10,000 barely-covered, rotting, human bodies lying outside Kremenets on the former firing range of the Russian Imperial Yakutsky Regiment that are lying there to no use whatsoever. How many candles could not have been made out of them? They could have illuminated all those tidy German dugouts along the Eastern Front, forming one gigantic Christmas tree. By the way, why shouldn't they also have been used to decorate Christmas trees? Why not? And wouldn't the wheat fields across Germany been richer thanks to the highly effective fertilizer? So many missed opportunities—and all because of haste.*

I was given the task of counting the thousands of soles that had been carefully removed from shoes—men's, women's, children's. I counted them by holding them in my own hands. They were stored separately—soles of men's shoes, women's shoes, and children's shoes. The order in the shoe storage eased calculation and summarizing. So-and-so many tens of thousands of men, so many women, and that many children. Most likely, however, this meticulous storage system was applied not for the sake of simplifying any future calculations, but only out of extreme perfectionism. Nonetheless, calculations were facilitated, and the grand total was about 100,000.

The soles were removed from the shoes in the search for carefully hidden valuables. I imagined that valuables hidden that way were only rarely found—if ever. Yet order is order, *Ordnung muss sein!* There was not a single pair of prisoner's shoes with soles in Sachsenhausen. For the same reason teddy bears, dolls, or whatever else children managed to bring along to Sachsenhausen was confiscated. The toys' bellies were cut open and their heads torn off, and not replaced. All these carefully dissected toys were also stored on shelves. There was a separate storage area for eyeglasses and one for smoking pipes and cigarette mouthpieces. There were rooms for the storage of trousers and other rooms for skirts. All this was waiting for some decision on its optimal utilization. Just like the bones . . . and the fat.

There were numerous sacks with hair—unbraided girls' braids, wiglets, and wigs—that were intended to be used for the manufacture of soft and durable mattresses.

The prisoners worked in workshops producing durable and comfortable military boots. Putting a new pair of boots on, a German soldier was supposed to feel the tender embrace of his *Vaterland.* That was why there was a square-shaped road paved with crude cobblestones and laid out on the camp premises. Prisoners marched along this road from morning till night, wearing boots for the *Wehrmacht* soldiers, to get them in shape. It was easily achieved—a prisoner received a pair of boots that was a size smaller than what he usually wore. That's how the boots were broken in quickly and efficiently.

What if someone couldn't endure it all?

There were many methods.

Repeated violators of the regulations were hanged in public, to the tunes of a camp band. Ordinary death row prisoners were shot dead in a shallow trench, the walls of which were lined with thick logs. People were put facing the wall and shot at the back of their heads. All those who have reason to deal with these issues know well: shooting at the back of the head is the most efficient way. Gradually, a crater some thirty centimeters deep appeared in the wood. There also existed a "medical block." When the prisoner's "height was measured," a bar was lowered unto the top of the head and immediately a shot at the back of the head followed. It was considered humane. If the capacity and effectiveness of such individual methods seemed to fail, then a system of mass sanitary "cleaning" was applied with the use of nerve gas. [Gas was used on a small scale in some concentration camps within Germany, indeed at Sachsenhausen-Oranienburg. Large-scale gassings took place in the extermination camps, *Vernichtungslager,* outside the prewar German borders. *Ed.*]

All these methods of extermination led to the crematorium furnace.

That was the wealth of knowledge that I accumulated during my short term of service at Sachsenhausen.

I hope my readers can forgive me for this account. I don't particularly like to read such accounts myself, but it belongs to my twentieth century. All this actually took place! I heard what had happened from the people in the striped uniforms, I saw the places and the things with my own eyes, and I held many of the described objects in my own hands. Nowadays there are people who say that these events never took place. Well they did! I testify!

A Close Shave

Some years of peacetime military service, from 1945 to 1949, followed for me there in Germany. Even now I occasionally get one of those sentry-duty dreams at night, though this is becoming less frequent now. In these dreams it's as if my service hasn't ended. In fact I was kept in military service for what today might be considered an eternity, seven years, including five years in Germany. Well, that was just how long many people served then. We were there instead of those who had been killed and for the sake of those who were growing up and working back home in order to fill in the void after the millions and millions who had disappeared into the black hole of the war.

In 1949 I was awarded a short leave to visit my family, ten days plus traveling time. At the Frankfurt Railway Station in Berlin I stormed and seized an upper—formerly luggage—bunk of a shattered third-class car of a passenger train that was called "Five Hundred Happy Souls." On this train I crossed Poland. At one of the stations, on a parallel track, there was a train going in the opposite direction carrying German POWs without armed guards—the Germans were going home. I talked to them from door to door in a friendly manner. There could have been a loud and bow-legged Vatter on this train. Or the junior *Luftwaffe* officer who chose not to hit me that time on Shirokaya Street. Or the one who didn't shoot from his Parabellum when Yuri tried to protect his Lyda. Germans were all different, just like us Russians. They were just more disciplined and more law-abiding. For centuries they have been taught to become that, consequently it was, as they say, under their skin. We are careless, and this, too, can be explained by our nation's history, with its dark times as an essential element until the present day.

At the Gdansk Railway Station in Warsaw I got out of the car to stretch my legs and take a stroll along a temporary wooden platform beside low barracks that had been raised instead of stone buildings. At a distance I saw the half-ruined towers of St. Florian's church and the onion dome of an Orthodox Church a bit to the left of it. The house where I spent my childhood was there next to it. My heart pinched slightly.

In the huge and noisy border-town railway station of Brest I waited for an operating train to Zdolbunov. The old and very worn local train cars were dark and empty. From Zdolbunov I traveled on the open platform of a freight train to Dubno, jumping off as the train went on.

There were forty kilometers left until I reached home. After a year of the war and five years of separation I was ready to walk all that distance, so I set off walking. Soon an old GAZ pickup truck going my way picked me up and gave me a ride.

Then somewhere in the middle of that forty-kilometer ride the truck came under machine-gun fire coming from the forest. Sitting in straw, with my back to the truck cab, I saw chips flying off the truck, leaving three ugly holes behind. The driver sped up and we passed the place.

In Kremenets, a neighbor of ours, a shoemaker, ran to my parents' house, out of breath.

"Alexander Vassilievich! Come soon! There, from Dubno, your son, Romka, is walking home! He has nice leather boots, with nails! He is a *starshina* and he has medals! He has certainly grown, your Romka." In a little town news spreads with a speed inexplicable by physical laws.

Thus I returned and was drowned in the warm hugs of my family, standing on our hillock.

At home I noticed a freshly-made bullet hole in my duffel bag and discovered that bullets had pierced some of my gifts to my family.

I also found a PPSh submachine gun with a full drum magazine next to my brother, Yuri's, bed, and hand grenades in the drawer of his bedside table. At that time telephone lines were being set up in the area. Yuri was the head of the local Communications Center and frequently had to work outside town, therefore this instrument—weapon—was necessary.

Gloomily smiling, sitting at the table, Yuri told me many stories that were akin to frontline stories, and we shared drinks as equals. [Although few are aware of it today, Ukrainian nationalist guerrillas continued to fight the Soviet authorities until about 1955. *Ed.*]

I think it was a happy moment for my father to sit and listen to his slightly tipsy sons, soldiers of their Motherland.

The following day, wearing polished boots we went out together to the center of the town—my father, Yuri, and I. We walked by a recently planted park where the ghetto used to be. We walked by carefully whitewashed houses that had survived here, throughout that very long night that was the Second World War. We walked by clean, emptied spaces that were turning green, and by new construction sites that were appearing here and there.

We were walking in step.

A man we knew stopped, tipped his hat and said, "Hello, Alexander Vassilievich! Gee, what a fine pair of sons you have!"

I was happy for my father.

Occupation Duty in Berlin

The years of military service in occupied Germany were filled with events that my memory has preserved well. I have enough stories about those events, snapshots of years long passed, to write another book.

"When I was involved in exhumation, . . ." I sometimes begin to tell. If the truth be told, I didn't do it directly, at least not with my own hands, and naturally it all took place after the war was over. During the war the dead were buried, if possible, where and when circumstances allowed. After the war, they were re-buried. Even today, however, the bones of our soldiers keep being found everywhere. No memorial date of that big war passes without mournful reburial ceremonies. [Some sixty years after WWII, in the area of the Soviet 14th Army alone, some fifty Soviet soldiers are found annually above ground or in shallow field-graves. These human remains are collected by idealistic groups of *poiskoviki* (literally: seekers). If an identity can be ascertained, relatives are notified. Finally these soldiers are buried on 7 October each year, the date when the last offensive of the 14th Army began in 1944. Similarly, Soviet soldiers are put to final rest all along the former Eastern Front on the most significant date of that particular stretch of the front. The latest development is that the remains of German soldiers missing in action are also being transferred to proper burial grounds. *Ed.*]

For some time I was assigned as a military interpreter to an inter-Allied group that dealt with this ghastly business in the Soviet-occupied zone of Germany.

The Americans and English took their dead home. What about our boys? Our boys still rest in Germany in numerous mass cemeteries, everywhere, in the middle of German towns and cities. The cemeteries are neat and well maintained. Occasionally new graves appear here and there, marked "Unknown Soldier." When another one is located, that is a good thing. One also hopes that this soldier has never been officially listed as "missing in action," because when this was the case his family was sure to have hard times in Stalin's years—as "missing in action" was equated to having surrendered to the enemy. Those who, for one reason or the other, became prisoners of war were also branded as traitors. I, too, in my short war service, was close to placing also this burden on the shoulders of my loved ones, but I was fortunate to escape this fate. So here I am now, with my snapshots. I remember one from my experience in the Inter-Allied group.

<hr>

For some weeks we in the Inter-Allied group were connected by a common task. We traveled all over Germany, reviewed cemetery records, questioned witnesses, and dug the ground. The Americans and the English were amazingly well informed. We would come to a certain location, for example, and would begin taking measurements: along the road from a house on the edge, x meters that way, then turn right toward the forest, a few more meters. Dig here! Then some half meter down we would come across remains. Pilots. Their plane had been shot down and they had jumped out with parachutes. They were captured, taken down this road, and here, in the ditch, they were executed and buried. In another instance a cockpit of an American bomber was raised from the bottom of a lake. The pilots were still inside, or rather what was left of them. The commanding pilot's briefcase had navigation maps that were amazingly well preserved, as well as thirty dollars in one-dollar bills. Following some instruction, our captain took care of them. The currency was to be turned over to our state bank. I remember how we later washed and ironed those bills. Yet the stench remained. I don't think that those who accepted this deposit and counted the bills in the bank enjoyed the stench either.

In that inter-Allied group there was a French captain whose last name was Gorodetsky. I think I remember him so well because he was of Russian origin, and he even held some high French military order. To the other officers of the group, a Soviet captain included, I was a translator, a military interpreter. For Captain Gorodetsky I also constituted a potential discussion partner, although I wore only sergeant's stripes. He assessed both of us, our captain and me, and then preferred communicating with me, although such contacts in particular were not advisable for us, to put it mildly. Work, fulfill your duties—and no chit-chat.

Our captain, that is, the Soviet captain, was from *SMERSh*, the counterintelligence service. Of course he did not introduce himself that way. I figured it out myself. Actually he should have had an interpreter from that service as well, but most likely none was available at that time.

The captain had obviously thoroughly reviewed my record and once surprised me with the following diagnosis, "Yes, kid, your father sure gave your biography quite some fascinating parts. This is all rubbish, though. Your father being a Czarist officer—rubbish. He was just as silly as his son is now. Look at you, you're still a child. We are vigilant, though. And you, kid, must study. You must complete your elementary education, then graduate from a university. You have to become a real man. All this living abroad, in Poland, is also rubbish. Your folks, they never really emigrated anywhere. The border moved to the east in 1920—that's what really happened. If not for this, who knows? We're vigilant and cautious. And the occupation is rubbish, too. Many millions were trapped. This will all be forgotten and ignored in a decade from now. You need to have less of that cultured air about you, that's all," he summed it up. He felt sorry for me and he had said words that he should not have said—and I understood that very well. This could be explained by our direct everyday human contact. I wondered about how *SMERSh* could have taken on such a person. Or perhaps things were not the way they seemed, not at all. . . .

The French captain (who may well have been affiliated with a secret agency similar to that of our captain's) was torn apart by contradicting emotions. On the one side, he experienced a natural antipathy to the lowlifes who forced his parents to leave Russia. On the other hand, he was astonished by the heroic deeds of the Russian nation (Red Army) during the war.

The "Frenchman" was shocked by the manners of our captain, his table manners in particular. When our captain used his knife to pick out a piece of the canned Madagascar monkey that the French treated us to, then skillfully put it into his mouth, the corners of the French captain's mouth drooped slightly. At those moments I tried not to meet his eye since he presumed I was a like-minded person. As a child, at home, I was taught good manners and traces of that education were still obvious. During the war, however, forks were not provided—we had just a spoon and a pocketknife, or a bayonet from the rifle. What kind of manners could we talk about? Besides, I felt like making a face myself: eating a close relative—that monkey meat I mentioned— evoked not only psychological but also purely physiological revulsion in me. Yet I had to bear it all.

When I recall snapshots from the past, I rarely get a reason to crack a joke. Drama prevailed during those times, inseparable as it is from the word "war." We were completing an assignment, though. Human remains in plastic bags were loaded into boxes and we would set off on the road again. Our convoy included a car in the lead position, followed by army trucks with personnel, carrying unpainted wooden boxes. Captain Gorodetsky was riding in front, alongside a driver from Marseilles. Our officer and I sat in the back. Our vehicle was an old and worn trophy Opel. (The Americans and the English came to us riding their regular army cars).

We rustled newspapers. Having finished reading his, after a pause, the "Frenchman" asked us, carelessly, over his shoulder, "So, what do they write about in your *Pravda?*"

We had explicit instructions: to mind our own business—which meant doing nothing but exhumation, and not to partake in any political discussions. We were not to play Ministry for Foreign Affairs. Our captain was not inclined to hide in the bushes, however, covering up under some instructions. Or perhaps he had his own instructions? Making a face and casting a glance on me, he paused and responded to the challenge, "They write about Vietnam."

"That's interesting," the Frenchman said with his archaic aristocratic haughtiness. "And what do they write about *our* Vietnam?"

The dark-haired and always jovial driver from Marseilles looked at us, hearing a familiar word. Our captain paused again and then continued, "They write that the French once proclaimed a motto of liberty, equality, and brotherhood. *Liberté, égalité, et fraternité,*" he added in French, making the driver look back again. "And now they oppress the nation which fights for the very same liberty." Most likely our captain had paused not so much to decide whether to answer or not, but rather to prepare this concise response, so that it would be in compliance with the instructions and rules.

Captain Gorodetsky was silent. Then, without turning his head back and without any emotion, he said, "The Vietnamese are lowlifes." This phrase was not improvised or accidental. His mother and father, trying to save their family's lives from the menace of home-grown lowlifes in Czarist Russia, had moved to a flourishing and prosperous France. Obviously equating the two situations, he referred to the Vietnamese in the same way.

We continued our trip in silence. The following day swords were crossed again. It was a kind of a duel between a French descendant of Russian aristocrats and an intelligence officer, who wore a Soviet Guards badge.

There were many such illuminating lessons in the years that I spent as a sergeant in post-war Germany. I had been out of school for almost a decade by then, yet I couldn't say those years of my life were wasted, not at all. Besides, I believe it was that decade that left me with a spark of friendly sarcasm, which occasionally comes in handy when talking to the younger generation—those who long since "know it all." They learned from sources where the information is preserved in a compact and convenient form. It is a bit more of a hassle to deal with original sources! It is also so much better, though, for the heart and for the mind. That decade left me with a wealth of knowledge including the knowledge of languages. Because of that knowledge I'm needed in the new era and because of that I have a valuable opportunity for communication—the essence of our lives. (They say that motion is the essence of life and I agree, but there is more to motion than walking legs. There is also motion within the brain, there are eyes moving to look at one another. There are hands that type on a keyboard. After all, then, there is the tongue, out of flesh and blood.)

In this new era of opening the doors, French descendants of Russian aristocracy (like Captain Gorodetsky) travel to Bordeaux to meet the President of the new Russia and to shake his hand. Our president, in fact, is a former intelligence officer (like my *SMERSh* captain). That's how it works today.

1949: The "Glorious" Finale

From Germany we were brought to an assembly and reassignment station in Kuibyshev—not accompanied by armed guards yet, but without our vital personal documents and under escort. A strict search followed in which anything "excessive" was confiscated. In particular, I even had to yield *A Short Introduction to the History of the VKP(b),* published in German—you never know what those demoralizers might bring into the country! [*VKP(b):* Russian abbreviation for the All-Russian Communist Party of Bolsheviks. *Trans.*] What happened next was the consequence of our glorious five-year mission abroad and the logic of ideologues in action: we'd communicated for a long time with foreigners, which to the ideologue meant we couldn't help but get "contaminated" by foreign ideas. Obviously their faith in their own ideas wasn't very strong.

We were marching along the street to a bathhouse. A major was walking by our side, on a sidewalk, holding a boy by his hand. The boy said, "Dad, who are those?"

"They are traitors to their motherland." Obviously the major knew that we had just been branded as traitors due to some standard procedure.

Our reaction to the major's words? Our ranks broke apart immediately. I had never before in my life seen any major that could run so fast. We didn't catch him; we were stopped and calmed down by a shout of our senior officer—one of us appointed in charge of all of us for the bath assignment. We obeyed the shout because, as we had been taught, "a commander's order is the law for his subordinates." All of us in that column had served way too many years, and thus army laws had become an integral part of our lives. Even today I'm disgustingly punctual. I'm certain that today's chaos in the army was not inherited from us.

Then, in that assembly and reassignment station, had I had a gun, I would have shot myself. I would have killed myself before realizing that my return from Germany to the homeland via that humiliation was, in fact, a blessing in disguise sent to me from above.

What I'm writing now seems to be memoirs, yet this is not really so. I'm not writing about myself here. I write about the fate of my generation.

From Kuibyshev we traveled individually, now with our documents, "for continuation of the service," transferred to various *stroybats* (military construction engineering battalions). Some of us were sent to the Komi Republic, some to the Donbass region. We would "serve in the army" but actually we were now something similar to convicts. All because the authorities reckoned we had stayed too long in the west. We were punished for crimes we had not yet committed. Punished for *perhaps* having become unreliable.

I was sent to Yenakievo, to the *Yunkom* mine, *Yunkom* being the acronym for Young Communard. When I saw the kind of people who were serving in these military construction engineering battalions, how decorated they were, and saw the number of stripes for military wounds they had, I realized that my fate was not bad fortune at all. Besides, the village had an evening school for adults.

I couldn't imagine why a lieutenant colonel who had been decorated with an Order of Lenin, three Orders of the Red Banner, and many other things that covered his chest would end up commanding our construction battalion. In those years one was supposed to wear one's decorations just about all the time, and the "collection" on his chest sure was an impressive sight. Of course he drank like a fish. What was the cause and what was the consequence, however? On one of my days off, I was walking along a village street that was black with coal dust. I almost stepped on an Order of Lenin; it was without its medal-ribbon brooch. I knew that in the village our Lieutenant Colonel was the only one who had that order. Or perhaps someone among the miners had it, too? Anyway, not many people had been bestowed with this high award. I thus went searching for the Lieutenant Colonel. There was a wedding taking place in one of the barracks. I walked in. He was sitting at the head of the table next to the newlyweds, with his well-decorated jacket unbuttoned, among already-drunk miners. They couldn't get a traditional ceremonial "wedding-general" anywhere, so they went for a real fighting lieutenant colonel! He was definitely tipsy, but he recognized me, looking for him from the doorway. He demonstrated a boss-like frown and motioned with his finger for me to come up. I made my way through the singing and arguing guests. On his jacket, in the place of the Order, the brooch was hanging empty; the Order of Lenin was missing. I handed the Order to the Lieutenant Colonel. He touched the left side of his chest with his hand and got ashen. His eyes sobered up instantly. I saluted, turned around in a military manner and left the buzzing room.

I was allowed to go to the evening school where they believed me, admitting me without school documents, initially on one month's probation, to the final—tenth—grade. I think that Order of Lenin I picked up off the ground played a part in it, too. Indeed, the Lord moves in mysterious ways. . . . (The official at the Education Department let me in without papers because he was simply a normal *human*. He understood my situation—seven years of military service, and so on—felt for me, and helped me. I suppose that my commander, the lieutenant colonel, out of gratitude allowed me to leave the location of the unit every evening for study. It was never discussed.)

In the summer of 1950 when I received my certificate of general education. My period of forced labor had a silver lining. I was given a short-term leave to go home, for ten days. It was the second leave in my seven years of military service.

Years
of Peace . . .
and Terrorism

The North

In October 1950 my long awaited army discharge came. Soon afterward I was admitted as a student of the Physics Faculty at Lvov University. Why physics? There had been other dreams, but by then I had figured out what would be a worthwhile aim for me. I had identified all the "buts" in the records about me. Well, Thank God, they gladly admitted me to the Physics Department, even though classes had started much earlier. Why Lvov University? I wanted to be close to my home, to my family.

A term of pride, "frontline veteran" was very common in those days. There were two of us in my class, Volodya Sur and myself. We studied in one group and, naturally, we became friends. Until now we have been staying in touch, exchanging letters. As a result of a serious contusion Volodya has lost his eyesight. For several years now I have been receiving wonderful messages from the town of Moskovey in Moldova, written by some friend of his, but dictated by him. Volodya was assigned to teach in Moldova after graduation. I'm sure that even today Vladimir (Volodya) Yanovich Sur, frontline veteran, the blind teacher of physics, is a highly respected man in those lands—it simply cannot be otherwise.

Volodya and I differed from our classmates in age and we were highly respected for our wartime achievements. We were experienced "fogies." At that time they were showing a huge Indian movie called, "The Vagabond" on the few city screens. The lines to get tickets for a night show were incredible. Its star actor, Raj Kapur, sang pitifully, "I'm a vagabooooond, aaah, I'm a vagaboooond. . . ." while a beautiful barefoot actress, wrapped into some endless fabrics, conquered our hearts with her elegant dancing movements. We were there, together with them, in suffering India that had just freed herself from the colonial yoke. In the darkness our girls sobbed, and even we guys quietly sniffed. How could we have stayed in the lectures when our instructor was late? We left for the movies. Later, at a meeting of the *Komsomol* group, my classmate Nelya, ablaze with righteous rage, cauterized me with scathing words, "How could *you,* a grown-up man, a frontline veteran, not stop us from acting so carelessly?" though she was the one sobbing in the darkness right next to me. I was ashamed for my behavior. We—Volodya and I—were older than everybody else by some six or seven years; for the first time, we were considered to be *you,* not with everybody else.

During our university years we stood out from all other students because we were still wearing our military uniforms. Once our financial well being increased we could purchase regular pants. Then, when I got my University badge, I added a jacket to my wardrobe so I could wear it. In the second year of studies I came to the October Revolution parade wearing my army greatcoat, polished boots, and a bright blue fedora, and was greeted by a sarcastic question from the dean, "Kravchenko, why have you gotten so spiffed up?" Totally proud of my new acquisition and my holiday looks I didn't even notice his sarcasm.

Then we were obsessed with an incredible desire to catch up on what we had missed.

My diploma work in 1955 turned out to be quite interesting. It was about the optical properties of a synthetic ruby at the temperature of liquid oxygen. I had noted an unexpectedly bright emission of light in the absorption range, something very similar to the effect of a laser. It was an observed phenomenon, but also inexplicable. I was recommended to make a report at an all-Union technical meeting that was held at that time in the University. Two tall burly men came up to me during a break. They praised my work. They started inquiring about my plans. By then I already had some plans for the future: I was going to get a graduation certificate, then go to Kiev and enter the research fellowship program at the Institute of Physics in the Ukrainian Academy of Sciences, and a fellowship was already reserved for me there.

The conversation that lasted for half an hour ended with an agreement—if I got an invitation—I would go to the North, to Kirovsk, for three years, joining the Kola Branch of the Academy of Sciences to purchase equipment, build up a laboratory, introduce modern methods. Funds and my own discretion of their use were guaranteed. The fellowship could wait.

Those three years have not ended yet. Those men's names were Alexander Vassilievich Sidorenko and Igor Vladimirovich Belkov. The names are quite known in their field. Sidorenko later headed the Kola Branch of the Academy of Sciences; became a corresponding member, then full member of the Academy of Sciences; Minister of Geology and Vice President of the Academy of Sciences of the USSR. He was the one who founded and developed the Academic Campus—the pride and beauty of the Arctic city of Apatity. There, he took care of the surrounding area, and bulldozers didn't erase the untouched pristine forest, which is even today full of mushrooms. Old ladies like to pick them up. It is very convenient—you walk along a paved asphalt path and look around for them. For decades Belkov was my director. He was, as they say, a God-inspired artist, and his works—painted landscapes of our area—were the object of admiration of everyone and anyone. In that year of 1955, however, that was all yet to come. Back to then. . . .

The invitation came. My family sighed. Father was already gone by then. I swore to come every year and spend vacation at home (this promise I kept diligently while they were alive). In late August 1955, with a suitcase and my army duffel bag I got off the train at the station of Apatity. A crate full of books and some simple household items were to arrive separately.

It was snowing and raining simultaneously and my first thought was whether I had made the right choice or gotten hooked up with some dubious adventure. Hadn't I had enough adventures in my life by then? Well, at any rate I thought I could manage through three years somehow. I had gone through things much worse before.

A rather small statue of the Leader was dripping, in a little garden with strange plants next to the homely-looking building of the railway station. Adjacent blackened wooden buildings were not a joy to the eye. . . .

Almost fifty years have passed since then. Life is like a roll of toilet tissue, the less that is left, the faster it rolls. I can't slow down the process, and I don't want to stop it completely, because I'm very curious about what is going to come next. My first years in the North were filled with a memorable series of events, scenes, and sketches. I remember the further decades much less intensely. My own getting older couldn't help but play an important part in all this. Age dulls the acuity of the perception and emotions, or what?

In February 1956 I was in the village of Kukisvumchorr, also known as "The Twenty-Fifth Kilometer" because of the distance to Apatity's railway station. A crowded auditorium of the Kolsky Branch of the Academy of Sciences was filled with an overpowering, tense silence; someone read aloud the resolution of the 20th Congress of the Communist Party, "On the Cult of Stalin's Personality."

I recalled a scene that had happened not so long before. It was March 1953. I remembered mourning displays with the portraits of the country's leader decorated with flowers, on all floors of the University buildings. A round-the-clock guard of honor was set up by each display, and this lasted until the day of the funeral. My shift in the guard was at three o'clock in the morning. I lived far away, and streetcars didn't go at that hour. I was running across an empty, sleeping town, right along the streetcar tracks. When out of breath I climbed the stairs to my floor, a change of guards was already stepping in toward "my" display. I was late! Someone had stepped in for me, but I was still totally devastated and had no idea where to go. I then sensed that nobody seemed to know me; I was surrounded by a void.

The following day a session of the *Komsomol* Bureau made a suggestion to dismiss me from the *Komsomol*. Somebody summoned courage to speak up for me, and I got away with a strict admonition. I believe that was the first reprimand in my adult life. That was one memorable snapshot.

"There Hadn't Been"

I have another snapshot from 1954, an episode of my life that illustrates our quite recent history. It also shows the fate of my father and other family members.

It was one of those times when for some reason I was going through the rather chaotic accumulation of papers that are pretentiously called the family archive, when I pulled out a letter—or rather a copy of a typewritten text. The letter was mailed (no, actually it was put into a slot in a Kremlin gate marked 'For mail') and addressed to G. M. Malenkov. It started with the following words, "Highly respected Georgy Maximilianovich!" Of course today, at the beginning of the 21st century, not very many people, even in Russia, will remember the person behind that name, Malenkov's. His last name may even cause an amused question of "say again?" *The Soviet Encyclopedic Dictionary* published in 1980 didn't mention this man at all, there simply hadn't been such a person! OK, he wasn't a Iossif [Joseph] Vissarionovich [Stalin], or even a Lavrenty Pavlovich Beria. Even today these two names are not empty sounds for a great many people. By the way, speaking of Beria, who, incidentally, wasn't listed in the above-mentioned *Dictionary* either (I'll divert somewhat from the main line of my current narration as Beria and his men have a direct bearing on my main story). The dark blue postwar edition of the *Big Soviet Encyclopedia* in 50 volumes had a detailed and long-winding article about this "'one of the most prominent leaders of the *VKP(b)* and the Soviet Union, a dedicated follower and closest comrade-in-arms of J. V. Stalin" in Volume 5. It went on and on, with a full page-size portrait—according to the level of his importance. (They say that collectors now offer big amounts of money to purchase such an authentic portrait!) Then Beria was gone. Soon afterward I received a package from Moscow, from the publishers of the same encyclopedia. The package had a recommendation to "remove pages 21, 22, 23, and 24 from Volume 5 of the Big Soviet Encyclopedia as well as the portrait in between pages 22 and 23, instead of which you will find enclosed the pages with a new text. You should cut the mentioned pages out using scissors or a razor, retaining blank margins close to the binding spine, and new pages should be glued to those margins." Voilà, yet another person who hadn't been there! It was an amazingly well thought-out technique and a very interesting approach toward history. I was struck by the following: in any part of this gigantic information source one could remove any given number of pages, substitute them with new ones, with absolutely new articles, without disrupting their strict alphabetical order and maintaining total compliance with the previous and following texts!

Because of my sometimes spiteful character I chose to preserve both the old and the new page versions in my volume 5. Come visit me, and I will show it to you—a true rarity these days.

Now let us get back to Malenkov, though. Why were such lofty words used to describe him?

Then, in the years after Stalin's death, the term "group leadership" was quite popular. Malenkov became the Chairman of the Council of Ministers of the USSR. Khrushchev was the First Secretary of the Central Committee of the Communist Party of the Soviet Union (CPSU). All of a sudden important state documents that used to be published under the full front-page headline "In the Central Committee of the CPSU and the Council of Ministers of the USSR," were reversed without any comments whatsoever and instead read: "In the Council of Ministers of the USSR and the Central Committee of the CPSU." Thus it became apparent who was running the country now. Nikita Sergeyevich Khrushchev didn't tolerate such an outrageous discrediting for long, however. The term "anti-Party group" appeared and order was restored, this time without executions, to the credit of Nikita Sergeyevich. To teach others a lesson, soon afterward Khrushchev filled both positions himself. Now let me return to the episode of the early post-Stalin period when I was forced to address G. M. Malenkov, who was then, as I have pointed out, the highest official in the country. The overture turned out to be quite long. . . .

In 1954 I was in my fourth year of studies. My family was still living in Kremenets. My father was engaged in "green engineering," that is, he was busy landscaping the park at the site of the former ghetto. My brother was the head of the Communications Center. His position required membership in the Communist Party. There were relevant instructions to attract local cadre to the Party membership. The cadre was indeed valuable: educated, knowledgeable, cultured, "committed to the cause of Lenin and Stalin," as it was phrased in his references. Yuri was not known to steal and didn't like to drink, which was slightly alarming, "is he really one of us?" Well, the bottom-line was that Yuri was admitted to the Party.

In the peak of my spring midterms, on the eve of an extremely difficult exam in quantum mechanics, that had us all trembling in spite of the fact that we had a week to study, I received an invitation to a long-distance telephone center, to answer a phone call. Yuri was calling me. "Dad has had a heart attack. Come over."

"You know, I have this exam. It's quantum . . ." I began.

"I understand, but you have to come, don't delay. It's a serious situation."

I left everything behind and set off to Kremenets. Yuri met me at the bus station and as we were walking along Dubenskaya, he updated me on the situation; it was indeed very serious, and not only was there father's health.

He said, "Last week I got a call from the district Party Committee, 'Come urgently to the First Secretary. Do you have the Party membership card at hand?' I said that certainly, I did. I took it out from my safe, and went across the street. The entire Bureau was in the office of the First Secretary. He said, 'Let's continue, comrades. On the agenda today is the personal case of Communist Kravchenko-Berezhnoy. The head of the district Department of State Security will report now.' The head of the Department said, 'We have information that Kravchenko's father was an active participant of the White movement during the Civil War. Kravchenko concealed this information when entering the Party.' The First Secretary said, 'What will be your opinion, comrades?' 'Right. For deceiving the Party, Kravchenko-Berezhnoy must be dismissed from the Party membership.' In short, twenty minutes later I walked out without my Party card. Two days later I was relieved of the position as head of the Center and became a deputy—which was quite humane, actually. I kept quiet about it at home; you know Dad. And yesterday Dad was going home from work, and met an acquaintance, 'Hello, Alexander Vassilievich, how are you doing? And how is your son doing? No, not your younger, your elder son. What, you don't know anything? He was dismissed from the Party.' Dad managed to make it home. And that's all. . . ."

A few days later Dad passed away. He was always true to himself. He couldn't use a bedpan; he felt humiliated. And he tried to stand up. . . .

Now some reader is bound to say or think, "He should have stayed in bed; as he had been told to, that's all he had to do."

That's possible. It's also possible that, in such a medical condition, when you don't try to stand up, you may live longer. Is it a more decent life, though? Father never moralized us, never said we had to do this and not to do that. He was simply our ideal. I never heard my parents raise their voices at each other. They never took off their wedding rings. When on the second day of the German-Soviet war, in prison, they ordered my father to remove his clothes and place everything on the table, a NKVD man who was supervising this procedure immediately took Dad's ring and put it on his own finger. He never put it back or returned it—an arrested man would never need it. They say that after the war this fellow returned to Kremenets, to his job. And people even saw the wedding ring on his finger. Perhaps he still wears it, in his honorary retirement? Or perhaps somebody has inherited it? Out of solidarity Mama stopped wearing hers. I have it now. The diminutive "Shura" is etched on the inner side of it. And Dad's ring had "Yultsya." That's what they called each other their entire lives. The descendants of that NKVD man can check it out; it's a true story.

My father was known, respected, and loved in Kremenets. The entire town attended his funeral. The coffin was carried on arms along Shirokaya Street— that year still called Stalin Street—and traffic was briefly stopped. Literally thousands of people came to see my father off on his last road, to the cemetery, behind the monastery wall.

Father never held any significant positions in his life. Well, at least not in his civilian life. In the army he was a battalion commander at the age of twenty-two, commanding 500 Russian soldiers, and in 1916 he participated in the Brusilov breakthrough, the Lvov offensive, coming all the way to the Carpathian mountains. His entire life was checked against his notions of duty, honor, and dignity. He was a *human being*, and he never compromised this high title.

I returned to Lvov, to the university. The midterms were almost over, and the exam in Quantum Mechanics had already taken place. I entered the department. Professor Abba Efimovich Glauberman stood up from behind his desk, going toward me. He was a theoretical physicist, a brilliant lecturer who ended up in this provincial university as the result of the struggle against "rootless cosmopolites and Zionists"—and these were incidentally the best years of our Physics Department. Abba Efimovich looked me in the eyes and shook my hand in silence. Then he extended his hand toward me again. Confused for an instant, I pulled out my record book and gave it to him. Having written a record in it and closing the book, the Professor let me go, encouragingly pressing my arm above the elbow. He didn't say a word. Only outside, I mustered myself to open the book. In the section for Quantum Mechanics there was a grade, "Excellent". I have been fortunate in my life because I have had many encounters with people of whom one wants to say, "This is a human being!" They are, in fact, the reason life goes on. . . .

I researched and wrote my course and later my graduation work about that very same synthetic ruby, in Moscow, on the Pyzhevsky Lane, at the Institute of Crystallography of the Academy of Sciences. Good people were working in the Institute. They fed me—some with a spread cheese, and some even with a chicken pate. Occasionally the laboratory alcohol was used for "cleaning an optical axis" and this, too, stimulated appetites. I was extraordinarily skinny then. Making use of that kind attitude toward me and the opportunity to work in the laboratory all night long, I typed a letter addressed to Malenkov. I told him about the misadventures of our family. In my request I insisted on putting an end to the issue of my late father's participation or non-participation in the White movement. From his stories we knew only that he returned an invalid from the fronts of World War I. Back in Kremenets, he successfully avoided any kind of "registrations" that often led to a bullet at the back of the head. I described the circumstances of his death and his "funeral that looked more like a demonstration." Today I'm confident that the last words of that sentence became a "keyword" for those who read that letter in Moscow. What, a non-sanctioned demonstration? This was way too much.

I was in my fifth year classes when Yuri called me again. "A man came from Moscow. A major. He is here, in the district Department. He summons elderly people. They talk about Dad. You didn't write to Moscow, did you?"

"I did, when I was in Moscow," I said. "To make sure it would get to where it should get."

"I can't believe it."

"Well, we don't have anything to lose."

"Well, I don't know. Everything seemed to have calmed down. I work. Now it's starting all over again. I can't believe it," He repeated.

A month later there was another call from Yuri, "They summon both of us to appear at the district Committee tomorrow. So, come over."

The major greeted us politely, introduced himself and offered us to sit down.

"You wrote to Comrade Malenkov. I was sent here to check everything out on site. While here I have questioned almost three hundred people, those who had known your father for a long time. The anonymous letter that accused him of participating in the Civil War on the side of the Whites didn't prove to be correct. That's what I'm going to report."

I went back to the University. The major left Kremenets. Some time later my brother was summoned to Ternopol, to the regional Committee. There his dismissal from the Party was confirmed, and the Department of Communications was advised to reconsider his employment, "in the view of non-compliance."

"See? And you thought everything was going to get better. . . ."

Soon afterward my brother was summoned to Kiev, to the Republic's Central Committee. A Central Committee official took out my brother's Party card from a safe and handed it to him, explaining, "There was *no* dismissal from the Party. There's just the problem that you haven't paid Party dues for half a year now. . . ."

The head of the district Department was transferred somewhere. Rumors had it that he got reprimanded, without any trace or written record of the incident. My brother was reinstated in his position and he worked there for almost a quarter of a century after that. His name was nominated for an Order of some kind on the occasion of some anniversary date, but then, on the stage of approval his name disappeared from the list; they never forgot their pain. For me the gates were lifted only in the late 1960s; my wife and I were allowed to go to Bulgaria, where we were even personally honored by having an "escort" assigned to us there. He was an athletic young man with pleasant yet common looks, in a way reminding us of a then famous actor by the name of Nozhkin. He spoke Russian well. He treated us to wine. He asked us what we thought of Solzhenitsyn and the dissidents. He was not bothersome, yet omnipresent. He didn't even bother to use some undercover identity. I could feel plain human curiosity emanating from him; he really wanted to know who this "client" was for the sake of whom he had been sent from Sophia to the mountain resort of Borovets. Well, we spent two very pleasant weeks in Bulgaria and even started missing the homeland.

Yuri was dying from a septic infection, after an unsuccessful appendectomy. The antibiotics he needed were not available. The ones that my Moscow friends managed to get hold of only slightly extended the process. The Department of Communications sent a helicopter and we took Yuri to the regional hospital. There, now in a single-person ward, he saw a technical novelty on my wrist—an electronic digital watch, and his eyes lit up for a moment. Throughout his life Yuri couldn't remain indifferent to electronics. When the sounds of mourning music from the Communications Center reached the district Party Committee, the new First Secretary interrupted his speech and said, "They are burying our communist over there. Those who want, can go." Nobody dared to leave the session of the Party Bureau, however. In small towns people have always been good at assessing the current political environment.

Mama soon followed Yuri. Children shouldn't go before their parents; this is against nature. Mama, who kept our family hearth and home, survived with the memory of my father for quarter of a century. She visited us here, in the North. She flew in a jet plane. I took her picture next to huge Czar-Bell after Nikita Khrushchev had opened up the Kremlin for tourists. Yuri's death was the end for her. I continued coming to Kremenets every year; such promises are kept by all means. During our last meeting Mama suggested I take our family heirlooms with me to the North—an icon with an oil lamp, military paraphernalia of my father, and their wedding picture: a brave officer much decorated with orders and medals and a young *gymnasium* graduate in a modest bridal veil. The picture was dated October 1917. Well. . . .

Mama said, "You know, Romukha, I don't really believe there is something out there. Everything is here. I feel sorry there will be no you, there will be no morning bird songs in the garden. . . ."

We found a little bundle under Mama's pillow, carefully tied with a ribbon. Those were my folded, triangular letters from the front, with thick ink stamps reading, "Checked by the Military Censure." Separate words and complete sentences were covered up with black ink. [No envelopes were issued to WWII Red Army soldiers, but by a special folding method the letter also served as an envelope. *Ed.*] A priest ran a funeral service for Mama; custom required that. Those present at the service watched closely whether I crossed myself or kissed the cross in the priest's hand. I crossed and kissed—I didn't care, I was not a Party member. It would have been difficult for Yuri. Mom was eighty-two. Dad and Yuri were both fifty-nine; they could have lived so much longer.

The family heirlooms decorated a corner in our apartment in the North, a memory from a past generation, and a reminder to future ones. It was an icon of the Apostolic Saint and Prince Alexander Nevsky, an Order of Saint Anne presentation dagger inscribed "For Bravery," a massive pocket watch from the once famous Swiss manufacturer Doxa. There is one thing I cannot explain: when our apartment was burglarized—a common thing nowadays—the thieves took a lot, and, of course, our computer among the first things. It was standing in the very same corner. They didn't touch the family heirlooms, though. Were they shocked by the rich catch? Or perhaps Saint Alexander, my father's patron saint, protected the family relics? I had started writing down these snapshots on the computer. I was very mad when we were robbed of it. After asking around, however, I was able to borrow a laptop computer, focused my strength and brought the project to its completion. My thanks go out to those burglars. You kind of stimulated me.

What about Rostislav, our Rostyu? He found his bliss eventually—Galina, or Galochka—and they were the sweetest couple in town. They lived in a separate house, and bees buzzed in beehives under their windows. We still treat ourselves with honey and beeswax coming from those beehives.

After my family was gone, I began visiting Kremenets less frequently; I wasn't getting younger with every year either, with different ailments along the way. Then it even became a foreign country, with *Gryvnas*. [The *Gryvna* is the currency of the sovereign state of Ukraine, where Kremenets now lies. *Ed.*] My conscience kept telling me that Rostyu was there, I mustn't be late. He turned ninety-three. We went there, filling up a full compartment in a train car and surprising the new border control officers with our modest luggage and non-businesslike purposes: homeland, graves. We arrived and the very same day we went to Rostislav's. He barely recognized us, but as always he was civil although a little bit estranged. Having looked intently at me and smiling with his eyes only, he asked half-inquisitively, "Heil Hitler?" Some association with that time must have flashed in his mind. He died the following day, between two spoons of water that Galya was giving him upon his request. He simply closed his eyes and never opened them up again. We arranged a dignified burial for him there, in the old cemetery beyond the monastery wall. There is a cohort of people among us, very small yet indestructible, who have similarities with Dmitry Sergeyevich Likhachev [a Russian intellectual and a literary historian who devoted his life to defending Russia's cultural heritage, a survivor of Soviet forced-labor camps. *Trans.*]. When one encounters such a person in one's life, the heart feels warmer. Rostislav Alexandrovich Kikets was one of those.

My mission in Kremenets was over.

※◦◦◦

In the Arctic Russian town of Kirovsk in the second half of the 1950s, the central square was called simply "the Square." The lawn of the square was covered with oats. It was bright green during the short summer season (decades later it was established that even roses can bloom here. If a man tries hard enough. . .). A new town was being built not far away and was called simply New Town.

Once there was a railway station called Apatity. [Russian for "apatites," the mineral mined nearby. *Ed.*] There was a small settlement next to the station with the same name, pretty gloomy, too. Through the forest, the first white brick houses of New Town were beginning to shine through. The village of Apatity and New Town then merged and in 1966 became the new Arctic city of Apatity (pop. 100,000 some years ago). New buildings popped up like mushrooms in a frenzy of careless construction. The word "ecology" was not yet common, however, only a few years later the entire community was involved to restore the damaged ground, on *Subbotniks* and *Voskresniks,* calling it "planting of greenery." [*Subbotniks* and *Voskresniks* (from the Russian words for Saturday and Sunday, respectively), collective work actions, usually initiated by Party organizations and state institutions, when the entire staff or town population had to volunteer (the idea was about volunteering, but participation was mandatory). *Ed.*] There is something bright and joyful in the recollections of those events and now I can't really believe that I dragged that birch tree on my back, the one by our house, which is now four stories high. How very young and strong we all were then.

Children from what we still called New Town went to school in Old Apatity, also in wintertime, in darkness, in blizzards. Parents would go to meet them after school, helping them to make it back. These kids, who are now well close to fifty, have scattered since then all over the world. Coming back to their hometown, though less frequently now, they are filled with nostalgic sentiments when recalling those daily hikes with frostbitten noses and tears freezing on their cheeks. There was something very special in all this, and I know exactly what it was. It was a feeling of motion, moving forward. Of "it may be bad and difficult today, but tomorrow it will get better."

I don't miss the past. I am not in favor of going backward to continue the unjustified *experiment* with our country. (This word appeared and firmly settled in my mind long before mass media began using it to describe Soviet Communism.)

One also can't purge one's memory of events that took place. Whatever happened stays there, both bright and dark moments. I know today from literature and museum displays how the mining towns of our region were created, who had to build them (forced labor), and at what price.

More recently the many construction cranes that soared above our town started to slow down and eventually stopped completely. Will they come alive and resume creating? I wish to live long enough to see it. There is a strong need today for faith in a tomorrow. Although when speaking of the North, the people who think practically about the new times have already spoken, "is it really necessary?" Wouldn't it be more beneficial and efficient to spend time up here on a rotational basis? I doubt that, and our town has already become a homeland to tens of thousands. The graves of their ancestors are here. We are drawn here—to our home—after long and far and exotic journeys.

━━━━◦◦◦◦━━━━

When I set off to work in the far North I didn't think I would be there for long. I thought that the North is a place of work, while your home remains in the South. Then gradually I turned into a veteran of the North. An all-around veteran, too. There, in the South, I am only a visitor nowadays, and one coming less frequently. Only graves are there now. Nobody's waiting for me there. Besides, my old homeland is now a foreign country and the lines to the clinic down there are longer than most people can even possibly imagine. Here I have my own doctor who knows everything about my blood pressure, cardiogram, and everything else. Then you find out that the North has actually changed your systems and become a resident within you—yes, you remain a northern person, even if you leave the North. You may spend your days, for instance, in sunny and rich Krasnodar, picking grapes in a vineyard, but all your stories begin with, "Well, up north. . . ." You remain a northern person, just like a sailor always remains a sailor.

Now we are persistently advised to leave the North and change climate. It's not doctors who are telling us this, but people who have looked at the economics of living up here. We are glad that we now live in a more pluralistic society so that we can disagree with the economists and stick to the North. We are on a continuous lookout, too; we are waiting for our children. What if they come back? We also stay simply because we like this land. For us this land is not an issue of economic calculations. The North is our home.

That's how it is.

But now let's return to Germany, modern Germany, so that the story does not end on a sad note.

A Last Encounter, or How I Became a Colonel

This happened on the eve of the reunification of Germany [which took place on 3 October 1990. *Ed.*], when thousands of East Germans flooded west. We had *perestroika* and *glasnost*. This meant that the quick and effective tank method to "restore order," used in the previous decades, was no longer allowed.

So in this new era, in Hanover, West Germany, they were planning a major international conference on gases in deep rock. As always they sent out a first call for papers. We got a copy, too. Then the second notice came, now with the list of planned reports, including a report on gases in our Kola super-deep borehole written by a friend of mine. My friend was an expert in these matters and after the first call, he had sent his proposed abstract to Hanover, just to try. He never imagined he'd be accepted. The Germans wanted this report badly, though. First of all, he was from Russia, which had just recently started to open up a new window to Europe. Secondly, we were from a very exotic corner of Russia, with our polar bears and polar night. And, finally, our borehole was indeed the deepest in the world. [To this day the Kola super-deep borehole outside Zapolyarny remains mankind's deepest borehole, 12,262 meters deep, *Ed.*]

We prepared the first response together. He wrote and I translated. The official language of the conference was English. My friend, however, had no language skills—neither English nor any other. He had studied during the war, but those things were not a priority then. Finally, my friend said that he would just have to give up the idea and that we had started it all in vain. After some hesitation we decided to go for an all-or-nothing.

We wrote them that if a translation from Russian wasn't secured, then the oral report was not possible, however, we added, he could bring a colleague with him, who spoke foreign languages. The Germans contemplated for a while. And then they sent one more invitation, to me, with all expenses covered. Thus, not really thinking about it, I got into this trip.

A German professor, Manfred Schidlowski, was the heart and soul of the conference. The professor was paralyzed, yet this didn't stand in the way of him being extraordinary communicative, active, and cheerful. His young and very sweet wife, *Frau* Ingrid, skillfully and even a bit breezily maneuvered his wheelchair around.

Speaking in Polish, I asked the Professor whether he was Polish. He understood my question, but answered me in German. No, he was born in Eastern Prussia, where many used to have such typically Slavic names.

"And this German of yours, where did you learn it?" he asked.

"It's from Ukraine, occupied for almost three years, and then as a result of five years of military service in Germany, starting in 1945. At first I used a submachine gun, and then I served as a translator. Life taught me."

"And your English?"

"Same source. For almost ten years I didn't have the opportunity to attend school. So I learned what I could myself."

My friend's report went well and was well received. At the end of the conference there was a visit to the Institute laboratories. We moved from one working area to another in a small group, centered on the professor in his wheelchair. At some point we found ourselves in a laboratory that very much resembled the one my friend directed here in the Kola Peninsula. My friend began questioning a young German who worked there, asking about every little detail. The German felt awkward and then said, "*Herr* Doctor is asking so specialized questions that it is hard for me to speak in English. If only I could respond in German."

And here Professor Schidlowski laughed with a Mephisthophelean laughter and pointing his finger at me exclaimed, "*The Colonel speaks all languages!*" I didn't object to such a promotion! The Professor mistakenly assumed I was a KGB agent, and, as is well known from the movies, all KGB agents are colonels.

Still flattered by my "promotion" and feeling adventurous, that evening I left my cautious friend behind in his hotel room and went out to take a walk around town.

I was looking at some sight when two young girls walked up to me. One of them, having made a slight curtsy, very politely asked me if I had a *Groschen* (coin). I didn't know what denomination they needed, so I poured on my hand a bunch of change that had accumulated in my pocket and offered it to the *Fräulein*. She pulled the coin she needed, thanked me along with a curtsy, and the girls rushed off to a payphone. Most likely they were trying to make plans for a date. Here I was, a Russian providing two Germans with some "humanitarian aid"—that topped my "promotion" to colonel!

During a weekend break of the conference, we were invited to visit the conference organizer's family at their country home. There, during an utterly hospitable reception a meeting with several German *Ostfeldzug* (the Eastern campaign) veterans took place. It was a human, warm meeting. Friendly contacts with this German family continue to this very day.

And after that conference, we soon met with Manfred Schidlowski again. The lively professor took an Aeroflot flight to our Arctic town, with his wheelchair and his inseparable companion. He was hosted by our Kola Science Center of the Russian Academy of Sciences. Some local bodybuilders lifted him in his wheelchair down the stairs and put him into a van. The rest of the program went smoothly, too.

On the evening before their departure the Schidlowskis invited us all into their hotel suite. My wife and I brought a big bucket of daisies, which moved *Frau* Ingrid. The professor kept asking questions, and there was no end to them, for example, why we had two different abbreviations that both meant a collective farm (*kolkhoz* versus *sovkhoz*). Not among the easier questions you can get. Again I had to explain that one should not ask "Why?" in our parts. Why? As a brief reply was mostly impossible, and the full answer will start with the words, "Because in November of 1917 the October Revolution took place in Russia, and. . . ." This was immediately followed by a question, "Why is it called the October Revolution if it happened in November?" I am positive, the Professor knew the answer at least to this question. He just wanted to joke.

The evening turned out to be an interesting one. Saying good bye, I asked him, "Are you satisfied, *General*?" He paused with my hand in his, looked into my eyes, and broke out laughing. We laughed well then.

Such was my last encounter with Germany. I put to rest the idea of Germans as enemies and now appreciated them as friends. I never expected to have to take part in a war again, at least not against Germans. There would still be one more occasion, however, when my past as a military interpreter would come in very handy.

My Longest Hours

On 30 June 1990, together with my daughter, Nataliya, I was returning to the North from Kremenets where we had visited the family graves. Yuri's widow, Lyda, remained as the sole occupant of the house by the hillock. It was hard to say good bye—the chance that we'd meet again was small indeed.

It was very hot, above 30 degrees Centigrade (86 degrees Fahrenheit). People were lingering in and around the terminal of the Lvov airport, which was being renovated. As is normal in these stories, there were not enough refreshments and beverages. The silence was surprising: no take-offs, no landings. Finally they announced the check-in for our flight, 8678, though delayed. If according to schedule, our arrival in Leningrad [today: Saint Petersburg] should be after 11 PM, we would barely make it to the subway and to our friends on Petrogradskaya before midnight, when the subway shut down for the night. At our friend's place we were going to meet my wife who had just come from Krasnodar, where her family's graves were. We were supposed to spend the night at our friend's, and in the morning continue our trip together. Homeward.

The security check went fast, but the luggage was still left with the passengers. Then we were all put on regular city buses that pulled over and took us somewhere far away from the airport, and even out of town. Nataliya supposed that perhaps it was a new kind of service by Aeroflot: taking people by bus straight to Leningrad. The ride was some forty minutes long and then we came out near some obviously not civilian airport; there a huge crowd formed, with a no less huge amount of luggage; in those days, everybody was bringing something tasty and good from the South. One couldn't grasp that all of this could fit inside one plane, but the Tu-154 was a spacious jet.

Instead of 9:00 PM we took off at 10:30 PM. The overnight stay with our friends in Leningrad became highly unlikely. Our entire itinerary was falling apart.

That was how it worked. "Fly with Aeroflot!"

There were two cabins on board; our seats were up front. They turned on the air, and breathing got easier. There were almost two hours of flight ahead of us, and I could finally relax. It had been a hard day; the sad face of Lyda, now the sole resident of the home where I had lived with my family, a three-hour ride in a heated tin of a bus, the hassle and fuss around Lvov, the uncertainty about the departure

Nataliya was napping, and I fought slumber, being afraid to miss the moment they would serve water—I was very thirsty. A smiling flight attendant soon appeared with a tray. Then, some twenty minutes later she was passing my seat again. This was surprising, a most unfamiliar thing on an Aeroflot flight. With the same smile on her face, the flight attendant entered the cockpit a few times, and left it.

We were in the air for almost an hour and I started to doze off, but then something clicked, and a female voice said calmly, "If there is a passenger on board who can speak English, please come to the flight attendant post." I waited for a while, then looked back in the aisle but nobody was approaching the attendants. I stood up and went there. Nataliya accompanied me with an understanding look on her face, "You, Dad, are always looking for some adventure." Both flight attendants were there and there was someone else, a man from the crew, with a trying look.

"Do you speak English?" I nodded. "You will have to follow me to the cockpit," said the flight attendant, with a smile.

Life taught me not to ask extra questions. If you have to, you have to. I had never been in a pilot's cockpit before, and even more so—on a flying jet. Passing by my daughter, I met her eye, and slightly shrugged my shoulders. The attendant knocked, the door got opened and we entered the cockpit. The door was locked behind us. There were four men in the cockpit, all wearing uniform blue shorts, with rolled up sleeves and unbuttoned collars. There was an enormous amount of gauges. Massive headphones, microphones. . . .

The flight attendant said, "Here, this comrade speaks English."

The captain (the one who was in the left-side seat, as we know from the movies) turned his head toward me and studied me for a second, "Do you speak English perfectly?" there was an obvious emphasis on "perfectly." I mumbled something intelligent regarding the *Russian* language, saying that one couldn't even, but the captain interrupted me.

"Fine. Do you already know that we have been hijacked?" Not waiting for my answer, he continued. "The hijacker demands a landing in Stockholm.

Nobody speaks English in the crew. Will you be able to secure the communication with the Swedish air services? To translate our commands, our inquiries, and their answers?"

Which meant if the communication would be secured we would fly on to Stockholm. If not, the "ground" wouldn't permit us to leave national airspace, and perhaps the "perfectly" was also demanded by the "ground" . . . and for the "black box"?

There was nothing else to do. I was standing behind the captain's back and saw what the pilots were seeing: the ground that was bright and green, disappearing at a distance in a bluish smoky air.

The people in the cockpit were absolutely calm. Exchanging brief phrases. Doing their job. I only had to join them.

I was put into the place of the air communications officer, at the captain's back. They gave me headphones and showed me how to use the microphone. My task was to answer when called "Aeroflot eight-six-seven-eight," translate everything that was directed to them, and repeat in English everything that the captain would direct to the ground.

For the time being Russian was heard in the headphones. So, on the back side of the navigator's map I hastily scribbled from the depths of my memory those English words that resembled aviation terminology: altitude, direction, descent, runway. I couldn't then recall the word "runway" in English. The pilots didn't know it, either. It was the most important word. How could one land not knowing where?

The captain said melancholically, addressing the second pilot, "As I've been telling you, Yuri, study English. . . ." Distressed, Yuri admitted his fault and promised that as soon as we'd be back he'd immediately.

For the time being we were not coming back, however. Instead, we were flying away.

The ground took good care of us. I believe Riga was directing us. Near Ventspils we planned to make a turn to Stockholm, I knew about Ventspils, which is in Latvia, from the fall of 1944; we fought somewhere near there. We received queries regarding the situation on board, remaining fuel reserves, behavior of the hijacker—where he was sitting, what he was armed with, whether he had any accomplices with him. The information on the further course followed, the weather conditions near Stockholm. At some point there was a query from the Minister of Civil Aviation himself.

Many of those who were supposed to rest didn't sleep that night. Somebody said, "Most importantly, do not panic." Those words were not needed; the people in the cockpit worked calmly, they stayed focused and even maintained an atmosphere of slight jest. They were tough, reliable men.

The second pilot took off his gun and from time to time went to the tail section of the plane to negotiate with the hijacker. The captain advised him, "Yuri, tell him not to do anything stupid. We're on our way to Stockholm." The hijacker didn't believe us and threatened us with his hand grenade, which he demonstrated by showing the inside of his jacket. He claimed he had three more accomplices sitting behind him. I remember thinking, "They should have paid attention to the jacket when we were boarding the plane. Everyone else had been wearing just T-shirts and tank tops."

The flight attendant brought some water. I asked her to go to the sixth row, seat "D" and calm down my daughter. In response Nataliya sent me some validol. [Validol, a common pharmaceutical agent used to relieve angina attacks and prevent heart attacks. *Ed.*] "Darn doctor!" I thought, with warmth, as she had recently received her MD degree.

The Russian voice from the ground informed us that we were leaving our zone. When approaching their zone, he said that we would be met by two interceptors of the Swedish Air Force. Then, almost in whisper, "Break a leg!" The captain said, just as quietly, "Thanks."

For a while the air was silent. Standing up a bit, I looked over the captain's head. In front and below us there were the enormous jagged teeth and dots of the Swedish reefs, coming out into the golden sea. These were the very same reefs where allegedly someone's submarines occasionally were having problems. It was way past midnight, but we were far north so the sun was still above the horizon.

I heard a clear voice in my headphones, "Aeroflot eight-six-seven-eight!"

The captain ordered, "Respond to them. Translate everything." So I tried to translate everything. I also echoed every word I was told by ground control, to exclude every chance of an error. With the permission of the captain I reported that I was not a member of the crew and did not know airline terminology, asking them to speak slowly and clearly. The invisible guardian answered with an encouraging "Okay!" Only the most important and necessary words were said both from our side and their side. There was only our dialogue; all others on the same frequency got silent. Only once somebody's voice broke in, "What is the matter with them?" And a short reply, "They have been hijacked." Then silence. It seems to me that I didn't even say two dozen words during the approach and landing.

Again our flight number came, and further instructions followed, "You'll be accepted by the Arlanda Airport. Runway 01 is clear for you." Runway! That was the word I hadn't been able to remember. Runway 01 was clear for us! Runway! I remembered it for the rest of my life. As it turned out, I wouldn't be getting many more opportunities to fly during the remainder of my life. It became extremely expensive soon after this trip.

Ground control obviously believed that the crew of the Russian airliner had information about Arlanda, its landing and take-off runways, their dimensions, and orientation. It all could have been stored in an on-board computer, and having received the information about runway 01, the crew could have been capable of further independent action. Perhaps it was not exactly so, but it sure seemed to me that the pilots did not know anything about the airport or the runway. The navigation officer was leaning above a map with a slide-rule in his hands. Was it an anachronism? Or an error-proof device? I repeated not to make a single mistake, "Arlanda, Runway 01." The flight continued in the same direction, at the same altitude. Then a closer voice came in (perhaps that was a pilot from one of the fighter jets, although we didn't see them. They could have stayed out of our field of vision, as there was no particular need for them, and they might have distracted our pilot in this complicated and stressful situation). Our flight number sounded, and then after our response there followed an order to make a turn to course two seven zero, straight to the west. The line of the horizon immediately stood up, smoothly, clockwise, and returned to the previous position. *Wow! Such a huge machine, and it can do such a smooth turn. Just like a military plane.* Then, we were directed to course three hundred, an additional turn in the reverse direction, to the north. Another leap of the horizon line. The navigation officer calmly reported, "I see the runway." I stood up and also saw the runway, which was far away and below, straight ahead of us. That voice directed us wonderfully. I think that it was the high point of all that adventure; once we saw it, we'd land. We never really thought that we couldn't land, however. Then we could see the runway clearly ahead and far below—and it seemed so incredibly short, some five centimeters. When the details of its width and length came on the radio, however, the captain and the navigation officer smirked with satisfaction.

The navigation officer requested information on the atmospheric pressure in the area of the airport and received an answer. Then the report of the captain, "We see the runway," followed by an encouraging "okay!" and an order to descend.

The runway approached quickly underneath us. The navigation officer called out clearly the remaining distance and altitude—fifty . . . twenty . . . ten . . . eight . . . four . . . two . . . two . . . two . . . touchdown. I realized that in the moment of landing the pilot cannot see the ground. He has to rely on the information of the gauges and equipment. The navigation officer reads them while the plane flies above the runway almost touching it. We, the passengers, when looking outside the window, keep thinking, "Why don't the pilots land it? Why, the runway will soon end, they might not make it if they keep on going like that. . . .

We landed and the brakes were instantly applied. There was no familiar clicking from passing over the concrete slabs, or rather, this airport's tarmac was not made up of slabs, like we were accustomed to. There was an order to taxi following a yellow car. We were redirected into some faraway corner, near some forest. The forest looked just like a Russian pine forest, though it was filled with cars with blue siren lights. On the airfield, a bit to the side, there were tall figures with submachine guns. The radio said they were going off the air now, and police would contact us. Then a Russian voice broke in, a representative of Aeroflot, who would now take care of the contact with the Swedish authorities. He asked the captain, "Do you have clearance to fly abroad?"

"No," answered the captain.

"How did you . . . ?"

"We have a man on board, he speaks English *perfectly,*" said the captain.

That was the biggest compliment said to me in my entire life. I wish I could get a paper stating that, certifying it with a seal.

The Aeroflot representative said, "We shall decide whether you will fly back yourselves, or if we shall get a plane from the Soviet Union a crew with clearance." Half a day later it became clear that the question was resolved in favor of our crew.

I was free to go—conditionally—back to my daughter. I felt instantly that calmness reigned in the cockpit only, and not in the cabin. People surrounded me and started asking questions. I told them all I knew. There was a woman from the second cabin sitting in my seat next to Nataliya; she was shaking terribly—her seat had been the one next to the hijacker.

Nataliya felt all right and brave, although a well-wisher sitting next to her had whispered to her in my absence that we were flying in the wrong direction and that I must have been taken hostage in the cockpit. Then after the plane had stopped, one man, a heavy sleeper, woke up and started getting ready to leave. He thought we were joking telling him about Stockholm. Only the sight of the serious-looking armed figures outside the window convinced him that this wasn't the airport in Leningrad.

Some negotiations followed between the hijacker and the Swedish side. An announcement that originated from the Swedish authorities followed: those wishing to seek political asylum in the country may leave the plane with the hijacker. We exchanged glances. How was that possible? We didn't wish to leave. We wanted to get back home, to the North. Some dark-haired man jumped up from his seat and began pacing the aisle nervously back and forth. A woman grabbed his hand and asked him to sit down. The flight attendants also asked people, both kindly and strictly, to take their seats, to maintain order. These ladies were beautiful, the way they were supposed to be. One was tall, with a permanent or, as Nataliya said, glued (ah, women!) smile on her face, and the other was petite and strict. She was the one who called us to calm down when necessary, and it was necessary. People rushed to one side of the plane to look at the submachine gunners in black— "They look like true fascists!"—or to the other side, to watch the hijacker coming down the ladder. He threw something into the box prepared by the SWAT team, and following an order he lay down on the smooth Swedish tarmac. He lay there, lonely, pressing his face to the concrete, and then he was taken away.

Then the order to come out followed; the entire thing was paced out. We had to leave the plane in groups of ten, with all our luggage, women and children going first. There were many women and children. The process of leaving the plane lasted through the morning.

The number of people on board was getting smaller and smaller. The pilots stayed inside the cockpit, the door was open. At that moment we all were one team. I was very thirsty.

Nataliya and I were leaving the plane among the last ones, the crew members were the only people left on board. The sun was already up in the sky. We were stopped with a gesture next to the stairs. The cars with flashing lights were standing in a dense row behind the tail, unseen from the windows. We were directed there, one after another, with a gesture. The men on the field were tall, young, athletic, wearing black fatigues, polished boots, black gloves, and knit hats. Their weapons were small, black, and looked more like toys. They had walkie-talkies on their chests, totally unemotional faces, and obvious total preparedness. It was clear that if anyone made a sudden movement, their reaction would be instantaneous. You didn't want to make any sudden movements.

We were the only ones left, standing together, side by side. The one man standing some three meters away, was looking straight at us, but it seemed like he looked straight through us. I thought to myself, *Here's a young, charming girl beside me and you won't show the slightest human reaction? Damn it!* But then, Nataliya also looked at him as if he was a figure in a waxworks exhibition. A Swedish mosquito was buzzing, obviously not as big as our Russian ones, yet just as annoying. It didn't seem to attack the men in black, though. Perhaps they even wore some repellent?

A young woman in the same uniform, but unarmed, motioned with her finger, "One," and made another inviting gesture. I said, "Come on!" but Nataliya decided to be the last one.

Walking to where I was called, I glanced back. An empty jetliner stood on the tarmac and by the stairs I could see a young woman's figure with a little suitcase. Opposite her, with his legs wide apart there stood a killing machine of a man with a submachine gun. That's how my memory has preserved the scene. He was a "human weapon," but still didn't make you feel very uncomfortable. He didn't make you feel any way at all. He simply was one tough son-of-a-bitch. That's the way the guys in SWAT teams should be, I guess.

Having reached the woman in black, I blurted "Morning!" Her face gave way to half a smile and she responded with a polite "Morning!" Thus I exchanged my first courtesies on Swedish soil. Folding tables stood behind the cars and the passengers' belongings were being carefully examined, a very polite and professional examination. Once again I was glad we didn't have much luggage. My daughter's stethoscope caused a friendly smile. The security sweeper blipped next to my pocket and I said, "Small knife" and pulled out my pocketknife. They nodded—okay. After a "thank you" gesture we were invited to a gigantic bus that was shining with cleanliness, as if it had just come off the production line. I must add that everything that we managed to see in our few hours on Swedish soil impressed us with cleanliness, neatness, and order. Everything seemed as if it had just been set up. Had I seen this at home, I would have thought it was a show-off, yet here such a thought didn't cross my mind. We fight for cleanliness all the time. *They* have it naturally. Well. . . .

Our bus, escorted by motorcyclists, rolled toward some low buildings that we could see in the distance. We arrived in a very spacious room that looked more like a restaurant—tables, chairs, bar stools, and a bar. Everything was in plastic and metal. The rest of the passengers were already there. They were milling around, sitting, sleeping, if they could. The morning was cool and those who were dressed lightly had been offered warm, orange, fuzzy blankets that were piled high next to the entrance. The result was a group of strange-looking figures wearing orange togas, like the ones Buddhists wear!

We spent a few hours in this room. A man with a submachine gun sat in an armchair by the door, so nobody seemed to feel any urge to go outside and get some fresh air. Still, the room itself with the adjacent bathroom was comfortable enough. The food was good and tasty and offered by two ladies who radiated elegance and white-toothed smiles. Bananas and other similar things were gone before the last group arrived, however. The Swedish buffet hadn't been prepared for a full-scale Russian assault. That was why there was a slight concern written on the ladies' faces. In any case, orange juice, coffee, and extremely scrumptious high-calorie sandwiches were available for everyone. Once back on the plane, we were each handed an additional beautiful little "packed lunch." In fact, these boxes were so nice that they qualified as souvenirs and were not consumed, but taken home. The boxes even contained small cans with the text "Fresh spring water from one of the most remote areas of Norway." I am still saving this can, as it might soon be the last clean water on earth.

A Swedish doctor, a tall man with a name badge on his jacket, kindly brought me to a bathroom where I managed to clean up and even shave. I felt much better. Having seen me again, the doctor asked me, "Was it too dramatic?" I later, at home, got the very same question, albeit in a less sophisticated variant, "did you freak out?" I tried to analyze my emotions and it boiled down to the following: there was a task and it had to be tackled. To be more precise, I couldn't refrain from answering the call; there were 160 people on board, including my daughter. It turns out when you're busy with such an important thing, no emotions get in your way. It's like it was in the war, on the frontline.

The whole crew came into the room and was greeted with applause, which felt really good. Then quickly completing his breakfast, the captain walked up to me and said, "bring your daughter and your luggage. We are going back to the plane. We've got work to do."

So we were to be airborne again. Meanwhile the plane was taxied almost to the doors of the restaurant. Again I was in the cockpit. The Aeroflot representative came up to me, shook my hand, thanked me, and offered to write down some terms needed for taking off. So I took off almost professionally.

I said, "Captain, we ought to thank ground control."

"Yes, we'll climb to the altitude, get on our course, and then transmit."

Somehow it all went so fast. Have you ever noticed such a phenomenon when the trip *back* always seems to be shorter than trip *there*? The captain ordered, "Transmit words of gratitude."

I pressed the necessary button and said, "Aeroflot eight-six-seven-eight. Arlanda. Stockholm. The passengers and the crew would like to thank you for your help and hospitality. Thank you very much. Good bye!"

Stockholm replied with a few kind words, adding, "You're welcome!" meaning "any time." The crew laughed in unison. Soon Russian voices were again in our headphones.

My mission was nearing its end. The captain asked my name and where my home was. I showed him my Great Patriotic War veteran's ID. It's a rare thing when demonstrating this ID is a pleasant experience. Its not the same thing on a bus or beside a really long line for tickets, where everybody hates you for the privileges that go with this document. No, here it was very appropriate.

The captain then took my sheet of the navigation map and on its clean corner he wrote the following:

"Tu-154, Aircraft 85334, Flight 8678 Lvov-2–Leningrad
Captain of the flight—Bukharov Alex. Nik.
2nd Pilot Reztsov Yur. Vlad.
Navigation Officer Golovkin Ser. Vikt.

Flight Engineer Smirnov Iv. Al.
We thank you for your help in a critical situation."

Everybody in the cockpit signed it. Four strong handshakes followed.

I must confess that it is very flattering to have such a document in the family museum. I should definitely get it framed.

The captain, sitting down comfortably in his seat, said with satisfaction, "As I've been telling you, Yuri, study English."

Yuri answered with readiness, "I'll enroll myself tomorrow!"

━━━━◦◦◦◦━━━━

My wife must have been going insane, pacing from corner to corner of the Leningrad airport. Using "connections" I asked if I could send some comforting information to Leningrad. I was certain from decades of experience of Soviet life that the people who were waiting for the flight didn't know anything, "they were not supposed to." The times were beginning to change, however, and soon the public address system in the airport announced, "Lyudmila Ivanovna Polezhaeva [the Author's wife's name], waiting for flight eight-six-seven-eight from June thirtieth from Lvov. Please come up to the information desk."

Everyone who was anxiously waiting for this flight rushed toward the information desk. Lyudmila Ivanovna picked up the phone and the airport dispatcher told her the words that all those who were waiting needed.

━━━━◦◦◦◦━━━━

Leaving the plane I told the flight attendants, "Ladies, flying with you was an absolute pleasure. How about Madrid next time? They say, it's a beautiful place." And I earned very sincere smiles in response. What an old flirt!

There was a special interview in one of the least accessible rooms of the airport. A young soldier stood at the exit to the room and when leaving, we handed him our special entrance passes. He poked them onto his Kalashnikov's bayonet—just like in a famous scene from the Revolution of 1917. Coming out of this room, we went downstairs and entered the Arrivals area from the side opposite the one usually used for arrivals. There we could see my wife, who was pacing the hall nervously. We walked up almost next to her before she saw us and I asked her quietly, "Why are you running around?"

The most amazing thing was that after all our adventures we managed to make our connection, We were supposed to arrive in Leningrad on the evening and spend the night at our friends. Instead, we spent the night in the hijacked plane and the morning in Stockholm. We arrived in Leningrad about midday. The flight to Kirovsk that was scheduled to depart at 10:00 AM started with a 4-hour delay "due to the weather in Kirovsk," so we managed to catch our flight. We later found out, the sun was shining brightly in Kirovsk with my favorite temperature of 9 degrees Centigrade. Aeroflot moves in mysterious ways! I wish we could fly more nowadays. I'd like to get to Madrid. . . .

I told my daughter, "Do you remember I promised something as a reward for excellent graduation from the medical school?"

"You promised a trip abroad," she said.

"See, I keep my promises."

"I never doubted it," she replied. "And Stockholm is a nice city, isn't it?"

"Certainly! Especially that restaurant in the airport," I laughed.

"And that young man in the armchair, with the small submachine gun, by the entrance."

"Please, you two," my wife said. For some reason, she seemed on the verge of crying all the time.

Conclusion

So I have been fortunate in life. Now, when it's almost over, I'm inclined to believe that there has been some interference from above; my luck has just been too incredible at times. My *entire twentieth century experience* was marked by the fact that every turn in my life that, at first, was thought to be a tragedy, a drama, or at least a major nuisance, turned out to be, some time later, a good thing sent my way. Well, occasionally it took me decades rather than moments or days to realize this fact, and yet the cliché saying that "whatever happens, it will turn out for the best" has always been true for me.

In the fall of 1944 in the Baltics, by the village of Vainede, during the German artillery preparation, my foxhole received a direct hit. The shell entered one of my "walls," covered me generously with dirt from the breastwork, and left behind a perfectly round hole half a meter away from my eyes, but *for some reason* no explosion followed. If there had been one, I would have been listed among the missing in action for the rest of my folks' bitter lives. It didn't happen, although it should have. German quality ammunition, after all. At the time my acquired atheism stood in the way of my understanding of the interference from above. It was like a severe disease, but a treatable one, with such lessons. . . .

Here I believe it will be appropriate to stop for a second on this topic.

My work for decades in an academic institution entailed lecturing activities, collaboration with the *Znanie* [Knowledge] Society. It so happened that during these lectures I was repeatedly asked the same question, "Do you believe in God?" I gradually formed an answer that was acceptable for the listeners of *that time* and for myself. With the inevitable self-censorship, it looked approximately as follows.

"Mankind has perceived an extremely small share of the surrounding world, and the wider and deeper our knowledge gets, the greater is the scope of what yet remains unknown. The belief in things not capable of being known or comprehended that, in fact, exist around us and inside us and perhaps that determine the fate of everyone does not contradict a materialistic outlook. Spatially it could be presented that, for example, the world that is accessible to our cognition is only a particle, a molecule of some super-world, super-organism, that lives according to its laws—laws not accessible to our minds. If this super-creature will have issues, so to say, with what our world is, where you and I are, then, . . ." Thus my reply to the "do you believe?" question was evasive, I didn't really say "no" and could continue my lectureship with a more or less satisfied conscience. Today, frankly speaking, based on my own personal experience I would like to say that there are things and events outside and inside us that are directly related to us and yet cannot be explained by the laws of nature known to us. Everyone decides for himself or herself how to name these things and in what form the attempt to explain them should be put. As for the religiousness, gradually, with the course of years and decades, I have come to perceive the great similarities between religion and an ideological system that observes rituals in accordance with certain accepted works. This standpoint, however, doesn't stand in the way of being impressed by the music and festive solemnity of Orthodox services. I have been affected by them since my early years, they are close and exciting to the soul. This is in the very same way that kindness can be accepted as kindness, regardless of the religion of the person doing the good deed. As far as faith is concerned, I think it is relevant for two parties only: Him and me. Intermediaries are not necessary.

Along the same topic of supernatural interference: when not so long ago I fell from a cherry tree, falling spine first with the likely perspective of breaking my neck, for some reason I didn't close my eyes, but grabbed a branch that passed by, which slowed my fall. The end result was a mere two broken ribs, two *sprained* collar bones (very rare indeed), some torn ligaments and a broken finger. I still walk around bravely and truly enjoy when people ask, "What were you doing up that cherry tree?" obviously hinting at my age. Here the understanding of interference from above was instant, right after the hit, together with the restored breathing.

The trip to Stockholm together with my daughter on the hijacked Tu-154 left the most pleasant memories, and there have been many things like that in my life.

There were several "blots" on my record—hereditary hassles with the Party; in spite of the years of immaculate military service in Germany, non-promotion to the officer's ranks (but *had* they promoted me, I would have served until retirement!); and add to this my not-very-brilliant career (head of a laboratory at an academic institution was tops, for thirty-three years, though!). Only now I realize how big of a *blessing* it all was, allowing me to preserve and develop the most important thing: internal freedom, ability to perceive myself without excessive seriousness. Speaking of the officer title. I did become one in the end, a Second Lieutenant, commander of a reconnaissance unit of divisional artillery upon graduation from university. There was a military department at the university, and we received adequate training in correcting the fire of 76-mm guns, in fact very well according to professional artillerymen. In any case, the training targets were blown to pieces. Basically, we spent our time well with the physics and mathematics faculty. Later, after some reserve duty training courses, we were promoted to the next higher rank. When I reached the point of removal from the reserve lists, due to my age, I was again promoted, to First Lieutenant. Then in May 2000 I unexpectedly received a nicely decorated citation from the order of the Supreme Commander of the Armed Forces of the Russian Federation, dated 27 April 2000, No. 2:

"For bravery and self-sacrifice, demonstrated when defending the homeland and to mark the 55th anniversary of the Victory in the Great Patriotic War of 1941–1945, First Lieutenant Roman Alexandrovich Kravchenko-Berezhnoy is promoted to the military rank of captain. [signed] V. Putin, Supreme Commander of the Armed Forces of the Russian Federation."

Of course this order embraced all participants of that war who were lieutenants and were still alive in May 2000. Perhaps I'll make it to my centennial anniversary and be promoted to the rank of colonel. There are actually several factors that point toward the possibility that I may attain that vintage. My wife, who is ten years younger than me, is extremely enthusiastic and motivated me to lead an active lifestyle, including skiing; working with Internet and with youth, mostly of the opposite sex. Morning exercises—bell bars, running, knee-bends (now more likely semi-knee-bends), water gymnastics, and finally there is the author's theory of conservation of the organism in the low temperatures of the North, mentioned earlier. Plus limitations in alcohol consumption (although it is known that alcohol consumed *moderately* is not harmful even *in the biggest amounts*) (a joke that students of Russia will appreciate) and a total tobacco abstinence, as noted earlier by the *starshina*. The list of adverse factors to long life is not a small one either, of course, and the question here is, as always—which side will win? Most importantly I try to extend my years by laughing at myself.

I have been lucky in my life to meet many good people. In October 1949 in our unexpected, non-ceremonial and urgent—two hours to pack and get ready!—departure from Germany, the commander gave me, already with escorts [performing the duties of guards, *Ed.*], an envelope to be opened when back in the motherland. The envelope contained a recommendation for admittance to the Party, properly written out. This was the biggest thing that Guards Colonel Murachyov and his deputy Major Bushtedt could ever have done for me. They were taking a big risk then, too. They signed as a result of their own *opinions,* this differed from the *instructions.* I keep this document as a valuable family relic. The Colonel was a true *human,* and so was the Major. When decades later I met him, he told me, clicking our glasses in a raised toast, "You, Roman, even then were a dissident." I lived, though, only according to Marx—doubt everything.

Ah, Major Bushtedt. . . . In the late 1940s I went on a business trip with him from the eastern side of Berlin to Potsdam, in a commuter train. At that time, the supreme headquarters were in Potsdam. The train crossed all occupied sections of the city: Soviet, French, American, and British. On one stop two Americans entered the compartment. They sat down across from us and started eating cakes out of a box that they put on a little table in the compartment. One of them took a cake with his rather dirty hands (perhaps he was a driver) and gave the now dirty cake to Bushtedt. He paused for a second, put the gift on his palm, and then pressed the cake into the American's forehead. We all jumped up and reached for our guns. Then the second American, looking at his friend's crème-covered face, started laughing and we joined in. There could have been an international conflict but, thank God, instead we started laughing. That's some snapshot.

Sergey Viktorovich Bushtedt was a man capable of making his own decisions—a *human.* By the way, we could have gotten off that train at any stop and asked for some kind of asylum, but this thought never really crossed our minds. And yet we were bound to be sent to some assembly and reassignment station after Germany (that is, assigned for forced labor).

Then there was the school official in Yenakievo, who turned a blind eye to the absence of my documents, and wrote across the left top corner of my application: "Allowed to enroll in the 10th grade with a month of probation." (The 10th grade was the last year of school, giving the certificate of general education) signed under the statement. He was truly *human.* I'm absolutely confident that at any time, under any rule, those who can be called humans are in the majority. No matter how aggressive and brazen "the young and tough" of a new generation are, the *humans* will be in the majority.

I was born in 1926. Those born in this year were the last ones to be drafted to the war's slaughterhouse, and those who survived the baptism of fire were battered in the gigantic victorious battles of 1944 and 1945. I was at the graves of other guys born the very same year, in Warsaw, Prague, Berlin, and on the Seelow Heights. Their dates of death were in April and May 1945. They were only weeks or days short of Victory. They turned into dust . . . and I go on living. I am indebted to them. Somewhere, somehow they covered my back. Therefore I'd like to say, this book is to your memory, guys, from one who was to lead a lucky life.

I was lucky when instead of making use of my Kiev postgraduate fellowship I decided to move to the Far North with my fresh honors degree in Experimental Physics—to the land of people strong in spirit. I've been here for over fifty years now. Here I met a reliable and loyal partner—for life. In addition she is a proofreader, editor, and uncompromising critic of this book. I'm sure she will want me to delete these lines—but I'll stand up for them.

I was lucky when in the midst of the "raging democratization" in the late 1980s the employees at my lab ousted me by a closed vote; after thirty-three years they had grown tired of me, just as much as I had of them. While there was no pressure from above to retire, I thought it was time to go. Thanks to my wealth that "didn't weigh down my pockets"—foreign languages—I remain useful, keep working, and in my former laboratory I also keep raising toasts with my former colleagues on holidays and anniversaries.

As a result of the economic drama of the recent decade there was almost nothing left of my laboratory. Had I remained the head of the lab, I could hardly have survived such a fate for the fruit of my work without a heart attack or paralysis. Besides, in the course of years—my years, being the head of the lab—I felt how the rate of progress gradually decreased. I left of my own accord and feel completely satisfied with that decision.

I also didn't turn lazy. I didn't get carried away with ambition, greediness or, God forbid, some kind of intolerance—ideological, political, religious, racial, or nationalistic, which is so much in vogue and is even demonstrating itself in our land. I have persevered in my ability and inclination to look at myself with a smile, and at others, too. Many don't even have an inkling what a *bliss* it is to be able to do this.

Dear reader! You haven't found here a word about atomic and hydrogen bombs, about Yuri Gagarin and the first men on the moon (or even about the water on the moon—a discovery containing a promise of emigration for mankind); about lasers and Einstein; about clones and AIDS; about Afghanistan and Chechnya; all this—and so much more—are the events, achievements and losses of our twentieth century. I promised to write about *my* century, however, which I now have done to the best of my ability. I could have continued, pulling other images of my past from my memory (they are particularly abundant when you've got insomnia), but would it be worthwhile? Anyway, the final punctuation mark has to come pretty soon now. As you see, *that* period, World War Two, took up the biggest portion of my twentieth century. It is not my fault; it turns out that a slow and good life doesn't leave that many marks.

Here someone may say, "Well, and what about the most important thing? Didn't you notice the most important thing? The break-up of the Soviet Union?"

Of course I noticed. This is also our common thing. That's what happened in the last decade of our twentieth century. And yet this was not only our thing—and there were precedents in that century, too. The October Revolution, and particularly the Brest Peace Treaty, was followed by the dissolution of the Russian Empire, wasn't it? It was the time when Finland, Poland, the Baltics, Ukraine, and the Caucasian nations split away. Central Asia remained restless for a long time. So, there are always precedents. Separations. Unifications. This has been and will be again. I would only hope that in the future it will happen without bloodshed. Nobody else shed as much blood as our people did in the twentieth century, ever or anywhere. Perhaps that was enough? Perhaps we could learn and thus stop feeding and sustaining hatred and images of enemies within ourselves. We would do better by using some *perestroika,* that is, reconstructing.

Many different things happened in our lives. Yet in the future, though perhaps not in mine, I do not see Russia in darkness any more. I see a country where the *humans* will be in charge. I dream of this time.

We are getting to the close now, and I feel sad. I have become so used to sitting at the computer and leading this conversation. Frankly, I don't want to press the key with the period, but I have to. One should be able to end things. . . .

Dear reader, now you have seen them, my most memorable snapshots.

Now I hope that having written this book, God willing, and taking a rest, I will be back at my computer. And I will continue: capturing "new" snapshots from the depths of my memory.

Apatity, on the eve of the year 2007

Rank Equivalents

US Army	Red Army	German Army	Waffen-SS
—	Generalissimus	—	
General of the Army	Marshal Sovetskogo Soyuza	Generalfeldmarschall	
General	General Armiyi	Generaloberst	SS-Oberstgruppenführer
Lieutenant General	General Polkovnik	General (der Infanterie, der Artillerie, etc.)	SS-Obergruppenführer
Major General	General Leytenant	Generaleutnant	SS-Gruppenführer
Brigadier General	General Major	Generalmajor	SS-Brigadeführer
—	—	—	SS-Oberführer
Colonel	Polkovnik	Oberst	SS-Standartenführer
Lieutenant Colonel	Podpolkovnik	Oberstleutnant	SS-Obersturmbannführer
Major	Major	Major	SS-Sturmbannführer
Captain	Kapitan	Hauptmann	SS-Hauptsturmführer
1st Lieutenant	Starshiy Leytenant	Oberleutnant	SS-Obersturmführer
—	Leytenant	—	—
2nd Lieutenant	Mladshiy Leytenant	Leutnant	SS-Untersturmführer
Sergeant Major*	—	Stabsfeldwebel	SS-Sturmscharführer
Master Sergeant/ First Sergeant	Starshina	Oberfeldwebel	SS-Hauptscharführer
Technical Sergeant	Starshiy Serzhant	Feldwebel	SS-Oberscharführer
Staff Sergeant	—	Unterfeldwebel	SS-Scharführer
Sergeant	Serzhant	Unteroffizier	SS-Unterscharführer
Corporal	Mladshiy Serzhant	—	—
Private First Class	Yefreytor	Hauptgefreiter Obergefreiter Gefreiter	SS-Rottenführer
—	—	Obersoldat (Obergrenadier, Oberkanonier, etc.)	SS-Sturmmann
Private	Krasnoarmeyets	Soldat (Grenadier, Kanonier, etc.)	SS-Mann

*Not a rank in the US Army during WWII. NCOs serving as sergeants major during that era were usually master sergeants.

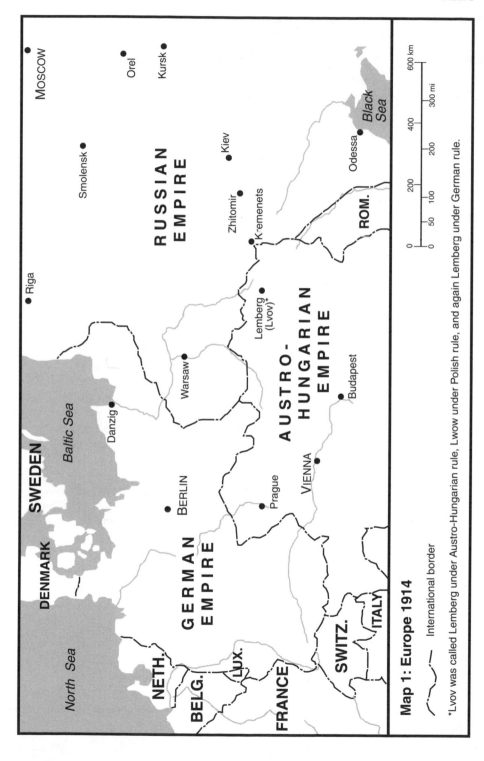

Map 1: Europe 1914

— — — International border

*Lvov was called Lemberg under Austro-Hungarian rule, Lwow under Polish rule, and again Lemberg under German rule.

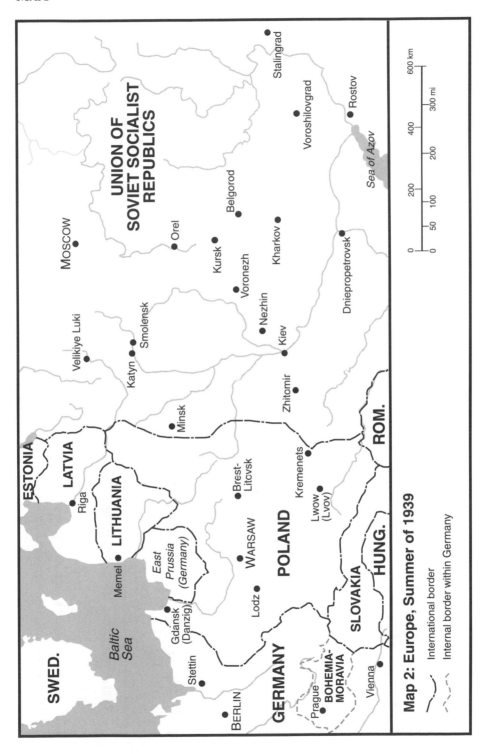

Map 2: Europe, Summer of 1939

International border

Internal border within Germany

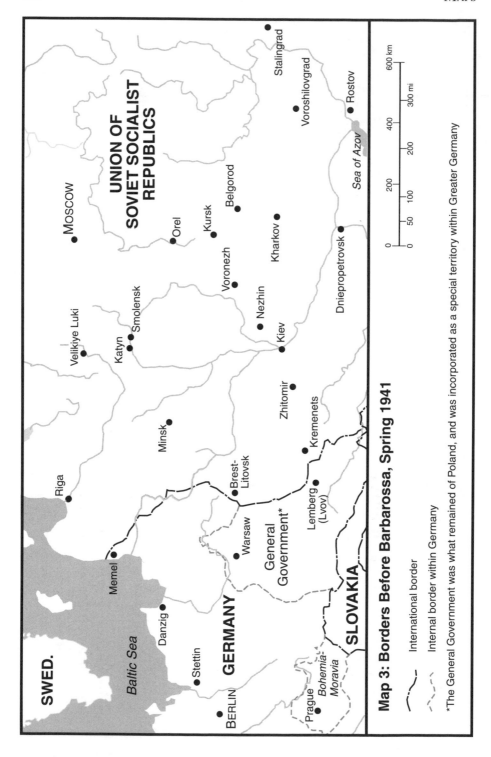

Map 3: Borders Before Barbarossa, Spring 1941

International border

Internal border within Germany

*The General Government was what remained of Poland, and was incorporated as a special territory within Greater Germany

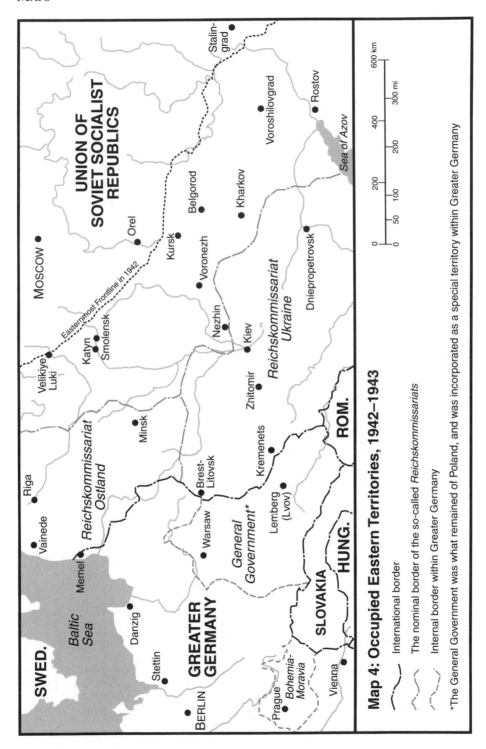

Map 4: Occupied Eastern Territories, 1942–1943

International border

The nominal border of the so-called *Reichskommissariats*

Internal border within Greater Germany

*The General Government was what remained of Poland, and was incorporated as a special territory within Greater Germany

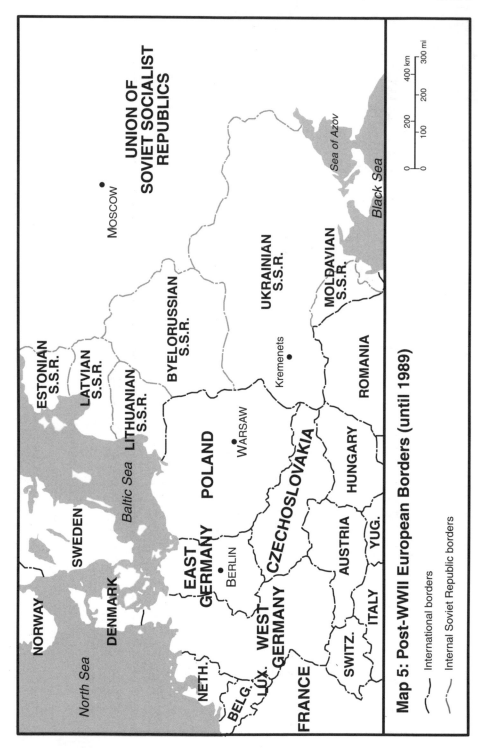

Map 5: Post-WWII European Borders (until 1989)

— International borders

—·— Internal Soviet Republic borders

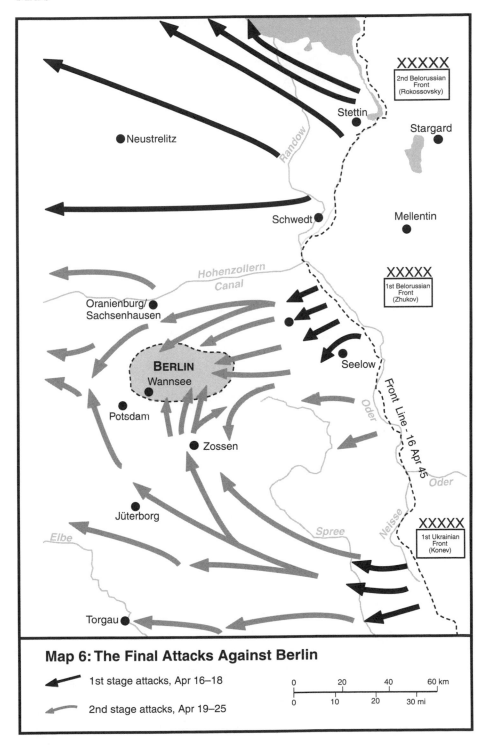

Map 6: The Final Attacks Against Berlin

1st stage attacks, Apr 16–18

2nd stage attacks, Apr 19–25

About the Author

Roman Kravchenko-Berezhnoy was born in 1926 in Poland. His family was Russian, his father a former Tsarist officer. His town was incorporated into the Soviet Union in 1939, and in 1941 it was made part of German-occupied Ukraine. After having experienced and documented the Nazi occupation, the author joined the Red Army in the spring of 1944, where he at first served as a simple rifleman (with a submachine gun) in the 61st Army's 356th Rifle Division. When his language skills were noticed he was transferred to a reconnaissance detachment in the same division. He fought in Latvia, Poland, and Germany up to the seizure of Berlin. In occupied Germany he served as a military interpreter for about five years, including an Inter-Allied group searching for the remains of Allied aviators. Because of the nature of the Stalinist system he was then "rewarded" for his long service abroad and contacts with westerners with banishment to a construction battalion in the Motherland. This was a penalty, but thanks to it he could graduate his secondary education. After almost 7 years of service in the enlisted ranks of the Red Army, he entered Lvov University in 1950.

After graduation in 1955 from Lvov University, for more than fifty years Kravchenko-Berezhnoy has lived in the extreme north of Russia with his wife, Lyudmila Ivanovna. Both physicists, they met in 1957 as colleagues, married in 1963, and both received their PhDs for research work at the Kola Centre of the Russian Academy of Sciences. Their daughter, Natalia, has a PhD in medicine, and their son, Vasily, is a Doctor in physics and mathematics. They have two grandchildren. Roman's elder son, Igor, has a PhD in geology and is also an expert in translation of scientific literature to English. Roman, now 80, still works at his institute in Apatity, Kola Peninsula, Russia.

About the Translator

Marina Guba was born and grew up in Dnepropetrovsk, Ukraine. She was trained as a linguist and received her degree majoring in English language and literature. A practicing translator and interpreter since 1990, in 2002 she moved to the United States and in 2006 became a citizen. An independent contractor, Marina translates fiction and non-fiction as well as medical, legal and corporate documents. Among her non-fiction work are: *We Are the Only Survivors: Testimonies of Holocaust Witnesses and Survivors* (Middlesex, UK: Valentine Mitchell, 2005); *Year 2020: Who Will Survive Depression?* by M. Lezhepekov (Bloomington, Ind.: Authorhouse, 2006); two other translations of personal memoirs are forthcoming. She lives in Southern Indiana with her husband and a dog.

Other Titles by The Aberjona Press

Sledgehammers: Strengths and Flaws of Tiger Tank Battalions in World War II
by Christopher Wilbeck
> "This detailed, yet readable study, enhanced by fascinating photographs and superb maps deserves to be on every tank warfare devotee's bookshelf."—*WWII History* magazine

272 pages. 35 Original Maps. 42 Photos.
Paperbound. ISBN 13: 978-0-9717650-2-3.
$19.95; plus $4.00 U.S. shipping

Slaughterhouse: The Handbook of the Eastern Front *David Glantz et al.*
> "A virtual treasure trove of information and lore for all those who can't get enough of the personalities, equipment, unit histories and orders of battle related to the war in which Hitler fought Stalin. . . . *Slaughterhouse* is a 'must have'."
> —*Armchair General* magazine

520 pages. 9 Maps. 88 Photos. Extensive 16-page bibliography. Paperbound. ISBN 13: 978-0-9717650-9-2.
$29.95 plus $4.50 U.S. shipping

Waffen-SS Encyclopedia:
by Marc J. Rikmenspoel
> "Few units arouse such intense interest as the Waffen-SS: love them or hate them, the Waffen-SS has had more books printed about them then probably any other unit. Unfortunately, some of them are more about the 'SS cult fetish' then tangible information. Thankfully, Marc Rikmenspoel has supplied us with a one-stop reference tool worth its spot on the bookshelf."— *Broadsword Military Magazine*

300 pages. 82 Photos. Extensive 20-page bilbiography.
Paperbound. ISBN 13: 978-0-9717650-8-5.
$19.95 plus $4.00 U.S. shipping

Seven Days in January: With the 6th SS-Mountain Division in Operation NORDWIND *by Wolf T. Zoepf*
> "The balanced, integrated account of American and German experiences is exemplary. . . . The evolving German perception of their American foe is fascinating. . . . The maps are perfect. . . . Anyone with any interest in the European campaign will find this a compelling, valuable read."—*World War II* magazine

312 pages. Maps. Photos. Index.
Hardbound. ISBN 13: 978-0-9666389-5-0.
$12.95; plus $4.00 U.S. shipping
Paperbound. ISBN 13: 978-0-9666389-6-7.
$12.95 plus $4.00 U.S. shipping

Into the Mountains Dark: A WWII Odyssey from Harvard Crimson to Infantry Blue *by Frank Gurley*
> "Yet another Aberjona Press classic. . . . A profound coming of age story of a young man's transition to manhood. Emotionally charged, meticulously edited, and expertly packaged, *Into the Mountains Dark* is a wonderful WWII memoir."
> —*Military Heritage* magazine

256 pages. Maps. Photos.
Paperbound. ISBN 13: 978-0-9666389-4-3.
$14.95 plus $4.00 U.S. shipping

Five Years, Four Fronts:
The War Years of Georg Grossjohann, Major, German Army (Retired)
by Georg Grossjohann
> "This is not an *All Quiet on the Western Front* or another *The Forgotten Soldier*. In my opinion, it is a better book."
> —*The Journal of Military History*

218 pages. Maps. Photos. Index.
Paperbound. ISBN 13: 978-0-9666389-3-6.
$14.95 plus $4.00 U.S. shipping

Black Edelweiss: A Memoir of Combat and Conscience by a Soldier of the Waffen-SS
by Johann Voss
> "A fascinating and unique contribution to our knowledge of the motivations of the men who comprised not only the Waffen-SS, but much of the rest of the German armed forces in the Second World War. . . . It is highly recommended."—*The Journal of Military History*

224 pages. Maps. Photos.
Paperbound. ISBN 13: 978-0-9666389-8-1.
$19.95 plus $4.00 U.S. shipping

The Final Crisis: Combat in Northern Alsace, January 1945
by Richard Engler
> "Quite remarkable. . . . Superbly researched and well written. . . . What emerges is a clear sense of just how important the individual American soldier was in winning the war in Europe and just how effectively he generally performed in combat." —*Military Heritage* magazine

368 pages. Maps. Photos. Index.
Paperbound. ISBN 13: 978-0-9666389-1-2.
$29.95 plus $4.00 U.S. shipping

The Good Soldier: From Austrian Social Democracy to Communist Captivity with a Soldier of Panzer-Grenadier Division "Grossdeutschland"
by Alfred Novotny
> "[Novotny's] wartime experiences . . . come vividly to life. . . . [His] sharply etched memories . . . are compelling in their detail."
> —*The Peoria Journal-Star*

160 pages. Photos.
Paperbound. ISBN 13: 978-0-9666389-9-8.
$14.95 plus $4.00 U.S. shipping

Audio CD, 6-disc set, 6.5 hours
ISBN 13: 978-0-9777563-0-8.
$29.95 plus $4.00 shipping

Odyssey of a Philippine Scout: Fighting, Escaping, and Evading the Japanese, 1941–1944
by Arthur Kendal Whitehead
304 pages. Maps. Photos.
Paperbound. ISBN 13: 978-0-9717650-4-7.
$19.95 plus $4.00 U.S. shipping

American Illiad: The History of the 18th Infantry Regiment in World War II
by Robert Baumer
> "Exceptionally well done . . . seamlessly weaves together the unit's operational history with the personal experiences of the 18th's soldiers. Readers hoping to get a real feel for the intensity of World War II combat are advised to get this must-have book."
> —*Armchair General* magazine

424 pages. Maps. Photos.
Paperbound. ISBN 13: 978-0-9717650-5-4.
$24.95 plus $4.00 U.S. shipping

Forthcoming

Defending Fortress Europe: The War Diary of the German 7th Army, June–August 1944
by Mark Reardon

Swedes at War: Willing Warriors of a Neutral Nation, 1914–1945
by Lars Gyllenhaal and Lennart Westberg

Victory Was Beyond Their Grasp: With the 272nd Volks-Grenadier Division from the Hürtgen Forest to the Heart of the Reich
by Douglas Nash

For much more information, visit our website at:
www.aberjonapress.com

THE ABERJONA PRESS Setting the highest standards . . . in *History*
P.O. Box 629, Bedford, PA 15522; **toll free: (866) 265-9063;** aegis@bedford.net